JAMES BAMFORD

The Shadow Factory

James Bamford is the author of *Body of Secrets*, *The Puzzle Palace*, and *A Pretext for War*, and has written on national security for *The New York Times Magazine*, *The Washington Post Magazine*, and the *Los Angeles Times Magazine*. His *Rolling Stone* article "The Man Who Sold the War" won the 2006 National Magazine Award for reporting. Formerly the Washington investigative producer for ABC's *World News Tonight with Peter Jennings* and a distinguished visiting professor at the University of California, Berkeley, Bamford lives in Washington, D.C.

THE
SHADOW
FACTORY

ALSO BY JAMES BAMFORD

A Pretext for War

Body of Secrets

The Puzzle Palace

THE
SHADOW
FACTORY

■

THE ULTRA-SECRET NSA FROM 9/11
TO THE EAVESDROPPING ON AMERICA

JAMES BAMFORD

ANCHOR BOOKS
A Division of Random House, Inc.
New York

FIRST ANCHOR BOOKS EDITION, JULY 2009

Copyright © 2008 by James Bamford

The Library of Congress has cataloged the Doubleday edition
as follows:
Bamford, James.
The shadow factory : the ultra-secret NSA from 9/11 to the
eavesdropping on America / James Bamford.
p. cm.
Includes bibliographical references and index.
1. United States. National Security Agency—History.
2. Intelligence service—United States. 3. Electronic
surveillance—United States. 4. United States—Politics and
government—2001– I. Title.
UB256.U6B38 2008
327.1273—dc22
2008026448

Anchor ISBN: 978-0-307-27939-2

Book design by Michael Collica

www.anchorbooks.com

PRINTED IN THE UNITED STATES OF AMERICA
10 9 8 7 6 5 4 3 2

To Mary Ann

And to my father, Vincent

In memory of my mother, Katherine

And to Tom, Paula, and Christina

I'm very grateful for their

constant support and

encouragement.

Contents

Acknowledgments

Whenever I write about the NSA, it is like trying to reassemble a puzzle after the pieces have been scrambled. Thus, I am deeply grateful to the many courageous people who helped me fit the pieces together. Although they must be unnamed, they will not go unheard or unthanked.

I am also very grateful to Doubleday's editor-in-chief, Bill Thomas, for suggesting this book and for his help, encouragement, and friendship. Many thanks also to my editor, Kris Puopolo, who helped me put the pieces of the puzzle in their proper places and was always full of good ideas and support. And thanks to Stephanie Bowen for her excellent eye and help with managing the manuscript and for keeping me on schedule. I also greatly appreciate the years of excellent advice and direction provided by Kris Dahl, my agent at International Creative Management.

THE
SHADOW
FACTORY

Introduction

In northern Georgia near the South Carolina border, a few miles from Leburda's Grits N' Gravy and the Cracker Barrel Old Country Store, one of the most secret facilities in the world is undergoing a major expansion. When completed, it will likely be the largest eavesdropping facility ever created, employing more than four thousand civilian and military "voice interceptors" and other specialists. Run by the ultra-secret National Security Agency, it is where the agency eavesdrops on the Middle East and North Africa, thousands of miles away. Inside, behind barbed-wire fences, heavily armed guards, and cipher-locked doors, earphone-clad men and women secretly listen in as al-Qaeda members chat on cell phones along the Afghan border, and to insurgents planning attacks in Iraq. They also target and record American citizens in that region, including businesspeople, journalists, and Red Cross workers, as they engage in intimate conversations with their spouses back home and discuss confidential matters and business deals. "A lot of time you could tell they were calling their families," said one of the NSA intercept operators who listened in on the Americans, "incredibly intimate, personal conversations . . . Basically all rules were thrown out the window, and they would use any excuse to justify a waiver to spy on Americans."

By 2008, the NSA had become the largest, most costly, and most technologically sophisticated spy organization the world has ever known. It had also become the most intrusive, secretly filtering millions of phone calls and e-mails an hour—international and domestic—through equipment programmed to watch and listen for hundreds of thousands of names and phone numbers. To sift through it all, the agency has the world's largest collection of data-eating supercomputers. Its newest, code-named "Black Widow," is a colossal $17.5 million Cray computer made up of sixteen tall cabinets crammed with thousands of processors. It is able to achieve speeds of hundreds of teraflops—hundreds of trillions of operations a second—and the NSA predicts that it will soon break the petaflop barrier, plowing through phone calls, e-mails, and other data at more than a quadrillion operations a second.

In its manic drive for information, the agency requires a city-sized headquarters complex that consumes so much energy that it is now in real danger of running out of power and going dark. It has already run out of space to store all of its data—data in which it is now drowning, according to the Congressional Research Service. "Whereas some observers once predicted that the NSA was in danger of becoming proverbially deaf due to the spreading use of encrypted communications," the report said, "it appears that NSA may now be at greater risk of being 'drowned' in information." The report added, "Some intelligence data sources grow at a rate of four petabytes per month now . . . and the rate of growth is increasing." In a year at that rate, the NSA's massive database would hold at least 48 petabytes, the equivalent of nearly one billion four-door filing cabinets full of documents. It would also be equal to about twenty-four trillion pages of text.

Among the few who know just how much data flows into the NSA is Eric C. Haseltine. The former head of Disney's "Imagineering" labs, Haseltine was appointed as the agency's associate director for research in 2002. Two years later he noted that even the NSA's enormous computer power has trouble keeping up with the flow. "We in the NSA are encountering problems with the flood of information that people [in the outside world] won't see for a generation or two," he said. "We've been into the future and we've seen the problems" of a "tidal wave" of data. He added, "We can either be drowned by it or we can get on our surfboard and surf it and let it propel us. And, of course, that's what we're trying to do."

If indeed the data flowing into the NSA is what the outside world will see two to four decades from now, the amount of information the agency is ingesting is truly astronomical. In fact, it may be rapidly moving from measuring the data by the petabyte to measuring it by the exabyte, which is 1,000 petabytes. By way of perspective, 200 petabytes is the equivalent of all printed material. Five exabytes (5,000,000,000,000,000,000 bytes), on the other hand, represents enough information to fill 37,000 new Libraries of Congress and more than all the words ever printed. This is the annual equivalent of a thirty-foot stack of books for every man, woman, and child on the planet.

No longer able to store all the intercepted phone calls and e-mail in its secret city, the agency has now built a new data warehouse in San Antonio, Texas. Costing, with renovations, upwards of $130 million, the 470,000-square-foot facility will be almost the size of the Alamodome. Considering how much data can now be squeezed onto a small flash drive, the new NSA building may eventually be able to hold all the information in the world.

The principal end product of all that data and all that processing is a list of names—the watch list—of people, both American and foreign, thought to pose a danger to the country. Once containing just twenty names, today it is made up of an astonishing half a million—and it grows rapidly every day. Most on the list are neither terrorists nor a danger to the country, and many are there simply by mistake. Some of the many innocent people on the list may discover their situation when they are tossed off a plane, as happened numerous times to Massachusetts senator Ted Kennedy. Others, however, may never know. Instead, their application for a Small Business Administration loan may be turned down without their being given a reason; or the application of a bright son or daughter for admittance into one of the military academies may be rejected without explanation; or, because the names are shared with foreign governments, a person could be turned away after landing in London for a vacation or business trip—without being told why.

Known as the Terrorist Identities Datamart Environment, or TIDE, it is the mother of all watch lists—the watch list from which all others, including the Do Not Fly list, are derived. Nevertheless, it sits ingloriously on a dated and inexpensive Dell laptop in the basement of the National Counterterrorism Center, maintained by the CIA.

In early September 2001 there was no TIDE, and the NSA was a little-noticed agency attempting to downsize by a third and searching for a mission. A few days later it found its new mission—a mission that began with a phone call intercepted from a house on a dusty backstreet in Yemen.

BOOK ONE

ATTACK

Sanaa

It was late December and Yemen's capital of Sanaa lay cool beneath the afternoon sun. A fine powder of reddish sand, blown southward from the vast Arabian Desert, coated the labyrinth of narrow alleyways that snake throughout the city. On crowded sidewalks, beneath high walls topped with shards of broken glass, women in black chadors paraded with men in drab suit coats and red-and-white checkered scarves that hung loose like long shawls. It is a city of well-oiled Kalashnikovs and jewel-encrusted daggers known as jambiyahs, a place where former comrades from the once Marxist south sit on battered sidewalk chairs chewing qat and puffing from hookahs with wrinkled imams from the tribal north.

At the northwest edge of the city in Madbah, a cluttered neighborhood of cinder-block homes and yapping dogs, was a boxy, sand-swept house. Across the street sat a vacant lot littered with stones, bits of concrete, and tufts of greenish weeds. Made of cement and surrounded by a black iron fence, the house had a solid, fortresslike appearance. On the flat roof were three chimneys, one for each floor, and open balconies that were wide and square, like bull pens at a rodeo; glass arches topped the windows and doors.

It was the home of Ahmed al-Hada, a middle-aged Yemeni who had become friends with Osama bin Laden while fighting alongside him against the Russians in Afghanistan. Hada came from a violent family tribe based for generations in Dhamar Province, about sixty miles south of Sanaa. In a valley of squat, mud-brick houses and green terraced farms, the region was sandwiched between two volcanic peaks in the Yemen Highlands. The area had achieved some fame as a center for the breeding of thoroughbred horses. It also gained fame for kidnappings.

A devoted follower of bin Laden, Hada offered to turn his house into a secret operations center for his friend in Afghanistan. While the rugged Afghan landscape provided bin Laden with security, it was too isolated and remote to manage the day-to-day logistics for his growing worldwide terrorist organization. His sole tool of communication was a gray, battery-powered $7,500 Compact-M satellite phone. About the size of a laptop computer, it could transmit and receive both voice phone calls and fax messages from virtually anywhere in the world over the Inmarsat satellite network. His phone number was 00-873-682505331; the 00 meant it was a satellite call, 873 indicated the phone was in the Indian Ocean area, and 682505331 was his personal number.

Bin Laden needed to set up a separate operations center somewhere outside Afghanistan, somewhere with access to regular telephone service and close to major air links. He took Hada up on his offer, and the house in Yemen quickly became the epicenter of bin Laden's war against America, a logistics base to coordinate his attacks, a switchboard to pass on orders, and a safe house where his field commanders could meet to discuss and carry out operations. Between 1996 and 1998, bin Laden and his top aides made a total of 221 calls to the ops center's phone number, 011-967-1-200-578, using the house to coordinate the 1998 bombings of the U.S. embassies in East Africa and to plan the attack of the USS *Cole* in the port of Aden in 2000.

Also living in the house was Hada's daughter, Hoda, along with her husband, Khalid al-Mihdhar. Standing 5'6" and weighing 142 pounds, Mihdhar had an intelligent face, with a soft, unblemished complexion and a neatly trimmed mustache. Wearing glasses, he had the appearance of a young university instructor. But it was war, not tenure, that interested Mihdhar. He had been training in secret for months to lead a massive airborne terrorist attack against the U.S. Now he was just waiting for the phone call to begin the operation.

Khalid al-Mihdhar began life atop Yemen's searing sandscape on May 16, 1975. Shortly thereafter, he and his family moved to the Kingdom of Saudi Arabia. It was the beginning of the oil boom and the Mihdhars, like thousands of others in the poverty-racked country, hoped to take advantage of the rivers of petrodollars then flowing into the Kingdom. They settled in the holy city of Mecca, Khalid's father was successful, and the family became Saudi citizens.

For centuries the Mihdhar tribe was prominent in the remote Yemen provinces that merge invisibly into Saudi Arabia across an endless expanse of drifting sand dunes. Known as the Empty Quarter, the provinces are a geographical twilight zone, a void on the map where governments, borders, and lines of demarcation have scarcely intruded. Horizon to horizon, there are only the occasional Bedouins who pass like a convoy of ships on a sea of sand. In the city of Tarim is the al-Mihdhar mosque, with its strikingly beautiful minaret reaching more than seventeen stories into the sky, the tallest such structure in southern Arabia. It was built in honor of the fifteenth-century religious leader Omar al-Mihdhar, the grand patriarch of the tribe.

When Mihdhar was growing up, one of his neighborhood friends was Nawaf al-Hazmi, whose father owned a supermarket and a building in the Nawariya district in northwest Mecca and whose older brother was a police chief in Jizan, a city in southwest Saudi Arabia across the border from Yemen. Darker, more muscular, and a year younger than Khalid, he came from a prominent and financially well off family of nine sons. His father, Muhammad Salem al-Hazmi, described both Nawaf and his younger brother, Salem, as "well behaved, nice young men who have been brought up in a family atmosphere free from any social or psychological problems." Nevertheless, Nawaf would later complain that his father once cut him with a knife, which left a long scar on his forearm.

Soon after turning eighteen, Hazmi packed a duffel bag and left for Afghanistan to learn the art of warfare. But by 1993 the war against the Soviet occupiers was long over and Osama bin Laden had returned to his contracting business in Sudan. Undeterred, Hazmi called his family from Peshawar, Pakistan, near the Afghan border, and told them he was going to fight in Chechnya. Very concerned, Muhammad al-Hazmi went to Peshawar to bring his son home. "I went to Peshawar," he recalled. "I found him there. He said he was staying in Pakistan as a trader of frankincense and we returned home together. I asked him to help me in my commercial ventures, including shops and hotels." Speaking of his sons, he added, "In fact, I planned to open branches for them and to find brides for them. But they did not stay for long."

Returning to Mecca with his father, Hazmi met with a key al-Qaeda member and in 1996, bubbling with enthusiasm, convinced Mihdhar to join him in a new war, this one in Bosnia defending fellow Muslims from attacks by the Serbs.

What drove Mihdhar, Hazmi, and thousands of others was a burning need to defend Muslim lands from the West, which had a long history, as they saw it, of invading and occupying their territory, killing and humiliating their families, and supporting their corrupt rulers. The victory in Afghanistan over the Soviets, a superpower, was their first real win and gave many Muslims across the region a sense of unity, fueling an ideology that viewed their separate countries as a single Muslim nation—what they called the "ulema." An occupation or invasion of one Muslim state was therefore an aggression against all Muslim states.

Now with the taste of victory over Russia still sweet in their mouths, adrenaline still pumping through their veins, and a new sense of Muslim nationalism, many were no longer willing to sit and wait for the next encroachment on their lands. The West had long waged war on Islam, they believed; now it was Islam's time to defend itself and fight back. The time had come to go on the offensive.

On August 23, 1996, Osama bin Laden issued his call to action: "My Muslim Brothers of the World," he said. "Your brothers in Palestine and in the land of the two Holy Places [Saudi Arabia] are calling upon your help and asking you to take part in fighting against the enemy—your enemy and their enemy—the Americans and the Israelis. They are asking you to do whatever you can, with your own means and ability, to expel the enemy, humiliated and defeated, out of the sanctities of Islam."

Turning his attention to the United States, he said, "[We] hold you responsible for all of the killings and evictions of the Muslims and the violation of the sanctities, carried out by your Zionist brothers [Israel] in Lebanon; you openly supplied them with arms and finance [during Israel's bloody Grapes of Wrath invasion]. More than 600,000 Iraqi children have died due to lack of food and medicine and as a result of the unjustifiable aggression [the sanctions] imposed on Iraq and its nation. The children of Iraq are our children. You, the U.S.A., together with the Saudi regime, are responsible for the shedding of the blood of these innocent children."

The charges resonated with Mihdhar and Hazmi, and in about 1997

Hazmi returned to Afghanistan, formally swore his loyalty to bin Laden, and fought against the Northern Alliance, possibly with his brother, Salem. Mihdhar followed, and swore his allegiance to the al-Qaeda leader in 1998. They would become the elite of al-Qaeda, among the first seventeen to join from the Arabian Peninsula. Bin Laden would call them "The Founders." Early on, the al-Qaeda leader had developed a special affection and trust—almost father-son at times—for Mihdhar. They shared a common heritage, both sets of ancestors having come from the remote, desolate Yemeni province of Hadramont.

In the spring of 1999, bin Laden and his operations chief, Khalid Shaikh Mohammed, worked out a plan to bring their war to the doorstep of the enemy. Using large commercial airliners, they would in one swoop bring mass destruction to America's financial, political, and military centers: the World Trade Center, the White House, and the Pentagon. During the meeting, bin Laden told Khalid Shaikh that he wanted Mihdhar and Hazmi to travel to the U.S., begin pilot training, and lead the operation. The two were so eager to participate, he said, that they had already obtained U.S. visas.

That fall, bin Laden began setting the air attack operation in motion by sending Mihdhar and Hazmi to an elite training course at his Mes Aynak training facility. But Mihdhar may have been having second thoughts about the U.S. plot. That fall he learned that his wife, Hoda, was pregnant with their first child, and he returned to Yemen rather than continue on to specialized training led by Khalid Shaikh. For Mihdhar, it was a complex situation in a difficult time. His father-in-law, whose house he shared, was one of bin Laden's most loyal supporters and ran his Yemen ops center. And he himself was one of bin Laden's favorites and had sworn his life to him. But all that was before the news of his future child.

Shortly after Hazmi completed Khalid Shaikh's course, in late December 1999, Mihdhar was at the ops center when he received the phone call he had been waiting for. He and Hazmi were instructed to leave in a few days for Kuala Lumpur, Malaysia, where their final, fatal mission to the U.S. would begin. Now Mihdhar had to make a decision.

At that moment, seven time zones and 7,282 miles to the west, the phone call was captured and recorded by America's big ear, the ultrasecret National Security Agency.

Intercept

Michael Vincent Hayden stood at the window of his large corner office looking west through rimless glasses with rectangular lenses. Balding, with dark, graying hair cropped close on the sides, he had a broad globelike forehead, cheeks that were full and friendly, and a slight chin that quickly disappeared into his neck. At fifty-six, he was in good shape—stood as straight as a plumb line but carried a slight paunch that pressed tight against the buttons of his starched, powder-blue shirt. On each shoulder was a cloth epaulet with three silver stars, the rank of an air force lieutenant general.

Unrecognizable to most Americans, the man at the window was the nation's top electronic spy, overseeing more analysts and operatives than anyone else in the country and possibly the planet. In addition to people, he controlled the largest collection of eavesdropping tools the world had ever known: constellations of billion-dollar satellites that could hear whispers on a cell phone from more than twenty-two thousand miles in space; moonlike listening posts around the globe with dozens of giant white orbs containing satellite dishes capable of pulling in tens of millions of phone calls, e-mail messages, and faxes an hour; and, to sort it all out, the largest collection of supercomputers on earth. In addition, he controlled the agency's own secret military force, the little-known Central Security Service, with its fleets of ships, submarines, and aircraft that quietly vacuum the world for telltale voices and data.

The vast and mysterious city stretched out below Hayden was the largest, most powerful, and most intrusive eavesdropping machine ever created. Made up of tens of thousands of people, more than fifty buildings, dozens of receiving antennas, and the planet's most powerful number-crunching supercomputers, it had one overriding goal: access. Access to billions of private hard-line, cell, and wireless telephone conversations; text, e-mail, and instant Internet messages; Web-page histories, faxes, and computer hard drives. Access to any signal or device that might contain information in any form regardless of protection—firewalls, encryption, or passwords. Never before in history had a single person controlled so much secret power to pry into so many private lives.

The NSA was once a backwater agency whose director had to fight to sit at the same table with the CIA chief, but by the time Hayden arrived it had become the largest, most expensive, and most technologically advanced spy organization on the planet. Supplying nearly 80 percent of all intelligence to the rest of government, it needed an entire city to house it—a city that, if incorporated, would be one of the largest municipalities in the state of Maryland. At the same time, it remained nearly as dark and mysterious as when Harry Truman secretly created it, without the approval—or even knowledge—of Congress, nearly half a century earlier. To those who worked there, NSA still stood for No Such Agency and Never Say Anything. To those on the outside it was virtually invisible, hidden from the world behind a labyrinth of barbed wire and electrified fences, massive boulders, motion detectors, hydraulic antitruck devices, cement barriers, attack dogs, and submachine gun–toting commandos in black ninja outfits nicknamed "Men in Black."

Inside, upwards of 30,000 employees and contractors traveled over its 32 miles of roads, parked in lots covering 325 acres, and entered one of more than four dozen buildings containing more than seven million square feet of floor space. More than 37,000 cars were registered in the city, and its post office distributed over 70,000 pieces of mail a day. The secret city's police force employed more than 700 uniformed officers and a SWAT team, ranking it among the top 5 percent in the country in terms of size. Its fire department responded to 168 alarms and 44 automobile accidents the year before Hayden arrived.

Like a powerful political boss, Hayden oversaw his city from a suite of offices on the top floor of the agency's massive headquarters/operations building, an interconnected maze of over three million square feet that stretched in all directions. The complex is so large that the U.S. Capitol Building could easily fit inside it—four times over. Modern and boxy, it has a shiny black-glass exterior that makes it look like a giant Rubik's Cube. But hidden beneath the dark reflective finish is the real building, a skinlike cocoon of thick, orange-colored copper shielding to keep all signals—or any other type of electromagnetic radiation—from ever getting out. Known by the code name Tempest, this protective technique, used throughout much of the secret city, was designed to prevent electronic spies from capturing any escaping emissions. Like a black hole, NSA pulls in every signal that comes near, but no electron is ever allowed to escape.

Like the walls, the window through which Hayden was looking that bright December morning was specially designed to prevent eavesdropping. Made of two thick, bulletproof-style panes, they contained hair-thin copper wires to seal in even the faintest electronic whisper. And to prevent sophisticated laser devices from capturing the telltale vibration of his voice on the glass, music played between the panes.

But despite the metal walls and unbreakable windows, when Hayden arrived the NSA's vast city was a land under siege. Congress was lobbing mortar rounds. Morale was lower than a buried fiber-optic cable. Senior managers had become "warlords" and were locked in endless internecine battles.

Among the agency's most vocal critics was the conservative Georgia Republican Bob Barr, who began his government career working for the CIA. A dapper dresser with a dark-gray mustache, he was also the first member of Congress to call for the impeachment of President Bill Clinton. But a desire for privacy and the right to be left alone by the government was as much a traditional conservative and libertarian value as it was a core liberal principle. In May 1999, a month after Hayden arrived, Barr stood on the floor of the House of Representatives and addressed the issue of the NSA's spying within the U.S.

Barr pointed a finger at an operation known as Echelon. The program, he said, "engages in the interception of literally millions of communications involving United States citizens over satellite transmissions, involving e-mail transmissions, Internet access, as well as mobile phone communications and telephone communications. This information apparently is shared, at least in part, and coordinated, at least in part, with intelligence agencies of four other countries: the UK, Canada, New Zealand, and Australia."

The Georgia congressman then proposed legislation requiring the NSA to turn over to the committee highly secret details about Echelon, including "the legal standards for interception of communications . . . to or from United States persons." Congress, Barr said, is "concerned about the privacy rights of American citizens and whether or not there are constitutional safeguards being circumvented by the manner in which the intelligence agencies are intercepting and/or receiving international communications." He added, "I ask Members on both sides of the aisle to support this very straightforward amendment, which not only will help guarantee the privacy rights for American citizens, but will protect the oversight responsibilities of the Congress which are now under assault by these bogus claims that the intelligence communities are making."

Barr's amendment to the 2000 Intelligence Authorization Act was enthusiastically backed by the Republican chairman of the House Permanent Select Committee on Intelligence, Congressman Porter Goss of Florida, who would later be picked by President George W. Bush to head the CIA. "It is intolerable to think of the United States Government, of big brother, or anybody else invading the privacy of an American citizen without cause," he warned. "I believe that the amendment offered by the gentleman from Georgia (Mr. Barr) will help in that debate, and I am prepared to accept it." Goss was also harshly critical of the NSA's refusal to turn over Echelon documents and warned that such a denial could "seriously hobble the legislative oversight process" provided by the Constitution and would "result in the envelopment of the executive branch in a cloak of secrecy." Jumping on the bandwagon, the Republican chairman of the House Government Reform and Oversight Committee, Dan Burton of Indiana, then announced he would hold hearings on the NSA's Project Echelon.

Spurred on by the House Republicans, newspapers, magazines, and television shows began reporting the dangers of Echelon and the NSA. "Is Uncle Sam illicitly reading your e-mail? Listening in on your telephone calls? Scanning your faxes?" asked ABC News. Even the conservative *BusinessWeek* got in on the act with an article titled "They're Listening to Your Calls: Echelon Monitors Phones, E-Mail, and Radio Signals." Referring to Echelon, the May 1999 article warned: "Run by the supersecret National Security Agency, it's the granddaddy of all snooping operations. Business and political leaders are waking up to the alarming potential of this hush-hush system." The worry about Echelon became so great among a number of privacy and civil liberties groups that several organizations got together and created "Jam Echelon Day," where the public was invited to flood phone lines and the Internet with words likely to trigger the NSA's surveillance system. Among the words were "CIA," "NSA," "assault rifle," "bomb," "assassinate," "Mossad," and even "George Bush."

Overseas, the European Union was alarmed by the potential of Echelon to spy on private companies throughout Europe and pass the information back to American competitors. In response, the EU announced it was also launching a full-scale investigation into the surveillance network. Their preliminary report, issued by the European Parliament, warned: "All e-mail, telephone and fax communications are routinely intercepted by the [NSA], transferring all target information from the European mainland via the strategic hub of London, then by satellite to Fort Meade in Maryland." Among those outraged was Glyn Ford, a British member of the European Parliament. "Almost by accident we've stumbled on to what we believe is a substantial problem for the 15 member states of the European Union and their citizens with respect to their human rights," he said. "We're hoping we can use our position to alert other parliaments and people throughout the EU as to what's going on. And hopefully that will lead to a situation where some proper controls are instituted and [where] these things are done under controlled conditions."

It was against such a backdrop that the NSA picked up the call to Khalid al-Mihdhar in late December 1999. By then, the agency had known of the Yemen ops center and its link to Osama bin Laden and his embassy bombings in East Africa for more than three years. Earlier in 1999, as bin Laden was formulating plans for a sea attack in the Yemeni port of Aden against an American warship and the air attacks in the U.S., an intercept from the ops center had picked up, among other things, the full name of Nawaf al-Hazmi.

The new message clearly identified the two people who would be traveling to Southeast Asia by their first names: "Khalid" and "Nawaf." Another name mentioned in the conversation was "Salem," who analysts correctly determined was Nawaf's brother. Yet despite the fact that the agency had had Nawaf's full name and other details in its database for nearly a year, no one thought to do a computer search before sending a report on the new intercept to the CIA and FBI, and the report went out with first names only. It was a troubling oversight given the importance of the ops center—the place where they knew bin Laden's embassy bombing operation was coordinated—and the fact that three suspected terrorists, closely linked to bin Laden, were suddenly on the move to another part of the world.

If the agency had passed the name "Nawaf al-Hazmi" to the State Department, analysts there would have quickly turned up the fact that Hazmi—a suspected terrorist—had recently been issued a visa to visit the United States. They would also have discovered that a visa had been issued on almost the same day, and in the same place—Jedda—to someone named Khalid al-Mihdhar. And now the two, along with a third suspected terrorist, were on the move.

But within the NSA, isolated in its rarefied world of signals and ciphers at Fort Meade, a universe away from rest of the spy community in the Washington area, analysts felt it was not their job to research the suspected terrorists' identities—unless they were specifically asked. This despite having what was likely the largest database of intelligence information on the planet at their fingertips. Part of the reason was hostility toward their counterparts at the CIA's Counterterrorism Center (CTC) for treating them not as equals but as subordinates—"like an ATM for signals intelligence," said one NSA analyst. They also were angered by the CTC demand that they exclude their own comments on intercept reports when in fact it was the NSA's duty to analyze the messages, not just send out raw transcripts. Finally, NSA analysts complained, if a dispute arose over the interpretation of an intercept, Director of Central Intelligence George Tenet would always come down on the side of his own people at CIA. So in this case, they did the minimum.

The message said that "Nawaf" would fly to Kuala Lumpur on January 2 and that "Khalid" would follow three days later, on January 5, traveling via Dubai. The NSA noted that the intelligence came from a "suspected al-Qa'ida logistics facility" and indicated that "an operational cadre" made up of "terrorist operatives" was planning an important meeting in Malaysia. The NSA message added that "Salem may be Nawaf's younger brother."

At the CIA, there was immediate concern within a crowded, window-less room in the basement of the agency's New Headquarters Building. Four stories underground, Room 1W01 had no name on the door but was known as Alec Station, set up as a "virtual station" and named after the son of its first chief. Its purpose was to find, track, and capture or kill Osama bin Laden. It was a bureaucratic subdivision of the agency's CTC, and its staff, which started out at about a dozen, had doubled by 1999 and included FBI agents.

Alec Station viewed the move by al-Qaeda to organize a meeting in Malaysia as both a troubling development and also an opportunity to dis-cover the group's next move before it happened. "We knew that some guys that looked as though they were al-Qaeda-associated were traveling to KL," said a senior CIA official, referring to Kuala Lumpur. "We didn't know what they were going to do there. We were trying to find that. And we were concerned that there might be an attack, because it wasn't just Mihdhar and Hazmi, it was also 'eleven young guys'—which was a term that was used for operatives traveling. We didn't have the names of the others, and on Hazmi we only had his first name, 'Nawaf.' So the concern was: What are they doing? Is this a prelude to an attack in KL—what's happening here?"

The NSA report wound up in front of a desk officer who began seeing connections. Because the report originated at the Yemen ops center, the travelers were likely members of al-Qaeda. The desk officer was then able to discover Khalid's last name: al-Mihdhar. With that information, Alec Station dispatched a cable to CIA stations in the area. Titled "Activi-ties of Bin Ladin Associate Khalid Revealed," it warned that "something nefarious might be afoot" and that "Nawaf's travel may be in support of a terrorist mission."

The first task was to find out exactly who "Nawaf" and "Khalid al-Mihdhar" were, so CIA station chiefs in Pakistan and the United Arab Emirates got in touch with their counterparts in the local intelligence or-ganizations and asked them to surreptitiously obtain copies of the men's passports as they passed through airport immigration facilities on the way to Malaysia. But because Hazmi changed his flights at the last minute, and because the CIA never considered that possibility, he slipped through the net.

CIA officials had more luck with Mihdhar. As planned, he boarded a plane on January 5 at Sanaa International Airport. Landing in Dubai, he was in the process of transferring to his flight to Kuala Lumpur when he was pulled aside by customs officers. At the request of the American embassy, they took his Saudi passport and secretly photocopied it before letting him go on his way. UAE officials then passed the copy to the CIA station chief in Dubai, who faxed it on to the CIA's Alec Station.

What was striking was that Mihdhar's Saudi passport contained a valid multi-entry visa for the United States. And his visa application, faxed from the American embassy in Jedda, Saudi Arabia, showed Mihdhar's destination was New York. Doug Miller, one of three FBI employees at Alec Station, took one look at the faxes and became instantly alarmed. A possible terrorist, whose travel was arranged by bin Laden's ops center, was on his way to a secret al-Qaeda meeting and would soon be heading for America's largest city. At 9.30 a.m., Miller started pecking out a message to alert his superiors at FBI headquarters, who could then put Mihdhar on a watch list to bar him from entry.

But inexplicably, the message—known as a Central Intelligence Report (CIR)—was spiked by his CIA boss, Tom Wilshire, the deputy chief of Alec Station. At about 4:00 p.m., one of the CIA analysts assigned to the station, a twenty-nine-year-old woman, typed a note onto it: "pls hold off on CIR for now per Tom Wilshire." Without Wilshire's approval, Miller could not pass on the information, even verbally. He had done everything by the book. A potential terrorist and member of al-Qaeda was heading for the U.S., the FBI's jurisdiction—its turf—and he was putting the FBI on notice so it could take action. There was no reason to kill the message.

Miller then told his FBI colleague Mark Rossini what had happened. Rossini had spent many years working on terrorism cases in the bureau, from the first World Trade Center bombing to the attacks on the U.S. embassies in East Africa, and had been assigned to Alec Station for several years. He was both perplexed and outraged that the CIA would forbid the bureau's notification on a matter so important. "Doug came to me and said, 'What the fuck?'" said Rossini, who took the matter up with Wilshire's deputy. (Because she is still actively working for the CIA, her name cannot be revealed.) "So the next day I went to her and said, 'What's with Doug's cable? You've got to tell the bureau about this.' She put her hand on her hip and said, 'Look, the next attack is going to happen in

Southeast Asia—it's not the FBI's jurisdiction. When we want the FBI to know about it, we'll let them know. But the next bin Laden attack's going to happen in Southeast Asia.' " It made no sense to Rossini. The potential terrorists were coming to the U.S.—not to Southeast Asia. Neither Rossini nor Miller was questioned by the 9/11 Commission.

"They refused to tell us because they didn't want the FBI . . . muddying up their operation," said one of the FBI agents assigned to the station, expressing his anger. "They didn't want the bureau meddling in their business—that's why they didn't tell the FBI. Alec Station worked for the CIA's CTC. They purposely hid from the FBI, purposely refused to tell the bureau that they were following a man in Malaysia who had a visa to come to America. The thing was, they didn't want . . . the FBI running over their case."

The person most disliked by CIA officials in Alec Station was John P. O'Neill, the flashy chief of the FBI's National Security Division in New York, both for his style and his expanding turf. In his double-breasted Valentino suits, O'Neill rubbed shoulders with the media, hung out at celebrity-filled Manhattan watering holes, and was constantly pushing to expand the FBI's presence overseas. "They despised the FBI and they despised John O'Neill," said the FBI agent, "because of his personality, because of his style, because he was John, because they couldn't be John."

Having forbidden Miller and Rossini from notifying their headquarters about Mihdhar's planned travel to the U.S., the CIA then proceeded to lose Mihdhar and Hazmi when they took off for a brief visit to Bangkok, en route to the U.S.

Thus Mihdhar and Hazmi had successfully dodged the intelligence capabilities of the NSA, CIA, and FBI. There was only one obstacle left: U.S. passport control. It was the last line of defense between al-Qaeda and America. But since Alec Station had not bothered to submit Mihdhar's name to the State Department for inclusion on its terrorist watch list—and the NSA had not bothered to look up Hazmi's last name, let alone notify the State Department—no one was looking for them. "What we had was an al-Qaeda guy, all his passport information, and a visa to the U.S.," said the senior CIA official, shaking his head slowly back and forth. "If you look at the State Department standard for watch-listing, that met it, not a question about that. And we didn't do that."

On January 14, the chief of Alec Station told senior CIA officials that the search for Khalid al-Mihdhar and the others was still going strong. In fact, it had been over for days. The next day, the FBI agent Doug Miller sent an e-mail to Tom Wilshire asking what happened to his CIR to FBI headquarters warning of Mihdhar's plans to travel to the U.S. "Is this a no-go or should I remake it in some way?" he asked. He never received a response.

At almost that same moment, Mihdhar and Hazmi's plane touched down at Los Angeles International Airport.

San Diego

When United Airlines Flight 002 pulled up to the jetway at LAX on January 15, Los Angeles, like the rest of the country, was taking a nap. The long Martin Luther King weekend looked to be quiet, cool, and wet.

Few likely paid much attention to a front-page story in that weekend's *Los Angeles Times*: "Some See U.S. As Terrorists' Next Big Target." Written by John-Thor Dahlburg, it warned that the U.S. was increasingly "hated by many radical Muslims" and "at the center of this web . . . is Saudi militant Osama bin Laden." One senior French law enforcement official noted: "Terrorism is like the weather: there are zones of high pressure and low pressure, and they change with time. More and more in the future, the United States is going to be a target that will replace the traditional targets, like France." The Swiss journalist Richard Labévière agreed and indicated that the U.S., because of its actions in the Middle East, had largely brought the terrorism on itself. "For America," he cautioned, "the bill is now coming due."

Waved through immigration with barely a glance, Mihdhar and Hazmi had little interest in the morning papers. Neither knew more than a few words of English and neither had ever spent any time in a Western culture. It is thus highly unlikely that they would have embarked on such an enormously complex and important mission without having first arranged for someone with a good command of English to help them get acclimated. According to new information, it is quite possible that one of Mihdhar's own clan members had long been planning for their arrival. He may have met them at Los Angeles International Airport, driven them to San Diego, and helped them get settled.

A year and a half before, in the summer of 1998, Mihdhar Mohammad al-Mihdhar Zaid had arrived in Canada from Yemen. Fluent in English, Mihdhar Zaid was born May 8, 1978, in a remote part of South Yemen. Miles from any paved roads, the village of Al Hamra' was once part of the mini-kingdom of Awsan. Several millennia later it sits forgotten in time on a rocky edge of a dry river valley called Wadi Markha.

Arriving in Ottawa in August 1998, he moved into a small apartment at 1067 Bakerville Drive and signed up for a computer course at Algonquin College, a small school a few blocks away that specialized in business and technology. Mihdhar Zaid was quiet but friendly and wore a short, narrow, neatly trimmed beard that began at his sideburns and circled his chin like a strap. On December 10, four months after arriving, Mihdhar Zaid was finishing his first semester. On a mild Thursday beneath a heavy layer of dark gray clouds in Ottawa, he boarded a red-and-white OC Transpo bus, got off at the American embassy, and walked out with a visitor's (B-2) visa good for a three-month stay in America. Six days later he boarded a plane for San Diego via Los Angeles.

Now safe in the U.S., Mihdhar Zaid's next objective was to remain permanently. He destroyed his Yemen passport, changed his name to Mohdar Mohamed Abdoulah, and applied for asylum at a local immigration office. He was from Somalia, he told them, where he had been subject to harsh persecution. Eventually granted asylum, Mihdhar Zaid enrolled in computer studies at a small local school, Grossmont Community College.

Passing through airport immigration control, Mihdhar and Hazmi indicated that they would be staying at the Sheraton Hotel in Los Angeles. But they never showed up. Instead, shortly after arriving—the same day, according to an FBI chronology—they turned up in San Diego. There they quickly became close friends with Mihdhar Zaid, who may have met them at the airport. With the help of Omar al-Bayoumi, a Saudi who came to the United States in 1993 and was also a close friend of Mihdhar Zaid, the two moved into the Parkwood Apartments, Room 152. Bayoumi then hosted a party to introduce them to the local Muslim community. Mihdhar Zaid would later claim that Bayoumi asked him to acclimate

Mihdhar and Hazmi to San Diego, but Bayoumi would deny it. It may have been that Mihdhar Zaid asked Bayoumi to introduce the two to the community.

Mihdhar and Hazmi's new home at the Parkwood Apartments was a two-bedroom flat in a bland, two-story building. It was located at 6401 Mount Ada Road in Clairemont, a section of the city teeming with students and other young Muslims. Nearby was a large Islamic center, a community college, and a row of strip clubs. Inside the apartment, except for a television set, there was little more than bare walls and a carpeted floor. While Hazmi was outgoing, stopping by the rental office in the mornings to say hello to the managers and join them for coffee and cookies, Mihdhar would breeze by.

To get around, the two paid $2,300 cash for a blue 1988 Toyota Corolla, purchased an insurance policy at the Huggy Bear Agency, and obtained California driver's licenses. But soon the nearly $1,000-a-month rent got too expensive. To help them, Abdussattar Shaikh, a Muslim from India who was a retired San Diego State University English professor and member of the local police commission, offered them a bedroom in his house for free. Mihdhar and Hazmi agreed, but insisted on paying Shaikh $300 a month.

Located in the sleepy, working-class town of Lemon Grove, the house at 8451 Mount Vernon Avenue was perched on a bluff overlooking a valley in east San Diego County. Despite the fact that Shaikh had been a longtime "asset" of the local FBI office, he passed on little but the first names of his two boarders, largely because they never gave any signs of violence or hatred of America. "They never gave me any indication of hate," said Shaikh. "They never showed any anger, any temper." Hazmi would often sit silently, lost in thought. "I'd ask him, 'Is there something bothering you?' He'd just smile and say, 'Oh, no, no.' "

The one person they did trust with their real feelings right from the beginning was Mihdhar Zaid. He was apparently the only one who knew Mihdhar's true background—including his involvement with the pro–bin Laden Islamic Army of Aden back in Yemen. Mihdhar Zaid also shared Mihdhar and Hazmi's anger at the U.S.

During their time in San Diego, Mihdhar Zaid acted as their guide, tutor, trusted confidant, and dining companion. Known as someone "very quick with English" whose conversations were often sprinkled with

American colloquialisms, he translated for them and helped them apply for language training and, later, for flight training in Florida. He even took them to the United Airlines ticket counter to help them trade in the unused portions of their round-trip tickets from Kuala Lumpur to Bangkok. To everyone else, the two claimed they had just arrived from Saudi Arabia.

Mihdhar Zaid lived at the Southridge apartments, just a few miles away from Mihdhar and Hazmi, at 7200 Saranac Street in La Mesa. A fashionable bedroom community east of San Diego, it was dotted with picturesque restaurants, quaint antique shops, and trendy tea and coffee houses. But like many other places around the country and around the world, just below its placid surface there was a groundswell of anger and resentment among young, alienated Muslims. And the anger increased every time a U.S. submarine-launched cruise missile was fired toward Baghdad.

In La Mesa, the epicenter for much of that anger was a Texaco gas station on Spring Street near University Avenue, where Mihdhar Zaid worked as assistant manager. Known as Sam's Star Mart, it had become a hangout for bitter and frustrated young Muslims. Crowded around an outdoor picnic table, they would chat and argue and sip dark coffee. Mihdhar and Hazmi soon became regulars and Hazmi briefly worked the pumps himself, earning six dollars an hour.

Soon frustrated and homesick, their few attempts at flight training a disaster, Hazmi and Mihdhar began spending much of their time calling back to relatives in Yemen and Saudi Arabia, usually on cell phones. Nevertheless, probably out of laziness, they would also occasionally breach security and make calls back home from the landline in their apartment. On March 20, for example, Mihdhar used the cell phone for a sixteen-minute call to his home at the ops center in Yemen, probably to check on his then pregnant wife, Hoda, who lived there with her father, Ahmed al-Hada. "Anytime you saw them, they were on their cell phones," said a former neighbor, Ed Murray. Shaikh, their landlord, also noticed something odd: they would usually go outside when using their cell phones.

They also spent a great deal of time surfing the Web and sending e-mail messages over the Internet using free computers at the San Diego State University library or else borrowing the one owned by their landlord. In March 2000, Mihdhar signed up for WebTV Networks, a service that would let him go online using his television instead of a computer and monitor. His e-mail address was kkhd20002@yahoo.com and Hazmi's was hzi2002@yahoo.com. It was through e-mail that Mihdhar and Hazmi kept in communication with bin Laden's operations chief, Khalid Shaikh, in Pakistan.

By March, the NSA had been eavesdropping on their calls for months without passing on their location. They were living in the home of an FBI informant—without the FBI knowing they were there. And the CIA knew that at least Mihdhar was planning to travel to the U.S. Worse, in early March the CIA's Bangkok station reported to Alec Station that it had identified one of Mihdhar's traveling companions as Nawaf al-Hazmi. The cable reported that Hazmi had traveled to Bangkok on January 8 and had subsequently traveled on a United Airlines flight to Los Angeles on January 15. It also stated that Mihdhar had likewise arrived in Bangkok on January 8 but that it was unknown if and when he had departed. Given the circumstances, however, traveling with Hazmi to Los Angeles would have been a logical guess—especially since they both had visas issued about the same time from the same place.

Now Alec Station definitely knew that one and possibly two of the suspected terrorists linked to bin Laden's Yemen ops center had just flown to California following what appeared to be a terrorist summit. Still, Tom Wilshire never notified the FBI. Nor were any of the three FBI agents inside Alec Station even alerted to the cables. While they had access to the system, none had seen the messages. At that moment, Doug Miller's CIR to FBI Headquarters was still sitting unsent in his computer. At any time, had the FBI been notified, they could have found Hazmi in a matter of seconds. All it would have taken was to call nationwide directory assistance—they would have then discovered both his phone number and address, which were listed in the San Diego phone directory. Similarly, if the NSA had traced any of the incoming calls to the ops center, they would have located two of the callers on California soil.

Deaf

t had been a bitter winter in Maryland, and icy patches of snow had turned General Mike Hayden's driveway into a black-and-white checkerboard. His redbrick house on Fort Meade's Butler Street, the official living quarters for the NSA director, had a dignified but tired look about it. It was in a small, tree-lined enclave reserved for flag-rank officers and off-limits to anyone else. On military bases, privates live with privates, majors live with majors, and generals live with generals. Inside was an eclectic mix of furniture: a shiny black cabinet from Korea, his last post, in the living room; a long, dark wood table in the dining room that probably came from a government warehouse; and a bedroom set upstairs that had banged around the world for a dozen or more years. In the back, protected by a flimsy carport, was the family's only car, a dark blue Volvo.

In the NSA's Ops 2B building, counterterrorism specialists continued reading the cryptic conversations between Mihdhar and the Yemen ops center that had been picked up while targeting the center. But inexplicably, the fact that the calls from Mihdhar had a U.S. country code and a San Diego area code—something that should have been instantly obvious to the NSA's signals intelligence experts—was never passed on to the FBI, CIA, or anyone else. Overly concerned about being accused of domestic eavesdropping, Hayden made a drastic decision. He secretly pulled the plug on intercepting all international communications to and from the U.S., even those involving terrorism. The ban apparently went even so far as to not reveal the fact that suspected terrorists were present in the U.S. Thus, as analysts and agents searched for Osama bin Laden, they had no idea that his men were already here.

Rather than the suave, bullet-dodging Bond in Ian Fleming's thrillers, Michael Vincent Hayden more closely resembled a character out of a John le Carré novel—a wizened, cynical spymaster. He also lacked the background of the stereotypical super-high-tech spy chief. Shortly after his arrival at the NSA, he told his staff that arithmetic had never been his best subject. "I'll state right up front," he admitted, "I am not a mathematician or a computer scientist and I won't pretend to be one. I will be relying heavily on all of you who are."

Irish through and through, Hayden was born on St. Patrick's Day, 1945, in a predominantly Catholic blue-collar area of Pittsburgh's North Side. Known as "the Ward," the neighborhood was near the confluence of the city's three great rivers, the Monongahela, the Allegheny, and the Ohio. It was an era of tin lunch buckets, steel-toed boots, and Iron City beer; a place where smoke from coughing funnels painted the sky white and heavy trucks hauling slag and shiny rolls of new steel made the earth tremble. His father, Harry, worked the swing shift at the city's Allis-Chalmers plant, applying a welding torch to giant electrical transformers, while his mother, Sadie, stayed home to care for Mike and his brother, Harry III, seventeen years his junior, and his sister, Debby.

The Age of Aquarius dawned during Hayden's college years, and by 1967, as he was completing his final year, the country was undergoing a seismic shift in social and political attitudes. In January, twenty thousand people jammed into Golden Gate Park to hear Timothy Leary tell the assembled crowd to "turn on, tune in, drop out." It would be a prelude to the Summer of Love in Haight-Ashbury.

Half the world away, the United States launched a bombing campaign against the North Vietnamese capital of Hanoi as U.S. military presence in the country exploded to nearly half a million troops. That same year more than eleven thousand of them would return in body bags. In April, Martin Luther King Jr. decried "the madness of Vietnam" and said it represented a "malady in the American spirit." Two months later, on June 1, Vietnam Veterans Against the War was born, and in polls taken that summer, American support for the war fell below 50 percent for the first time. In October, fifty thousand protesters marched across the Potomac to the Pentagon, which was protected by more than twenty-five hundred army troops with bayoneted M-14 rifles. A photograph showing a protester putting a daisy into a police officer's gun quickly became an iconic symbol of the anti-war movement.

In Washington, the CIA launched Operation Chaos to find a link between antiwar groups and foreign interests. Soon, the program had indexed 300,000 names, built up 13,000 subject files, and intercepted large numbers of letters to and from American citizens. At the same time, the NSA began targeting the telephone calls and telegrams of thousands of Americans involved in peaceful protest activities, including the singer Joan Baez, the baby doctor Benjamin Spock, and the actress Jane Fonda.

But at Duquesne University it was as if the protests over the war and the collapsing social order were taking place in a different dimension of space and time. What became famously known as the "Duquesne weekend" in February 1967 had nothing to do with a student sit-in or a massive rally. It was the coming together of ultraconservative Pentecostals and Charismatics to give birth to the Catholic Charismatic Renewal movement, an evangelical group that promoted, among other things, the speaking in tongues during Catholic religious services. Like many of his religious and conservative classmates, Hayden rejected the antiwar movement and the social revolution and instead would embrace the military.

After receiving his bachelor's degree in history in 1967, he married Jeanine Carrier, a fellow student from the village of River Grove, Illinois, about a dozen miles from Chicago. He then stayed on at Duquesne for another two years to earn his master's degree in modern American history, writing his master's thesis on the effects of the Marshall Plan on post–World War II Europe. As Jeanine typed up and proofread his manuscript, Hayden drove a cab around the city, worked as a bellhop at the exclusive Duquesne Club, and coached football at St. Peter's. When he graduated in 1969, the war in Vietnam was continuing its slide to disaster and the antiwar movement was growing in strength and power.

As his family prepared to move to nearby Brighton Heights, Hayden joined the air force. "He was so interested in history that I guess he wanted to become part of it," said his brother, Harry. But instead of combat in Vietnam, the young second lieutenant was sent to America's heartland: Omaha, Nebraska, home of Offutt Air Base and the Strategic Air Command Headquarters, where he worked as a briefer. Two years later he was assigned to Guam. As chief of current intelligence for the headquarters of the Eighth Air Force, he helped plan massive bombing raids against Vietnam. Beginning in 1975, he spent the rest of the decade in various schools, mostly teaching ROTC at St. Michael's College in rural Vermont.

In June 1980 Hayden, newly promoted to major, was sent to Osan Air Base in South Korea as chief of intelligence for a tactical fighter wing. Two years later it was back to school and then air attaché in Sofia, Bulgaria. "I've crawled in the mud to take pictures of MiG-23s taking off from Bulgarian airfields so I could understand what type of model it was," said Hayden. From there he moved into a policy job in the Pentagon and then over to the Bush White House in the National Security Council until 1991. After an intelligence assignment at U.S. European Command Headquarters in Germany, he took over the Air Intelligence Agency and became director of the Joint Command and Control Warfare Center at Kelly Air Force Base, Texas. There he became heavily involved in the concept of information warfare. Finally he was assigned as deputy chief of staff for the United Nations Command in South Korea, where he dealt with the issues of missing servicemen from the Korean War.

Hayden was in Seoul, Korea, in late 1998 when he received a call from George Tenet, the director of central intelligence, asking him to come back to Washington for an interview. The meeting took place at the Wye Plantation on the Eastern Shore of Maryland during the Arab-Israeli peace talks. Tenet was there playing an active role but broke away for the interview with Hayden. The CIA chief liked what he heard and Hayden flew back to Korea virtually assured that he had the job as director of the NSA.

Shortly afterward, on a Friday night, he took his wife to the movie theater at Yongsan Army Garrison. Playing was a film he had not heard of called *Enemy of the State,* in which Will Smith portrays an average citizen caught up in the NSA's secret eavesdropping net, and Gene Hackman is a retired NSA official worried about the agency's enormous power. In the opening scene, the NSA's director of operations, played by Jon Voight, assassinates a congressman who refuses to approve a bill expanding the agency's power to spy on Americans. Thereafter, agency thugs spend much of the rest of the movie doing their best to kill Smith's character, who witnessed another NSA assassination.

"Other than the affront to truthfulness, it was an entertaining movie," Hayden told the author in his NSA office on February 2, 2000. "But I'm not too uncomfortable with a society that makes its boogeymen secrecy and power. That's really what the movie's about—it was about the evils of secrecy and power . . . making secrecy and power the boogeymen of political culture, that's not a bad society."

As Hayden spoke those words, Mihdhar and Hazmi were moving into Room 152 at the Parkwood Apartments in the Clairemont section of San Diego and establishing communications with bin Laden's Yemen operations center. Their phone was even listed on page 13 of the 2000–2001 Pacific Bell White Pages: "ALHAZMI Nawaf M 6401 Mount Ada Rd. 858-279-5919." But Hayden's decision to secretly turn a deaf ear to nearly all international communications entering and leaving the U.S.—even when they involved known terrorists within the country—would have momentous consequences.

It would also be an area completely unexplored by the 9/11 Commission, which, astonishingly, virtually ignored the NSA in its investigation. "No one from the commission—no one—would drive the twenty-seven miles from downtown Washington north to the headquarters of the NSA, in Fort Meade, Maryland, to review its vast archives of material on al-Qaeda and terrorist threats," according to the *New York Times* reporter Philip Shenon, author of the book *The Commission*. "There was no problem on the commission's staff finding people willing, eager, to spend their days at the CIA's headquarters in Virginia to review its files," said Shenon. "But no one seemed worried about what the NSA knew." He added, "For the commission's staff, Fort Meade might as well have been Kabul." Shenon interviewed the commission staffer Lorry Fenner, an air force colonel with an intelligence background, who found that both the commissioners and staff "did not understand what the NSA was and what it did." And because Fenner herself was assigned to other tasks, the NSA completely escaped scrutiny.

Hayden's decision was based on his concern that the NSA would once again be caught illegally targeting American citizens as happened in the mid-1970s. Back then, many senior officials were read their Miranda rights by FBI agents and came close to being prosecuted. Hayden was also concerned about his agency's growing image as America's secret and powerful "boogeyman." The best way to avoid both outcomes, he believed, was to keep his agency's operations as far away from U.S. territory as possible. If a terrorist in the U.S. was communicating with his masters in a foreign country, Hayden reasoned, that was the FBI's responsibility, not his.

But the problem was that Hayden did not coordinate coverage with the bureau either, leaving them largely in the dark and the international circuits to and from the U.S. largely unmonitored. And even had they notified the bureau, the FBI, light-years behind the NSA technologically and with little capacity for translating languages such as Arabic, would not have been able to pick up the slack. Thus, although the NSA picked up conversations between Mihdhar (identified as "Khalid" in NSA intercepts) in San Diego and the ops center in Yemen by targeting the ops center, it never made the effort to reveal where Mihdhar was actually located.

Had the NSA wanted to, it could have easily discovered Mihdhar's exact location in the U.S. from the technical metadata that preceded the calls—the same information that the telephone companies use to bill their customers. With that, they could have gotten a warrant from the Foreign Intelligence Surveillance Court and begun full-scale targeting of Mihdhar's international communications—telephone as well as e-mail. All that was required for a FISA (Foreign Intelligence Surveillance Act) application was showing that the targets were likely agents of a foreign terrorist organization, an easy task since both Mihdhar and Hazmi were being directed by bin Laden's ops center in Yemen.

Hayden's decision was not made lightly. Almost from the moment he arrived at the NSA, in March 1999, the agency was under seige. As the Cold War ended and the digital age began, the NSA became a convenient target for those fearful of the U.S. government's growing surveillance capability. At the center of the controversy was Echelon, the agency's system for eavesdropping on worldwide private communications, which involved sifting through billions of telephone calls and e-mails continuously zipping around the globe.

And as Mihdhar and Hazmi landed in Los Angeles, the NSA's computerized brain that ran Echelon was on the verge of a devastating aneurysm.

After dinner on Monday, January 24, 2000, a little more than a week after the two arrived in the U.S., Hayden took a seat on his living room couch and flipped on the television. The undefeated Syracuse Orange-men were scheduled to play the University of Connecticut Huskies at the Carrier Dome on nationwide TV, and it was expected to be an exciting game. But just as he sat down, his secure STU-III telephone began buzzing upstairs in his vaultlike SCIF. Pronounced "skif" and officially known as a Sensitive Compartmented Information Facility, it was a bugproof room where he could read and store supersecret NSA documents and communicate with the agency's headquarters, about a mile away.

Hayden inserted his black plastic crypto-ignition key into the phone, enabling it to receive information at the highest classification level, and in a small window the words "Top Secret Codeword" appeared. On the other end of the line was the operations center with some very bad news. The NSA, he was told, had just suffered a massive systemwide meltdown. "Give me a sense," he asked. "How many computers are down?" It was the worst possible answer. "All of them," the operations officer told him. "The whole system is down." Hayden was in disbelief. Every computer in the agency's secret city—including those in its two-story supercomputer facility—had suddenly crashed and could not be restarted. While it was 7:00 p.m. in Washington, it was midnight deep within the computers, which operate on Greenwich Mean Time. For some reason, at that moment a piece of software snapped, setting off the enormous shutdown.

"It was the whole net by which we move, use, abuse, process — everything we do with information here at Fort Meade went down," said Hayden. "Everything on the Fort Meade campus went down. Everything!" There was no way to minimize the problem, Hayden said. "NSA headquarters was brain-dead . . . This was really bad . . . We were dark. Our ability to process information was gone." Hayden called George Tenet, the director of central intelligence, and then immediately ordered an emergency response. Computer scientists, electrical engineers, mathematicians—anyone who could shed light on the problem was told to report in. But then, adding to the chaos, Washington was suddenly hit by a powerful snowstorm that shut down the entire federal government, including the NSA, for two days.

By Thursday, as snowplows finished clearing the secret city's 325 acres of parking lots and employees crowded into the seventeen thousand spaces, Hayden wondered how to keep such an enormous disaster secret from foes such as Osama bin Laden, who might seek to take advantage of the agency's sudden deafness. "I called [NSA director of corporate communications] Bill [Marshall] in here and I said, Bill, I need a concept; we need to communicate this to the work force," he recalled. "What should we do?" Marshall suggested a town meeting. "And that's exactly what we did."

Taking the stage in the William F. Friedman Auditorium, Hayden warned everyone not to breathe a word about the crash. "I said the fact that we're down is an operational secret. Our adversaries cannot know that our intelligence capabilities have been crippled." He pulled no punches. "We are the keeper of the nation's secrets," he told the code breakers and the intercept operators, the cryptolinguists and the area specialists. "If word of this gets out, we significantly increase the likelihood that Americans will get hurt. Those who would intend our nation and our citizens harm will be emboldened. So this is not the back half of a sentence tonight that begins, 'Honey, you won't believe what happened to me at work.' This is secret. It does not leave the building!"

That night, Hayden and his wife, Jeanine, took a long drive to the Stone Manor, a romantic inn near Frederick, Maryland. It was their thirty-second wedding anniversary and he had long ago made the dinner reservations. But on the drive back to Fort Meade, he received a call from his deputy director for technology, Robert Stevens, who said he needed to speak to Hayden on a secure line the minute he arrived home. A short while later, Hayden climbed the stairs to his SCIF and dialed Stevens on his STU-III. Despite the fact that the system was slowly improving, Stevens believed the fix was going in the wrong direction and wanted permission to bring the whole system down once again and start all over. Hayden agreed, but by then the NSA's customers were becoming hungry for their daily ration of secrets.

Desperate for intelligence, Hayden's deputy, Barbara McNamara, contacted the agency's British partner, GCHQ (Government Communications Headquarters). "We actually got in touch with them," she recalled, "and said: 'Would you please ensure that the information that you are providing in support of military operations or ongoing world events, crises, conditions, also gets to our customers here in the U.S.?' " Meanwhile, on the second floor of the Tordella Supercomputer Building, scientists pulled apart spaghetti-like mazes of multicolored wires, covered desks and floors with unwieldy schematics and wiring diagrams, and probed, millimeter by millimeter, the nervous systems of the computers. The hard work paid off and the cause of the crash was pinpointed to an outdated routing protocol. The solution was a massive hardware and software upgrade.

On Friday, after spending thousands of man-hours and $1.5 million in repairs, the network was patched together. After more than three days, the NSA awoke from its electronic coma, its memory still intact. But like water faucets stuck in the open position, millions of intercepts per hour had continued to pour down from the agency's satellites during the crash—enough data every three hours to fill the Library of Congress. But instead of being processed and analyzed, they were simply collected in vast memory buffers capable of storing five trillion pages of data.

"We had the ability to store that which we collected over this three and a half day period," said Hayden. "When we were able to go back and process the information when that capability came back, it took eight to twelve hours to process and analyze the information that we had collected." Hayden concluded, "The network outage was a wake up call." Others familiar with the NSA's fragile state of technology agreed. "We went deaf for seventy-two hours because of an antiquated system that should have been upgraded years ago," said Tim Sample, staff director of the House Intelligence Committee.

The next day, as Hayden and his wife went cross-country skiing on the nearby Fort Meade golf course, the supercomputers in the Tordella complex continued crunching through the mountains of backlogged data. Batches of intercepts at last arrived on analysts' desks. And in the agency's counterterrorism center, the bin Laden specialists finally began reading the communications between Mihdhar and the Yemen ops center.

Hayden spent much of the spring defending his agency from attacking Republicans. On April 12, 2000, he took the witness chair in an open session of the House Intelligence Committee. It was a rare sight. The last time an NSA director had appeared in such a setting was a quarter of a century before, when another air force general, Lew Allen, squirmed in his seat from hostile questions about decades of illegal spying. Determined not to let that happen to him, Hayden ensured that his agency's giant ears were pointed as far away from the U.S. as possible. Rather than tens of thousands of targets in the U.S., as some reports had speculated, the NSA was targeting only about three individuals within the country. It was a cautious approach, made necessary because of the enormous focus on the NSA by Hollywood, the media, and Congress. But caution also had its dangers; terrorists might be missed—terrorists like Mihdhar and Hazmi.

Committee chairman Porter Goss, a Republican from Florida, led off the hearing with a bit of humor. "There are concerns that the NSA operates in a very secret environment, without any oversight or legal strictures in place to guide and control their conduct," he said. "These concerns were dramatized quite notably in the recent film *Enemy of the State*—a very exciting motion picture. Considering the fact that the character playing me was killed off in the first half hour of the film, I am very pleased to report that the movie was nothing more than a very entertaining work of fiction, and we'd like to keep it that way."

But Goss quickly got down to why they were there. "Congress imposed the Foreign Intelligence Surveillance Act of 1978 upon the NSA and other elements of the intelligence community because the NSA was found during the sixties and seventies to have engaged in indiscriminate electronic surveillance of U.S. persons. This was not a good period. This was not a proper thing."

Sitting arrow-straight in the witness chair, three silver stars on each shoulder flashing in the television lights, Hayden immediately went on the defensive. "What I'm here to tell you today," he said, "is that the laws and regulations under which we operate are, one, observed, and two, sufficient for both our conducting our mission and conducting it in a way that protects the rights guaranteed by the Fourth Amendment . . . The law requires us to do everything we can to prevent touching American privacy even at the very front end of that process, in the collection."

Hayden then addressed the charges that, as he put it, "NSA illegally spies on American persons." A key issue, he noted, was the definition of "American person." "We use the phrase within the agency that we protect the rights of American persons. Now, let me define in more detail who is an American person . . . An American person is an American citizen anywhere. An American person is also a permanent resident alien of the United States." To make his point, Hayden used an example. "Let me put a fine point on this. If, as we are speaking here this afternoon, Osama bin Laden is walking across the Peace Bridge from Niagara Falls, Ontario, to Niagara Falls, New York, as he gets to the New York side, he is an American person. And my agency must respect his rights against unreasonable search and seizure, as provided by the Fourth Amendment to the Constitution."

It was an ironic example. As Hayden was speaking that afternoon, bin Laden's men had already arrived. Just two days earlier in San Diego, Hazmi took his first flight lesson. And three days later he would receive a wire transfer of $5,000 from bin Laden's moneyman in the United Arab Emirates to continue the lessons.

Hayden's testimony was deliberately aimed at disarming his critics, but it was also misleading. His hypothetical suggested that NSA eavesdroppers would have to remove their earphones the second bin Laden stepped onto U.S. territory and became a "U.S. person." In reality, the NSA would be monitoring his every move, before, during, and after his arrival. While he was a foreigner in a foreign country—Canada—the agency would have had no legal problem eavesdropping on him. And as he walked into New York, the agency could have continued monitoring his communications without skipping a beat. FISA allowed for emergency eavesdropping without a warrant for up to two days. In that time, the agency could have easily obtained a full FISA warrant to continue the surveillance because of bin Laden's status as someone associated with a foreign terrorist organization, al-Qaeda.

Another sensitive area Hayden touched on was data mining—obtaining telephone calling records from the phone company—which he said was illegal. "The information you get in your phone bill, if it is about an American person, is beyond my reach. It is protected communication," he said. "All that comes about by the statutes and laws that are provided to us. They all devolve from the Fourth Amendment, FISA, Executive Order 12000, which indeed was promulgated in 1981, but has been reviewed by every administration, Democratic and Republican, since that time. And then finally by USSID 18, United States Signals Intelligence Directive 18, which takes the provisions in those broader statutes and executive orders and turns them into a specific cookbook that can be understood by every eighteen- or nineteen-year-old airman, soldier, sailor, or marine who comes to work for the National Security Agency."

Finally, Hayden brought up one area that appeared to be a giant loophole, if a president wanted to secretly take advantage of it. It was simply to have one of the NSA's partners in Canada, Britain, or another country eavesdrop on targets beyond the legal reach of the NSA and then pass the information back to the agency. Such an action had been considered in the past. In 1973, for example, the CIA refused to help the NSA illegally eavesdrop on American citizens within the U.S. But according to the NSA's deputy director at the time, Dr. Louis Tordella, they could have done it using foreigners in a foreign country. Hayden suggested that such activity was not prohibited by federal law. Instead it was prohibited only by presidential executive order, and executive orders can be canceled or changed at the whim of a president. "By executive order," Hayden said, "it is illegal for us to ask others to do what we cannot do ourselves, and we don't do it."

By the end of the hearing, Hayden had succeeded in convincing the committee and much of the public that his agency had not become the Orwellian nightmare portrayed in the movies. There was also little question, however, that all it would take for life to imitate art was a few secret decisions. But as he made his way out of the hearing room on that crisp afternoon in April 2000, the NSA director had no idea that his agency's greatest threat came not from studio executives in Hollywood, but from a pair of flight students 125 miles farther south in San Diego. "Mike Hayden's challenge," noted George Tenet at the hearing, "is not only to manage today, but to get ready for the next century . . . and anticipate how our adversaries will surprise us."

Mesa

Bored with life in San Diego, Mihdhar was getting anxious about his wife, Hoda, whom he would call often. Then in late May he learned that he had just become a father for the first time and he made the decision to return to Yemen and see his new daughter. Notified of this decision, Khalid Shaikh was infuriated. Not only was his soldier planning to go AWOL in the middle of the operation, Mihdhar's partner would be left abandoned in San Diego. Mihdhar, who barely knew Khalid Shaikh but was very close to bin Laden, ignored his demands to remain. Besides, he told him, there would be no problem in returning since he had not overstayed his visa. In a mad rush, Mihdhar pulled all $4,888.69 from his bank account and gave it to Hazmi, transferred the Toyota's registration to him as well, and then made plane reservations.

On June 9, Mihdhar piled his bags in the back of the Toyota and set off for Los Angeles with Hazmi driving and Mihdhar Zaid giving directions. After spending the night at a motel, the next morning they drove to Los Angeles International Airport. At the time, the idea of hijacking a plane from there was still being considered as part of the ultimate operation. Thus, soon after entering the terminal the three began casing it out. One stood near the security area with a video camera and slowly began turning in a circle to capture the entire panorama.

At 2:15 p.m., Mihdhar boarded Lufthansa Airlines Flight 457 for Frankfurt, where he would change for Flight 636 to Kuwait and then on to Sanaa, where Hoda and his new baby daughter were waiting.

Abandoned by his friend Khalid, Hazmi remained in San Diego like a jilted lover. By December 2000, he had been there almost a year. As Mihdhar saw his new baby in Sanaa, took part in the bombing of the USS *Cole* in Aden, and was busy in Saudi Arabia recruiting a dozen or more soldiers for the operation, Hazmi spent his days in his small Lemon Grove room. During the day he would surf the Internet on his landlord's computer following the news of fighting in Chechnya and Bosnia, call home and send e-mails, pump gas with Mihdhar Zaid at Sam's Star Mart—and wait. He had long ago given up any idea of becoming a pilot and had even stopped taking English lessons. But he continually received messages from Khalid Shaikh—and later from Tawfiq bin Attash, another top bin Laden lieutenant—that the operation was still going forward and that he would soon receive a new partner.

Six months earlier, at the start of the summer, the man picked to run the operation, Mohamed Atta, arrived on the East Coast and began flight training with a number of his associates. For bin Laden, it was good fortune falling in his lap. At the same time that it seemed neither Mihdhar nor Hazmi were going to become pilots, Atta and a number of his friends applied to join al-Qaeda. Fluent in English, well educated, and with a technical background, Atta seemed the perfect candidate to take over the operation. While Mihdhar recruited the soldiers in Saudi Arabia, Hazmi would become Atta's deputy—as soon as they found him a partner.

Finally, as the early snows of winter pushed deep across the country, Hazmi received the e-mail from Tawfiq bin Attash that he had been waiting for, and a few weeks later, on December 8, Delta Airlines Flight 43 from Paris touched down at Cincinnati's international airport. On board was Hani Hanjour, a quiet, determined twenty-nine-year-old on a stopover from Dubai to San Diego. Medium height and weight with short black hair and dark, soulful eyes, he was returning to a place very familiar to him, a place where he had once lived with a family in Florida, studied English in California, and earned his commercial pilot's license in Arizona.

Hanjour was born in 1972 into a prominent family of landowners and food supply merchants. The middle child of seven, he lived in a sprawling two-story villa on a tree-lined street in Al Faisaliyah, an upscale neighborhood in Saudi Arabia's summer capital, Taif. For many Saudis, Taif is a place to escape to, a cool mountain refuge a mile above the sweltering streets of Mecca. Set in a hollow between granite hills rising from the eastern slope of the Hejaz, it is also a city where the old and new have achieved a degree of harmony. Ultramodern marble and glass government offices tower over old mud homes with wooden louver windows and carved wooden doors. Elsewhere are pink palaces and the Corniche, a road that spirals down the sheer cliffs of the Taif escarpment to the fiery sandbox below.

Like the rest of the operatives, Hanjour was a member of the first generation of Muslims to witness the successful defeat of an invading Western superpower, shoved back across its border like a bully pushed out of a school yard. Growing up, their heroes were the men who at last stood up to the West, drew a line in the sand along the Afghan border, and then succeeded with little more than dented Kalashnikovs and worn sandals.

By the time Hanjour reached his teenage years, in the late 1980s, he was off to Afghanistan to join in the fight. But by then the Soviets had been defeated and he instead spent six weeks working for a relief agency. His battle would have to wait for another time and place.

Following the war in Afghanistan, buoyed by the victory over the mighty Soviet empire, many in Hanjour's generation turned their attention to another superpower with a long and unsavory history in the Middle East: the United States. The list of grievances was long. There was the CIA's coup that overthrew Iran's democratically elected leader and replaced him with the brutal quarter-century reign of the Shah and his Savak secret police. Then there was the unstinting support, backed by cash and carrier strike forces, for the region's most despised and corrupt dictators. And then the harsh sanctions imposed on Iraq that had no effect on Saddam Hussein but brought death and illness to hundreds of thousands of the young and poor. And finally it was America's iron-fisted support for Israel's half century of humiliation, oppression, and occupation of the Palestinians as well as its wars, occupation, and massacres in Lebanon.

For Atta, the breaking point came in April 1996 with the start of Israel's massive bombardment of Beirut and Arab villages in southern Lebanon in an attempt to end the shelling of northern Israel by Hezbollah.

In the southern Lebanese town of Qana, the attack turned horrific, and while largely ignored by the American press, it made the front pages of newspapers throughout Europe and the Middle East. "It was a massacre," said a front-page story in London's *Independent*. "Israel's slaughter of civilians in this terrible 10-day offensive—206 by last night—has been so cavalier, so ferocious, that not a Lebanese will forgive this massacre."

Even some in the Israeli press were harshly critical of the attack. Arieh Shavit, a columnist for the Israeli daily newspaper *Ha'aretz,* noted: "How easily we killed them [in Qana] without shedding a tear. We did not denounce the crime, did not arrange for a legal clarification, because this time we tried to deny the abominable horror and move on." And the international edition of *Time* magazine noted, "Around the Middle East . . . Qana is already a byword for martyrdom."

For Atta, Israel's Grapes of Wrath invasion was the final shove, pushing him over the edge. He was "enraged," said his friend and fellow student Ralph Bodenstein. Shortly after the invasion began, Mohamed Atta walked to the al-Quds mosque in Hamburg, Germany, with several of his friends and signed his last will and testament, naming it his "Death Certificate." He was twenty-seven years old. According to one of his friends, by signing the will during the attack he was offering his life as a response to Israel's invasion. All that was left was to find the right target.

For millions throughout the region, their emotions had been deprived of expression for decades. Afghanistan showed them there was an alternative. To Hanjour, Atta, Mihdhar, Hazmi, and the rest, the United States was *their* generation's Soviet Union, and they dedicated their lives to continuing where the last generation left off. As America bombed Berlin and Tokyo during its great war, they would bomb New York and Washington during theirs.

It was dark when Delta Flight 1661 passed over Balboa Park and finally touched down on Lindbergh Field in San Diego. For Hani Hanjour, it was the end of a long journey, but it was also a journey to the end.

There, happy to greet him, was Nawaf al-Hazmi, who after six long months finally had a new partner, a new companion, someone who knew his secret. His time in purgatory was over; the operation was again moving forward. They were also both in a hurry. Now as second in command under Atta, Hazmi was concerned because the soldiers Mihdhar was recruiting and preparing would start arriving on the East Coast in the spring and they had to be there to handle them. And Hanjour, the last of the pilots to arrive—half a year after the others—knew he needed to catch up very fast on his flying and was eager to get back to Arizona for a few months of practice.

Within a day, and with little time to rest from his exhausting flight, Hanjour climbed into Hazmi's aging blue Corolla—now packed with all his belongings—as they prepared for a long cross-country odyssey. But first Hazmi made a last trip back to his rooming house in Lemon Grove to bid farewell to his friend and landlord, Abdussattar Shaikh. Introducing Hanjour simply as "Hani," Hazmi told Shaikh that they were headed north to San Jose to take flying lessons and that he would stay in touch, and he promised to return soon. Next they stopped by Sam's Star Mart, where Hazmi now introduced Hanjour as a "longtime friend from Saudi Arabia." After he said his good-byes to Mihdhar Zaid and the rest of the crowd, they were off.

On December 12, they pulled into Mesa, Arizona, where Hanjour was going to begin his training on multi-engine aircraft. At Jet Tech, a company in nearby Phoenix that offered instruction using a highly sophisticated Boeing 737-200 simulator, Hanjour couldn't wait to get started. Strapped in his pilot's seat, he perfected his turns, his control, and his stabilization. Pushing the throttles fully forward, he also perfected his speed and his aim as he prepared for his first multi-engine solo, and his last.

Thinthread

ar away from Hayden's modern suite high atop Ops 2B, Rich Taylor's ornate, wood-paneled office was almost a museum piece. Located on the second floor of Ops 1, it was in the agency's original A-shaped building, now the home of its signals intelligence directorate. When the agency first moved to Fort Meade in the late 1950s, at a time when even its name was top secret, it was the office of the director. A few years later, during the Cuban missile crisis, it was where many intercepts of both the Russian naval forces and the Cuban missile crews were read.

As the NSA's deputy director for operations, Taylor was Hayden's electronic spymaster. A native of Kentucky and a 1969 graduate of the Air Force Academy, Rich Taylor spent five years in the air force before signing on with the NSA as a program manager in the agency's research and engineering organization. From then on he spent nearly his entire career involved with the NSA's satellite eavesdropping program, from design of the spacecraft during several years at the National Reconnaissance Office to analysis as the manager of the overhead systems division within the operations division. He then became the executive director, the agency's number three position. But the choice job in the agency had always been the chief of the operation directorate, where all the action happened—which Taylor took over in November 1997.

Frustrated by the agency's lumbering bureaucracy, Taylor sent a long and secret memorandum to Hayden within weeks of the general's arrival outlining his view on fixing the agency's growing problems. "We need help," he wrote. "The first and most important issue for NSA/CSS [Central Security Service] is to reform our management and leadership system . . . we have good people in a flawed system." Next, he said, was "strengthening and leveraging our strategic alliances," in other words, working more closely with the CIA and the NSA's foreign partners, such as GCHQ.

The problem with the foreign partners, Taylor complained, was the NSA's tendency to leave them in the dust both operationally and technologically. "The U.S. maintains the lead, both in technology and operational readiness," he said. "We bring our partners along." By not helping them keep up, Taylor suggested, the NSA might one day lose their cooperation. Finally, because so much of the NSA's success in the age of the computer depended on getting secret access to foreign machines, databases, and software—with the help of the CIA's clandestine officers—it was more important than ever to closely merge the two disciplines. "Our relationship with CIA is absolutely vital to our future success," he wrote. "It is essential that NSA and CIA put our relationship on a sound basis."

Before Hayden arrived, Taylor had been tackling the issue of how best to reduce the ocean of intercepts flowing into the agency and at the same time have the ability to trace back the suspicious calls to the U.S., including those from Yemen, without violating the law. Code-named Thinthread, the project was intended to develop complex digital filters to sift through the Nile-size rivers of phone calls, e-mail, faxes, and other communications signals channeled into the agency by satellites and ground stations. Made up of diabolically complex mathematical algorithms and protocols, these filters would isolate and trap the key conversations and messages while discarding the rest, unheard and unread.

The system was designed for intercepting communications within or between foreign countries. But Thinthread also had a unique component that allowed the agency to trace signals back to the United States without violating the Foreign Intelligence Surveillance Act. That law forbade monitoring communications to or from individuals in the U.S. without a warrant. The catch-22 was that to get a warrant the agency needed probable cause, but without being able to intercept the message and follow it to its U.S. destination there was no way of knowing to whom or where it was going. And without that information, there was no way to apply for a warrant.

The idea behind Thinthread was that the agency would automatically encrypt the body of all the messages and phone calls entering and leaving the U.S., thereby protecting the privacy of the content. All that would be visible would be the "externals," the exact destination or origin of the communications. As a further safety check, Thinthread also employed an automated auditing system to ensure that analysts were not abusing the system and "peeking" at the contents.

With such a system, the agency would be able to see the links between suspected targets overseas and destinations in the U.S. without the ability to read the contents of the communications. And if a pattern began to emerge—such as frequent calls and e-mails from the Yemen ops center to several phone numbers and computers in San Diego—that would be enough to show probable cause that the people in San Diego were agents of a foreign terrorist organization. With that, the agency could then obtain a FISA warrant to identify the individuals, decrypt the contents of the communications, and begin reading and listening to the complete messages and phone calls. At the same time, the FBI could begin its own investigation on the ground. The system would also allow the agency to target those communications that simply transited through the U.S., such as an e-mail from Frankfurt to Mexico City via the Internet hub in Miami.

Tests of the program throughout 1998 proved very successful and Taylor advocated for its full implementation. But when Hayden arrived the following March he flatly opposed it. His opposition was largely based on objections by his legal staff, who felt the program pushed the agency too close to the edge. Hayden also had a personal desire to avoid even the appearance of eavesdropping on Americans in America, which he considered the FBI's responsibility. Instead of Thinthread, he came up with a different concept to help with the information overload problem. Code-named Trailblazer, the project, like Thinthread, attacked the massive data flowing into the agency with a combination of powerful computers and complex filtering software. But where Thinthread encrypted all traffic entering, leaving, or transiting the U.S.—thus allowing the NSA to analyze where it came from and where it was going without violating the law—Trailblazer offered no such protection.

By the fall of 2000, the battle between Thinthread and Trailblazer cul-

minated in a "very emotional debate" between Taylor and Hayden, with
the director siding with the lawyers. Taylor, pushed out of his position
by Hayden, then decided to leave the agency altogether at the end of December, the same month that the NSA released a request for proposals to
defense contractors to begin bidding to work on Trailblazer.

Hayden knew the agency was in trouble. "We are digging out of a deep
hole," he said. "NSA downsized about one-third of its manpower and
about the same proportion of its budget in the decade of the 1990s. That
is the same decade when packetized communications—the e-communi-
cations we have all become familiar with—surpassed traditional communications. That is the same decade when mobile cell phones increased
from 16 million to 741 million—an increase of nearly fifty times. That
is the same decade when Internet users went from about 4 million to 361
million—an increase of over ninety times. Half as many landlines were
laid in the last six years of the 1990s as in the whole previous history of
the world. In that same decade of the 1990s, international telephone traffic went from 38 billion minutes to over 100 billion."

Out of those 100 billion minutes, however, the NSA needed only a few
dozen to discover and stop bin Laden's planned air attack—and those few
dozen were sitting nearby in a cavernous tape library collecting dust.

Totowa

On February 21, 2001, Hani Hanjour was awarded his certificate for completing sixty hours of Boeing 737-200 Systems Ground Training. At Jet Tech in Phoenix, he underwent lengthy sessions in the company's Boeing 737-200 simulator at $250 an hour, as well as classroom study. Although his performance sheet has no checkmarks in the box opposite "Taxi," it does contain a large check opposite "Steep Turns," which, for Hanjour, was far more of a priority. In his final evaluation, his instructor noted that "Hani absorbed a great deal of information and is very intelligent," but, he concluded, "he will need much more experience flying smaller a/c [aircraft] before he is ready to master large jets." With his commercial pilot's license in his pocket and advanced training in flying a passenger jetliner, Hanjour was now up to speed with the other three pilots. To celebrate, he and Hazmi drove to the Grand Canyon for some sightseeing.

As Hanjour trained in the simulator, Hazmi was busy with research. He sent away to Sporty's Pilot Shop in Batavia, Ohio, for training videos for Boeing 747-200, Boeing 747-400, and Boeing 777-200 flight decks, as well as a video titled "How an Airline Captain Should Look and Act." But both he and Hanjour were now anxious to get to the East Coast as soon as possible. Hazmi needed to begin making preparations for the cadre of soldiers his friend Khalid al-Mihdhar would soon be sending his way. At the same time, Hanjour would be able to get in some additional flying time on smaller aircraft at local airports. Getting ready for the trip, Hazmi drove down to Wide World of Maps in Phoenix and purchased a

National Geographic road atlas, a Unique Media map of the United States and another of New York City, and a world aeronautical chart covering the northeast portion of the United States.

Around dawn on Sunday, April 1, they departed Mesa in their battered blue 1988 Toyota Corolla, packed with wrinkled shirts, blue jeans, and flight videos. The two turned onto I-40, the 2,400-mile highway that wraps the country's heartland in a ribbon of asphalt. For Hazmi and Hanjour, it was a road to war, a payback for treating their lands as little more than gas stations for road-hogging SUVs and targets for military firepower. To them, it would become a road to redemption.

Because it was Sunday, they were able to make good time as they dashed through New Mexico and then into the northern tip of Texas, zipping past miles of monotonous scrub plains and farmlands. When they crossed into Oklahoma at about 5.30 p.m., the sun was beginning to set behind them, and the road ahead grew dark as Hazmi cruised along at about eighty-five miles per hour. Approaching Elk City, they tripped the radar in the car of C. L. Parkins, an Oklahoma Highway Patrol trooper. Parkins stayed with them for a dozen minutes; then at 6:06 p.m. he pulled Hazmi over. "I asked him to come back to my car and he sat there, and I visited with him a little bit," Parkins recalled. Hazmi appeared calm and collected and Parkins thought he spoke English well. "We did our normal checks—check to see if the vehicle's stolen, check to see if he's wanted, if his driver's license status is valid—try and see if there's anything we need to look further into."

Apparently, no one was looking for him—not the NSA, CIA, or FBI, or the State Department. Thus, said Parkins, "we didn't see anything to go any further with the contact . . . I wrote him a ticket for speeding and the seat belt." Hazmi promptly mailed in his tickets with money orders covering the $138 in fines to the Washita County court clerk and the matter was quickly forgotten.

Hazmi and Hanjour were lucky; America's intelligence system was broken. Six year earlier another Oklahoma Highway Patrol trooper, Charles Hanger, made a similar routine stop not far away and arrested Tim McVeigh less than two hours after he blew up the Murrah Federal Building in Oklahoma City. Although at the time no one knew he was responsible, McVeigh was put in jail for carrying an unregistered handgun. Two days later, before McVeigh made bail, the FBI named him as a chief suspect and immediately flashed his name to law enforcement organizations around the country. As a result of the quick actions by FBI and police, McVeigh never got away.

Back on I-40, Hazmi pressed ahead. In some ways, the car's occupants were a study in contrasts. Hanjour was dour, secretive, often unapproachable, with a tendency to cut Hazmi off when he thought his partner was becoming too open with strangers. He could sit for hours in the car without speaking, his hat pulled tight on his head. Hazmi was the extrovert, outgoing, made friends easily. He liked to wear colorful shirts, have a coffee with friends, laugh. More puzzled than annoyed, he would always ask why when Hanjour cut him off.

As the odometer spun, there would be no stopping at motels, just catnaps at rest stops. The soldiers would be coming soon and Hazmi needed to find a place to put them up where they could blend into the background. It was also essential to get them some type of ID, perhaps even driver's licenses, so they would have no problem boarding the planes.

Two days after they left Mesa they reached Front Royal, Virginia, on the outskirts of Washington. Hazmi got gas and Hanjour withdrew $100 from a cash machine with his Citibank card. It was an easy way to get access to the $11,000 deposited into his UAE Citibank account by bin Laden's moneyman in Dubai. Hanjour also had another $9,600 in a Saudi British bank account. Back on the road, they continued for another hour to the Hillwood Motor Lodge, a decaying relic of the 1950s awaiting the wrecker's ball, just off Sleepy Hollow Road in the busy Seven Corners section of Falls Church, Virginia, a suburb of Washington.

On May 2, Hazmi and Hanjour drove their blue Toyota Corolla to Washington's Dulles Airport to meet United Flight 925 from London, arriving at 7:40 p.m. On board were the first two members of Hazmi's crew, Majed Moqed, a law student at King Saud University in Riyadh, and Ahmed al-Ghamdi, a university student in Mecca who grew up in a prominent family in the southern Saudi city of Beljurashi. They had flown into Britain on Emirates Airlines Flight 1 from Dubai. Hazmi was no doubt happy to have some additional friendly faces around. On the previous evening he had been mugged in front of his apartment by a man who had been hanging around his place for several weeks. He immediately called the police and when the Fairfax County officers showed up, he gave his full name and his current address. No one, however, was ever arrested.

The arrival of the two soldiers put more pressure on Hazmi to quickly find a good location near New York City for the other members of his crew as they began arriving. To help them out, Eyad al Rababah, someone they met at a local mosque, suggested that the pair consider Paterson, New Jersey, and agreed to take them there and show them around. "It was somebody asking you for a favor, and you don't lose anything by saying yes," he said. Still, Rababah thought it was odd that while they professed to be practicing Muslims, he never saw them engaged in prayer. "Even in the mosque, I never saw them praying," he said. Then when he showed up at their apartment for the trip he received another surprise: instead of two there were now four of them. On the morning of May 8, Rababah headed north with Hanjour seated next to him in his Honda Civic, and Hazmi followed behind in the Toyota Corolla with Moqed and Ghamdi.

Seven hours later they pulled into Rababah's new hometown of Bridgeport, Connecticut, where he got them registered at the nearby Fairfield Motor Inn and took them on brief tour of Paterson, about ninety minutes away, and to dinner there at a Chinese restaurant. After returning them to the hotel, Rababah said good-bye and left Hazmi and his crew to make their decision. They got right to business, making over seventy-five local phone calls to area flight schools and real estate firms. Joe Macy, owner of the inn, recalled that his guests "behaved very gentle like."

For Hazmi and Hanjour, Paterson seemed just the place to disappear. An old, gray industrial town of 170,000 residents, it contained thousands of new immigrants attracted by the low cost of housing and, for some without the right papers, the promise of anonymity. Begun in 1792 as a sketch on the drawing board of Alexander Hamilton, two hundred years later the city's eight square miles contained seventy-two distinct nationalities, a polyglot of cultures and languages, colors and hair styles, smells, sounds, and tastes. The two liked the gritty, blue-collar neighborhoods of African Americans and Hispanics. Also nearby was a growing Middle Eastern community and just twenty miles northwest was New York City.

For $650 a month, they rented a one-room apartment at the top of an aging three-story redbrick building at 486 Union Avenue. With graffiti on the white door and pried-open mailboxes in the hallway, it sat on a shabby block in Totowa, next to Paterson. Down the street was St. Mary's, a Romanesque, ochre-colored church decorated with pots filled with yellow mums. It had been built a century before, when the area was predominantly German and then Irish. Newly arrived Hispanic families now filled the pews and overflowed onto the sidewalk on Sundays. Nearby was Inner City Blues, a clothing store selling hip-hop Phat Farm sweatshirts, and across the street was a storefront converted into an Islamic mission where Muslim men, mostly from Bangladesh, kneeled for afternoon prayer.

Moving into Apartment R3 on May 21, Hazmi, Hanjour, Moqed, and Ghamdi attracted little attention. But Jamie Diaz, who lived one floor below, noticed that they only brought with them two carry-on bags and a dark green garbage bag stuffed with clothing. They had no furniture for the unfurnished apartment and their only major purchase was a used air conditioner for thirty dollars. Nevertheless, for the next three months, as the dreary flat became the operations center and living quarters for Hazmi's growing crew, he and the others blended in with little difficulty.

Dressed in jeans, shirts, and sometimes sandals, they would walk beneath the yellow awning of the bodega on the first floor to buy water, soda, juice, bread, toilet paper, napkins, and individually wrapped doughnuts—sometimes half a dozen at a time—or load up with Chinese food in brown stapled bags from the nearby Wo Hop III restaurant. Hanjour and Ghamdi would frequently stop in El Fogon, a Mexican restaurant a few doors down Union Street, where owner Modesta Gomez would sell them packs of Salem or Parliament cigarettes and Budweiser beer.

Totowa also had the advantage of being between two local airports with flight schools, each only about a fifteen-minute drive, and Hanjour was eager to climb back into the cockpit. On the very day they moved into their new apartment, Hanjour drove the eight miles to Air Fleet Training Systems in Teterboro, New Jersey, where he started receiving ground instruction. His goal was to fly solo along the Hudson Corridor, a low-altitude "hallway" along the Hudson River that passes such New York landmarks as the World Trade Center. But heavy traffic in the area can make the corridor a dangerous route for pilots with insufficient experience. Over the next few weeks he would fly along the corridor with an instructor and eventually do a solo run. He then switched to Caldwell Flight Academy eight miles in the opposite direction in Fairfield, New Jersey, where they permitted him to rent aircraft, and for much of June, Hanjour continued to improve his flying skills.

Now certain of his decision to complete his mission, Hanjour decided to make a final phone call to his family back in Saudi Arabia so they would not become suspicious. Telling his mother he was calling from a pay phone in the United Arab Emirates, where they believed he had gone in 1999 to find a pilot's job, he said he would telephone again when he had his own number. He might, he added, return home for a visit in about a month.

With Hazmi now settled in Totowa and Atta living in Florida, the two decided it was time for their first summit meeting to coordinate the various attacks. It would also be their first face-to-face meeting. Until then, both communicated via cell phones and e-mail, using public computers at libraries, Internet cafés, or Kinko's. When Atta arrived in June 2000, he went into Manhattan and purchased a Motorola "flip" cell phone plus a fifty-dollar prepaid calling card from Datavision Computer on Fifth Avenue. The number, 646-479-0432, was activated the next day, and Atta quickly used it to call back to the Middle East more than a dozen times.

After about a month he got rid of what was, in essence, a throwaway phone. From then on he primarily relied on more secure untraceable calling cards, bought for cash at grocery stores and pharmacies, and pay phones when calling back to the Middle East. Thus, while in New Jersey to meet with Hazmi, Atta called his sister in the Middle East from a pay phone at the busy Cibao grocery store on Union Avenue in Paterson. He then made several other calls to the UAE from a wall phone near a stack of tires at Happy's Garage in Elmwood Park. In all, the group used at least 133 different prepaid calling cards, defeating the NSA's ability to track them.

When communicating with each other, Hazmi and Atta would always talk in coded language, but there was only so much they could discuss in such a limited way. So both had hoped to get together in April when Hazmi first arrived in Virginia, but they just could not find the time. Finally, on June 19, Hazmi went to Newark International Airport and boarded Continental Airlines Flight 1471 for Miami.

Around the same time, bin Laden decided to put the United States and Israel on notice about his planned attack, as he had done prior to previous attacks. In June, Bakr Atyani, the Pakistan bureau chief for the London-based MBC-TV network, received an unusual message asking if he would like to interview Osama bin Laden. The Arabic-language network was widely watched throughout the Middle East and the Islamabad-based journalist had reported on both bin Laden and the Taliban in the past. Atyani agreed, and on June 21 he drove to Chaman, a dusty Pakistani frontier town just across from Afghanistan.

Eighty miles from Quetta, with its cool air scented with jasmine, Chaman was reached by a road that cuts through a low, wide desert plain of sun-bleached bluffs, sandy dunes, and deep gullies. It then climbs sharply up the eight-thousand-foot Khojak Pass, finally reaching the border post situated at the crest and often hidden in a shroud of sandstorms. There Atyani was placed in a car with blackened windows and driven for hours over a rock-strewn road with near-meteor-size potholes toward Kandahar—and then three hours more into the desert, past slowly moving waves of sand.

The final destination was a mud-walled room in a remote compound. Atyani was greeted by bin Laden, who rose from a series of low silky cushions splashed with color. Also greeting him was bin Laden's deputy, Ayman al-Zawahiri, and his military chief, Muhammad Atef, who Atyani thought was "a very sharp person." After a *mensaf*—an Arabian dish of rice and meat—bin Laden said that because of an agreement with the Taliban, he would not give any press statements. Then he added, "You are here because there is some material which we are going to give you and some news."

Then Muhammad Atef gave Atyani the news in the form of a stark warning. "The coming weeks will hold important surprises that will target American and Israeli interests in the world," he said. Atyani knew that meant a coming attack. "I am 100 percent sure of this, and it was absolutely clear they had brought me there to hear this message," he later said. He then asked bin Laden to confirm the message but, in keeping with his agreement with the Taliban, he just smiled off camera. Bin Laden seemed "happy with the talk of his aides," said Atyani.

Atef indicated that he was aware of the consequences of such an action. "We are expecting an American strike," he said. But the men in the camps were able to "dismantle their equipment and move to other hideouts in less than half an hour," he added. Jamal Ismail, another journalist working as a television correspondent in Pakistan at the time, recalled that some bin Laden aides informed Atyani unofficially that they hoped the attack would be of great assistance to the Palestinians in their struggle against Israel. "We have big plans for the Intifada," they said. "We are going to strike against American interests more than the *Cole.*"

Chatter

In late June, the NSA suddenly picked up a large number of very worrisome intercepts, filled with talk of attacks, throughout the Middle East. "Unbelievable news coming in weeks," said one intercept. "Big event—there will be a very, very, very, very big uproar," said another. "There will be attacks in the near future," said a third. At the same time, bin Laden also released an al-Qaeda-made videotape that opened with shots of the USS *Cole* shortly after its attack by suicide bombers eight months earlier and included shots of terrorist training exercises. Bin Laden then declared: "To all the mujahideen, your brothers in Palestine are waiting for you; it's time to penetrate America and Israel and hit them where it hurts most."

The "chatter" and bin Laden's warning hit Hayden like a thunderclap. He knew that shortly before the embassy bombings, bin Laden had allowed in a reporter from ABC News and offered a similar warning, which was also followed by a great deal of chatter from target areas. But now bin Laden's warning was crystal clear to anyone who listened to it: he was intending "to penetrate America" and hit it "where it hurts most"— likely Washington and New York. As the NSA sent reports of the chatter throughout the national security community, red alerts began flashing.

At the State Department, a "Worldwide Caution" was issued regarding the risk of terrorist attack and specifically mentioning groups linked with bin Laden and al-Qaeda; U.S. military forces throughout the Persian Gulf were placed on a heightened state of alert; a Marine Corps contingent in Jordan cut short its training session and returned to its ships; the U.S. Fifth Fleet sent its ships out to sea from ports in Bahrain.

While worrisome signals had been arriving for weeks, the red flag went up on Thursday, June 21. Top-secret intercepts of confidential messages exchanged between the reporter Bakr Atyani in Islamabad and MBC-TV in London, likely picked up by GCHQ—Britain's NSA—revealed bin Laden's latest dire warning. NSA analysts were well aware that similar warnings had preceded the attacks on both the U.S. embassies in East Africa and the USS *Cole*.

Immediately the agency flashed major alerts about "UBL"—Usama bin Laden—throughout the national security community. The U.S. Central Command raised the force protection condition level for U.S. troops in six countries to Delta, the highest possible level. A U.S. Marine Corps exercise in Jordan was halted. U.S. embassies in the Persian Gulf conducted an emergency security review, and the embassy in Yemen was closed. The State Department's Foreign Emergency Support Teams were readied to move on four hours' notice and kept up the terrorism alert posture on a "rolling twenty-four-hour basis."

On Friday, the CIA sent out a cable to all its stations. "Threat UBL Attack Against US Interests Next 24-48 Hours," it said. The same day the FBI issued its own warning to its field offices in its daily "UBL/Radical Fundamentalist Threat Update." More CIA warnings continued on Saturday. "Bin Ladin Attacks May Be Imminent," said one. "Possible Threat of Imminent Attack from Sunni Extremists," said another.

On Sunday, June 24, Bakr Atyani's report on MBC-TV finally aired, triggering a cacophony of chatter throughout the Middle East. On Monday, the warnings throughout Washington continued: "Bin Ladin and Associates Making Near-Term Threats," said a CIA cable. It reported multiple attacks planned over the coming days, including a "severe blow" against U.S. and Israeli "interests" during the next two weeks. And at the White House, longtime National Security Council counterterrorism coordinator Richard Clarke sent a Terrorism Threat Update to National Security Advisor Condoleezza Rice indicating the possibility of near-term "spectacular" terrorist attacks resulting in numerous casualties. He also said that six separate intelligence reports showed al-Qaeda personnel warning of a pending attack.

Clarke believed that the detailed threats contained in the intercepts were far too sophisticated to be merely a psychological operation to keep the United States on edge, a view with which the CIA agreed. The intercepts were incredibly consistent: the attacks would be calamitous, causing the world to be in turmoil, and would consist of possible multiple—but not necessarily simultaneous—attacks.

On Thursday, June 28, Clarke wrote to Rice that the pattern of al-Qaeda activity indicating attack planning over the past six weeks "had reached a crescendo." "A series of new reports continue to convince me and analysts at State, CIA, DIA [Defense Intelligence Agency], and NSA that a major terrorist attack or series of attacks is likely in July," he noted. Finally, two days later the headline of a briefing to top officials pulled no punches: "Bin Laden Planning High-Profile Attacks." The report stated that bin Laden's operatives expected near-term attacks to have dramatic consequences "of catastrophic proportions."

At the NSA, where intercepts containing frightening new threats appeared almost every three days, the tension seldom let up for Mike Hayden. "Throughout the summer," said Hayden, "we had more than thirty warnings that *something* was imminent." But the questions were always the same—where, when, and how?

Cambrils

For Hazmi, the Fourth of July would be a reunion. Stepping off Saudi Arabian Airlines Flight 53 at JFK that morning was his old buddy and partner Khalid al-Mihdhar. Now that all of the soldiers were in the U.S., it was time for Mihdhar to rejoin Hazmi and his crew. With no problems going through passport control, Mihdhar may have enjoyed the irony of arriving on the day America celebrated its independence, casting off its British shackles. He had come to help break his lands free of America's shackles. In another touch of irony, Mihdhar listed as his U.S. address the Marriott Hotel at the World Trade Center. In fact, Hazmi would put him up at the Quality Hotel Eastside, a low-cost hotel a few blocks from another skyscraper, the Empire State Building.

For the American intelligence community, it was yet another humiliating blunder. Once again, the U.S. embassy in Jedda, Saudi Arabia, issued Mihdhar a B-1/B-2 (tourist/business) visa. And once again he was able to enter the U.S. and disappear, just as he had done more than a year and a half earlier. In all that time, his name had never been placed on a watch list. Prior to obtaining the visa, Mihdhar had obtained a new "clean" passport, but like the previous document it also contained a secret coded indicator, placed there by the Saudi government, warning of a possible terrorist affiliation. U.S. passport control officers, however, had no knowledge that such a code system existed. In addition, his visa application contained at least one false statement, indicating that he had never traveled to the U.S. before. And his passport was technically invalid since it had no expiration date (apparently an accident)—a fact the inspector at JFK failed to notice that could have triggered closer scrutiny or even barred him from entry.

That evening, Hazmi drove Atta to Newark International Airport for his 6:30 p.m. Delta flight back to Fort Lauderdale, where his crew had been enjoying a few days off. While Wail al-Shehri was driving through Lion Country Safari, his brother Waleed al-Shehri and Satam al-Suqami were working out at Body Perfect Fitness Center, and Marwan al-Shehhi was purchasing pornographic videos at Video Outlet in Deerfield Beach, where he became a regular customer.

A few days later, with the complete team now assembled in the U.S., Atta boarded Swissair Flight 117 from Miami to Zurich, where he would change planes for Madrid. He was traveling to Spain for a summit with Ramzi Binalshibh, his former roommate and the man who was helping bin Laden and Khalid Shaikh Mohammed coordinate the operation from his base in Germany. Making use of his two-and-a-half hour layover, he withdrew 1,700 Swiss francs from an ATM, bought a box of Swiss chocolates, and began looking for sharp knives in the duty-free store. One that caught his eye was a red Swiss Army Camper Knife that featured a large blade, a sharp, jagged saw, and nearly a dozen other attachments. The other was a Swiss Army Soldier's Knife, which also had a large stainless-steel blade but was more compact. Atta took both of them. He then telephoned Marwan al-Shehhi back in Florida and learned that Binalshibh, in Hamburg, had been unable get a ticket to Madrid because of the holiday travel season. The only thing available was a ticket the next day to the small Catalan city of Reus on Spain's Costa Dorada, its Gold Coast. Atta figured the easiest thing would be to simply drive there to meet him. At a computer stand in the airport, he logged on to Travelocity and reserved a car in Madrid from July 9th to the 16th.

Atta landed at Madrid-Barajas Airport in the early afternoon on July 8, too late to leave on the long drive, so after using a public Internet terminal he stopped at a small airport travel kiosk to find a hotel. What he wanted, he told the woman at the counter, was the hotel that was cheapest and closest to the airport. The travel agent called the Diana Cazadora, a three-star hotel near the cargo terminal, confirmed the reservation, and showed Atta where to wait for the minibus. After checking into Room 111, he called Binalshibh to confirm that everything was still on schedule for the meeting the next day. Then the following morning he paid cash for the hotel room, slid behind the wheel of a silver Hyundai Accent rented from the SIXT agency next door, and got started on the three-hundred-mile trip to the Mediterranean shoreline.

At 7:00 p.m., the small Aero Lloyd plane carrying Binalshibh pulled into the Reus Airport, a single terminal ringed by olive groves. There to greet him was Mohamed Atta. The two then drove to the tiny seaside village of Cambrils on the southern outskirts of Salou. By the time they arrived, the exodus of tourists from the town's long, honey-colored beaches was over and the sidewalk cafés were starting to buzz. It was a good place to become invisible in plain sight, lost among the constantly changing faces, like cards in a shuffle. Arriving without reservations, Atta and Binalshibh found a space at the four-star Hotel Monica, overlooking six miles of gentle surf, and they checked into Room 412.

Despite the carefree nature of the venue, their weeklong series of meetings was deadly serious. Binalshibh told Atta that bin Laden wanted the attacks carried out as soon as possible because he was concerned about the large number of operatives in the U.S. at the same time. But Atta said he was still unable to provide an exact date for the attacks because he was too busy organizing the arriving soldiers. In addition, he still needed to coordinate the timing of the flights so that the crashes would occur simultaneously. Atta said he needed about five to six more weeks before he could provide an accurate attack date.

In whispered talk in their room and along the beach, Binalshibh told Atta that bin Laden wanted the date of the attack kept from the other operatives until the last minute and that Atta was to provide Binalshibh with advance notice of at least a week or two. In that way Binalshibh could travel to Afghanistan and report the date personally to bin Laden. Turning to targets, Binalshibh reminded Atta that one of bin Laden's chief aims was to destroy the White House. Atta said its low position surrounded by taller buildings made it a difficult target, but he had asked Hazmi and Hanjour to evaluate its feasibility and was awaiting their answer. He explained that Hanjour had been assigned the Pentagon and he and Hazmi had rented small aircraft and flown reconnaissance flights near the building.

With regard to the rest of the targets, Ziad Jarrah would crash into the Capitol and both he—Atta—and Marwan al-Shehhi would hit the World

Trade Center. In the event a pilot could not reach his intended target, he was to crash the plane wherever he could. Atta said that if he was unable to strike the World Trade Center, his plan was to crash his jet directly into the streets of New York. Each pilot, he said, had volunteered for his assigned target, and the assignments were subject to change.

A few days after they arrived, they were told the hotel was fully committed for the rest of the week and they would have to find a new place to stay. Climbing into the silver Hyundai, they drove a few miles up the coast toward Tarragona and turned onto the Via Augusta and into the Hotel Sant Jordi, a small, amiable establishment near the sandy shore of Playa Sabinosa. The hotel had space and the clerk handed Atta the keys to Room 206.

Turning to the mechanics of the hijackings, Atta said he, Shehhi, and Jarrah had encountered no problems carrying box cutters on cross-country surveillance flights. During those flights, he said, the best time to storm the cockpit was about ten to fifteen minutes after takeoff, when the cockpit doors typically were opened for the first time. Because he was confident that the doors would be open, he said, he had not planned for any contingency actions, such as using a hostage or claiming to have a bomb. In looking for planes, Atta said he wanted to select aircraft departing on long flights because they would be full of fuel, and that he wanted to hijack Boeing aircraft because he believed them easier to fly than the Airbus, which he understood had an autopilot feature that did not allow them to be crashed into the ground.

Finally, Atta confirmed that all the soldiers had arrived in the United States without incident. He said he planned to divide them into teams according to their English-speaking abilities, and in that way they would be able to assist one another before the operation. Each team would also be able to command the passengers in English. One problem Atta brought up was the desire by some of the pilots and soldiers to contact their families to say good-bye, something he had forbidden.

Before they parted, Atta expressed his concern about his communications being intercepted. To help reduce the threat, he instructed Binalshibh to obtain new telephones as soon as he returned to Germany. One phone would be used to contact him in America and the other would be used to speak with the leaders in Afghanistan and Pakistan. Binalshibh then gave Atta eight necklaces and eight bracelets that Atta had asked him to buy when he was recently in Bangkok. He believed that if the hijackers were clean shaven and well dressed, others would simply stereotype them as wealthy Saudis and give them less notice.

By the time they were finished it was Monday, July 16, and Atta drove Binalshibh back to the Reus Airport for his Aero Lloyd flight back to Hamburg. It would be the last time they would ever see each other. Five years earlier, as Israel began its bloody Grapes of Wrath invasion of Lebanon with American support, Atta had signed his last will and testament vowing revenge. It was time for the endgame.

Warning

If June was a bad month for Mike Hayden, July was even worse; the chatter was indicating that an attack could happen any day. What caused the sudden spike in warning indicators was the news on June 20 that President Bush had invited Israeli prime minister Ariel Sharon to the White House—their second meeting—while at the same time once again snubbing Palestinian leader Yasir Arafat. There were few people on earth bin Laden detested more than Ariel Sharon, and as a result he sent a strongly worded letter to Khalid Shaikh Mohammed ordering that the attack take place in July as a statement of support for the Palestinians.

It was the second time bin Laden exploded over Israel and ordered the immediate launch of the attack. The first time was in October 2000, while Atta and the other pilots were still undergoing flight training. The trigger that time was the killing of twelve-year-old Mohammed al-Dura, a Palestinian boy in Gaza who was shot by Israeli troops when gunfire broke out between the Israeli forces and Palestinian civilians. The entire event was captured by a French television camera crew and then broadcast around the globe, setting off a firestorm throughout the Middle East. The news also quickly reached Afghanistan, sending bin Laden over the top. As an act of revenge, he ordered Khalid Shaikh to immediately launch the attack in the U.S., even though none of the pilots had yet been trained. He argued that now was the time to make their point, and it would be enough for them to hijack the planes and then simply crash them into the ground, killing everyone on board, rather than fly them into specific targets. Khalid Shaikh, however, was not willing to throw away years of planning and work for a quick moment of revenge, and he talked bin Laden into keeping the original timetable.

Now, as a result of the Sharon visit to the Bush White House and the snub to Arafat, bin Laden was again on the warpath. His order this time was so serious that a general warning went out through his training camps in Afghanistan. His al-Farooq camp suddenly went on a high state of alert, and trainees began practicing evacuation drills. At the moment their commanders gave the order, they would run to the gates of the compound and into the mountains where they would remain until it was safe to return. Al-Qaeda members dispersed with their families, security was increased, and bin Laden moved to a safe location. But in the end, Khalid Shaikh once again succeeded in keeping the air attacks in the U.S. on track, arguing that the teams were not ready, and the alert was called off.

As the alert was taking place, Khalid al-Mihdhar was in Saudi Arabia, having flown there from Sanaa on May 26 to spend about a month taking care of some final details. While there, he told his cousin in Mecca about the coming attacks in the U.S. He said that five were planned and that they had originally been scheduled for May and then July (because of Sharon) and finally September. "I will make it happen even if I do it by myself," he quoted his mentor, bin Laden. Finally, Mihdhar asked his cousin to watch over his home and family because he had a job to do.

At the end of July, the NSA issued a report noting that the spike in intelligence about a near-term al-Qaeda attack had stopped, and Hayden breathed a sigh of relief. At the White House, Richard Clarke passed the report on to Condoleezza Rice and her deputy, Stephen Hadley, warning that the attack had just been postponed for a few months "but will still happen."

A few days later, on August 1, the FBI issued an advisory that although most of the reporting indicated a potential for attacks on U.S. interests abroad, the possibility of an attack within the United States could not be discounted. The CIA brought the same issue to the president's attention five days later when it included a report in its President's Daily Brief (PDB) titled "Bin Ladin Determined to Strike in U.S." It was the thirty-sixth time so far that year that bin Laden or al-Qaeda had been discussed in a PDB.

In the August 6 brief, the CIA noted that bin Laden had warned that "his followers would follow the example of World Trade Center bomber Ramzi Yousef" and "bring the fighting to America." Also, after the U.S. missile strikes on his base in Afghanistan in 1998, bin Laden "told followers he wanted to retaliate in Washington." At another point the document discussed a 1998 report indicating that bin Laden "wanted to hijack a U.S. aircraft to gain the release of 'Blind Shaykh' Umar Abd al-Rahman and other U.S.-held extremists." Finally, the PDB noted that "FBI information since that time indicates patterns of suspicious activity in this country consistent with preparations for hijackings or other types of attacks, including recent surveillance of federal buildings in New York." Despite the wake-up call, the president showed little interest.

As the lights flashed and the sirens wailed from the tops of the spy factories, some of the analysts and operatives inside began attempting to put the pieces together. At the CIA, Khalid al-Mihdhar and Nawaf al Hazmi had never been far from the thoughts of Tom Wilshire, the deputy chief of Alec Station. In January 2000 he had spiked the message drafted by Doug Miller, one of the FBI agents assigned to the station, alerting his headquarters to Mihdhar's U.S. visa and New York travel plans. Wilshire also never alerted the State Department, which would have put Mihdhar on a watch list and stopped him at the border. Then, when Wilshire learned in March 2000 that Hazmi had actually flown to Los Angeles two months earlier, he again failed to notify the FBI or even the agents working for him in his office.

In May, Tom Wilshire was transferred to FBI headquarters as the CIA's chief liaison to the bureau's counterterrorism division. Soon after he arrived, he began focusing closely on the Kuala Lumpur meeting out of concern that al-Qaeda might next target a location in Southeast Asia. Shortly before Wilshire left Alec Station, Margarette Gillespie began "getting up to speed" on the Malaysia meeting, too. An FBI IOS (intelligence operations specialist) detailed to Alec Station as a desk officer, she had been asked to help Wilshire on the project in her spare time. That meant reading all the relevant cable traffic and reviewing the stack of memos and e-mail messages previously sent.

Looking for something but unsure of just what, on May 15 Wilshire downloaded the March 2000 cable indicating that Mihdhar and Hazmi had traveled from Malaysia to Bangkok on January 8, 2000. From there, according to the cable, Hazmi flew to Los Angeles a week later. Consid-

ering how concerned Wilshire was about the meeting, it seems astonishing that he would not be interested in why Hazmi might have flown to Los
Angeles and what he was doing in the U.S. And yet there is no evidence
that he was.

To help him unravel the mysteries surrounding the meeting in Kuala
Lumpur, Wilshire turned to Dina Corsi, one of the FBI's intelligence operations specialists at headquarters. Because the information gathered by
the FBI's criminal investigators would be used to prosecute people and
put them in jail, or even execute them, they needed to show to a court
a high degree of likelihood—"probable cause"—that the target of their
investigation was involved in criminal activity. Only after that burden
was met would a judge in a criminal court issue a warrant authorizing
electronic surveillance or a physical search.

Signals intelligence specialists at the NSA, on the other hand, looked
for information not to put someone in jail but to discover threats from
foreign governments or foreign terrorist organizations. As a result, their
requirements for obtaining an eavesdropping warrant—known as a FISA
warrant—were much less stringent. Instead of criminal courts, attorneys
from the Justice Department representing the NSA would appear before
the highly secret Foreign Intelligence Surveillance Court. There, rather
than demonstrate that their target was involved in criminal activity, all
they would have to show is that he or she was connected in some way
to a foreign government or foreign terrorist organization and that useful
intelligence would result from the eavesdropping. The burden was lower
because the consequences were fewer; privacy would be breached but no
one would be going to jail.

The worry had always been that overeager criminal investigators, hoping to get a tap on a suspect with little or no probable cause, would simply
apply for a FISA warrant by showing some nebulous foreign connection—for example, that the person works for a company headquartered
in London. They would then be able to, in essence, go on a fishing expedition by listening in on the person's communications for three months,
hoping to find something—anything—in that time. The Constitution, under the Fourth Amendment, protects against such unreasonable searches.

To keep the two types of eavesdropping activities—intelligence and
criminal—completely separate, an artificial "wall" was created. This was

designed to prohibit those monitoring private conversations with much easier FISA warrants from "cheating" by passing their result "over the transom" to criminal investigators, who required a much tougher probable cause standard for a criminal warrant.

Beginning in October 2000, as a result of extremely sloppy and questionable work by the FBI, the FISA court ordered the wall between the FBI's criminal investigators and the NSA's eavesdroppers heightened considerably. The court found errors in approximately one hundred applications for FISA warrants, mostly in affidavits submitted by FBI supervisory special agents. The errors involved both omission of information and misrepresentations about criminal investigations of FISA targets. In addition, instead of having separate criminal and intelligence squads working on separate criminal and intelligence investigations, FBI agents were constantly moving back and forth between groups. This was exactly what was prohibited.

To remedy the situation, the FISA court issued a new order. It now required that anyone who reviewed FISA material, such as transcripts of the NSA's FISA-authorized domestic electronic surveillance, sign a certification acknowledging that the court's approval was required before the information could be shared with criminal investigators. The FBI then decided to allow only agents and analysts assigned to intelligence duties access to FISA materials, not the criminal investigators.

At the NSA, Hayden had looked at the new requirements with anguish. From then on, before the agency could send intercept reports to the FBI, it would first have to review the documents, determine whether any of the information in them came from FISA surveillance, and then include a warning notice, or "caveat." Still, because the agency only had a few—less than half a dozen—FISA-authorized domestic surveillance targets at the time, the additional work would be minimal. All that needed to be done was to put a warning notice on those limited intercepts while leaving the thousands of others unchanged.

The NSA soon discovered a drastic way around the minor inconvenience. Instead of simply placing the warning notice, or caveat, on just the data from the FISA-authorized targets, it would put the notice on *all* counterterrorism-related intelligence provided to the FBI. The caveat, in the form of a computerized "stamp," read:

Except for information reflecting a direct threat to life, neither this product nor any information contained in this product may be disseminated to U.S. criminal investigators or prosecutors without prior approval of NSA. All subsequent product which contains information obtained or derived from this product must bear this caveat. Contact the Office of General Counsel of NSA for guidance concerning this caveat.

This shifted the burden from the NSA to the FBI. From then on, *everything* pumped out of the NSA that related to terrorism would contain the caveat, even though just a minute fraction of the NSA's counterterrorism-related intercepts came from FISA surveillance.

For the FBI, the NSA's policy was a nightmare. Before *any* information from an NSA report was passed from the intelligence side to the criminal side it would first have to be routed back to the NSA and then approved by the agency's general counsel, a process that could take up to five days. It was a very onerous task and one that largely fell on the backs of the bureau's cadre of analysts, the intelligence operations specialists such as Dina Corsi.

Unlike the special agents, who traditionally entered the bureau as lawyers, CPAs, or ex-military, the IOSs came from a wide variety of backgrounds. Some entered from graduate schools where they had specialized in area studies or international relations. Others, like Corsi, rose from within the administrative side of the bureau. Arriving as a clerk in 1988 while attending college, Corsi graduated in 1995 and entered the bureau's language training program. Emerging as a Russian language specialist, she worked on foreign counterintelligence issues and then switched to intelligence work on counterterrorism cases, becoming an IOS in 2000. Since then she had worked in the bureau's bin Laden unit, focusing primarily on the investigation into the *Cole* bombing—a bombing in which they now believed Mihdhar was involved.

Throughout the summer, Mihdhar continued to be a key focus for Maggie Gillespie at Alec Station and Dina Corsi at FBI headquarters, and they often e-mailed each other or met in Washington. On August 7, Corsi asked Gillespie for a copy of the flight manifest for Mihdhar's January 2000 trip to Malaysia. "I plan to write something up, but perhaps we should schedule another sit down to compare notes on both sides," Corsi wrote. "Let me know." "Okay, all sounds good," replied Gillespie.

Given the high level of NSA intercepts and bin Laden's warning, by then the head of the CIA's Counterterrorism Center, Cofer Black, feared an attack was imminent. On August 15, he concluded a briefing to the Department of Defense's Annual Convention on Counterterrorism with the comment, "We are going to be struck soon, many Americans are going to die, and it could be in the U.S."

Six days later, on August 21, Gillespie was scanning through CIA cables at Alec Station when she suddenly stopped. It was the March cable indicating that Hazmi had flown to the U.S. and entered Los Angeles. It was a breathtaking moment. Suddenly "it all click[ed] for me," she said. One of the possible terrorists she had been tracking for months on the other side of the world might be just on the other side of the continent. With her adrenaline pumping, Gillespie checked with Customs and discovered that Mihdhar had also entered the U.S.—just weeks before, on July 4—and had not departed. A pair of suspected terrorists were loose somewhere in the U.S.

Fort Lee

Back in Germany, Ramzi Binalshibh followed Atta's instructions. He purchased two phones, one with which to keep in touch with Atta and another to communicate with everyone else. If the NSA picked up the calls from Binalshibh to the Middle East, Atta believed, they would not be able to link the number to calls from Binalshibh to Atta. To further obscure the nature of the communications and frustrate any interception, the group had worked out a series of code words, and using those terms, Binalshibh passed on to Khalid Shaikh the highlights of the meeting.

With everything again on track, the planning shifted into overdrive. A week after returning from Spain, Atta flew to Newark, where Hazmi picked him up in his blue Toyota Corolla and took him to the King's Inn in Wayne, New Jersey, a nondescript, two-story transient way station. Atta paid $69.90 in advance in cash and checked into Room 230, a few doors down from Khalid al-Mihdhar. He was there to fill them in on the meeting with Binalshibh and to coordinate the next few weeks. Ever concerned about the NSA, when he had to make an overseas call, he would duck into Tony's Hair Stylist or Julian's Hardware and use the pay phone and an AT&T prepaid calling card.

By now the teams had chosen their targets, and Hanjour, Hazmi and his brother Salem, Mihdhar, and Majed Moqed volunteered to attack the Pentagon, the five-sided heart of America's war machine. A week before, Hanjour and Hazmi had rented a plane at Caldwell Flight Academy, a few miles away in Fairfield, New Jersey. On their first surveillance flight over the Washington area, they flew down to a suburban airfield in Gaithersburg, Maryland, a route that would have allowed them to see from the air many of the capital's landmarks.

While Atta decided to hit the North Tower of the World Trade Center and Marwan al-Shehhi volunteered to crash into the South Tower, there was still some disagreement over the target for the fourth pilot, Ziad Jarrah. In a series of e-mails, Atta and Binalshibh discussed the matter. But to hide their true meaning from the NSA or any other intelligence agency that might be intercepting the messages, they used coded language. They pretended to be students discussing various fields of study: "architecture" referred to the World Trade Center, "arts" the Pentagon, "law" the Capitol, and "politics" the White House. Once again Binalshibh reminded Atta that bin Laden wanted to hit the White House.

And once again Atta cautioned that such an action would be difficult. But when Binalshibh persisted, Atta agreed to include the White House but suggested they keep the Capitol Building as an alternate target in case the White House proved too difficult. Planning for maximum casualties among senators and members of Congress, Atta also suggested that the attacks not happen until after the first week in September, when Congress reconvened.

For months Binalshibh had been communicating bin Laden's impatience and his desire for a date for the operation, and by mid-August, Atta was ready to give it to him. Again to defeat any NSA analyst who might be listening, he used a riddle to convey the date to Binalshibh, a riddle containing two branches, a slash, and a lollipop. In other words 11/9, the European way of writing 9/11. Just to be sure before he passed the message on to Khalid Shaikh, who would then pass it on to bin Laden, Binalshibh called Atta back to confirm the date.

With the date now set in stone, Atta again flew up to Newark to meet with Hazmi and begin coordinating the complex task of picking just the right seats on just the right flights on just the right type of aircraft at just the right times. He wanted the attacks to happen with maximum explosive power, in the morning when most people were at work, and as simultaneously as possible. Once officials in Washington began to understand what was happening, Atta knew, they would immediately make every effort to ground all aircraft. Timing would be everything.

It was just after ten on a warm and muggy late-summer evening when

Atta stepped off Spirit Airlines Flight 460 at Newark. The next day, Friday, he briefed Hazmi and Mihdhar on the dates and they discussed flights and schedules. Then on Saturday, August 25, they were finally ready to start booking the September 11 flights. In this new type of war in which cheap motels are used as barracks and commercial jets become powerful weapons, public libraries and Internet cafés are quickly transformed into communications centers. Thus, Mihdhar and Majed Moqed drove ten minutes from Totowa to William Paterson University, a state school on 370 wooded acres in Wayne.

Cutting across the campus, they entered the squat, concrete-block David and Lorraine Cheng Library, a state-of-the-art building with high ceilings, colorful abstract art on the wall, and, in the Electronic Resource Center, a bank of thirty-six computers open to the public free of charge. Mihdhar logged on to his e-mail account, kkhd20002@yahoo.com, pulled up Travelocity.com, and began looking for a morning nonstop flight on American Airlines from Washington's Dulles Airport to Los Angeles on September 11. The best flight was 77, which departed at 8:10 and used the same equipment in which they had conducted their surveillance trip. Mihdhar then logged on to AA.com, the airline's Web page, and booked two seats in coach, 12A and 12B, using Moqed's Visa card.

To keep from looking suspicious, the group logged on to the Internet at computers in a variety of locations around the area. That same afternoon, Atta went to Yuricom, Inc., a small computer repair shop on Main Street in Fort Lee, New Jersey, and searched on Travelocity for 8:00 a.m. flights on September 11 from Boston to Los Angeles and from Dulles to Los Angeles, both for two people. A few doors down the street was The Web Station, where the day before Mihdhar had opened an American Airlines Advantage account, enabling him to book and pay for a flight online. On Sunday, Atta and Mihdhar were back at the keyboard searching for flights on Travelocity, this time at Cyber Café on West Main Street in Fort Lee. Atta made his final decision and purchased two tickets.

But despite Atta's focus on tight security, that weekend Hazmi may have telephoned his old friend from San Diego, Mihdhar Zaid, who helped Hazmi and Mihdhar get settled when they arrived. Beginning around August 25, according to his friends, Mihdhar Zaid began acting strangely and he stopped making phone calls from his telephone. Others in the group that hung out at Sam's Star Mart, the Texaco gas station where Mihdhar Zaid and Hazmi worked, may also have received word that something big would happen soon.

Later, in October, after Mihdhar Zaid was arrested on immigration charges, several fellow inmates claimed he bragged that he knew both Hazmi and Mihdhar were planning a terrorist attack. According to one inmate, Mihdhar Zaid claimed someone had notified him that Hazmi and Mihdhar would be arriving in Los Angeles with plans to carry out an attack. Mihdhar Zaid also allegedly said that he had driven the two from Los Angeles to San Diego. As new information came up years later, the FBI would begin taking a second look at Mihdhar Zaid, but by then he had already been deported back to Yemen.

On Monday, August 27, Hazmi drove Atta to their new staging area in Laurel, Maryland.

Discovery

Gillespie could hardly wait to tell Corsi the news of her discovery, that both Mihdhar and Hazmi were somewhere in the U.S. On Wednesday, August 22, the two met in the FBI's tan, fortresslike headquarters. Corsi was stunned. She then discovered that Mihdhar and Hazmi had flown into Los Angeles together on January 15, 2000, listing their destination in the city as the Sheraton Hotel. A check with the INS revealed that Mihdhar had departed from Los Angeles on June 10, 2000, aboard Lufthansa Airlines, but no departure record could be found for Hazmi. Corsi thus assumed that Hazmi had departed at the same time. But Hazmi had never left. The data flowed in quickly now. Another INS message indicated that when Mihdhar reentered the U.S. on July 4, he had come in through New York and listed his destination as the Marriott Hotel in New York City, the one at the World Trade Center.

Later that day, the two rushed over to Wilshire's FBI office and gave him the news. But it was like a rerun of an old movie. He apparently made no mention of the fact that he had known most of the details for a year and a half or more and actively kept the information secret from the bureau. All agreed that an intelligence investigation to locate Mihdhar should be started immediately. Back at Alec Station, Gillespie asked another CIA official to draft a message to the State Department, INS, Customs, and the FBI requesting the placement of Mihdhar and Hazmi on U.S. watch lists.

On August 23, Corsi contacted the State Department to get a copy of

Mihdhar's most recent visa application from the U.S. Consulate in Jedda, Saudi Arabia. Later, after obtaining permission to open an intelligence investigation into Khalid M. Mihdhar, she called the New York agent on the bin Laden squad to give him a "heads up" alert that the paperwork would soon be coming. She was eager for the case to get under way before Mihdhar left the country. Finally, she called Wilshire and told him she had found another link in Malaysia between Mihdhar and the *Cole* bombing. "I am still looking at intel," she said, "but I think we have more of a definitive connection to the *Cole* here than we thought."

Corsi was also hoping to help the criminal investigators working on the *Cole* bombing by getting them details on the highly secret link between Mihdhar and bin Laden's Yemen ops center. But the only place to obtain such permission was the NSA, and on Monday, August 27, she sent over the urgent request.

That afternoon, Hayden must have been shocked. He had at last discovered that Mihdhar, whose conversations they had been recording for the past eighteen months, along with his partner, Hazmi, had been living in the country, on and off, for much of that time. He approved Corsi's request immediately, and must have known how difficult it would be to now find them. They could be almost anywhere.

At that moment, Hayden could have almost seen Atta, Mihdhar, Hazmi, and the others from his eighth-floor window. That same afternoon, the hijackers were having their penultimate summit meeting at their new base, the Valencia Motel in Laurel, Maryland, a shabby truck stop just two miles away from Hayden's office.

Laurel

It was the ultimate irony. At long last, the hunter and the hunted were now living next door to each other—without either knowing of the other's presence. For years Laurel had been the agency's "company town." Since the NSA first moved to the area in the late 1950s, Laurel had served as its bedroom community. As the agency grew, so did Laurel. It was where nearly everyone seemed to work simply for "the government," or "the Department of Defense." Merchants and neighbors understood the code; whenever they heard the phrase they knew that it meant the NSA and that they should inquire no further.

That Monday afternoon, August 27, Ziad Jarrah flew into Baltimore-Washington International Airport from Fort Lauderdale and joined Atta, Hazmi and his brother Salem, Hanjour, Moqed, and Mihdhar. It was a major operational meeting and the group was spread out among three hotels in Laurel: the Turf, the Pin-Del, and the Valencia. In the afternoon Hazmi went to the local Kinko's store in Laurel, logged on to Travelocity, and purchased his and Salem's tickets for September 11 on American Flight 77 to Los Angeles. Then at about 2:30 he went to the Target store on Fort Meade Road and purchased a Leatherman Wave folding tool knife. A fat hunk of stainless steel, it contained two knives, two wire cutters, a saw, a scissors, and an assortment of other sharp instruments.

Over the next two weeks, the terrorists and the eavesdroppers would coexist in the NSA's close-knit community like unseeing ghosts. Together, they would eat gooey cheese at Pizza Time, pump iron at Gold's Gym, and squeeze tomatoes at Safeway. For eighteen months, since the agency first identified Mihdhar and Hazmi as likely al-Qaeda terrorists, NSA analysts had been listening to their phone calls and reading their e-mail; now they were in touching distance. Registered under their real names, they ate, sweated, and banked alongside their pursuers. Like neighbors, they shopped at J.C. Penney and Wal-Mart, bought groceries at Giant Foods, dined at the Food Factory, and banked at the First Union National Bank and the Dime Savings Bank.

Hazmi's entire team, all five, would consolidate into Room 343 of the Valencia Motel. A $308-a-week suite, with two beds, a small living room, and a kitchenette, it was a crossroads for truckers, transients, budget travelers, and welfare recipients placed there by the state. Every morning and night, thousands of NSA employees would pass Hazmi's blue Toyota Corolla with its California tags, parked in front of his room, as they crawled in heavy traffic down Route 1, the main drag through town to the NSA.

Despite the significance of the investigation, an FBI analyst simply gave the hunt for the suspected terrorists a "routine" precedence, the lowest of three, and on Thursday, August 30, a novice FBI intelligence agent transferred to the FBI's bin Laden unit just weeks before was assigned to it. It was Special Agent Rob Fuller's first intelligence investigation. He had graduated from the FBI Academy in June 2000 and over the past year had worked briefly on an applicant squad, a drug squad, and a surveillance squad.

The day Fuller was assigned the case, Mihdhar, Hazmi, and Hanjour were back in Totowa closing the lease on their top-floor apartment. Hanjour picked up their security deposit from owner Jimi Nouri, who never bothered to check the apartment for damage "because [Hanjour] was a gentleman," he said. They then lugged out the same two suitcases and garbage bag stuffed with clothing they brought with them more than three months before. "They left as quietly as they came in," said neighbor Giselle Diaz.

Because Fuller was busy with other cases, he was not able to even pick up the Mihdhar/Hazmi case folder until Tuesday, September 4, when he completed a lookout request on Mihdhar for the INS. But instead of checking off the box on the form indicating he was wanted for "security/terrorism," and was to be considered "armed and dangerous," he mistakenly checked the "witness" box. He also contacted a Customs Service representative and verified that they too had a lookout for Mihdhar. He then requested a local criminal history check on Mihdhar through the New York City Police Department. Eventually, Fuller also noticed Hazmi's name on the investigative order, so he did the same checks on him.

As the FBI's search began, the hijackers were having a leisurely day in Laurel. Mihdhar was shopping at The Shoe Department for a pair of Timberland shoes and several MUDD Ripstop Cargo bags; Hazmi was nearby buying an ID bracelet at the Gold Valley jewelry store; and Hanjour was at the local DMV office getting a new Maryland ID with the address 14625 Baltimore Avenue in Laurel, the location of the group's mail drop. Later, Mihdhar, Hanjour, and Salem al-Hazmi went for a workout at Gold's Gym.

On Wednesday, Fuller requested a criminal history check and a search of motor vehicle records for any information on Mihdhar and Hazmi. He then contacted the Marriott hotels in the New York area since Mihdhar had listed on his customs form that his destination was the New York Marriott at the World Trade Center. But the six Marriotts he contacted all said Mihdhar had never registered as a guest. Fuller then conducted a Choicepoint search, which checks a variety of public records, but turned up nothing. At 10:17 a.m., Mihdhar and Moqed were at the American Airlines ticket counter at Baltimore-Washington International Airport. Counting out hundred-dollar bills, they were paying $2,300 for their tickets on Flight 77 on September 11 from Dulles to Los Angeles.

By Friday, September 7, every check had thus far turned up zero. That day, Atta sold his 1986 Pontiac Grand Prix to Sun Auto Leasing in Fort Lauderdale for $800 and then again flew up to Baltimore-Washington International Airport for a final coordination conference with Hazmi in Laurel. One of the key details was to close out all remaining bank accounts and send the remaining money back to bin Laden's bankers in the UAE. On Saturday, Hazmi, Mihdhar, and Hanjour emptied their accounts and gave the cash to Atta. Then, while many NSA employees were doing their weekly grocery shopping, he went to the Giant store in Laurel and, via Western Union, wired $5,000 to the Wall Street Exchange Center in Dubai. He then went to a nearby Safeway and wired an additional $2,860.

For the meeting, Ziad Jarrah had driven down to Laurel from the Marriott Hotel at Newark International Airport, the staging area for his flight into the White House. That night they went to dinner at their favorite restaurant, the Food Factory, an inexpensive eatery specializing in kebabs and Afghan and Pakistani cuisine. With the twangy sounds of the sitar and the rhythmic beat of the tabla playing in the background, Mihdhar paid the $54.82 tab. It was past eleven when Jarrah left the Valencia and headed back to Newark. In a hurry after the long day, he leaned heavily on the accelerator as he sped through Maryland on Route 95. Then a few minutes past midnight, just across the Susquehanna River Bridge in the small town of Port Deposit, Jarrah saw a red light flashing in his rearview mirror and he pulled over. After everything, he must have thought, on the eve of the mission, trouble.

Stepping out of his patrol car, Maryland state trooper Joseph Catalano walked up to the passenger window of Jarrah's red Mitsubishi Galant. "How are you doing today?" he asked and then brusquely told him he was clocked at ninety in a sixty-five-mile-per-hour zone. "Can I see your license and registration, please?" He then checked Jarrah's Virginia driver's license, which gave a phony address, 6601 Quicksilver Drive, Springfield, Virginia. It was a parking lot near the Springfield Mall. "You still live in Springfield, on Quicksilver Drive?" Jarrah calmly said, "Yes." A few minutes later, after checking that the car was not stolen, Catalano returned to the passenger window and handed Jarrah a ticket. "Okay, sir, ninety miles an hour in a sixty-five zone is a two-hundred-seventy-dollar fine. I need your signature down here at the bottom," he said. "You are free to go." Jarrah said nothing, turned on his left-hand blinker, and pulled back into traffic. Seven minutes after it began, the last opportunity to stop the plot was over. Catalano would later say that Jarrah was extremely calm and cooperative throughout the stop.

On Sunday, Atta flew to Boston as the four teams consolidated at their staging areas. Hanjour's Pentagon crew was in Laurel, and Jarrah's White House team was in Newark. But because both Twin Tower attacks were to originate from Boston's Logan International Airport, Atta was likely worried about the image of ten Arabs, most of whom spoke little English, suddenly showing up at the same time at Logan for two flights. He therefore searched for the closest airport to Boston with a flight early enough to connect to American Flight 11, which was due to depart Logan for Los Angeles at 7:45 a.m. What he came up with was Portland, Maine. Thus, instead of leaving from Boston, on Monday he and Abdulaziz al-Omari would drive to Portland and catch U.S. Airways Flight 5930, operated by Colgan Air, departing for Boston at 6:00 a.m. Tuesday.

After Atta left Laurel, Hazmi and Mihdhar began planning a final celebratory meal for their crew. Hazmi went to the Giant supermarket in Laurel and bought $158.14 worth of groceries, and Mihdhar went back later for another $57.60. That night at the Valencia, behind the door to Room 343, the five men cooked over a small stove and ate in the crowded kitchenette. For all, like the other members of the cabal, it was the end of their journey, a journey from different places over different roads but with the same final destination.

Early Monday morning, Mihdhar, Hazmi, and the others loaded up their beat-up Toyota Corolla as a conga line of NSA employees, heading in to work, passed slowly by a few feet away on Route 1. By then, the agency's secret city was already buzzing. At 7:15 a.m. Hayden, swiveling in his high-back, padded maroon chair, focused his attention on one of the two television sets in his office. It was time for his private intelligence briefing, broadcast from the agency's war-room-like National Security Operations Center. On this day, the topic was suicide bombers; Ahmed Shah Massoud, forty-eight, a key rebel leader fighting the Taliban in Afghanistan, had been assassinated. The chief suspect was Osama bin Laden.

Following the televised briefing, Hayden convened his "Breakfast Club," as he called it. "A stand-up meeting in here with just my personal staff," Hayden said, "public affairs, inspector general, lawyers, each of the key components represented. It's real quick. Literally a stand-up, everyone's standing, including me. The room is about a third full. We'll go quickly around—hot news of the day." By Monday, few items were hotter than bin Laden. The previous week, the FBI had notified him that Mihdhar and Hazmi were loose somewhere in the country, and now bin Laden and the Taliban appeared to be launching a new war in Afghanistan.

Later that day, two intercepts were received that may have referred to the attack either on Massoud or on America. One said, "Tomorrow is zero hour," and the other said, "The match begins tomorrow." They were between targeted pay phones in a highly dangerous area of Afghanistan and people in Saudi Arabia. But despite the importance of their points of origin, they sat unread throughout the day.

At the time, Mihdhar and Hazmi were a few miles down the road, checking out of Room 343 at the Valencia Motel. In a series of deposits to his First Union National Bank account that morning, Mihdhar deposited nearly $10,000 in cash and traveler's checks. They then went to Mail Boxes, Etc. in Laurel, where Hazmi mailed a package addressed to their financial contact in Dubai. Among the items inside was a handwritten letter in Arabic from Mihdhar to his wife in which he expressed his deep love for her and their daughter and his desire for her to have the money in the account. His bank card and PIN were included with the letter.

Hazmi may also have called his old friends back at the Sam's Star Mart Texaco station to give them a heads up about the attack. Early on Monday morning, Mihdhar Zaid and a number of others began behaving suspiciously. One allegedly said, "It is finally going to happen," as the others celebrated by giving each other high fives.

While Hazmi and his crew were in Laurel tying up loose ends, FBI special agent Rob Fuller was hoping to find the two in Los Angeles, where they had first landed a year and a half earlier, claiming to stay at the Sheraton Hotel. Fuller drafted a memo for the FBI's Los Angeles field office asking them to begin a search of Sheraton Hotel records concerning any stays by Mihdhar and Hazmi in early 2000. He also requested that the Los Angeles office check United Airlines and Lufthansa Airlines records for any payment or other information concerning Mihdhar and Hazmi.

At three o'clock, Hazmi checked the group into Room 122 at the Marriott Residence Inn at 315 Elden Street in Herndon, Virginia, where they would spend their last night. The hotel had two advantages; it was a short drive to the airport and it contained a Gold's Gym.

Surprise

The clock radio went off at 5:45 a.m., an hour before sunrise. "Defense secretary Donald Rumsfeld says he can trim a billion dollars or more in Pentagon operating costs by reducing waste and inefficiency." Host Bob Edwards was introducing a story about military spending on National Public Radio's popular *Morning Edition* program. "In a speech yesterday, Rumsfeld told Defense Department workers that he's declaring war on bureaucracy." As he usually did, Mike Hayden lay in bed, eyes closed in the darkness, until after the six o'clock news summary. It was Tuesday, September 11, and the Pentagon had just declared war on itself. "Some might ask how in the world could the secretary of defense attack the Pentagon in front of its people," Rumsfeld asked rhetorically. "To them I reply, 'I have no desire to attack the Pentagon.' "

But at 6:22 a.m., as they checked out of the Marriott Residence Inn in Herndon, that was exactly what Hazmi and his crew had in mind that day. A few minutes later he climbed behind the wheel of his Toyota Corolla one last time for the short drive to Dulles International Airport. Like Hazmi, who was wearing a neatly pressed blue oxford shirt and tan khaki pants, the crew all dressed casually but conservatively. With no mustaches or beards and their hair neatly trimmed, they might have been going to a Rotary Club meeting.

Arriving at the Dulles parking garage, the team separated into groups of no more than two and entered the American Airlines ticket area, where Mihdhar and Hazmi faced their final security hurdle. Having evaded the CIA, NSA, FBI, INS, State Department, and assorted other intelligence and security organizations for close to two years, now they just needed to get through airport security and they were free to carry out their deadly mission. At 7:15, Mihdhar and Majed Moqed presented their Virginia ID cards, fraudulently arranged in the parking lot of a 7-Eleven, to the American Airlines ticket agent at the check-in counter.

By now, with numerous domestic flights behind them, including dress rehearsal practice missions, they knew how the system worked—as well as where it didn't. At the time, the principal tool to screen for potential terrorists was a program known as the computer-assisted passenger prescreening system (CAPPS). Used by all airlines, the program was designed to identify the most questionable passengers—those who purchased their tickets with cash, for example, or purchased one-way tickets.

Once selected by the computer, a passenger's checked baggage would be screened for explosives and held off the plane until the passenger boarded. The procedure was to avoid the problem of passengers checking luggage containing explosives and then not boarding the plane. If a person boarded the plane, the theory went, the odds are they would not have a bomb in their bag. However, neither those selected nor their carry-on luggage would be subject to additional scrutiny in the security checkpoint area. The program also contained the names of potential terrorists, who would be flagged at the counter, denied a ticket, and possibly arrested.

Both Mihdhar and Moqed were flagged by CAPPS, but since Mihdhar had no checked luggage and Moqed wasn't carrying any explosives, the procedures had no effect on their mission. Also, at the time, there were only twenty names of potential terrorists in the computer database—none belonging to any of the nineteen hijackers.

Within the next twenty minutes the Hazmi brothers and Hanjour would also check in. Hanjour, arriving at the counter by himself, was also flagged by CAPPS, and the Hazmi brothers were flagged by the American Airlines ticket agent because one of them had no photo identification and could not understand English, and because the agent found both to be suspicious. But, again, because Hanjour had only carry-on luggage, and no one was carrying any explosives anyway, the selection process proved useless. Ahead lay the final barrier: the security screening checkpoint.

After a quick shower, Mike Hayden climbed into his Volvo and drove the three miles across Fort Meade to the NSA's Ops 2B building, arriving about 6:50. With only one vehicle in the family, his wife or son would often drop him off and then keep the car. Entering the lobby, he slipped his blue security badge into the CONFIRM card reader, pushed through the turnstile, and turned the key in the lock of his private elevator. On the eighth floor he walked past a receptionist and walls lined with large framed pictures of antenna-covered listening posts, then took a left through an unmarked wooden door and entered his spacious corner office.

Taking a seat in his maroon leather chair, Hayden was surrounded by the accoutrements of power, knickknacks and souvenirs of a long air force career. On his walnut desk was a penholder from his days as the number two commander in Korea, a notepad printed with the word DIRECTOR, and a Brookstone world clock. On a table behind him, next to his NSA flag, sat two computers, one for classified and the other for unclassified work. The table also contained a series of telephones. One was for internal calls; another, the STU-III, was used for secure, highly secret external calls; a black "executive phone" connected him to other senior officials; and a white phone could put him through instantly to Secretary of Defense Rumsfeld and the chairman of the Joint Chiefs of Staff. No phones, however, connected him directly to the White House.

At about 7:15 Hayden began looking over his schedule for the day—a schedule he knew would be made more complicated by Rumsfeld's declaration of war on Pentagon bureaucracy. There would be calls for more cuts to his already depleted budget, reduced by 32 percent over the past decade.

Three minutes later, Mihdhar and Moqed entered Dulles Airport's west security screening checkpoint, where they placed their carry-on bags on the belt of the X-ray machine and proceeded through the arched magne-tometer. Both set off the alarm, and they were directed to a second metal detector. Mihdhar did not trigger the alarm and was permitted through the checkpoint. After Moqed set it off, a screener quickly passed a wand around him and he was allowed to pass.

At 7:35, Hani Hanjour placed two carry-on bags on the belt and pro-ceeded, without alarm, through the magnetometer. A short time later, Nawaf and Salem al-Hazmi entered the same checkpoint. Salem cleared the metal detector and was permitted through, but Nawaf set off the alarms for both the first and the second metal detectors. In his pocket or in his hand luggage he had the heavy Leatherman multitool utility knife he had purchased at the Laurel Target store. But at the time, as they knew from their test flights, such a knife was permitted to be carried on board as long as the blade was less than four inches. A screener waved a wand over Nawaf and, as with Moqed, let him go without ever bothering to check what set off the alarm. A minute later another screener swiped Nawaf's over-the-shoulder carry-on bag with an explosive trace detector, producing negative results. The last security barrier had been successfully breached.

The drab waiting area for American Flight 77 to Los Angeles was un-crowded; Tuesdays were generally among the slowest flying days of the week. At 7:50 Mihdhar walked down the Jetway with a black bag slung over his shoulder, wheeling a black carry-on behind him. He and Moqed entered the fuselage of the silver Boeing 757-223 and took seats 12A and 12B in coach, with Mihdhar in the center and Moqed at the window. In their section of the plane the flight was barely a quarter full, with just 43 of the 154 seats occupied.

A few minutes after Mihdhar, Hanjour walked on with a black bag draped over the shoulder of his white shirt and another, larger one in his hand. A flight attendant directed him to the left into first class and he took seat 1B, on the aisle directly in front of the cockpit door. The Hazmi brothers fol-lowed and took seats 5E and 5F on the right side of the first-class cabin, and at 8:16, the wide-body jet began to taxi away from the terminal.

At 8:00, as he did every Tuesday and Thursday, Mike Hayden took the elevator down to the third floor and walked across to the National Security Operations Center in Ops 1 for his regular morning meeting with his senior staff. "It's something I started here because I wanted the seniors to get a sense of the ops tempo," he said. Among the more worrisome items the ops officer brought up that morning was the assassination of Massoud. The action seemed to have touched off a new offensive by the Taliban against Massoud's Northern Alliance forces. Also, although the White House was cautiously avoiding discussing whether Massoud was dead because of some conflicting reports from his group, intelligence reports were indicating that Massoud had died on a helicopter en route to Dushanbe, the capital of neighboring Tajikistan.

Then there was the usual assortment of other items—in the Middle East, Israeli tanks ringing the West Bank city of Jenin began shelling Palestinian security positions just outside town; in Istanbul, Turkey, a female suicide bomber killed two police officers and injured at least twenty other people. About seven minutes after the briefing began it was over. "I keep beating them to keep it shorter," Hayden said. Following the ops briefing, the group moved into the small conference room next door for a quick staff meeting. "By eight or eight thirty we've kind of gotten the burst communications and now you're into your work schedule."

"American 77, Dulles tower," said the controller. "Runway three zero, taxi into position and hold. You'll be holding for landing traffic one left and for wake turbulence spacing behind the DC-10." Seated in the front row, Hanjour kept his eyes focused on the cockpit door. As soon as it opened— when the flight attendants brought the flight crew their breakfast, or one of the crewmembers left to use a rest room—it would be time to make their move.

At 8:20, American Airlines Flight 77 nosed upward into a cloudless, Tiffany-blue sky.

Following the ops briefing, Hayden returned to his office for a meeting with a small number of senior officials. A few minutes after it began, about 8:48, he was standing a few feet from his desk, behind a tall wooden speaker's table, when his executive assistant, Cindy Farkus, walked in. A plane had just crashed into the World Trade Center, she said. "The immediate image I had was a light plane, off course, bad flying," said Hayden, who glanced at CNN just as they began showing scenes from Mohamed Atta's attack on the North Tower. "I thought that was a big fire for a small plane," he said, and then continued with his meeting.

At about that same moment aboard Flight 77, Hazmi and his crew sprang into action. They had trained the scenario many times: they would pull out their knives and box cutters and take command of the aircraft, ordering the crew to relinquish their aircraft, leave it on autopilot, and move to the back of the plane with the passengers. Then as Hazmi, Mihdhar, and the rest cleared out the cockpit, first class, and the front of coach, Hanjour would walk into the cockpit with the case he brought onboard containing maps, charts, and flying aids.

The entire operation appears to have worked like clockwork. At 8:50:48, Indianapolis Control transmitted the navigation message "American 77 cleared direct um Falmouth," and the crew responded three seconds later, "uh direct Falmouth American 77 thank you." Less than four minutes later, at 8:54, Hanjour was at the controls as the plane made its first deviation from its assigned course by turning slightly to the south. And two minutes later the transponder was switched off, causing the aircraft to disappear from primary radar.

With the transponder switched off, the plane had become virtually invisible to the controller on the ground who had been tracking the flight. Desperate to find it, he began searching along its projected flight path and the airspace to the southwest where it had started to turn. But there was nothing there. He tried the radios, calling the aircraft directly, then the airline. Again there was nothing. Indianapolis Control then made the first of ten unsuccessful attempts over the next six and a half minutes to contact the aircraft via radio. Finally, shortly after 8:56, the controllers agreed to "sterilize the air space" along the flight's projected westerly route so that other planes would not be affected by Flight 77.

By 9:00 a.m., Hanjour had turned to the east and had begun to descend. Five minutes later the plane's blip again appeared on the radar scopes of

Indianapolis Control, but well east of where it should have been, leading to great confusion, including thoughts that the plane might already have crashed. After another seven minutes, Hanjour leveled off at twenty-five thousand feet and made a slight course change to the east-northeast. "You guys never been able to raise him at all?" asked a radar operator at Indianapolis Control. "No," said the air traffic controller. "We called [the] company. They can't even get ahold of him, so there's no, no, uh, no radio communications and no radar."

Pentagon

indy Farkus again broke into Hayden's meeting, but this time she was almost running. Another plane had hit the second tower, she said. "One plane's an accident, two planes is an attack," said Hayden, who immediately adjourned his meeting and asked Farkus to quickly summon the agency's top security officials to his office. L. Kemp Ensor, the National Security Agency's associate director for security, walked into the director's office with his assistants. "As they were walking through the door, I knew exactly what we needed to do and I said, 'All nonessential personnel out of here.' Out of the complex," said Hayden.

Throughout the NSA, loudspeakers began sounding. "All nonessential personnel are to leave the building," came the announcement over and over.

Within Alec Station, CIA officers and FBI agents stared at the television in disbelief. "I saw the second plane hit in the office and it was like, oh my God, we're under attack," said FBI agent Mark Rossini. "No one uttered it. We just knew, we just knew. It was just frantic. Then we were just trying to find information—trying to find everything we could that's on cable traffic, what's being written. In some respects, we had no idea what was going on—we couldn't really do anything. Everybody immediately suspected it was bin Laden."

Shortly after nine, Theodore Olson, the Bush administration's solicitor general, heard about the hijackings and quickly turned on his office television. His wife, Barbara Olson, forty-five, a talk-show regular, was flying to Los Angeles that morning, and he was worried that she might have been on one of the planes that crashed into the World Trade Center. A fixture on cable networks for her strident advocacy of conservative and far-right issues, Olson was on Flight 77 in seat 3E, a few seats behind and across from Hanjour.

After a brief mental calculation, Ted Olson figured his wife's plane could not have gotten to New York that quickly. Suddenly, a secretary rushed in. "Barbara is on the phone," she said. Olson jumped for the receiver. "Our plane has been hijacked!" she said quickly, but after a few seconds the phone went dead. Olson immediately called the command center at Justice and alerted them to the fact that there was yet another hijacked plane—and that his wife was on it. He also said she was able to communicate, though her first call had been cut off.

Minutes later, Barbara called back. Speaking very quietly, she said the hijackers did not know she was making this call. All the passengers, she said, had been herded to the back by men who had used knives and box cutters to hijack the plane. The pilot, she said, had announced that the plane had been hijacked shortly after takeoff. Ted Olson then told her about the two other planes that had been hijacked that morning and flown into the World Trade Center. "I think she must have been partially in shock from the fact that she was on a hijacked plane," Olson recalled. "She absorbed the information."

"What shall I tell the pilot? What can I tell the pilot to do?" Barbara said, trying to remain calm. Ted asked if she could tell where the plane was at that moment. She said she could see houses and, after asking someone, said she thought the plane was heading northeast. Then they reassured each other that the plane was still up in the air, still flying, and that it would come out all right. "It's going to come out okay," Olson told his wife, who agreed.

But Ted Olson knew the situation was anything but all right. "I was pretty sure everything was not going to be okay," he recalled. "I, by this time, had made the calculation that these were suicide persons, bent on destroying as much of America as they could." "I love you," she said as they exchanged feelings for each other. Then the phone suddenly went dead again. While waiting for another call, Olson remained glued to the television. It was now about 9:30.

At 9:24, the FAA had alerted officials at NORAD about the missing plane. Officials there immediately sent out a scramble order to their Air National Guard unit at Langley Air Force Base in Hampton, Virginia. At 129 miles away, it was the closest alert base to Washington. As Langley's scramble horn blared and the battle stations light turned yellow, Major Dean Eckmann, a Northwest Airlines pilot serving his regular National Guard rotation, ran for his fighter. Joining him were Major Brad Derrig and Captain Craig Borgstrom. Six minutes later, NORAD's three F-16s, each loaded with six missiles, were wheels up. The mission for Eckmann and his two fellow pilots was to somehow find Flight 77 before it found its target, and possibly shoot it down. But that would require the authorization of the president, then in an elementary school in Sarasota, Florida. "I don't think any fighter pilot in the United States would have ever thought they would be flying combat air patrols over American cities," Eckmann said. "That was huge, huge culture shock."

At 9:29, with the plane thirty-eight miles west of the Pentagon and flying at seven thousand feet, Hanjour turned off the autopilot and took control of the stick. At that same moment, Dulles tower air traffic control operator Danielle O'Brien spotted an unidentified blip on her radar screen. Although she didn't know it at the time, it was the missing Flight 77.

The alarmed controllers quickly called to warn their colleagues at Reagan National Airport, which was located close to downtown Washington. "Fast-moving primary target," they said, indicating that a plane without a transponder was heading their way. Tom Howell, the controller next to O'Brien, glanced over at her screen and his eyes grew wide. "Oh my God!" he yelled. "It looks like he's headed to the White House! We've got a target headed right for the White House!" At full throttle, American Flight 77 was traveling at about five hundred miles per hour directly toward P-56, the prohibited airspace surrounding the White House and the Capitol. Because of its speed and the way it maneuvered and turned, everyone in the radar room of Dulles Airport's tower assumed it was a military jet.

At the NSA, the one group Hayden could not move to Ops 1 was the counterterrorism unit, eight floors up on the top of Ops 2B. He visited the unit and described the employees working there as "emotionally shattered." "One of the more emotional parts of the day, for me," said Hayden. "I went into our CT [counterterrorism] shop and our logistics folks were tacking up blackout curtains because we can't move the CT shop in the midst of this." Hayden called his wife, Jeanine, at their home a few miles away and asked her to locate their children.

Hayden then ordered the counterterrorism unit to focus their attention on Middle Eastern intercepts and to translate and analyze them immediately as they were received, rather than starting with the oldest in the stack first, as was normally the case. It was then that analysts finally translated the two messages sent the day before, between pay phones in a highly dangerous area of Afghanistan and people in Saudi Arabia. To their shock, one said, "Tomorrow is zero hour," and the other said, "The match begins tomorrow." Whether they were referring to the attack or to something else, such as the assassination of Massoud, was unknown; the messages were too brief and vague. Still, the NSA would wait until the next day, September 12, before distributing the information to anyone else in Washington.

Within the tower at Dulles Airport, the tension rippling through the air was almost visible. The supervisor in the radar room began a countdown as the unknown plane got closer and closer to the White House. "He's twelve miles west," he said. "He's moving very fast eastbound—okay, guys, where is he now? . . . Eleven miles west, ten miles west, nine miles west." About that point, he picked up the phone to the Secret Service office at the White House. "We have an unidentified, very fast-moving aircraft inbound toward your vicinity," he said, counting down the miles. "Eight miles west. Seven miles west."

Many within Alec Station believed the CIA might be the target of Flight 77—a similar scenerio had once been planned by Ramzi Yousef, the man who bombed the World Trade Center in 1993. "We thought it was coming for the CIA," said FBI agent Mark Rossini. "So they evacuated the building, but we stayed. We were in the basement; I thought we'd be okay. We were in NHB [New Headquarters Building]. It was all underground up to the fourth floor, so I thought if the plane comes in it's not really going to hit us, it's going to hit the ground. Or it's going to hit OHB [Old Headquarters Building]; it's not really going to hit us. So we all stayed."

At the White House the warning came into the tightly packed Situation Room, down a flight of stairs from the Oval Office, where three watch officers continuously monitor computers carrying reports from the various intelligence agencies. A rush of fear suddenly washed over Franklin C. Miller, the director for defense policy. *The White House could be going down,* he thought. Then he had an aide send out an e-mail with the names of those present "so that when and if we died, someone would know who was in there," he said.

Secret Service officers quickly rushed into Vice President Dick Cheney's office. "We have to move," said one agent. "We're moving now, sir; we're moving." Once out, they hustled him down to the Presidential Emergency Operations Center, a special tubelike bunker under the East Wing of the building. The rest of the White House staff were told to get out and away from the building as quickly as possible. "Get out, get out, this is real," shouted members of the bomb squad running through the building. "All the way to H Street, please," one uniformed Secret Service officer yelled. "Women, drop your heels and run, drop your heels and run," yelled one Secret Service agent. "Suddenly, the gates that never open except for au-

thorized vehicles just opened and the whole White House just flooded out,"
recalled Press Secretary Jennifer Millerwise.

At 9:34, with the plane five miles west-southwest of the Pentagon, Hanjour began a complex, 330-degree right turn.

"Six miles," said the supervisor. "Five miles, four miles." He was just
about to say three miles when the plane suddenly turned away. "In the
room, it was almost a sense of relief," recalled air traffic controller Danielle O'Brien. "This must be a fighter. This must be one of our guys sent
in, scrambled to patrol our capital and to protect our president, and we
sat back in our chairs and breathed for just a second. In the meantime, all
the rest of the planes are still flying and we're taking care of everything
else."

Then at about two thousand feet and four miles southwest of the
building, Hanjour pointed the nose down and increased to near maximum speed. "He's turning back in!" O'Brien yelled. "He's turning back
eastbound!" O'Brien's fellow traffic controller Tom Howell also saw the
turn and began to yell to the supervisor. "Oh my God, John, he's coming back!" Arlington, Virginia, police officer Richard Cox could hardly
believe his eyes. He grabbed for his microphone and called dispatch. "It's
an American Airlines plane, headed east down over the pike, possibly
toward the Pentagon," he said excitedly.

Traveling at 530 miles per hour and with 36,200 pounds of jet fuel
aboard, Flight 77 smashed into the gray concrete wall of the Pentagon.
The jet hit with such force that it penetrated four of the five concentric
rings of corridors and offices surrounding a gazebo in the center court,
long nicknamed Ground Zero.

"We lost radar contact with that aircraft," recalled O'Brien. "And we
waited. And we waited. And your heart is just beating out of your chest
waiting to hear what's happened."

"Dulles, hold all of our inbound traffic," said a voice. "The Pentagon's
been hit." "I remember some folks gasping," recalled O'Brien. "I think I
remember a couple of expletives." "It's just like a big pit in your stomach
because you weren't able to do anything about it to stop it," said Tom
Howell. "That's what I think hurt the most."

At the Justice Department, Ted Olson heard on the television that an explosion had taken place at the Pentagon. Although no one identified the aircraft involved, he knew it was Flight 77, carrying his wife. "I did and I didn't want to," he recalled. "But I knew."

The NSA, made up of more than fifty buildings containing more than seven million square feet of space, was an easy place to hit. Following definite word that the Pentagon had been struck and that there were still one or more hijacked aircraft headed toward Washington, Hayden ordered the three to four thousand remaining essential personnel to immediately leave the agency's three tall towers. They were to relocate to the three-story Ops 1 building, the old low-rise A-shaped structure that was the agency's first home in Fort Meade. All four buildings were interconnected, so employees never had to go outside.

In Ops 1, Hayden and his top staff marched through the automatic glass doors of the third-floor National Security Operations Center, the agency's "war room." Normally quiet and sedate, the NSOC suddenly became a beehive of activity, with watch officers and signals intelligence officials fielding messages to and from the worldwide listening posts searching for answers in the dim light. All were watching for a CRITIC (Critical Intelligence) message—which took highest precedence—warning of where the next attack might come.

At 9:53 a.m., less than fifteen minutes after Flight 77 hit the Pentagon, analysts picked up a phone call from a bin Laden operative in Afghanistan to a phone number in the former Soviet republic of Georgia. The person in Afghanistan said that he had "heard good news," and indicated that a fourth target was yet to be hit—a possible reference to United Flight 93 that would crash in Pennsylvania before reaching its intended target in Washington.

"I got in touch with George Tenet," said Hayden. "He said, 'What do you have?' and I passed on whatever information we had." Hayden then called his wife back, said he was okay, and found out that his children had been located and were safe.

Over the next hours and days, it would become clear to Hayden that the men who attacked America lived, planned, and communicated not only within the country but even within the NSA's own community. It would also become clear to him that the pressures would be enormous to begin turning the NSA's massive ears inward, and to start filling its near bottomless data storage capacity with the words and voices of millions of Americans. For years, under his leadership, the agency had deliberately taken an overly cautious approach to eavesdropping and, possibly as a result, contributed to the intelligence failures that led to the attacks. Now he had a different priority. "Number one, security," he said. "We've got to defend ourselves."

BOOK TWO

TARGETS

Opportunity

Five miles north of the Pentagon, on a bridge crossing the Potomac from Maryland into Virginia, John Poindexter was on his way to work in Arlington at the moment Hani Hanjour drove Flight 77 into the building. On his finger was a large ring from the Naval Academy, where he graduated at the top of his class in 1958, and on his sleeves were cuff links with the White House seal. A retired rear admiral and former Reagan national security advisor, he had become deeply involved in the arms-for hostages scandal, where money from covert arms sales to Iran was siphoned off to illegally support counterinsurgents in Nicaragua. After disappearing from public life, he began turning his attention away from waging wars with guns and guerrillas and toward a new form of warfare, one that would instead use complex mathematical algorithms and computer-based pattern recognition techniques to defeat an enemy, focusing on the new emerging threat of terrorism. The idea was to find the enemy before he could find us.

Moments after the plane hit the Pentagon, Poindexter received an urgent call on his cell phone from his wife, Linda, who told him about the attack. "Mark is okay," she said, referring to their son, who was a commander on the staff of the navy's chief of naval operations. "He wasn't in the building." Poindexter's first thought was relief. Then he began seeing connections to the type of work he had been doing. "I realized this was a well-coordinated attack of the type that we had been working to prevent," he said.

The more he heard on the radio, about terrorists seizing aircraft and using them as weapons of mass destruction, the more he became convinced that his work was the answer to similar attacks in the future. In the Cold War, indications of pending attacks came via advanced radar systems— on land, on sea, and in the air—designed to detect incoming aircraft and missiles, or satellites that could discover their imminent launch. But the new terrorists turn everyday items into weapons, from cars and trucks to dinghies and jumbo jets. By the time they have struck, it is too late to detect them. What was needed was a way to find them at the earliest possible moment; what was needed were the ideas and techniques he and his colleagues at Syntek Technologies had been working on for years.

Arriving at work in time to witness the South Tower collapse on television, Poindexter became frustrated and discouraged. Despite six years of hard effort, they had not been able to convince the intelligence community of the need to adopt their ideas and concepts. As most of the staff departed early for home, Poindexter, the company's senior vice president, remained behind, thinking of how in a matter of hours the world had suddenly changed. "I stayed most of the day," he said, "thinking about what needed to be done."

Schooled at Annapolis and trained as a scientist, sixty-five-year-old John Poindexter was a man with a great understanding of schematic diagrams, wiring charts, and military order. Tall and bulky with a hairless scalp, a bushy white mustache, and a fondness for pipes, starched white shirts, and dull gray suits, he was the technocrat's technocrat. The answer to all things could be found in a test tube, a circuit board, or a mainframe. Thus Poindexter was convinced the answer to the complex problem of Middle Eastern terrorism was simply to place the everyday actions, public and private, of all Americans under a massive government magnifying glass.

Early on September 12 he contacted J. Brian Sharkey, an old friend who had previously worked for the Pentagon's cutting-edge laboratory, the Defense Advanced Research Projects Agency (DARPA). In 1999, as the deputy director of DARPA's Information Systems Office, Sharkey had introduced a program dubbed Total Information Awareness (TIA), a name George Orwell would have liked. Eventually TIA died on the vine and Sharkey left DARPA to become a vice president at SAIC, the giant defense contracting firm. But now, with America in the grip of fear, TIA's time had finally come.

Poindexter and Sharkey held a meeting in a parked car off a Maryland highway. Both were energized by the idea of turning information into a weapon, of vacuuming up everyone's digital trail, their parking receipts and Web searches, their bookstore visits and their gas station fill-ups, and then using supercomputers and complex algorithms to discover who among us is a terrorist. The data collected would be from public, private, and government databases, from Web browsers such as Google, from credit agencies and credit card companies, and from the Social Security Administration. Every bit had a history and every keystroke told a story. Known as data mining, it was automated surveillance on steroids.

On October 15, at a local Arlington fish restaurant—Gaffney's Restaurant, Oyster & Ale House Sharkey outlined TIA to DARPA's new director, Dr. Anthony Tether. By the time the oyster shells were empty, Tether wholeheartedly endorsed the idea and then suggested that Sharkey run the operation. Unwilling to give up his very lucrative defense contracting salary at SAIC, Sharkey instead thought of Poindexter. A few days later, while the two were sailing on the Chesapeake aboard Poindexter's forty-two-foot sloop *Bluebird*, Sharkey suggested to his friend that he talk with Tether about taking the job. Poindexter liked the idea and a meeting with Tether was set up. For the admiral, it would be a second chance to save the world—again in his own secret way. This time, instead of a covert arms-for-hostages deal he would build the information equivalent of an atomic bomb.

Not a man of small ideas, Poindexter arrived at the meeting with Tether prepared with a presentation titled "A Manhattan Project for Counter-Terrorism." He would become the Edward Teller of the information age. Like the old atomic-bomb development facility at Oak Ridge, Tennessee, the facility that Poindexter envisioned would employ the best and the brightest minds in computer science, physics, and information technology. But instead of intending to explode trillions of electrons and protons in a million different directions, Poindexter wanted to do the opposite. He wanted to collect into one "ultra-large" data warehouse billions of seemingly inconsequential bits of data and from that establish who might hijack the next plane or blow up the next building or take down the next bridge. He believed that with the right combination of hardware, software, and brainpower, he would be able to tie the purchase of a Leatherman knife at Target with a Web search on American Airlines and a speeding ticket in

Oklahoma and discover Nawaf al-Hazmi before he had a chance to board Flight 77. "How are we going to find terrorists and preempt them, except by following their trail?" asked Poindexter.

In an atmosphere of hysteria, and with an administration unable to shovel dollars into counterterrorism projects fast enough, it was an easy sell. Tether said he would fund the project if Poindexter would run it. Poindexter readily agreed, and by January 2002, what would possibly become the largest data-surveillance system ever built was placed into the hands of a man once convicted of five felony counts of lying to Congress, destroying official documents, and obstructing congressional investigations. If Poindexter was a man of big ideas, he was also a man of big scandals, a factor that didn't seem to bother Tether.

During the Reagan administration, Poindexter was the highest-ranking official to be found guilty during the Iran-Contra affair. He was sentenced to prison by a federal judge who called him "the decision-making head" of a plot to deceive Congress. Later, an appeals court overturned the conviction on a technicality, holding that the testimony Poindexter gave to Congress about Iran-Contra was immunized, and therefore couldn't be used against him at his trial.

Dubbed the Information Awareness Office, Poindexter's organization grew rapidly. With about $200 million in funding, Poindexter farmed out much of the research into how to build such a system to a wide range of corporations and universities that would do the heavy lifting. The companies were mostly large defense contractors such as Booz Allen Hamilton and Raytheon, and small boutique intelligence consultancies like Hicks & Associates. The universities ranged from Cornell and Columbia in the east to the University of California at Berkeley in the west.

Ted Senator, one of Poindexter's colleagues, used a metaphor to describe the difficult task ahead in creating TIA. "Our task is akin to finding dangerous groups of needles hidden in stacks of needle pieces," he said. "This is much harder than simply finding needles in a haystack: we have to search through many stacks, not just one; we do not have a contrast between shiny, hard needles and dull, fragile hay; we have many ways of putting the pieces together into individual needles and the needles into groups of needles; and we cannot tell if a needle or group is dangerous until it is at least partially assembled. So, in principle at least, we must track all the needle pieces all of the time and consider all possible combinations."

As with a prefabricated mansion, each contractor worked on a separate section of TIA. Among them was the Evidence Extraction and Link Discovery program, which Ted Senator described to a group of technologists in 2002:

> We've all seen what's meant by links and relationships in the past year. Many newspaper articles have appeared about the events of September 11, typically accompanied by very nice graphics that show the relationships between the hijackers—some roomed together in Hamburg, some had airline tickets purchased on the same credit card at the same time, some traveled to Las Vegas at the same time, and the pilots trained together and, most important to our ability to have detected the plot in advance, engaged in suspicious and unexplainable behavior that was reported during this training. These articles had as their theme: "we had the information but didn't put it together."
>
> And that is what EELD is all about: developing techniques that allow us to find relevant information—about links between people, organizations, places, and things—from the masses of available data, putting it together by connecting these bits of information into patterns that can be evaluated and analyzed, and learning what patterns discriminate between legitimate and suspicious behavior.

TIA also included Scalable Social Network Analysis (SSNA), which was projected to distinguish potential terrorist cells from ordinary groups of people through an analysis of various everyday activities, such as telephone calls, ATM withdrawals, and meetings; and Activity, Recognition, and Monitoring (ARM), which sought to develop computerized cameras capable of watching, recording, and learning how people act and behave—to "capture human activities in surveillance environments." In other words, the object was to develop hidden cameras to determine whether someone was acting out of the ordinary. Finally, oblivious to calling attention to the Orwellian nature of his new organization, Poindexter personally designed an official seal for the Information Awareness Office with a pyramid topped by a piercing, disembodied, all-seeing eye.

Within a month of opening for business, Poindexter began reaching out to the intelligence community—his future customers—and offering them a portal to his operation. This was a highly secret computer network through which the various agencies could interact with TIA's sophisticated systems. Agencies would access the network through a "node," a dedicated desktop computer located within each agency. Among the agencies interested was the NSA, which could never have enough computer help to sift through and analyze its ocean of intercepts. By tying into the TIA network, the agency would be able to experiment with new analytical software developed by Poindexter's group. To work out the arrangement, Poindexter met with Hayden and the agency began installing the TIA nodes. Once they were installed, the agency started running stacks of intercepted e-mail and other communications through the system, testing various programs and exchanging data with other intelligence community users.

In the fall of 2002, Poindexter's luck ran out when conservative *New York Times* columnist William Safire, a staunch and longtime privacy advocate, caught wind of both TIA and Poindexter. His resulting November 14 column, entitled "You Are Suspect," was merciless. Calling TIA "the supersnoop's dream," he went on to say, "Here is what will happen to you":

> Every purchase you make with a credit card, every magazine subscription you buy and medical prescription you fill, every Web site you visit and e-mail you send or receive, every academic grade you receive, every bank deposit you make, every trip you book and every event you attend—all these transactions and communications will go into what the Defense Department describes as "a virtual, centralized grand database."

Safire was no less severe on Poindexter himself, calling him "the disgraced admiral." Others, including members of Congress, quickly jumped on the bandwagon and TIA went on life support. The end for Poindexter finally came when it was discovered that one of his programs involved a bizarre use of stock-market techniques to predict potential terrorist attacks. He resigned on August 29 and a month later House and Senate leaders came to agreement on scrapping the funding for TIA.

Rather than truly dying, however, the controversial domestic data mining operation simply slipped deeper into the shadows—and ended up at the NSA.

Hunters

In the days immediately following the attacks, General Hayden had a major decision to make. He had to decide whether to continue to go forward with his massive, long-term reorganization plan, designed to revitalize the NSA's workforce and modernize its worldwide eavesdropping network, or quickly change gears to focus on the immediate terrorist threat. On September 13, he called a meeting in his office.

"We had all the senior leadership of the agency in this room," said Hayden. "About thirty-five people . . . all the key leaders. We had them all in the room. I said, 'Okay, we had a plan and we had a transformational road map and we made some decisions, now this [9/11] has happened. Do we need to revisit any of the trajectories that we put the agency on?' And this was one of those frank and wide-ranging discussions. Every man and woman in the room said, 'Go faster. No change in direction. If anything, accelerate all the changes under way.' "

Ironically, at a time when most of the intelligence agencies were recalling previously retired workers, the NSA went ahead with their plan to offer incentives for employees to take early outs. "This was within thirty days of the attack," said Hayden, "with the whole system stretched by the challenges of the new war. We had a lot of people leave and actually paid some people to leave."

The problem was that many of the people at the NSA had the right skills for the wrong targets. The agency had to move out many of the longtime Soviet linguists and high-frequency specialists to make room for Urdu and Dari speakers, and experts at dissecting and reverse-engineering the Internet. "We could not squeeze any more juice out of retraining," said Hayden. "We had spent a decade trying to retrain people for the new kinds of missions, and now it was time to get new people in here. And the only way you can get new people in here is to let other people go. And we were criticized for that. Someone who's as good at her job as [Congresswoman] Jane Harmon, the senior member on the [House Intelligence Committee, who] pays a lot of attention to us and is very conscientious and comes out to visit us and is very supportive, even she kind of said, 'What is this all about?' and said so in a public way. And I quietly pointed out to her, 'It was a tough decision, but it was a right decision.' "

The NSA's personnel problems began in the early 1990s with the end of the Cold War. "We were a third smaller at the end of the 1990s than we were at the beginning," said Hayden. "We downsized in the worst possible way—we shut the front door. For most of the decade of the 1990s, we hired fewer than two hundred people a year—civilians—in an agency that had over twenty thousand civilians in 1990; [we had] fifteen thousand by 2000." By 2004, according to Hayden, the new recruits had jumped to 1,500 a year.

But of those numbers, the largest group hired were not code breakers but security guards. "Garrison no longer equates to sanctuary," said Hayden. "So we're hiring guards. We're renting some, too. Number two, we've increased our polygraphers. Number three, linguists. Number four, analysts. And there almost ain't a number five . . . We focused on what I call wartime languages—Arabic, all the languages of Afghanistan, and then selected languages in other parts of the world, [like the] Horn of Africa." The man in charge of hiring and recruiting was Harvey Davis. "We let the hiring program atrophy," he said, referring to the 1990s. "But now there is a transformation under way, and we are recruiting and hiring at a feverish pace."

At the same time, entire departments quickly packed up and shipped out to the Middle East. Many took with them small, transportable "suitcase kits," packed with eavesdropping equipment for targeting suspected terrorists. Made by SWS Securities, a small NSA contractor, they could handle rugged terrain and track low-powered radio transmissions, the kind produced by people in hiding and using shortwave radios and generators. They were also capable of detecting smaller signals obscured by large transmitters. Designed only for short-term use before disposal, they lasted about six weeks.

But according to Steve Uhrig, the president of SWS, bin Laden and his men had the advantage. "Anyone with a little computer understanding could get something up and running for him," he said. "If he kept his transmissions short, moved frequently, he could even put the transmitter ten miles away from where he is, run a ground microwave relay to a hilltop, and bounce it off a satellite; put it under an oil company's name . . . It could provide the perfect cover." For security, employees and their kits were picked up at local parking lots, rather than at their homes or at the agency, and driven to Baltimore-Washington International Airport. Back at headquarters, many employees worked round the clock. "When people say they are going to meet at eight," said one, "you have to ask if they mean eight in the morning or eight at night."

On the eighth floor of Ops 2B, Michael Hayden sought to restore a feeling of normalcy and confidence at the NSA. He also knew that there would be an immediate effort to push the NSA to the brink of the abyss. "On the thirteenth of September," said Hayden, "I gave an address to an empty room, but we beamed it throughout our entire enterprise, about free peoples always having to decide the balance of security and their liberties, and that we through our tradition have always planted our banner way down here on the end of the spectrum toward security [possibly meant liberty]. And then I told the workforce . . . there are going to be a lot of pressures to push that banner down toward security, and our job at NSA was to keep America free by making Americans feel safe again. So this balance between security and liberty was foremost in our mind."

But it was Hayden himself who would grab the banner and lead the charge away from liberty and toward a security state. As the smoke cleared, and the details about Mihdhar and Hazmi and the Yemen ops center began to emerge, he knew exactly what had happened. Worried about congressional concerns over privacy, unhappy about the public's image of the NSA as an evil eavesdropper, and hoping to avoid the slippery slope that led to the Church and Pike Committee investigations of the 1970s, he had turned a deaf ear to signals heading into the U.S. from suspected terrorist locations overseas. This despite the fact that closely monitoring these communications was part of his responsibility—provided certain FISA court rules were followed.

Hayden had preferred instead to play it safe and leave those communications to the FBI, which had neither the technology nor the capability to do that type of collection. "I had an agency," said Hayden, "that, you know, for decades—well, since the mid-1970s—had, frankly, played a bit back from the line so as not to get close to anything that got the agency's fingers burned in the Church-Pike era." As a result, the agency limited the monitoring of international communications to foreign diplomatic establishments in Washington and New York and a half dozen other FISA targets. Mihdhar and Hazmi were not among them.

But the times had now changed, and Hayden changed with them. Civil liberties were out, Fortress America was in. Even Hayden's ever-present football metaphors became more aggressive. "We're going to live on the edge," he would say. "My spikes will have chalk on them." In Haydenese, launching war against al-Qaeda became "playing a little offense rather than having a perpetual first down and goal on the three-yard line in the homeland." He would often say that the NSA had long been "gatherers"— passively picking information from the airwaves as it passed by. Now they would become "hunters," actively going after that information wherever it was.

Almost immediately after the attacks, Hayden beefed up the coverage of communications between Afghanistan and the U.S. Then, on his own initiative and without White House approval, he dropped the FISA-mandated rule of minimization on those communications, leaving in the names and other details of American citizens without court approval.

Soon thereafter, Vice President Dick Cheney called George Tenet and asked him if the NSA could do more. "I called Mike to relay the vice president's inquiry," said Tenet. "Mike made it clear that he could do no more within the existing authorities." Nine months earlier, soon after Bush and Cheney were elected, Hayden had presented them with a top-secret transition book outlining the challenges and limitations his agency was facing, noting both the fiber-optic revolution and FISA's limitations.

"The volumes and routing of data make finding and processing nuggets of intelligence information more difficult," it said. The best way to find those nuggets, Hayden suggested in the report, was to tap into the worldwide tele-communications web—voice as well as data—to "live on the network," even though that meant picking up many American communications. Hayden's recommendation was to make the NSA "a powerful, permanent presence on a global telecommunications network that will host the 'protected' communications of Americans as well as the targeted communications of adversaries." In other words, tap into the international communications flowing into and out of the U.S., something he had been reluctant to aggressively pursue prior to the attacks on 9/11 due to concern over FISA.

"We went to see the vice president together," Tenet said. "Mike laid out what could be done . . . We began to concentrate on the possible connections between the domestic front and the data we were collecting overseas. We would identify al-Qaeda members and other terrorists overseas and often discover that they had relatives, acquaintances, or business ties in the United States. Each rock overturned abroad led to ants scurrying every which way, including many toward the United States."

The next meeting was in the White House with the president. Seated around the long conference table in the Situation Room with Bush, Cheney, and Condoleezza Rice were the key intelligence chiefs. Hayden, the kid from "the Ward," Pittsburgh's tough North Side, was a man impressed with power. He once beamed as he boasted of going to a baseball game with Rice. Now the president of the United States was putting his arm around him and calling him "Mikey," his childhood nickname. "Is there anything more we could be doing, given the current laws?" Bush asked the gathering. "There is," said Hayden. He then gave the president a brief summary of the NSA's signals intelligence operations against al-Qaeda.

"He showed me the plans for this country to pick up a conversation," said Bush, "listen to conversations from people outside the country, inside the country, who had an affiliation with al-Qaeda, or were al-Qaeda. He said, 'I think we can design a program, Mr. President, that will enable us to have a quick response to be able to detect and deter a potential attack.' I said, 'That's interesting, General.' I said, 'That makes a lot of sense to me.' I said, 'You're not going to listen inside the country.' [He said,] 'No, this is calls from outside the country in, or inside out, to people who we know or suspect are affiliated with al-Qaeda.' And I remember some of those phone calls coming out of California prior to September the 11th attacks by the killers—just thinking maybe if we'd have listened to those on a quick response basis, you know, it might have helped prevent the attacks. My second question was, is it legal?"

Hayden then brought up FISA and complained that it was designed for an earlier period of time. It was designed for the 1970s, he said, when international communications signals, its principal focus, traveled through the air and domestic calls, which they were prohibited from monitoring, were transmitted over wires. Thus the law placed most restriction on the wired communications. "When the law was passed," he said, "almost all local calls were on a wire and almost all long-haul communications were in the air. In an age of cell phones and fiber optic cables, that has been reversed . . . with powerful and unintended consequences for how NSA can lawfully acquire a signal." To correct the problem, Hayden proposed a new concept: "hot pursuit."

Under FISA, if the NSA was eavesdropping on the Yemen ops center and a call was made to the U.S., the intercept operator could legally listen in as long as the target was in Yemen. But as soon as the two parties hung up, the NSA intercept operator might want to begin targeting the American number immediately. "From that decision to coverage is measured in minutes," Hayden said. Because the person is in the U.S., however, the NSA would now have to get a FISA warrant to begin targeting that number, a process Hayden claimed was "slow and cumbersome." Instead he told the president he wanted authority to secretly bypass the court and begin monitoring all of the target's international communications immediately—in other words, "in hot pursuit." The standards for what represented a "reasonable" intrusion into Americans' privacy had changed, Hayden said, "as smoke billowed from two American cities and a Pennsylvania farm field."

FISA, however, already provided for "hot pursuit"—it allowed intercept operators to begin listening immediately, as long as they would apply for the warrant within three days. Yet even that was too cumbersome and time-consuming for Hayden and Bob Deitz, Hayden's top lawyer at the NSA, who argued that the whole exercise was a waste of both time and paper—a total bother. "The problem with the seventy-two-hour rule," he said, is that "it is not a freebie. It is not you get to do whatever you want for seventy-two hours . . . My concern is not lawyer time, although that is precious enough. My concern is analyst time, and the issue that most concerns us is your counterterrorism experts and analysts do not grow on trees . . . Analysts talk to each other. They do memoranda. They pass the memoranda on to shift supervisors . . . Then it has to go to our lawyers. Then it has to go to a group of lawyers at the Department of Justice; and then, ultimately, it has to go to the attorney general." And then there was all that paper. "FISA applications," he said, "now are approximately three-fourths of an inch thick. That is paper producing . . . I suggest that that is simply a waste of that paper and effort and analysts' time."

But in a democracy, eavesdropping on citizens, the most intrusive act a government can perform, has traditionally been done with care and deliberation, checks and balances, lest the government itself become the enemy. Eavesdropping in East Germany during the Cold War was very quick and efficient—and therefore pervasive. And during that same period, eavesdropping by the NSA rapidly accelerated due to limited outside oversight. Hayden's real problem today was not so much velocity—speed—as it was volume; he wanted to be able to target thousands of people simultaneously, some briefly and some long term, without the hassle of justifying them to anyone higher than an anonymous shift supervisor.

In fact, according to James Baker, the Justice Department official most familiar with the FISA court as the head of the Office of Intelligence Policy and Review since 2002, the warrants can be handled as quickly as in a matter of minutes. "We've done it in a matter of a day; we've done it in a matter of hours; we've done it in a matter of minutes," he said in 2007. "Very rapidly. Extremely rapidly . . . The point is, there's been no loss of foreign intelligence information. That's the key thing . . . The American people have not been put at any risk because of this process going on."

Nor, he said, were there any technical advances that prevented the court from doing its job. "The Congress in 1978," he said, "wanted to enable the government to collect all that information . . . I just want the American people to be reassured that there's not some pot of electrons out there floating around that we can't somehow get at technically because of the regime that FISA sets up . . . I submit that FISA works today. I believe that it's been effective in protecting the American people from threats from foreign powers, from hostile terrorist groups, from hostile foreign governments, and at the same time it's been effective in protecting the American people's privacy."

For years Hayden had avoided targeting Americans as much as possible. One slip and it was headlines and congressional hearings. But Michael Hayden was a man who spent his life tacking whichever way the political winds happened to be blowing, and now he would simply tack again, this time far to starboard. His goal was always to stay afloat and make it to the next larger port. For Hayden, that now required jettisoning the FISA court and launching his own top-secret eavesdropping operation at home against American citizens. The NSA would now become an agency of hunters.

FISA

As far as Michael Hayden was willing to go, Cheney wanted to go much further—to even allow the NSA to eavesdrop on purely domestic to domestic communications, phone calls as well as e-mail, without a warrant. If people within the U.S. with suspected links to al-Qaeda made calls, even to the house next door, Cheney believed the NSA should be tapping in, regardless of FISA. "Either we're serious about fighting the war on terror or we're not," he said. "Either we believe that there are individuals out there doing everything they can to try to launch more attacks, to try to get ever deadlier weapons to use against us, or we don't. The president and I believe very deeply that there's a hell of a threat, that it's there for anybody who wants to look at it. And that our obligation and responsibility given our job is to do everything in our power to defeat the terrorists. And that's exactly what we're doing."

Cheney's position was shared by his longtime aide and top legal advisor, forty-four-year-old David S. Addington, who became the chief legal architect of the warrantless eavesdropping program. He once told a senior Justice Department lawyer, "We're one bomb away from getting rid of that obnoxious [FISA] court." "He and the vice president had abhorred FISA's intrusion on presidential power ever since its enactment in 1978," said Jack Goldsmith, who headed the Justice Department's Office of Legal Counsel during the Bush administration—which he would later label "the terror presidency." "After 9/11 they and other top officials in the administration dealt with FISA the way they dealt with other laws they didn't like: they blew through them in secret based on flimsy legal opinions they guarded closely so no one could question the legal basis for the operations."

One reason why Cheney and Addington hated the court was its tendency to resist attempts by the Bush administration to push beyond the legal boundaries, even before the attacks of 9/11. Judges on the court kicked back more wiretap requests from the Bush administration than from the four previous presidential administrations combined. In its first twenty-two years, the court modified only two FISA eavesdropping requests out of the 13,102 applications that were approved. And in twenty of the first twenty-one annual reports issued by the court, up until 1999, the Justice Department reported that no orders were modified or denied. But beginning with the arrival of George W. Bush in 2001, the judges modified 179 of the 5,645 requests for court-ordered surveillance and rejected or deferred at least six the first outright rejections in the court's history—between 2003 and 2004.

Nevertheless, of all the courts in the history of the United States, it is likely none has ever been as accommodating to government lawyers. Such facts worry Jonathan Turley, a George Washington University law professor who worked for the NSA as an intern while in law school in the 1980s. The FISA "courtroom," hidden away on the top floor of the Justice Department building (because even its location is supposed to be secret), is a heavily protected, windowless, bug-proof SCIF. "When I first went into the FISA court as a lowly intern at the NSA, frankly, it started a lifetime of opposition for me to that court," said Turley. "I was shocked with what I saw. I was convinced that the judge in that SCIF would have signed anything that we put in front of him. And I wasn't entirely sure that he had actually *read* what we put in front of him. But I remember going back to my supervisor at NSA and saying, 'That place scares the daylights out of me.' "

The FISA judges are also agreeable to calls twenty-four hours a day if the NSA or FBI has an urgent warrant request. On one Saturday in April 2002, for example, four cars filled with FBI agents suddenly pulled up to the front door of the home of Royce C. Lamberth. A bald and burly fifty-nine-year-old Texan with a fondness for John Grisham novels, he was mowing his lawn at the time. But rather than arrest him, the agents were there to request an emergency court hearing to obtain seven top-secret warrants to eavesdrop on Americans.

As the presiding justice of the FISA court, Lamberth had become accustomed to holding the secret hearings in his living room. "My wife, Janis . . . has to go upstairs because she doesn't have a Top Secret clearance," he said. "My beloved cocker spaniel, Taffy, however, remains at my side on the assumption that the surveillance targets cannot make her talk. The FBI knows Taffy well. They frequently play with her while I read some of those voluminous tomes at home." FBI agents will even knock on the judge's door in the middle of the night. "On the night of the bombings of the U.S. embassies in Africa, I started the first emergency hearings in my living room at 3:00 a.m.," recalled Lamberth, who was first appointed to the court in 1995. "From the outset, the FBI suspected bin Laden, and the surveillances I approved that night and in the ensuing days and weeks all ended up being critical evidence at the trial in New York."

Lamberth, who first decided to become a lawyer at age seven, became a thorn in the side of the Bush administration soon after the inauguration. "Those who know me know the chief justice did not put me on this court because I would be a rubber stamp for whatever the executive branch was wanting to do," he said. "I ask questions." In March, he sent a letter to Attorney General John Ashcroft raising questions about a FISA request to eavesdrop on a member of Hamas, the militant Palestinian group. The issue involved whether the FBI was seeking authority to eavesdrop on targets without informing the court of pending criminal investigations involving the subject's status. FISA judges were always concerned that investigators might use the court, with its lower probable cause standard, as a back door to obtain eavesdropping warrants in standard criminal cases—something that was forbidden. Given Lamberth's conscientiousness and the fact that the court was rejecting an increasing number of FISA applications, Cheney and Addington began looking for a way to bypass the troublesome court altogether.

Enacted by a bipartisan Congress in 1978, FISA was a response to revelations that the NSA had conducted warrantless eavesdropping on Americans. To deter future presidents and NSA directors from ever again bypassing the court and the warrant procedure, Congress put sharp teeth

in the statute, making violation a felony punishable by a $10,000 fine and
five years in prison. Hard time. And each warrantless interception was a
separate violation.

Cheney was undeterred. The 9/11 attack occurred on his watch and
he was determined not to let something like it happen again. He also had
serious disagreements with even the existence of FISA, an impediment
on presidential power that he believed "served to erode the authority I
think the president needs to be effective, especially in a national security
area." He turned to Attorney General Ashcroft to find a way to get around
it. Ashcroft, in turn, handed the assignment to John C. Yoo, an extremely
aggressive, thirty-four-year-old Bush appointee who advocated for unprecedented presidential powers in times of war. He was also greatly
impressed with the NSA. "Sigint [signals intelligence] is even more important in this war than in those of the last century," he said.

Yoo argued forcefully to Ashcroft and Cheney that both the agency's
weapons and the law were a product of the last century. "The government
had to figure out how to tap into al-Qaeda's communications networks,"
he said. "We can't say well, that line is the devoted line for Osama bin
Laden to talk to his lieutenants. Or we know they use that frequency, because they use the Internet, and they use cell phones and telephone calls
just like you and I do. No. This is a good example of where existing laws
were not up to the job, because under existing laws like FISA, you have
to have the name of somebody, have to already suspect that someone's
a terrorist before you can get a warrant. You have to have a name to put
in the warrant to tap their phone calls, and so it doesn't allow you as a
government to use judgment based on probability, to say: 'Well, 1 percent
probability of the calls from or maybe 50 percent of the calls are coming
out of this one city in Afghanistan, and there's a high probability that
some of those calls are terrorist communications. But we don't know the
names of the people making those calls.' You want to get at those phone
calls, those e-mails, but under FISA you can't do that."

Ten days after the attacks, Yoo wrote an internal memorandum arguing
that the NSA could use "electronic surveillance techniques and equipment that are more powerful and sophisticated than those available to law
enforcement agencies in order to intercept telephonic communications
and observe the movement of persons but without obtaining warrants for
such uses." He noted that while such unprecedented and intrusive actions

might be rejected on constitutional grounds during normal times, they are now justified as a result of the 9/11 attacks. During such times, he said, "the government may be justified in taking measures which in less troubled conditions could be seen as infringements of individual liberties."

Yoo thought that constitutional guarantees instantly evaporate following a terrorist attack. "It appears clear that the Fourth Amendment's warrant requirement does not apply to surveillance and searches undertaken to protect the national security from external threats," he said. In another memo, this one to Alberto Gonzales, the White House counsel, he reiterated his view that the president's powers trump the Constitution. "Our office recently concluded," he wrote, "that the Fourth Amendment had no application to domestic military operations."

Hayden, not privy to the Justice Department's legal opinions, said he relied on the legal advice of his general counsel, Robert L. Deitz, and his staff for his decision to go along with the warrantless surveillance program. "Three guys," Hayden said, "whose judgment I trust; three guys who have advised me and who have told me not to do things in the past—and laid out the questions. And they came back with a real comfort level that this was within the president's authority . . . It probably would have presented me with a—with a bit of a dilemma if the NSA lawyers had said, no, we don't think so. But they didn't."

Given that neither Deitz nor any other NSA lawyer was trusted by the White House with the legal rationale for what they were doing, how could his lawyers evaluate the decision? It rather calls their "comfort level" into question. "Before I arrived [in October 2003]," said Jack Goldsmith, "not even NSA lawyers were allowed to see the Justice Department's legal analysis of what NSA was doing." He added, "They did not want the legal analysis scrutinized by anyone, even inside the executive branch."

Except for the presiding judge, Royce Lamberth, the FISA court was also kept in the dark about the NSA's warrantless program. But rather than being asked for his view on the legality of the operation, Lamberth, probably the most experienced person in the country on the topic, was simply told that this was a presidential decision, period. The meeting, with Hayden and Yoo, took place in the office of Attorney General John Ashcroft. During the meeting, which lasted nearly an hour, Lamberth said little and agreed to keep his fellow judges uninformed. "It was clear no one was asking him to approve it," said one person at the meeting.

"That was absolutely clear." Years later Lamberth would harshly criticize the program. "We have to understand you can fight the war [on terrorism] and lose everything if you have no civil liberties left when you get through fighting the war."

While Lamberth believed he had no legal power to prevent the president's actions—or even disclose them—he did make an attempt to keep any of the FISA cases that entered his court free of taint from the program. He did this by insisting that the Justice Department flag any FISA requests that were based, in any way, on the warrantless program. Lamberth had initially become alarmed when a number of requests crossing his desk failed to indicate the origin of the evidence of probable cause that was being presented—evidence, he believed, that originated from warrantless eavesdropping. By the time the NSA operation was up and running in the fall of 2001, between 10 and 20 percent of all the requests coming into the FISA court were tainted by what is known in the legal profession as "the fruit of the poisonous tree," that is, the warrantless program.

When Lamberth's tour on the court ended in 2002, he was succeeded by Colleen Kollar-Kotelly, like Lamberth a district court judge in the District of Columbia. She was also briefed on the program and continued to maintain the "firewall" separating legal FISA requests from the warrantless program. But the spillage into her court from the program became so bad that Kollar-Kotelly decided she had to take action. She insisted that the legal requests be accompanied by sworn affidavits—subject to perjury charges—attesting that the applications contained no product from the warrantless operation.

On October 1, Hayden gave a highly secret briefing to members of the House and Senate intelligence committees regarding his ad hoc decision to drop the minimization requirements on the intercepts between Afghanistan and the U.S. The fact that without even presidential approval the names of presumed-innocent Americans were now being sent to the FBI, CIA, and other agencies surprised and angered a number of those briefed, including Nancy Pelosi. A Democratic congresswoman from California and the House minority leader, she was also the ranking Democrat on the House Intelligence Committee. Hayden may also have touched obliquely on the warrantless eavesdropping, which at that time had not yet begun.

A few days later Pelosi sent a classified letter to Hayden expressing her concerns about the agency's legal authority to expand its domestic operations. In the briefing, she wrote, "you indicated that you had been operating since the Sept. 11 attacks with an expansive view of your authorities" with respect to electronic surveillance and intelligence-gathering operations. "I am concerned whether, and to what extent, the National Security Agency has received specific presidential authorization for the operations you are conducting." In his response, Hayden acknowledged that he had not gotten White House approval. "In my briefing," he wrote, "I was attempting to emphasize that I used my authorities to adjust NSA's collection and reporting."

Just days after the briefing, on October 4, Hayden received authorization to bypass the Foreign Intelligence Surveillance Court and begin eavesdropping on international communications to and from Americans without a warrant. Loaded with new money, freed of the FISA court, he now turned his attention to building his new worldwide surveillance empire.

Mission

In early October, Mike Hayden met a group of employees in a large windowless conference room just down the hall from his office. Sitting and standing around a giant doughnut-shaped table, they were the charter members of the most secret operation in the nation's most secret agency. They were also the first NSA employees since the mid-1970s to eavesdrop on the phone calls and messages of American citizens without a judicial warrant and in contravention to existing laws. In a very unusual move reflecting the questionable nature of the program, Hayden made participation in it voluntary. Each person also had to sign a special document acknowledging they had been briefed on the "special collection program" and agreeing under penalty of prison never to reveal any details of it to anyone not specifically cleared for the mission. And like its predecessors, Operations Shamrock and Minaret, it was also given a code word, which itself was secret.

"Let me tell you what I told them when we launched the program," said Hayden. "This is the morning of 6 October in our big conference room—about eighty, ninety folks in there—and I was explaining what the president had authorized, and I ended up by saying, 'And we're going to do exactly what he said, and not one photon or one electron more' . . . It was very closely held. We had to read people into the program specifically . . . This was walled off inside NSA; that's the compartment that it was in."

As the first intercepts began appearing on computer screens and digital recorders that first Saturday in October, less than a month after the attacks, one issue stood out above all others: whom to target. What criteria were the intercept operators to use to decide whether the American on the other end of that phone call or e-mail was linked to al-Qaeda or an innocent citizen constitutionally guaranteed the right to privacy? Under FISA, the Congress put that decision in the hands of the FISA court judges, independent arbiters with great experience and knowledge in the law, as well as extensive experience in determining whether there was probable cause—the high standard required by the Fourth Amendment—to begin targeting someone as a member of al-Qaeda.

Hayden's secret program bypassed the judges and instead left those decisions far down the food chain, to people with no legal training at all—"shift supervisors," according to both Hayden and his top lawyer, Bob Deitz. The NSA would become judge, jury, and eavesdropper all in one. "I don't make those decisions," said Hayden. "The director of Sigint out there doesn't make those decisions. Those decisions are made at the program level and at the level of our counterterrorism officer." Defensively, he noted, "I'm trying to communicate to you that the people who are doing this, okay, go shopping in Glen Burnie and their kids play soccer in Laurel. And they know the law. They know American privacy better than the average American, and they're dedicated to it . . . This isn't a drift net out there where we're soaking up everyone's communications. We're going after very specific communications that our professional judgment tells us we have reason to believe are those associated with people who want to kill Americans. That's what we're doing." Deitz added, "So this is not—this isn't simply Liberty Hall."

In addition to the issue of impartial judge versus partial eavesdropper, there is the question of different standards for deciding if an American is somehow affiliated with a terrorist organization. "They're targeted on al-Qaeda," said Hayden. "There is a probable cause standard. Every targeting is documented. There is a literal target folder that explains the rationale and the answers to the questions on a very lengthy checklist as to why this particular [phone] number we believe to be associated with the enemy."

But the term "probable cause" at the NSA is a misnomer. In fact, their standard is "reasonableness," which is much lower than that required by both FISA and the Fourth Amendment. "The standard that is most ap-

plicable to the operations of NSA," said Hayden, "is the standard of reasonableness, you know—is this reasonable?" He then gave an example
of how the warrantless system works. "NSA in the conduct of its foreign
intelligence work intercepts a communication from a known terrorist,
let's say in the Middle East, and the other end of that communication is
in the United States. There—one end of that communication involves a
protected person, all right? Everything NSA is doing is legal up to that
point. It is targeting the foreign end, it has a legitimate reason for targeting it, and so on, all right? But now, suddenly, we have bumped into the
privacy rights of a protected person, okay? And no warrant is involved,
okay? We don't go to a court. But through procedures . . . we must apply
a standard to protecting the privacy of that individual."

Inevitably, mistakes are made and innocent people are targeted.
"Clearly," Hayden acknowledged, "I think logic would dictate that if
you're using a probable cause standard as opposed to absolute certitude,
sometimes you may not be right." But, he added defensively, that doesn't
make the initial decision wrong. "To put someone on targeting under NSA
anywhere in the world . . . and at some point end targeting doesn't mean
that the first decision was wrong, it just means this was not a lucrative
target for communications intelligence."

The NSA's track record on accuracy, however, leaves much to be de-
sired. As even Hayden now admits, the agency got the war in Iraq completely wrong. "When we didn't find the weapons after the invasion and
the occupation," he said, "I brought our analysts in, NSA. Now, they're
not all source, they just do Sigint. And I said, 'Come on, we got five
things out there, chem, bio, nukes, missiles, and UAVs, give me your
confidence level on each one . . . zero to ten, how confident were you on
the day we kicked off the war?' . . . Nukes was lowest at three, missiles
was highest at ten, everything else was five, seven, and eight . . . As we
went further into this—I had them back in a month or two later—their
whole tone and demeanor had changed. There was a lack of confidence.
Everything was being marshmallowed to me, a lot of possibles and could
haves and maybes and so on."

The NSA scanned thousands of calls in the U.S. without a warrant,
some briefly and others for longer periods. Those considered suspicious—about five hundred people at any one time during the beginning
of the program and about one hundred people by 2007—would become

targets. Overseas the number of people targeted by the NSA on any particular day ranged from five thousand to seven thousand. Occasionally, following the capture of an al-Qaeda computer or terrorist, the numbers would jump as new names and phone numbers were discovered in databases or phone books. Also, there was a built-in multiplier effect: if one person was targeted and he was in communication with a dozen other people about whom the agency became suspicious, they also could end up on the NSA's phone-tree target list. And if a person in the U.S. seemed particularly important, the NSA could then go to the FISA court, meet the probable cause standard, and obtain a warrant to begin monitoring his or her communications. According to Hayden, "There were other circumstances in which clearly you wanted more than the coverage of international communications, and under this authorization, you would have to go to the FISA court in order to get a warrant for any additional coverage."

Had the warrantless eavesdropping system been in effect prior to 9/11, Hayden insists, both Mihdhar and Hazmi would have been detected. "I can demonstrate," he said, "how the physics and the math would work . . . Had this been in place prior to the attacks, the two hijackers who were in San Diego, Khalid al-Mihdhar and Nawaf al-Hazmi, almost certainly would have been identified as who they were, what they were, and most importantly, where they were." In fact, there was no need for such a system. If Hayden had simply done as his job allowed and traced the calls and e-mail back from the Yemen ops center and obtained a FISA warrant for the California phone numbers and e-mail address, he would have discovered who, what, and where they were back in the spring of 2000. And then by monitoring their domestic communications, the FBI could have discovered the other members of the group.

Those involved in the warrantless eavesdropping operation soon began to realize its limitations. By gaining speed and freedom they sacrificed order and understanding. Rather than focusing on the most important and potentially productive targets, which was required when going through the FISA court, they took a shotgun approach. They began monitoring thousands and thousands of "al-Qaeda affiliates," all of which proved unproductive, flooding the FBI with useless intercept reports, slowing down legitimate investigations, and placing thousands of innocent names on secret blacklists. The Do Not Fly list alone quickly ballooned from about twenty to over forty thousand names, many generated by the NSA's warrantless program as the agency zoomed from dangerously underreacting prior to 9/11 to dangerously overreacting afterward.

For nearly thirty years, the NSA's massive ear had been locked in place pointing outward. Now Hayden broke the lock and once again turned it inward, eavesdropping on Americans without a warrant. Nearly rusted on its pedestal and in need of new wiring, the NSA would require a major overhaul, from the intercept stations on the front end to the powerful supercomputers in the center to the analytical teams on the back end.

Highlander

The phone next to John Berry's bed rang shortly after 6:00 a.m. It was September 11, 2001, and his girlfriend, Sharilyn Bailey, had some urgent news. "She told me to turn on the television and asked if my army reserve unit had already called," he said. "I found the remote and clicked on the set." Berry was a thirty-seven-year-old reporter for the *Press-Enterprise,* a newspaper in the central California city of Riverside, where his beat was Moreno Valley. Once a dry cattle-ranching and citrus-farming town built around March Air Force Base, Moreno Valley by 2001 had become a sprawling, rapidly growing desert valley in the Inland Empire.

The day before, Berry had been covering the debate over whether to increase the town's landscaping fees. He never made it back to the city council meeting. "As soon as I saw it on TV, I knew that my life was about to change," he said. In addition to his work as a reporter, Berry was also a reserve army warrant officer and an NSA Arabic linguist with nearly twenty years of both active and reserve duty. "I knew the army would be calling soon."

In the days and weeks following the attacks of 9/11, as the agency's budget ballooned, General Hayden began an enormous building campaign. His key focus was the agency's four highly secret U.S.-based eavesdropping locations in Georgia, Texas, Colorado, and Hawaii. After the Cold War, the NSA closed down many of its listening posts around the world and replaced them with much smaller, remotely operated facilities. The intercept operators and analysts—mostly in the military—were then moved back to the U.S. and consolidated in four giant operational centers across the country, like eavesdropping factories. Three targeted separate parts of the globe while a fourth downloaded data from satellites and transmitted it to the others. To increase speed, the results would then be forwarded directly to the users—military commanders on the front lines and elsewhere around the world. A copy would also go to the NSA at Fort Meade, as would traffic too hard to break or too difficult to analyze. What Hayden needed most were Arabic linguists, and the military quickly began activating every one they could find. One of those was John Berry.

Like many NSA linguists, Berry had learned Arabic during an eighteen-month tour at the Defense Language Institute at the Presidio of Monterey in California. He was part of a small group of Arabic and Farsi (spoken in Iran) linguists assigned to the 345th Military Intelligence Battalion based in Georgia. Six times a year he would be flown there from California for weekend reserve training. He was thus little surprised when on September 28 he picked up his phone at work and heard the smoke-laden voice of the training sergeant. "Mr. Berry," he said. "You've been tapped." A little more than a week later, Berry had filled two seventy-pound duffel bags, stored his red 1996 Saturn in Sharilyn's garage (she also agreed to take his two cats), and made arrangements for the army to hire a moving company to clear out his apartment.

Berry's next stop was Fort Bragg, North Carolina, where he would be processed into active duty. He arrived on October 9, and when he wasn't in long lines getting shots, having eye exams, or trying on gas masks, he was running around looking for a phone jack for his computer in order to check his e-mail. "They took a sliver of us—the Arabic linguists and the Farsi linguists," he said.

Elsewhere on the same base was another Arabic linguist who had been activated. As Berry was hunting for outlets, twenty-four-year-old Sergeant Adrienne J. Kinne was sitting in a steel high chair being poked with a needle. A native of Utica, New York, she had spent four years on active duty, from 1994 until 1998. Before her recall she was studying for her master's degree at Augusta State University. The previous May she had graduated from the University of Virginia. Both Berry and Kinne were among the reservists called up from the 345th Military Intelligence Battalion because of their language training in Arabic and Farsi. "There were six of us from the 345th," said Berry. "I had known her [Kinne] since 1998. I was her language officer."

Kinne described the command structure at Fort Bragg as constantly in a state of confusion. "It's like one day we're going to go off to Uzbekistan, another day it's we're going to get stationed at NSA, another day we're going to be in Virginia somewhere. And then, lo and behold, they finally got us our year-long orders and we were assigned back at Fort Gordon."

Formerly known as the Georgia Regional Security Operations Center and renamed NSA/CSS Georgia, the facility seemed ill-suited for its purpose. It consisted of five buildings, including barracks and mess hall, spread out over several miles, with the majority of operations carried out in Back Hall, located on the corner of busy Chamberlain Avenue and Twenty-fourth Street. Inside the old 90,920-square-foot classroom building, intercept operators, analysts, and their equipment were crammed into small classrooms on opposite sides of wide hallways. It is there that analysts may have monitored the communications flowing between the Yemen ops center and Khalid al-Mihdhar and Nawaf al-Hazmi in San Diego.

During her first tour at the listening post in the mid to late nineties, Kinne eavesdropped on Arabic military communications intercepted by the NSA's signals intelligence satellites. "It would be collected by satellite over there and beamed back to us," she said. "It was all digital, so you would be sitting at your computer and you would call up your receiver . . . We had pre-programmed lists where it would target certain frequencies and you could scan through that. So a lot of time you would have four receivers going, two in each ear, and I would be just scanning . . . I remember a couple of times when I was just recording three different conversations at once."

One of Kinne's principal targets was the Syrian military. "I could transcribe it live, especially Syrian military," she said. "Pretty much you would record anything that you heard because usually they would only be on if they were talking about something militaristic or something." Kinne said the targets included a broad swath of countries from North Africa to most of the Middle East, including Israel. "We did have Hebrew linguists," she said. "They had different subgroups, so one was Syria, one was Levantine area—Lebanon and Jordan. The PLO, I think, was in there. And then there was Northern Africa Section—Egypt, Sudan, Algeria . . . We worked the Levantine mission, and then another group right next to us worked the North Africa mission . . . And eventually in that same room they stood up the Iraqi mission."

At the time, in the late 1990s, the listening post had about 1,200 people assigned to it. But following the attacks on 9/11, that number quickly doubled to 2,400 people. In the scramble for linguists, calls went out to contractors such as Titan, which supplied several dozen, and ads were placed in newspapers.

As Berry and Kinne arrived at NSA Georgia in late November 2001, technicians were overflowing into the hallways and crammed into temporary trailers. The two were among the 350 intelligence reservists called up and assigned to the 513th Military Intelligence Brigade following the attacks. Because of their signals-intelligence and linguistic backgrounds, the two were placed in the 201st Military Intelligence Battalion, which specialized in Sigint. Berry became officer in charge of a top-secret program code-named Highlander that cavesdropped on Inmarsat satellite communications within the Middle East. Kinne worked for the program as a linguist. "We were the pioneers. We got there before the system did. And one day we saw these boxes in this room," said Berry. "We needed to get thrown into the fight as soon as possible, and we got a system with no instruction manual, and so we literally figured it out one keystroke at a time . . . There was no guidance."

While much of the NSA was hunting for bin Laden by targeting the newer forms of communications, such as cell phones and the Internet, Berry noted, Inmarsat satellite phones still provided a wealth of intelligence. "Just because bin Laden drops that system, it doesn't mean other people will," he said. "Maybe if you go after his secretary, somebody who won't be using the latest technology, then it could be lucrative. It's like your boss may be having the best, most secure phone ever, but the office janitor won't be. They'll be using something you can intercept . . . Everybody goes after the golden ring, thinking, for example, bin Laden may be

on the latest, most expensive thing, and it turns out you go a few levels
below that, you find out a lot more . . . And that was absolutely amazing
what we pulled out. I look back on it and it was like, 'How did you guys
[NSA] miss this?' All along this was there."

To do this, the agency established a remote satellite interception capability at Camp Doha in Kuwait as the "front end" of the program. The
base was located within the spot beam of Inmarsat I-3 F1, launched in
1996 to cover the Middle East and Indian Ocean region, and the signals
were intercepted by a mobile antenna array known as Trojan Remote
Receiver-38 (TRR-38). The manager and her five coworkers on the site
were largely responsible for intercepting both sides of the conversations,
putting them together, and then relaying them in near real time—a few
minutes' delay—to NSA Georgia. "The two halves of the conversation
were recorded separately, but you could listen to them together," Kinne
noted. "They had one satellite phone and another satellite phone, and they
would match it up together. It's fairly close to live." According to Berry,
"It was like a big vacuum cleaner in the sky . . . We could listen to everything." Berry also said that safety was a very big advantage. "As a platoon
leader, I didn't have to worry about our guys stepping on a land mine or
getting shot. Because of technology it could all be done remotely—our
biggest concern was weak coffee and bad drivers."

The intercepted conversations, or "cuts" as they were called, were
transmitted to computers in the Highlander unit, where they would be
stored in a "queue" until Kinne and her fellow voice interceptors could
listen to them. "It would sort of collect everything from different satellites in the area and beam it back to us," she said. "All this stuff was
prerecorded. You could basically set up the front end to collect any conversation, automatically record it, and send it back. It's five minutes old.
It's very near real time. It prerecorded everything, and at first everything
was unidentified; we would just get these thousands of cuts dumped on
us and they would just come up in our queue, and it was just like searching blindly through all these cuts to see what the hell was what . . . and
we would slowly figure out some of the targets, like who went with what
phone number."

After matching up the phone numbers with the callers, the unit began
constructing a "phone book" of targets. "We got a phone number; we
had to figure out who was on that phone number and if it was worth it,"

said Berry. "So we constructed our own phone book." Even unproductive phone numbers were sometimes kept. "Six months later, Ahmed can pass it [a cell phone] on to his brother, and it goes from being benign to malicious . . . You constantly get this flow, and it came to be we were really good—we got good at separating the wheat from the chaff. We got a lot of momentum going so that by the time Iraq started we were going full steam, and I think we really contributed to the war effort."

Because the system pulled in communications from the entire Middle East, the conversations were in a wide variety of languages and dialects. "It was Iraq, Afghanistan, and a whole swath of area. We would get Tajik, Uzbek, Russian, Chinese," said Kinne. "It was just a big area—it was just like putting a vacuum in the sky and sucking it down," added Berry. "And it was up to us to figure it out as to whether it was good or not." Eliminating country codes from friendly countries, such as Kuwait, "would help a lot," said Berry, "but these were mobile—a lot of them were mobile. We don't know who it belongs to—here's a strange frequency showing up, and until you listen to it you don't know. There's these thousands of signals out there." When necessary, Berry could also call the NSA for help. "It's like, hey, I've got a cut in whatever language—can you bring somebody to come and look at it. And they would."

As Kinne would switch to a new conversation, the phone numbers of the parties as well as their names would appear on her digital screen. "In our computer system, it would have the priority, the telephone number, the target's name," she said. This may have been as a result of a secret agreement in which Inmarsat turned over to the NSA all of its subscriber information. "And you could actually triangulate the location of the phone if you wanted to. We could ask our analysts to figure out the exact location of the phone," said Kinne. Eventually, as the NSA gathered phone numbers from its warrantless eavesdropping program and from intelligence operations, those phone numbers would be sent down to NSA Georgia to be programmed into the computers. "At some point they started giving us, I don't know who, telephone numbers to program into the system to specifically collect."

But because al-Qaeda communicated far less by satellite phone after 9/11, and with little supervision of the intercept operators, much of what they eavesdropped on were communications involving journalists, nongovernmental organizations (NGOs) such as the Red Cross, and businesspeople. "There was no quality control; there were no senior linguists," said Kinne. Berry also said there was little oversight from above, but saw that as an advantage. "It was because we weren't being micromanaged is why I think we were so successful. Because we just did it on our own, we didn't have to clear it with anybody." Berry once asked a senior officer for guidance but received little more than a pat on the head. "I said, 'Is there any guidance you want us to follow?' And he said, 'Chief Berry, your bubbas are doing fine, so just keep doing what you're doing.' And I said, 'Yes sir, that's what we'll do.' "

Berry also briefed the NSA director Mike Hayden about the Highlander program in March 2003, but Hayden expressed little interest. "He said, 'Son, just tell me in five minutes.' And I had this whole presentation and I said, 'Sir, we did this, this, and this.' He shook a few hands, gave a coin to someone, and walked out the door. They said you have fifteen minutes, but then they cut it to five right when he walked in the door." The current NSA director, Lieutenant General Keith Alexander, was also briefed on Highlander by Berry when Alexander was head of army intelligence.

"As time went on we just saw the queue and it would just fill up with a lot of NGOs and humanitarian organizations and journalists," said Kinne. While the journalists and others were originally picked up at random, once in the system they then became permanent targets. "It's random at first, but once it's identified and you know who it is, the system is programmed to intercept those cuts and send it into the system at whatever priority we designated it as . . . And there was priority one through eight. Priority one was terrorists, which we rarely had anything related to that. And NGOs were priority five to seven, and journalists—all those were priority five to seven. Eight was we didn't have a linguist to translate it, and then nine was all the unidentified stuff."

Berry says his operation conscientiously avoided eavesdropping on Americans. "The thing is you can't listen to Americans, and I was very careful that we never did because, one, it's illegal. Two, I realized that we were in a kind of electronic minefield, so if I ever had a question about it then I would call the NSA's lawyers and I would describe the situation to them and they said yes, you can do this, you can't do that. They've got as many lawyers as they've got parking spaces." The problem, he said, was not knowing who was on the other end of an intercept. "You're sucking in someone you don't know who it is until you listen to it."

But Kinne said that even though the intercept operators knew they were eavesdropping on American journalists communicating with other journalists and their families in the U.S., the decision was made to continue listening to, recording, and storing the conversations. "Basically all rules were thrown out the window and they would use any excuse to justify a waiver to spy on Americans," said Kinne. "Because you could program the system to pick up specific phone numbers, you could also program the system to block phone numbers. And so we could have blocked the humanitarian aid organizations and all those other ones, but they said that we had to monitor them just in case they ever talked about—because they were eyes on the ground—just in case they ever talked about seeing weapons of mass destruction anywhere and gave a location. Or in case they ever lost their phone and some random terrorist picked it up and started using it . . . And for those two reasons, we could listen to all the NGOs, humanitarian aid organizations, and frigging journalists in the area—continue to even after they were identified and we knew who they were and that they weren't terrorists or terrorist-affiliated . . . So that was the excuse they gave."

Operation Highlander was an extraordinary and illegal expansion of the original purpose of the new program, which was to eavesdrop on Americans only when an NSA supervisor had a reasonable belief that the person on the other end was a member of al-Qaeda. "If you're talking to a member of al-Qaeda," said Bush, "we want to know why." But these people were not members of al-Qaeda, and they weren't talking to terrorists. Nevertheless, according to Kinne, the standard operating procedure was to keep recording them and not delete the numbers. "They were just hesitant to ever block phone numbers or drop them from the system," said Kinne. "There were no really clear-cut rules. They activated twenty reservists and stood up this elaborate high-tech mission and just said run with it."

Kinne had spent several years at NSA Georgia prior to the attacks on 9/11 and was shocked that they were now targeting Americans. The internal NSA regulations on handling communications involving U.S. persons were spelled out in a top-secret document known as United States Signals

Intelligence Directive 18 (USSID 18). "When I was on active duty before, we took USSID 18 incredibly seriously, and I just remember collecting a Syrian military cut once where in the report they mentioned an American diplomat who was visiting the region by name. And because they mentioned the American's name, we deleted the cut, we deleted everything. Maybe we didn't technically have to, maybe we could have just left his name out of the report, but we deleted everything, and I think that just goes to show the level to which we took USSID 18 incredibly seriously."

Worried about violating not only NSA internal regulations but federal law, Kinne says she brought her concerns to Berry. "I said we're not supposed to be listening to these people—not only are we not supposed to be listening to Americans, but there were five allied countries that we were not supposed to monitor either—the Five Eyes. But we listened to Australians, Canadians, Brits. And so it wasn't just the Americans but that whole idea that you weren't supposed to monitor those five countries either—citizens of those five countries . . . They told us that we could monitor calls from there to the States but that we could only report on the half of the conversation that took place in the Middle East. We couldn't report on the half that took place in America. And when they waived it, we could monitor these people in the Five Eyes. In reports, we just couldn't reference their citizenship country of origin. So you could report on the substance of the conversation, but not identify them as an individual."

Berry, however, again said his group never illegally eavesdropped on Americans. But when asked, "Did you ever pick up information from journalists, businesspeople, or humanitarian organizations?" he simply said the answer was classified. "I can't answer that," he said. "I can't talk about that." He added, "I made sure my soldiers did the right thing."

The idea of permanently recording incredibly personal conversations between Americans—husbands, wives, and lovers—greatly bothered Kinne, and she made a personal decision to go out of her way to erase them. "A lot of times I would just delete them," she said, "especially the halves that were taking place in America because they were picked up separately and recorded separately. I would just do that because I didn't feel comfortable leaving it in the system and I didn't . . . A lot of time you could tell they were calling their families, waking them up in the middle of the night because of the time difference. And so they would be talking all quiet and soft, and their family member is like half asleep—incredibly intimate, personal conversations—and I just can't believe they were frigging recording them, and I don't know why they would ever have to to begin with."

Another Arabic voice interceptor at NSA Georgia who became aware of the warrantless eavesdropping on Americans was David Murfee Faulk, who worked there until November 2007. Following the attacks on 9/11, Faulk, then thirty-two and a reporter at the *Pittsburgh Tribune-Review,* joined the navy to help in the fight against Osama bin Laden. With a master's degree in German from the University of Chicago, he had a knack for languages and was sent to the Defense Language Institute in Monterey, California, for sixty-three weeks of Arabic training. Upon graduation he was assigned as a cryptologic technician to NSA Georgia, where he specialized in eavesdropping on Iraqi cell phone conversations in Baghdad. Among his friends at the listening post was an air force Arabic translator working for an operation known as Cobra Focus, which provided Sigint support to U.S. ground forces in Iraq.

"One day he was ordered to transcribe every call that dropped in his queue," said Faulk. "And the calls were all in English, they were all American, and the guy goes back to his supervisor, a warrant officer, and says, 'Sir, these people are all Americans—are there any USSID 18 questions here?' He said, 'No, just transcribe them, that's an order, transcribe everything.'" According to Faulk, the calls included intimate conversations both within the Green Zone and to people back in the U.S. "There were people having affairs inside the Green Zone, talking about their meet-ups, just all kinds of stuff. And he transcribed everything word for word, and it just disappeared into the big NSA black hole. These were military, civilians, contractors. A lot of these people were having personal phone calls, calling their families back home, having all kinds of personal discussions, and everything just disappeared somewhere; someone's got it."

Faulk's friend eventually told his warrant officer that he was troubled by the work. "After a few days he said he didn't want to do it anymore, didn't think it was right," said Faulk. "So they got somebody else to do it. There is always somebody else who will do something like that. The whole agency down here, at least the way it operates in Georgia, there's a lot of intimidation, everybody's afraid of getting in trouble, and people just follow orders. They're told, 'Yeah, we already ran this by the legal department up at Meade and it's kosher,' and it may or may not be true . . . They generally aren't told the reason for the order—they just say we've cleared this, it's legal, so listen to it. I know about three cases where that was done . . . But people generally do what they're told. That's what really disturbed me down here with the whole discussion of warrantless wiretapping—if we wanted to just start tapping random Americans' phones, I think we'd have enough workers willing to do that. I think it's frightening. I think it's very frightening."

In 2002, one of the Inmarsat phone calls picked up by the NSA came from a group of suspected terrorists crossing a vast expanse of desert in a remote part of Yemen.

Assassination

For years, one of the people near the top of the NSA's target list was Qaed Salim Sinan al-Harethi, a native Yemeni suspected of belonging to al-Qaeda and of being one of the masterminds behind the attack on the USS *Cole* two years before. After listening to hours of tape recordings of his conversations, the small team assigned to locate al-Harethi was very familiar with the sound of his voice. But like most of the NSA's targets, al-Harethi knew that the United States was searching for him with an electronic dragnet, hoping to snag a brief satellite phone call and pinpoint his location. As a result he always carried with him up to half a dozen phones, each with multiple cards that could change the number. The NSA had a list of at least some of the numbers, and because he was a high-priority target, an alarm would go off if one of them was used.

On the afternoon of November 3, 2002, the alarm sounded, surprising one of the analysts on the team. "He knew this guy's phone number and he [al-Harethi] hadn't used it for a period of time—it was a satellite phone," said one knowledgeable source. "Then it came up." Using global positioning satellites, he was able to pinpoint al-Harethi in the Yemeni province of Mar'ib, a remote, sand-swept landscape controlled by well-armed tribal chiefs and largely off-limits to Yemeni police. The analyst quickly contacted a CIA team based across the Red Sea in Djibouti. From the small country on the Horn of Africa, the CIA operated a battery of unmanned Predator drones, each armed with deadly Hellfire missiles. From there, the drones could easily reach anywhere in Yemen, where at least one was already on patrol. Thus, almost immediately the CIA in Djibouti began directing the Predator toward the target.

But the NSA analyst, eavesdropping on the satellite call in near real time, was disappointed. Having listened to tapes of al-Harethi's voice many times over the years, he was convinced the person on the other end of the phone was not him. "This guy is listening and he realizes it's not the guy," said the source. "And all of a sudden he hears like a six-second conversation and it's the guy, he's in the backseat and he's giving the driver directions and it was picked up over the phone, and the analyst was that good that he heard over all the other stuff. He said, 'That's him.' But because they have to have a dual recognition, he called in the second guy, they played the tape, and they said, 'It's him.' Forty minutes later a Hellfire missile hit that car. The Predator was already up doing surveillance. The CIA said to the Predator team, 'Here's the general location—from NSA—that we have the satellite phone, go find the damn car and get the guy.' Those analysts get that good, they can recognize the voice. The CIA took credit for that because it was a CIA Predator that fired the shot that killed the guy. But the way they killed him was an NSA analyst listening."

The black all-terrain vehicle instantly burst into a ball of flames, killing all five of the occupants and leaving little more than charred metal and a sprawling oil stain on the desert sand. Also in the car was Kamel Derwish, an American citizen who had grown up in the Buffalo suburb of Lackawanna, New York, emigrated with his family to Saudi Arabia, and returned to Lackawanna in the late 1990s. He later recruited half a dozen other American Muslims to travel to Afghanistan, where they took part in an al-Qaeda training camp in 2001, months before the attack on 9/11.

It would be a milestone of sorts for the NSA—its first assassination. But it would not be the last. The agency created to passively eavesdrop on targets was now, with the CIA, actively assassinating targets. On January 13, 2006, for example, the NSA likely assisted the CIA in attempting to assassinate Ayman al-Zawahiri, bin Laden's deputy. Unfortunately, the missiles missed Zawahiri and instead killed as many as eighteen civilians, many of them women and children, triggering protests throughout Pakistan.

Assassinations carried out by intelligence employees had long been outlawed—by Presidents Ford, in 1976, and Reagan, in 1981. Also, a UN report concerning the 2002 Yemen killing called the strike "an alarming precedent [and] a clear case of extrajudicial killing" in violation of international laws and treaties. But as he did with the warrantless eavesdropping program, Bush brushed aside the law and instead claimed that the authorization to kill suspected terrorists was vested in him under congressional war powers following the 9/11 attacks.

By the time of the assassination, Hayden was well aware that war with Iraq was only months away, and he put his agency's workforce on notice that they should be planning accordingly and not waiting for the bombs to start falling. Speaking on the NSA's Top Secret/Codeword internal television show, *Talk NSA*, he said, "A Sigint agency can't wait for the political decision." He later told several subordinates, "It is my judgment in doing this for [more than] thirty years, I have never seen a condition like this when it didn't end in war. We're going to war."

In preparation, Hayden had the agency conduct what he called a "Rock Drill," a term taken from old army exercises where rocks—signifying fortifications—were moved around on a map. In an agency more familiar with routers than rocks, the exercise focused mostly on "hearability"—where best to place remote sensors to pick up communications. At another point, Hayden had his graphics department produce a stoplight chart indicating the agency's capabilities against various Iraqi targets. While much of northern and southern Iraq, where the U.S. had long been patrolling no-fly zones, was colored green, the Republican Guard was yellow—barely—and Saddam Hussein and his senior political and military leaders glowed bright red.

But a key problem for the NSA in launching a war against Iraq, according to the former NSA director William O. Studeman, a navy vice admiral, was that the U.S. had already let Saddam Hussein know many of its secrets during the Iran-Iraq war. "Having had about four years' or more worth of U.S. delivering intelligence to it with regard to Iran's conduct of the war, Iraq had a substantial knowledge and sensitivity of our capabilities in the area of imaging and other intelligence collection methods such as signals intelligence. If you go back to the fundamental principles of intelligence, we had already failed on the first count. That is, our security had been penetrated because we were dealing with this target to whom we had spent so many years displaying what our intelligence capabilities were. Add the fact that Iraq is a very secretive country itself and places a great premium on security, and you then have a target that is probably the most denial-and-deception-oriented target that the U.S. has ever faced. It is a country that goes out of its way to create a large number of barriers to allowing any Western penetration of its capabilities and intentions."

With the war in Iraq approaching, the tension and stress levels at the Middle East listening post mounted. Kinne had been opposed to the war from the beginning, but Berry was gung ho in favor of it and volunteered for a second year at NSA Georgia. "I agreed to stay army because I'm as angry as any affected New Yorker about the murder of about 3,000 innocents on September 11, 2001," he said. "Plus, because I'm an intelligence officer, I'm in a great position to avenge the holocaust I saw on TV that day." "He bought everything," said Kinne. "He thought Iraq was connected to 9/11."

As Kinne eavesdropped on Inmarsat communications, another group focused on a new competitor, an Arab communications satellite called Thuraya. Built by Boeing Satellite Systems and launched into orbit in October 2000, the satellite featured the world's most powerful satellite digital communications processor. The heart and brain of the spacecraft, the processor was a product of both Boeing and IBM technology and enabled the spacecraft to handle up to tens of thousands of wireless phone calls simultaneously throughout the Middle East. Owned by Thuraya Satellite Telecommunications Co. Ltd., based in the United Arab Emirates, the satellite system was marketed aggressively in an attempt to both draw customers away from Inmarsat and create a regional demand for their small, blue handheld phones. The campaign worked well and within a few years there were more than 65,000 of the company's phones in use and the minutes used per day were double the company's expectations.

Thuraya's satellite quickly became a key target of the NSA. Soon after the September 11 attacks, in a major change, Hayden ordered that determining the location of callers and receivers suspected of involvement in terrorism be placed on a higher priority status than deciphering and translating the actual conversations. This was a result of the continuing difficulty in acquiring adequate numbers of competent translators, an inability to decipher many of their targets' homemade verbal codes, and the need to quickly capture—or kill—suspected terrorists. Another factor was the growing use of encryption and the NSA's inability, without spending excessive amounts of computer time and human energy, to solve commercial systems more complex than 256 bits.

Fortunately for the NSA, among the people who communicated with the small blue phones, which could also be used for terrestrial mobile calls, were senior Iraqi officials. A key advantage for the spy agency was the fact that the phones contained Global Positioning System (GPS) chips that revealed their coordinates to the NSA. At Fort Meade, as the Bush administration began moving closer to its invasion of Baghdad, analysts studying intercepted Iraqi conversations were making progress. They successfully matched some of the phones to a number of senior officials and, at various times, were able to determine their locations within a broad geographic area. It was part of a plan to decapitate the Iraqi leadership at the start of the war.

But despite the NSA's enormous capabilities, as the rush to war began gathering steam, most of the intelligence that the NSA was able to pick up was ambiguous and far from solid with regard to weapons of mass destruction. "When I asked our best analysts to characterize our Sigint now, in comparison to the Humint [human intelligence], as an overall assessment, they characterized the Sigint as either ambiguous or confirmatory of the Humint," said Hayden. At the time, however, there was very little Humint. Adding to the ambiguity problem was the fact that much of the equipment that Hussein was receiving and the U.S. was monitoring was dual-use—items that could be used for either innocent or nefarious purposes. Hayden's Sigint analysts, he said, "brought up an additional fact that made this hard. Saddam was living under a sanction regime. Most commercial transactions which in other parts of the world would have been legitimate transactions were in many cases in Iraq violations of the sanctions. So an awful lot of commercial transactions were of an ambiguous nature that involved dual-use materials or dual-use equipment."

These transactions, said Hayden, "were conducted in an almost clandestine sort of way. Now, how do you distinguish that clandestinity as evidence of pursuing WMD, as opposed to simply a reflection of living under a regime in which commercial transactions that otherwise would be viewed as normal here have to be conducted in a secretive sort of way? . . . When you're looking at the evidence here, say you're a Siginter [a signals intelligence analyst] and you're looking at an intercept. It's admittedly ambiguous—you may give country X the benefit of the doubt, but if country X is Iraq, this is a guy who you know has lied about his weapons of mass destruction program, so there's a tendency here to be suspicious about even ambiguous activity."

Despite the doubts, Hayden raised no objections to the preparations for war and on January 13, he brought several hundred of the agency's senior managers together in the Friedman Auditorium for a highly secret "town meeting." Concerned about the criticism the agency received during the first Gulf War that valuable Sigint was never distributed beyond Washington, Hayden said this time that wouldn't happen. This time, he said, there needed to be a much greater effort to get key intelligence immediately to the soldiers on the front line, where it could then be acted upon immediately.

Then Hayden issued a formal "Statement of Director's Intent" for the war. "If directed," it said in part, "I intend to conduct a Sigint . . . operation that will meet the combatant commanders' objective of shock, speed, and awe while also providing policy makers information that is actionable and timely . . . We will push intelligence to those places it needs to be. I expect leaders at every level to actively remove obstacles to dissemination." One method of moving the Sigint immediately to the battlefield was through a new instant messaging system code-named Zircon.

Next Hayden turned his attention, and his agency's giant ears, toward the United Nations. Three months earlier, the Bush administration won support for its war from both houses of Congress. With the country largely convinced, Bush reluctantly went along with Secretary of State Colin Powell's recommendation to convince the rest of the world through a United Nations resolution authorizing the use of force against Iraq. As the vote on the resolution approached, Hayden intensified his eavesdropping on the UN, and especially Secretary-General Kofi Annan and the Security Council.

According to Annan's predecessor, Boutros Boutros-Ghali, "From the first day I entered my office they said, 'Beware, your office is bugged, your residence is bugged, and it is a tradition that the member states who have the technical capacity to bug will do it without any hesitation.' That would involve members of the Security Council. The perception is that you must know in advance that your office, your residence, your car, your phone is bugged."

In England, Member of Parliament Claire Short, a former member of Prime Minister Tony Blair's cabinet, set off a storm when she admitted that in the weeks prior to the launch of the Iraq war she had read secret transcripts of UN Secretary-General Kofi Annan's confidential conversations. The transcripts were likely made by the NSA and shared with its sister British eavesdropping agency, GCHQ, which passed them on to the prime minister's office.

"The UK in this time was also spying on Kofi Annan's office and getting reports from him about what was going on," said Short. She added, "These things are done. And in the case of Kofi's office, it's been done for some time . . . I have seen transcripts of Kofi Annan's conversations. In fact, I have had conversations with Kofi in the run-up to war, thinking, 'Oh dear, there will be a transcript of this and people will see what he and I are saying.' "

NSA was also eavesdropping intensely on the undecided members of the UN Security Council. On November 8, 2002, the members passed Resolution 1441, warning of "serious consequences" if Iraq did not take a "final opportunity to comply with its disarmament obligations." To Washington, that translated into an authorization to launch its war against Iraq if they failed to comply fully, but London disagreed. With a population far less supportive of military action against Iraq, Prime Minister Tony Blair's government suggested that a second resolution, specifically authorizing war, would be required before the launch of an all-out UN-backed invasion. Reluctantly, primarily as a favor to his friend Blair, Bush agreed to the recommendation.

By late January the Bush and Blair administrations had determined that Iraq had failed to fully disarm and as a result they were putting tremendous pressure on the uncommitted members of the Security Council to vote in favor of its tough go-to-war resolution. On the other side, arguing against the war, were France, Germany, and Russia. Thus the "Middle Six" on the Council, as they became known—Angola, Cameroon, Chile, Mexico, Guinea, and Pakistan—suddenly became top candidates for America's friendship, and key targets for the NSA's eavesdropping.

The NSA was like a cheat at a poker game; knowing what cards were in other players' hands would give the United States a critical advantage. By listening in as the delegates communicated back to their home countries, the NSA would be able to discover which way they might vote, which positions they favored or opposed, and what their negotiating positions would be. The agency also could pick up indications of what they needed, such as a highway, a dam, or a favorable trade deal, and, in a subtle form of bribery, the U.S. could provide the country with a generous "aid package" to help pay for the construction.

Among the things that the NSA tapped into was a secret meeting of the Middle Six, who were seeking, in a last-ditch effort, to come up with a compromise resolution to avert the war in Iraq by giving the weapons inspectors more time to finish their work. According to former Mexican ambassador to the UN Adolfo Aguilar Zinser, the Americans somehow learned of the meeting and intervened. They could only have learned of the plan, said Zinser, as a result of electronic surveillance. As soon as the Americans found out about the meeting, Zinser claimed, "they said, 'You should know that we don't like the idea and we don't like you to promote it.' "

Having already won over the U.S. Congress and the American public, the Bush administration was not about to let a half dozen Third World countries get between them and their war. Thus, on January 31, the NSA ratcheted up its targeting of the Middle Six. Frank Koza, the Sigint department's deputy chief of staff for Regional Targets, sent a Top Secret/Codeword memo to the NSA's Five Eyes partners in Britain, Canada, Australia, and New Zealand asking for help:

As you've likely heard by now, the Agency is mounting a surge particularly directed at the UN Security Council (UNSC) members (minus US and GBR [Great Britain] of course) for insights as to how membership is reacting to the on-going debate RE: Iraq, plans to vote on any related resolutions, what related policies/negotiating positions they may be considering, alliances/dependencies, etc.— the whole gamut of information that could give US policymakers an edge in obtaining results favorable to US goals or to head off surprises.

Koza added, "I suspect that you'll be hearing more along these lines in formal channels—especially as this effort will probably peak (at least for this specific focus) in the middle of next week, following the SecState's [Secretary of State Colin Powell's] presentation to the UNSC." It was during that address by Powell that the Bush administration would make its last major argument before launching the war—and the NSA was to play a leading role in the presentation.

War

Like Hollywood producers, the White House Iraq Group (WHIG) was looking for a media spectacular to sell not just the American public but the rest of the skeptical world on the need to go to war with Iraq. The answer was to replay the scene from the 1962 Cuban missile crisis when Kennedy administration UN ambassador Adlai Stevenson went on television to confront his Soviet counterpart in the Security Council over ballistic missiles in Cuba. While the whole world watched, Stevenson proved the Russians were hiding weapons of mass destruction on Castro's island. Four decades later, the role of Stevenson would be played by Secretary of State Colin Powell, backed up by a twenty-first-century sound and light show. As probably the most widely trusted member of the Bush administration, Powell would be the perfect choice and the Security Council the ideal venue to sell the WHIG's spurious claims against Iraq.

On February 5, 2003, Powell took his seat at the round Security Council table and made his case to the world. It was a powerful and convincing performance, particularly because of his assertive language and lack of qualifiers. "My colleagues," he said, "every statement I make today is backed up by sources, solid sources. These are not assertions. What we're giving you are facts and conclusions based on solid intelligence." He began with what he likely thought would be the most dramatic and convincing evidence—by playing actual NSA intercepts of Iraq military personnel.

"What you're about to hear is a conversation that my government monitored. It takes place on November 26 of last year, on the day before United Nations teams resumed inspections in Iraq. The conversation involves two senior officers, a colonel and a brigadier general, from Iraq's elite military unit, the Republican Guard." On the first intercept, the colonel says, "We have this modified vehicle . . . What do we say if one of them sees it?" He notes that it is from the al-Kindi company. "Yeah, yeah. I'll come to you in the morning. I have some comments. I'm worried you all have something left."

A second intercept, recorded on January 30, 2003, involves a conversation between Republican Guard headquarters and an officer in the field. "There is a directive of the [Republican] Guard chief of staff at the conference today," says headquarters. "They are inspecting the ammunition you have . . . for the possibility there are forbidden ammo . . . We sent you a message yesterday to clean out all of the areas, the scrap areas, the abandoned areas. Make sure there is nothing there . . . After you have carried out what is contained in the message, destroy the message." The officer agrees.

And a third intercept, said Powell, "shows a captain in the Second Corps of the Republican Guard being ordered by a colonel to 'remove the expression "nerve agents" from wireless instructions.' "

In years of monitoring Iraqi communications, that was the best the NSA had—comments about a "modified vehicle," an order to get rid of some "forbidden ammo," and an order to "remove the expression 'nerve agents' from wireless instructions." Even NSA director Hayden agreed that they were little more than ambiguous. "We were asked, what do you have," said Hayden in an interview. "And we surfaced several, including these three . . . If you take a textual analysis of that, they are ambiguous. That said, you don't have to be a dishonest or intellectually handicapped person to be very suspicious about when the guy's saying remove all references to this from your codebooks, or the other guy saying 'I've got one of the modified vehicles here.' "

Asked "Modified in what way?" Hayden said, "Well, we don't know. That's the ambiguity. So we went ahead and played them . . . In my heart, each one of them individually could be explained away as this, that, or the other. Collectively they made a reasonably good package . . . Now you say they're ambiguous. And I admit that, yeah, I can intellectualize and you can explain away some of these things . . . For example, let's just take the one about removing all references to 'nerve agents' in your codebooks. If I'm innocent and I'm on the other side of the fence [I might say,] 'Oh, give me a break, for God's sake, we all have codebooks, we all need references in it; you tell me you don't have codewords for nerve agents on the battlefield. All modern armies have those codewords, you idiots.' "

In fact, given the obvious ambiguity of the intercepts, Hayden was surprised that the Iraqis did not argue that case more strongly. "They didn't do that. What they said was, these are third-class forgeries that any high school student can fabricate. That was very interesting to me, because rather than taking the textual criticism and attacking [the intercepts] on their merits, or lack of merit, they dismissed them as forgeries. I just looked at it and said, 'Well, why are you going down that track?' It lessened the sense of ambiguity. Whatever lingering sense of ambiguity about these intercepts was in my mind got lessened by the Iraqi government's response to it."

Even within Powell's small task force, the NSA intercepts—the most dramatic evidence they had—was looked upon as ambiguous. "If Captain Hindi with a Republican Guard unit was saying, 'Take nerve agents out of his CEOI—out of his communicating instructions,' " said a senior official, "that could have a double meaning. I mean, we took it as having a meaning that they didn't want the inspectors to know they had nerve agents. But it could be the other side of the coin, too—they got rid of them, so they're taking it out of the CEOI because they don't need it anymore."

But the public was never told how weak and ambiguous the best evidence was. They would be told the opposite. In addition to hearing the intercepts, Powell brought up the frightening topic of biological weapons. "Saddam Hussein has investigated dozens of biological agents, causing diseases such as gas gangrene, plague, typhus, tetanus, cholera, camel pox, and hemorrhagic fever. And he also has the wherewithal to develop smallpox." Then he warned, "One of the most worrisome things that emerges from the thick intelligence file we have on Iraq's biological weapons is the existence of mobile production facilities used to make biological agents."

Finally, at 3:15 a.m. on March 20, 2003, an iron rain began to fall over Baghdad and the first of 29,199 bombs plunged toward earth. The Bush administration would call it "shock and awe." Six thousand miles away, the friction between Kinne and Berry continued as they listened to the bombs explode. "During shock and awe he [Berry] said, 'We're going to bomb those barbarians back to kingdom come,' " said Kinne. Berry then sent an e-mail to everyone in the Highlander unit in which he meant to write, "We're going to hit them with a fury of bombs during shock and awe." But he ended up saying "furry" instead of "fury." "It was hilarious," said Kinne.

Sitting at her station, Kinne was listening to several American NGO aid workers trying to get to safety and giving their position every few minutes to their headquarters. "That night, around the time of the initial invasion, I heard two Americans traveling somewhere in the region and they kept calling their main office because they were checking in and so they kept giving them updates on their location because they were kind of afraid. So I was monitoring them because I . . . would send out KL [high priority "Klieg Light"] reports updating their location—to whoever our consumers were." Kinne hoped the reports might warn of an attack in their area.

About the same time, an intercepted fax came in from the Iraqi National Congress, a group led by the Iraqi dissident Ahmed Chalabi. Close to the neoconservatives in the Bush administration, he had been pressing the U.S. government for years to launch a war against Iraq so he could replace Saddam Hussein as the country's leader. It was later discovered that much of his "evidence" that Hussein had weapons of mass destruction was fraudulent. "The fax came in, the analyst printed it off, gave it to me, I looked at it, and I could see that it said something about missiles," Kinne said.

Focusing on the two lost Americans, Kinne ignored the fax. "Part of me said that if we were going to be monitoring Americans, then if they need help that I was going to make sure I did whatever I could to see to that. So at the end of shift I told the people who were coming on mids [midnight shift]—that was around eleven o'clock at night—that these people were calling in, they were calling in every fifteen, twenty minutes for a while. And I also told them there was this fax. Well, they didn't get to the fax, and it wasn't till the next day on the day shift that somebody started translating the fax."

It turned out that the fax contained more allegations by Chalabi about supposed locations for weapons of mass destruction—information that should have been sent out immediately as a CRITIC, the NSA's highest-priority message, designed to reach the president's desk within five minutes. "So we all get called in because they realize the nature of what the fax was," said Kinne, "where all the weapons of mass destruction in Iraq were. This . . . got sent via CRITIC to the White House." In her defense, Kinne pointed out Chalabi's lack of credibility. "I made a point of saying to Mr. Berry, 'Just because this is all written down in a fax does not mean it's true. Why are we acting as if it's black and white and this is actually reflective of reality?' And that's when he said, 'You're not an analyst, you're an interceptor, and it's not your job to decide whether or not the intelligence is accurate, it's your job to collect.' "

Kinne later thought the entire incident was very suspicious. "It's really weird," she said, "because the fax—we had a lot of faxes that came in and we only had so many linguists so we didn't always get to faxes and a lot of times they would come and go and nobody ever said anything." The Chalabi message, she said, was the first time "where somebody called them and asked them what was going on with the fax . . . It was somehow called to the attention of people and [they were] asked where's this fax? Now I almost wonder if our government was telling the INC how to frigging pass information so we could intercept it . . . I just don't doubt that they could have done it intentionally just to get propaganda in the military . . . So when I got out of the military, and sometime in the beginning of 2004, I think I was at the gym and I was reading a *Newsweek* or *U.S. News and World Report* or something and there was a little blurb in there that said that we had determined that the INC had been feeding us misinformation about Iraq, and I just immediately thought about the CRITIC, and immediately your blood goes cold and you realize that it was all a bunch of bullshit."

That same night, Kinne discovered that among the locations on the military's target list during shock and awe was the Palestine Hotel in Baghdad, the main residence for journalists covering the war. As she eavesdropped, she could hear the frightened journalists calling home or calling in stories to their editors back in the States and thought someone should tell the military to avoid bombing the location. "During shock and awe," said Kinne, the journalists in the hotel were "calling family members in the States or even their employers or coworkers and talking about, just the fact that they were really concerned for their safety. And I don't even remember why we would have been given a potential target list but I just remember seeing the Palestine Hotel listed, and I knew there were journalists staying at the Palestine Hotel that thought they were safe. I went to Mr. Berry and said there are journalists staying there, they think they're safe, but it's a potential target, shouldn't somebody do something or say something? And he just kind of blew me off. He said somebody else, further up the chain, knows what they're doing."

At another point, Kinne was eavesdropping on a conversation between American and British aid workers. "The Brit, clear as day, said, 'Be careful because the Americans are listening.' And the American said, 'No, they're not; I'm protected by USSID 18; they can't spy on me; I'm an American.' That set off all the red alarms and people just went ape," calling it a major breach of security because uncleared civilians were not supposed to know about the NSA document.

Without any intelligence agents on the ground at the start of the conflict, the military was forced to rely on the NSA to locate members of Saddam Hussein's regime. But the agency had already found that Thuraya's GPS system was only accurate within a one-hundred-meter radius—more than three football fields. Thus the geo-location of the caller could be anywhere within a vast 31,400-square-meter area, much of it densely packed urban neighborhoods. This meant that killing Iraqi officials with Tomahawk cruise missiles and two-thousand-pound penetrator bombs was less a matter of precision targeting and more like firing blindly into very large crowds. While the weapons landed exactly where they were supposed to, not a single senior Iraqi official was hit—a 100 percent failure rate. Instead, large numbers of Iraqi civilians were killed.

While almost everything Operation Highlander received was unencrypted, Kinne did occasionally intercept a voice message that was simply a person reading a long series of coded letters and numbers. "At some point we started getting code, picking up conversations that were just code," she said. Those messages had to be sent to NSA headquarters for deciphering. "They wouldn't send us the key, so we weren't allowed to translate them ourselves or break the code. The mission before, in '96, they gave our analysts the key so they could break it themselves." One of those alphanumeric messages sent to the NSA was eventually returned, and Kinne was surprised by what it revealed. "One of the codes was Saddam Hussein's location. We collected it before he was captured, but they didn't tell us what the code broke out to until after he was captured. So I have no idea if that location was at all instrumental in his actual capture."

After Kinne intercepted calls, another group nearby used the phone numbers to create large charts in an attempt to find hidden links between them, a technique known as "call chaining analysis." "They would go through and they would do telephone diagrams of who was calling which numbers and kind of do these huge elaborate Inmarsat telephone diagrams," said Kinne. To do the call chaining, the analysts use a program known as PatternTracer, made by i2 Inc., a company in McLean, Virginia. "When suspected terrorists go to great lengths to disguise their call activity, PatternTracer can be used to find hidden connections in volumes of call record data," says the company.

In addition to PatternTracer, the analysts at NSA Georgia have an alphabet soup of data mining, traffic analysis, and social network analysis tools—secret and unclassified—within their computers. They include Agility, AMHS, Anchory, ArcView, Fastscope, Hightide, Hombase, Intelink, Octave, Document Management Center, Dishfire, CREST, Pinwale, COASTLINE, SNACKS, Cadence, Gamut, Mainway, Marina, Osis, Puzzlecube, Surrey, Tuningfork, Xkeyscore, and Unified Tasking Tool. The NSA also maintains large databases containing the address information, known as externals, on millions of intercepted messages, such as the Externals Data Global Exploitation (EDGE) database, the Communication External Notation list, and the Communications Externals Data Repository and Integration Center.

Kinne saw little in the way of major accomplishments by the Highlander operation. "I think I have some sense that we did get one al-Qaeda network over the course of the time, but I don't, I'm not really as familiar with that," she said. In her entire time there, the only CRITIC message sent out was the one from Chalabi; none were issued concerning terrorism or al-Qaeda.

"I am greatly fearful of what has been happening with our country, and our Constitution," concluded Kinne. "And I just kind of saw in those two years of service how things drastically and dramatically changed for the worse. Part of me will always regret not having upheld my oath of military service to the fullest extent that I should have. You know as a soldier we take an oath to defend the Constitution against all enemies foreign and domestic."

In Iraq, following the collapse of the government and the start of the American occupation, the NSA set up a large antenna farm within the Green Zone. Although there is no name on the compound, its nickname is Camp Alec, apparently derived from the CIA's bin Laden unit. About one hundred yards long and fifty yards wide, the facility consisted of four single-story buildings with double, bomb-proof roofs and a high tower containing a number of microwave horns and high-frequency antennas. Also within the compound, which was surrounded by two high steel fences, were a pair of medium-sized satellite dishes. The entire compound was part of an overall NSA security program code-named Viper.

The key targets were the thousands of cell phones within Baghdad and the surrounding areas, many of which were used by the growing numbers of insurgents as they planted roadside bombs. Once the intercepts were captured by the antennas, they were zapped into one of the four windowless buildings. "Where the information goes is a bank of computers," said one person who worked at the site. "We were under mortar attack there quite a bit." The data would then be transmitted both to the NSA's headquarters within the Green Zone, co-located with the CIA's offices, and also to NSA Georgia, where most of the analysis would take place. According to the source, "The data collected provides the Joint Special Operations Command with about 75 percent of the actionable intelligence that they're using to hit sites in Iraq."

"You would transcribe it word for word and then after the word *melon* you put a little 'op comment' in, to the effect that 'in terms of voice inflection it does not seem this guy is truly talking about melons.' It comes down to inflection, a lot of gut reaction to things," said Faulk. "The problem is, we never really got good feedback, post-mission feedback, about whether the targeted people were actually truly guilty of terrorist acts. After the house was blown up, did you indeed find weapons and bombs in it? You get these guys calling between one another using cover terms and speaking around issues. So you always run the risk that you'll kill some innocent people who really are selling melons and not IEDs. There's a guy going with a truck of melons somewhere and someone has to make the call—this is what really is kind of heart-wrenching about the thing— somebody has to make the call whether the guy moving melons is really moving melons or not. And you get a guy eight thousand miles away in a cubicle and he's supposed to know these things. It left me thinking we killed a lot of innocent people, but I have no real way of knowing . . . A lot of people don't really care about that . . . And that was one of the reasons I got out—to actually have to do that and know that people are going to live or die based on that is something I just can't live with. It's not the kind of mistake I want to make."

Despite the importance of Iraq to the Bush administration, few senior NSA officials ever left the comfort of their eighth-floor suite of offices and visited the war zone. One exception was Eric Haseltine, the iconoclastic former Disney imagineer who was brought aboard as assistant director for research to shake up the agency's institutional thinking. "Hayden wanted to really get an out-of-the-box person in there," said Haseltine, "so he got a headhunter to find a really out-of-the-box person, and I guess he figured he couldn't get more out-of-the-box than Disney."

It was an odd mix at the start, but Haseltine quickly fit it. "I was told that I was an alien," he said. "In some ways I fit in because I was a geek and it's an agency of geeks—you're either a linguist geek or a math or computer geek; and so one geek will resonate with another geek." He quickly earned his geek credentials when during a meeting he mentioned, "Cherenkov radiation is inherently vectorized so that you have an acceptance cone." According to Haseltine, "When I said vectorized Cherenkov radiation, I was a geek—I wasn't just a suit."

Haseltine found a wide gap in the cultures at the CIA and the NSA. "CIA is a very people-oriented place. It's a comfortable place to be—they have fabrics from around the world and objets d'art—it's a people-friendly place. NSA is a machine-friendly place. It's raised floors and converging lines of parallax down naked hallways forever. You tend to get a lot more extroverts at CIA who are good salesmen. At CIA you have people who are street smart, and at NSA you have people who are think smart." And because of the way technology was dominating most aspects of life today, "the future was pushing most intelligence missions toward Fort Meade."

"If you're talking about Russia, Humint is really important," said Haseltine. "If you're talking about al-Qaeda, Humint ought to be important, but Sigint turns out to be more important. If I'm a terrorist in Syria and wanted to communicate with a terrorist in Tehran and I'm using AOL or Hotmail, my conversation would go through Reston, Virginia, or Seattle. Geography is dead. We may have physical borders, but cyberspace does not recognize them." Eavesdropping, he said, is not the issue; the difficulty for the NSA is sorting through it all. "Our ability to collect stuff far outstrips our ability to understand what we collect—and that is the central problem, that is the core problem. What's probably surprising to most people—you know they think, how do we tap this cable or have a big antenna and scoop up these transmissions—that is so much not the problem."

Soon after he arrived, Haseltine was on a plane to Baghdad to view the agency from the perspective of the battlefield. "The wars we are in today are intelligence wars," he said. "And so if you believe that Sigint is number one, then the syllogism says NSA becomes the most important part of the war." He was surprised by what he found. "I spent a lot of time in Iraq. I went there three times when I was at NSA. The second time I came back from Iraq, I sat down with General Hayden and I said, 'Sir, there's good news and there's bad news. At corps [level] and above, everybody loves you. At division and below, they hate you like you wouldn't believe.' He had never heard that before from anybody. And the reason is there was no NSA presence below corps. The NSA information went down to a certain level and stopped. So the stuff that comes in at the top doesn't percolate down to the bottom."

Haseltine, who at the time was equal to a two-star general, received a shock on his first trip to the war zone. "I sat down in a lieutenant colonel's office in Baghdad who was in charge of intelligence for that division," he recalled. "And I said, 'Colonel, I'm here to help you help me help you.' And he said, 'Get the fuck out of my office.' I said I'll get out, but first tell me why. He said you're a mucky muck at NSA; you guys are such assholes. He knows I'm the associate director of the agency—he didn't care. He said, 'You guys are the huge rusty gear, and we're the fast gear—and there's no way your gears are going to engage in our gears and help us.' He says get out of here. You're just big and slow and bureaucratic. NSA had a very bad reputation below the senior levels because they never saw value from it. And it wasn't necessarily NSA's fault. That's the interesting thing. Was it the NSA's fault that the army chose not to share information down below the top echelon? But NSA got blamed for it." They didn't hate Hayden; they hated the NSA.

One of the colonel's major complaints was that he wanted the NSA to send him copies of the raw, untranslated, and unanalyzed intercepts, something the agency very rarely does. "They wanted the raw data," said Haseltine. "They said, 'Hey, you've collected some, you give it to us, we'll do the analysis.' Here's a couple of things he didn't understand. What if we gave you the raw transcripts in some dialect of Arabic? How many Arabic linguists do you have? Your worst nightmare would be if we gave you our whole collection. They didn't understand at least two things. One is that there is just unbelievable amounts of information— they would never have a prayer of finding their way through it. Number two, do they have the analysts to chomp on it? No way. Number three, there are legitimate legal issues involved."

Rather than give them the data, Hayden decided to assign an agency analyst to the division—it was a procedure the agency began repeating throughout government. "The bottom line is if you wanted to help somebody, you couldn't give them data, you had to give them a person, you had to give them a human body, because that person knew how to cope with information, and that person had the authority to give the information. So in my mind, NSA was transforming more from a product business to a service business. That was a paradigm shift that was going on, and I think I did help accelerate that with my conversations with General Hayden."

Despite his progress in integrating the NSA into the front lines, Haseltine made few friends and many enemies with this unorthodox approach. At a very senior meeting, the deputy director of a large intelligence agency—he wouldn't say whether it was the NSA or not— told him: "You know, Haseltine, you've got a bad reputation," he said. "You're a subcabinet-level official and you go out talking to sergeants in Iraq. You short-circuit way too many chains of command to ever get our cooperation."

With the U.S. in charge of rewiring Iraq's entire communications infrastructure, the NSA had a unique opportunity to turn the entire country into one giant acoustic bug. By 2008, over $1 billion in U.S. and Iraqi reconstruction funds and approximately $6 billion in private-sector investment had been spent on developing the national telecom architecture. This included six buried fiber-optic loops and a microwave network running north to south from Dohuk to Basra and west to east from the Jordanian border through Baghdad to Diyala Province and onward to Kirkuk and Sulaimaniya. Contracts were also given to interconnect the country with both FLAG Falcon and FOG 2 undersea cable systems. "What can be more important for Iraq today than a modern communications infrastructure?" said Minister of Communications Mohammed Tawfiq Allawi. "It is the technology thread that weaves our country together."

Yet despite this opportunity, more than five years after the war began the NSA may be as deaf to the actions of the Iraqi government as when Saddam Hussein was in power. For example, when Iraqi prime minister Nuri Kamal al-Maliki launched his military attack on the radical anti-American cleric Moktada al-Sadr's forces in Basra in March 2008, the CIA, the White House, and the commanders on the ground in Iraq were all caught completely by surprise. "You didn't know it was going to happen?" asked host Tim Russert on NBC's *Meet the Press.* "No more so than Dave Petraeus or Ambassador Crocker did," said Hayden, now the director of the CIA.

Among the highest priority intelligence operations within Iraq was the effort to locate computers used by the government of Saddam Hussein, remove the hard drives, and then send the drives to the CIA and NSA for forensic examination, translation, and analysis. The hope was to find either the locations where the weapons of mass destruction were supposedly hidden or Saddam Hussein's hideout. But with few capable Arabic linguists available and an equally scarce number of highly cleared computer experts, the operation produced a great deal of chaos and confusion but very little actionable intelligence. As a result, the CIA began paying out millions of dollars to scores of private companies, both long-established giants and small start-ups. Nicknamed "beltway bandits" because many had offices around the Interstate 495 beltway circling Washington, these contractors would recruit current and former CIA and NSA employees at up to double their salaries.

Once on board, they were frequently assigned back to the same offices at CIA and NSA doing the same work, but now the taxpayers were paying them up to twice as much. Others were assigned even less sophisticated work than they were originally performing. Because of the slapdash nature of the rush to expand, the quality of intelligence produced by some of those contractors quickly became questionable. "The money is incredible—I doubled my salary to go out and come back in and continue doing what I was doing," said one former CIA official who had been assigned to the Directorate of Operations (DO), now called the National Clandestine Service. "They're all former DO officers, and basically what these companies are doing, they have this net, and all these people trickling out of the agency, they're just catching them. It's like fruit on the ground, because the agency doesn't have the people that they need to do these jobs. But the problem is these jobs are mindless—because once again there's no structure applied to the task at hand. So we're all just sitting there looking at each other, and we're making a ridiculous amount of money."

According to one senior intelligence official, "The DO's chunk of the budget inside the CIA is now bigger than the entire CIA budget was when Bush came to office. Nobody can tell you [whether] what you're getting is any good or not. They're paying so much money to third-party countries for stuff, it's incredible. I don't think anybody even knows, really, how much money we're giving Pakistan."

Because much of the data in the hard drives was in Arabic or other languages that few analysts read or spoke, often the information simply collected dust. "The first contract I was on I left, because I said this is fraud," said a CIA officer turned contractor. "There was over a million dollars sitting in that [CIA] office—just the [contractor] salary we collected, not to mention the extra money that goes to these companies. We sat there all day and same-timed each other, which is like instant messaging. We would just same-time each other all day. And after about three months of that, I went to my company and I said you need to get me off this contract or I'm going to another company or I'm leaving altogether. Basically what we were doing," he said, "is we were looking for any ops leads in these hard drives—through e-mail—things that were found residually on hard drives. Anything you do in the computer is somewhere engraved in a hard drive, and so we could look for tools to mine . . . Sometimes we got hard drives that were probably a couple of weeks old, because these are hard drives from where we went out and either rendered people or we raided places and we would just scoop up—not we, but the agents who were out there—the military would just scoop up hard drives in a big old Santa Claus bag and send them back."

The problem came when the information was not in English, which was most of the time. According to the contractor:

A lot of it was in Arabic, and none of us spoke Arabic—just a little problem. It would just sit there. But none of us really knew what we were doing, and we had management who didn't know what they were doing either. The problem is, and I just can't stress enough what the agency [CIA] does to tackle their problems—they just throw people and money at the issue. It doesn't matter what the outcome is, it doesn't matter what the product of that is. It's just comforting to them to know that in this office next to me, he's got twenty people sitting there—doesn't matter what they're doing, but we've got them sitting there and that makes me feel like I'm getting something done, you know, that we're tackling this problem.

After September 11 happened, I think working from a position of chaos is understandable, because we were all shell-shocked. Everybody was, like, sleeping at the agency; we'll read traffic, we'll put out cables—whatever you want—we'll man telephones. There was a lot of momentum for out-of-box kind of thinking and freethinking and everything else. But it was a very chaotic time, and what we were able to accomplish was probably very good given what we were working under. Two years after September 11, it's not acceptable to continue to be working from that same position of chaos, because we haven't stepped back—we let the momentum carry us along, but we fell back on the old ways of doing things, which is just shove people on the problem.

According to the former official turned contractor, the surge in staffing the agency's Counterterrorism Center (CTC) left many of the agency's area divisions around the world depleted. Because of the "need to surge hundreds and hundreds at CTC," he said, "there's nobody in these area divisions anymore, everybody's working the CT target. Africa Division is smaller now than the number of people we have in Baghdad. The entire division. And the people in Baghdad are just sitting."

Afghanistan has also proved difficult for the CIA, according to a number of current and former agency officials. One said:

We were talking to teams in the field who were in Afghanistan every night. I was working the night shift all the time, and I would talk to the guys because that's when they were awake and doing things. [They were] using a secure phone via Inmarsat, and then we have a STU [Secure Telephone Unit] on the other end—we had several teams. I would ask, "What's going on? How are you all doing?" They weren't doing anything. And they were so frustrated.

People were leaving . . . There was one team that just left, they just up and left, because they were going to be extended and they had already stayed over their stay or whatever, and they had sent messages saying we're not doing anything here, and we've got family, and we have jobs, and we hear now that you're thinking of extending us—and this was probably a day before the helicopter was supposed to come and take them away. They got on that helicopter and they left.

Their job was to collect intelligence. But this is what was happening—you'd go into this village and you'd have ten or fifteen people come up to you and go, "I know where bin Laden is." So you give them a hundred bucks and you never see them again. [The informants were also given a handheld GPS to pinpoint exact locations.] The GPS was to be taken to wherever bin Laden was, and they would write down the latitude and longitude. And so a lot of cable traffic has come and gone based on all of this information, from all of these people who come in and say they know where bin Laden is.

And of course, they don't—they want the money. Or if someone does in all good faith, they only heard it through a cousin who heard it from their cousin who heard it from a cousin who heard it from a cousin. It's so ineffective. I'm not saying that that's not the right way to go about it, but what I am saying is it's not working . . . Let's think of another way to do that. Because the war in Iraq, which the Pentagon had promised would be over quickly—followed by happy, cheering crowds—instead quickly dissolved into a quagmire, the CIA was caught short. Instead of the eighty-five Clandestine Service officers it had originally planned to send, it was forced to rush to the battlefield four times that number.

Soon more than three hundred full-time case officers were packing the Baghdad station and more than half a dozen outlying bases. Overall, CIA personnel in the country soared to more than five hundred—including contractors—eclipsing even the Saigon station at the height of the Vietnam War more than three decades earlier. Despite the surge, quantity did not translate into quality. Many of the new arrivals had little or no training in the right languages, interrogation skills, or tradecraft. Even a year into the war, the total number of CIA employees fluent in Arabic was still only eighty-three, and many of them spoke a dialect not used on the streets in Iraq.

This required the CIA to become heavily dependent on outside translators, a problematic situation in terms of both security and effectiveness. Thus, there was little improvement in penetrating Iraqi resistance forces or learning who was behind the insurgency. To make up for the green arrivals, the CIA was forced to turn to hundreds of volunteers from its reserve force of homebound retirees, many of whom have long been away from the field and are of limited usefulness. Also, because they are rotated in and out so quickly—often for just ninety days at a time—there is little time to accomplish much. The confusion has also had a detrimental effect on the agency's relationship with a number of regional Iraqi leaders who have become frustrated over their inability to establish liaison relations with CIA officers. According to one former case officer who still maintains close ties to the agency, the CIA was stretched to the limit. "With Afghanistan, the war on terrorism, with Iraq, I think they're just sucking wind," he said.

Among the other handicaps faced by the station is the endless violence that has forced the agency to require that all employees leaving secure facilities be accompanied by an armed bodyguard. Under such conditions, developing sources and conducting clandestine meetings are all but impossible. "How do you do your job that way?" asked one former CIA official who had spent time in Iraq. "They don't know what's going on out there."

In addition to fighting wars in Afghanistan and Iraq, the NSA was also doing battle on a third front: the homeland. And for that they needed the secret and illegal cooperation of the telecommunications industry.

BOOK THREE

---■---

COOPERATION

Shamrock

Since the dawn of the space age, the NSA had eavesdropped on the world by mapping the heavens, determining the orbit of each communications satellite, analyzing its transponders, calculating frequencies, azimuths, and a thousand other details and then catching the signals as they poured down like rain. But by the late 1990s, more and more communications companies began switching their networks from satellites, with their half-second time delay and occasional atmospheric interference, to buried fiber optic cables. There on the muddy seabed, inside thick black cables encased in tar-soaked nylon yarn, millions of voices chat away and terabytes of e-mail zap back and forth. With its bundles of tiny, hair-thin glass strands, fiber-optic technology offers greater volume, more security, and higher reliability.

The problem for the NSA was that as telephone calls sank from deep space to deep oceans and deep underground, Echelon began living on borrowed time. "The powers that be are trying to kill it so fast because it's a legacy [outmoded] system," one NSA official told the author a few weeks before the attacks on 9/11. "We probably won't even use it in two or three years. It's an outdated mode of Sigint. Just 1 percent of the world's communications travel by satellite now—and much of that is U.S. communications. The amount of intelligence gained from Echelon is still relatively high, because we've been so slow in going to those other modes of communications. There's talk about a 300 percent growth in fiber-optic communications, and the packet switching [Internet and e-mail] is now up through the roof." Many of the satellite companies were making up for their loss in phone calls and e-mail by catering to the enormous growth in cable television channels.

Another NSA official agreed that Echelon has become largely obsolete but says it still provides useful, but limited, intelligence. "There are still things that you can pick up," the official said. "You can get some limited cell phone stuff where you have access to people using cell phones on the ground. You can get a little bit of cell phone stuff from space, but not as good as we'd like it. It's getting better, but it's hard. The bad guys are pretty disciplined about how they use it."

By 2000, there were more than ninety million miles of fiber-optic ca-ble in the U.S., and the NSA was facing a second, far more sophisticated generation of fiber technology. Also up was voice traffic, which had been increasing in volume at 20 percent a year. This was largely as a result of new digital cellular communications that were far more difficult for the NSA to analyze than the old analog signals. Rather than consisting of voices, the digital signals were made up of data packets that might be broken up and sent a myriad of different ways.

"Today you have no idea where that information is being routed," said one intelligence official. "You may have somebody talking on a telephone over a landline and the other person talking to them on a cell phone over a satellite. You don't know how it's being routed, it's going through all kinds of switches, the information is not where you think it is, and that's what has created the complexity and that's what we have to figure out how to deal with."

Tapping into cables had always been a problem for the NSA—legally as well as technically. FISA largely gave the agency free rein to eaves-drop on satellite signals in the U.S. at listening posts such as Sugar Grove in West Virginia—only requiring a FISA warrant when an American was actually targeted. But the rules of the game were completely different for wires, such as transoceanic fiber-optic cables. With wires, the NSA needed a FISA warrant just to tap in.

It was a rule that never made much sense to the agency's top lawyer, Bob Deitz. "The need for a court order should not depend," he said, "on whether the communications meet the technical definition of 'wire com-munications' or not. These factors were never directly relevant in prin-ciple, but in the context of yesterday's telecommunications infrastructure were used as a proxy for relevant considerations. Today they are utterly irrelevant."

Now that the NSA had decided to secretly ignore FISA, the issue was moot and the time had come to reinvent Echelon from the seabed up. While the cooperative worldwide satellite-tapping program would remain in place, the agency would develop a new version, what might be dubbed Echelon II, targeting the fiber-optic cables that were encasing the world like a spider's web. It would require an enormous change in technology, but more important, the NSA and the other members of Five Eyes—Britain, Canada, Australia, and New Zealand—would have to get access to the cables either through secret agreements or covertly, or both.

For Hayden it meant going to the telecommunications industry and secretly asking for their cooperation. Despite its questionable legality, it was a practice that had begun long before Hayden—and it ended in the mid-1970s with the worst trauma in the NSA's history, which came close to landing senior officials behind bars and exposing the NSA's deepest secrets for all the world to see. Now Hayden had to decide whether to risk putting his agency through the nightmare once again, and put employees at legal risk, by secretly climbing back in bed with the telecoms.

The rocky marriage between the NSA and the telecommunications industry began in a brownstone town house on Manhattan's East Side during the days following World War I. The building, a few steps off Fifth Avenue, was the home of the NSA's earliest predecessor, a highly secret organization known as the Black Chamber.

Formed in 1919 to continue the code-breaking activities of the military during the First World War, the agency was run by Herbert O. Yardley, a poker-playing Hoosier who had been in charge of MI-8, the army's cryptanalytic organization, during the war. To hide the Chamber's existence, the town house at 3 East 38th Street masqueraded as a commercial code company. But after hiring his first novice code breakers, Yardley was faced with an immediate problem: how to get the messages to and from the foreign embassies and consulates in Washington and New York. Without messages there could be no solutions.

During the war, companies like Western Union were required under censorship laws to turn over to the military all of those communications. But when the war ended, so did censorship, and the privacy of telegraph messages was again guaranteed by the Radio Communication Act of

1912. To the Black Chamber, however, the statute represented a large obstacle that had to be overcome—illegally, if necessary.

The first steps were taken by Yardley's boss, General Marlborough Churchill, director of military intelligence, who made a very quiet call on the president of Western Union, Newcomb Carlton. After the men "had put all our cards on the table," Yardley would later write, "President Carlton seemed anxious to do everything he could for us." Under the agreed-on arrangements, a messenger called at Western Union's Washington office each morning and took the telegrams to the office of the Military Intelligence Division in Washington. They were then returned to Western Union before the close of the same day.

All American Cable Company, which handled communications between North and South America, also agreed. Company executive W. E. Roosevelt had no hesitation. "The government can have anything it wants," he declared. Eventually, the Black Chamber obtained the secret and illegal cooperation of almost the entire American cable industry.

Concerned about ending up on a criminal docket, however, all the companies later withdrew their secret cooperation. One factor that may have had some influence was the enactment of the Radio Act of 1927, which greatly broadened the Radio Communication Act enacted in 1912. Whereas the 1912 act made it a crime only for the employees of the cable and telegraph companies to divulge the contents of the messages to unauthorized persons, the 1927 act closed the loophole by also making liable to criminal penalties those who received such unauthorized communications. One exception allowed for the acquisition of messages "on demand of lawful authority," but Yardley and his ultra-secret Black Chamber could hardly avail themselves of this channel.

Unwilling to give up in spite of the law and the refusals of the company executives, Yardley eventually resorted to a different method to obtain the messages needed to keep the Black Chamber in business: bribery. After developing sources in Western Union, Postal Telegraph, All American Cable, and Mackay Radio, he secretly put them on the Black Chamber's payroll, paying them in untraceable cash.

In the end, the Black Chamber faced doom not for lack of telegrams but for lack of support by Yardley's own government. In March of 1929, with the inauguration of Herbert Clark Hoover, the conservative Henry L. Stimson became the new secretary of state. Upon discovery of the Black

Chamber he became outraged that gentlemen would eavesdrop on other gentlemen—even if they were potential foreign adversaries. Branding the Black Chamber highly illegal, he at once cut off all money for it, and at midnight on Halloween 1929, the doors to the Black Chamber officially closed as quietly as they had opened.

But following World War II, history repeated itself. As in the First World War, the end of hostilities also brought the end of censorship and thus the end of access to the millions of cables entering and leaving the country each year. This time instead of Yardley it was Brigadier General W. Preston Corderman, the chief of the Signal Security Agency, successor to the Black Chamber, who faced the same problem. Hoping like Yardley to work out a secret agreement with the telecoms, Corderman, on August 18, 1945, sent two trusted representatives to New York City for the delicate purpose of making "the necessary contacts with the heads of the commercial communications companies in New York, secure their approval of the interception of all [foreign] Government traffic entering the United States, leaving the United States, or transiting the United States, and make the necessary arrangements for this photographic intercept work."

Their first overture, to an official of ITT Communications, met with complete failure. He "very definitely and finally refused," Corderman was informed, to agree to any of the proposals. Next, they approached a vice president of Western Union, who agreed to cooperate unless the attorney general of the United States ruled that such intercepts were illegal.

Armed with this agreement, the two went back to ITT the next day and suggested to a vice president that "his company would not desire to be the only non-cooperative company on the project." The implication was that to refuse was to be less than patriotic, so the vice president went to see the company president about the matter. A short while later he returned and indicated that ITT would be willing to cooperate provided that the attorney general decided the program was not illegal. That same day the two SSA officers shuttled across town to RCA corporate headquarters. With two-thirds of America's cable industry already in their pocket, they met with RCA's president, David Sarnoff, and asked him to join in the "patriotic" effort. The executive indicated his willingness to cooperate with the agency but withheld his final approval until he, like the others, had heard from the attorney general.

But a few days later the three telecom executives met with their corporate attorneys, who uniformly advised them against participating in the intercept program. The problem, the SSA officers told Corderman, was "the fear of the illegality of the procedure according to present FCC regulations." The memo also noted, "In spite of the fact that favorable opinions have been received from the Judge Advocate General of the Army, it was feared that these opinions would not be protected." Then the officers indicated a possible solution. "If a favorable opinion is handed down by the attorney general, this fear will be completely allayed, and cooperation may be expected for the complete intercept coverage of this material."

Nevertheless, despite the lack of an authorization by the attorney general and the warnings of their legal advisors, within a matter of weeks the chiefs of all three companies began taking part in what, for security reasons, was given the code name Operation Shamrock. By September 1, 1945, even before the Articles of Surrender were signed by Japan, the first batch of cables had been secretly turned over to the agency. Within a year, however, the complex arrangement threatened to come unglued when both Western Union and RCA again expressed concern over the illegality of their participation and the lack of attorney general approval. In a somewhat feeble effort to pacify the nervous executives, General Dwight Eisenhower, the army's chief of staff, forwarded to each of them a formal letter of appreciation.

Again, throughout 1947, the fear of criminal prosecution continued to hound the executives of all three companies. They were now demanding assurances, not only from the secretary of defense and the attorney general, but also from the president himself, that their participation was in the national interest and that they would not be subject to prosecution in the federal courts. To ease their concern, Secretary of Defense James Forrestal asked them to meet with him on Tuesday, December 16, 1947. It was an extraordinary meeting, attended by Sosthenes Behn, chairman and president of ITT, and General Harry C. Ingles, president of RCA Communications. Joseph J. Egan, president of Western Union, was invited but could not attend.

At the meeting, Forrestal, telling the group that he was speaking for President Truman, commended them for their cooperation in Operation Shamrock and requested their continued assistance, "because the intelligence constituted a matter of great importance to the national security."

Forrestal then said that "so long as the present attorney general [Tom C. Clark] was in office, he could give assurances that the Department of Justice would also do all in its power to give the companies full protection." One official was still unclear as to Shamrock's level of authorization, however, and asked Forrestal if he was speaking not just for the office of the secretary of defense, but in the name of the president of the United States. Forrestal replied that he was.

With an eye to the national elections, coming up in less than a year, Forrestal made it clear that "while it was always difficult for any member of the Government to attempt to commit his successor, he could assure the gentlemen present that if the present practices continued the Government would take whatever steps were possible to see to it that the companies involved would be protected." The next month, Western Union president Joseph J. Egan and the company's operating vice president were briefed on the December meeting.

Forrestal's assurances that Shamrock had the full backing of the president as well as the attorney general appeared to satisfy the three for the time being, but there was no guarantee just how long that would last. Then, on March 28, 1949, Forrestal resigned from office and in less than a week he was admitted to Bethesda Naval Hospital suffering from severe depression, anxiety, and acute paranoia. In the early morning hours of Sunday, May 22, he walked across the hallway into a small kitchen, tied one end of his dressing gown sash to a radiator just beneath a window, and knotted the other end around his neck. Seconds later, his body plunged from the hospital's sixteenth-floor window.

Among those stunned by Forrestal's death were the company chiefs he had secretly assured fifteen months earlier. On hearing of Forrestal's resignation and hospitalization, they had sought a renewal of the assurances against prosecution from his successor, Louis Johnson. On Wednesday, May 18, 1949, only four days before Forrestal's suicide, Johnson met with these officials and stated that President Truman, Attorney General Tom Clark, and he endorsed the Forrestal statement and would provide them with a guarantee against any criminal action that might arise from their assistance.

Confirming the fact that the knowledge of Shamrock went well beyond the office of the secretary of defense were two handwritten notes penned on the memorandum of the meeting. One approval bore the initials T.C.C., those of Attorney General Tom C. Clark; the other, signed by Secretary Johnson, stated, "OK'd by the President and Tom Clark." The May 18 meeting was the last time any of the companies ever sought assurances against prosecution from the government.

In 1952, the NSA was formed and took over the program, running it largely unchanged until the early 1960s, when the paper telegrams gave way to computer discs containing all messages entering, leaving, or transiting the country. NSA employees would secretly collect the discs from the telecom companies during the midnight shift, copy them, and then send the copies to Fort Meade and take the originals back to the companies before the end of the shift. The operation was discovered during the intelligence investigations of the mid-1970s and NSA officials came close to going to jail. To prevent future NSA directors from ever again turning this agency inward on the American public, Congress passed FISA in 1978 giving the FISA court the "exclusive" authority to approve or deny any NSA request to spy on Americans. The penalty was five years in prison for every violation.

Despite the law, like Yardley and Corderman before him, Hayden decided to ignore the court and secretly begin seeking the cooperation of the country's telecoms. Testing the water even before 9/11, Hayden made an initial approach to Joseph P. Nacchio, the head of Qwest Communications and one of the leaders of the fiber-optic revolution. On February 27, 2001, Nacchio was waved through the gates and quickly disappeared into the NSA's secret city.

Qwest

small, sassy upstart based in Denver, Qwest was building a world-wide infrastructure of hyperfast fiber-optic cables to channel e-mail, data, and phone calls to the exploding Internet. Packed tightly with hair-thin strands of glass, each capable of 1.5 million calls, the fiber-optic cables were quickly making the existing copper cables seem as archaic as smoke signals. By the time Nacchio joined the company in 1997, it had a thirteen-thousand-mile network of fiber-optic cable, laid alongside rail-road tracks around the country, serving four and a half million customers. With a goal of quickly extending the fiber coast-to-coast, Nacchio claimed that when his network was completed in the summer of 1999, it would have greater capacity than those of AT&T, MCI WorldCom, and Sprint—combined. He was also pushing to expand the company's European network and branching out to Japan.

Among those impressed by the young company and its new boss were senior officials at the NSA. At the time, the agency was looking to contract with a U.S. company for a secure fiber-optic network connecting a number of the agency's key listening posts in the U.S. to its Maryland headquarters. But because it would be used to pass encrypted, ultra-secret intercepts, it was essential that the network be both very secret and very secure. That meant an "air gap"—a physical separation between the NSA's fibers and those of other networks. Based on their analysis, agency officials determined that the best system for both speed and security belonged to Qwest.

Wasting little time, an official from the "Maryland Procurement Office," the cover name for the NSA's contracting department, telephoned a cryptic request to Dean Wandry, the chief of Qwest's government business unit. A general, said the caller, would like to meet with him and Nacchio very soon. Two weeks later the mysterious three-star lieutenant general turned up with a military aide at Nacchio's corporate suite atop Denver's fifty-two-story Qwest Tower. He said he had heard of Qwest's new network and asked to meet privately with Wandry, whom the agency had already secretly vetted. As the two stepped into a separate conference room, the general told Wandry he had looked at Qwest's network and wanted his agency to become a customer. Nacchio was excited; it would be his company's first major government contract—and his entrée into the black world of the cyberspies.

Although the agency solicited bids from other companies, it was mostly pro forma because only Qwest could provide the agency with a custom "virtual private network," complete with hardware, engineering, communications services, and network management. By May 1998—lightning fast by government standards—Qwest was awarded the ten-year, $430 million contract. Nacchio, who by then had also received his NSA clearance, wanted to publicly announce the deal to boost the company's reputation, but the NSA forbade even a whisper. That same year, Qwest also built a similar secure network for the NSA linking listening posts in Europe and the Middle East to a transatlantic cable.

Realizing the potential of the company's new cloak-and-dagger role, Wandry told Nacchio: "If managed correctly," the relationship with the NSA "would become extremely lucrative for Qwest." It would also become extremely lucrative for Nacchio. A man who once sprinted miles to the finish line of the New York marathon despite oozing blood from one foot, Nacchio had become the Gordon Gekko of the telecom world as growth, profit, and personal wealth quickly became obsessions. In meetings, his nervous energy would cause his hands to fidget and in conversations he would answer questions before they were completely asked. Above all, he thrived on taking calculated risks, combining gut instinct with hard analysis. It was a philosophy he dubbed "informed opportunism" while earning a master of science degree in management at MIT.

By 2000, thanks to a $45.2 billion merger with U.S. West, a "Baby Bell" that served fourteen western states, he had turned his small company into the fourth-largest telecom in the country. He started with fewer than a thousand employees, but following the merger Qwest ballooned to 71,000 employees, more than 29 million customers, about $18.5 billion in sales, and a 25,000-mile network extending from Los Angeles to New York and Washington, D.C.

Like hyperactive moles, Qwest employees crisscrossed the U.S. and Europe burying superfast cable in four-foot trenches to connect cities, towns, and companies to the Internet. The company's slogan became "Ride the Light," and Nacchio would boast that Qwest would soon be bigger than his previous employer, AT&T. "I feel like an emerging oil baron," he told one reporter. Addressing a crowd of executives, he declared, "Qwest is all about being aggressive. We're going to dominate."

With all the acquisitions, however, also came sky-high debt as Nacchio poured truckloads of cash into improving U.S. West's long history of lackluster customer service (giving it the nickname "U.S. Worst"). At the same time, with all the overbuilding there was a glut in capacity. While Qwest's extensive network was capable of carrying all the voice and data traffic in the entire U.S., its share of telecom traffic never exceeded 4 or 5 percent. That meant thousands of miles of unused or "dark" cable. Qwest's debt would soon balloon to more than $26 billion.

Fearing that Wall Street investors would nervously begin backing away from his company if they saw signs of a setback, Nacchio turned increasingly ruthless. He slashed eleven thousand employees from the payroll—mostly inherited from U.S. West—and created a culture of fear for those who remained. He demanded that managers continue to match or better Wall Street's predictions of double-digit revenue growth—or join the unemployment lines. The "most important thing we do is make our numbers," he warned employees in January 2001. During a sales conference at the swank Bellagio Hotel in Las Vegas, he threw out tennis balls stuffed with cash into a ballroom packed with his neatly attired marketing force. Then he laughed as they scrambled, pushed, and dived like hungry packs of wolves for the prizes.

To keep from being fired, managers resorted to shell games and smoke and mirrors in place of proper accounting methods. Revenue from deals spread out over years was instead counted as cash up front. One-time sales were recorded on the ledger as recurring revenue. Capacity was traded with other companies in trouble and made to look like profitable sales. "Our experience told us that any time you puff up the revenue like a giant souffle," said one vice president who quit, "sooner or later it all rushes back out."

By January 2001, the stock was sliding and Qwest executives and auditors began worrying about what the SEC would find if it started snooping around. Seeing the coming meltdown, that month Nacchio quietly began unloading more than $100 million worth of his stock in the company while at the same time telling stockholders, potential investors, and the public that Qwest's future could not be brighter. In the world of high finance, it was known as insider trading, a very serious crime.

As Nacchio was dumping his stock by the truckload, he learned of a new and potentially sweet contract with the NSA. Known as Project Groundbreaker, the plan involved allowing outside contractors, for the first time, to come in and upgrade and manage many of the agency's powerful computer and telecommunications systems. With the agency simultaneously falling behind technologically and needing to continue to downsize, Groundbreaker was designed to bring the agency into the twenty-first century technologically while also reducing its workforce.

Under the terms of the contract, the hundreds of employees who previously worked in the IT billets would be let go by the agency and then hired by the outside companies to work on the contracts. Thus, most would simply stay at their jobs while their paychecks came from a new employer. The idea was to free up the agency to focus on its core missions—eavesdropping, code breaking, and code making. "Essentially, the problem for this agency is we downsized a third [over the past twelve years] while the larger world has undergone the most significant revolution in human communications since Gutenberg," said Hayden. "We have got to get the technology of the global telecommunications revolution inside this agency."

On February 27, 2001, two weeks after Qwest inaugurated local broadband service in Washington and Baltimore, Nacchio and the new head of Qwest's government business unit, James F. X. Payne, arrived at the NSA. They had come to present their proposal to become part of the Groundbreaker project. Although the company was on the list of potential subcontractors, Nacchio was looking to up the ante by outlining a much larger role for the company. Neither, however, was prepared for the agency's counteroffer: to give the NSA secret, warrantless access to

Qwest's database containing the calling records of its millions of American customers. And possibly later, to give Nacchio's blessing to install monitoring equipment on the company's Class 5 switching facilities, the system over which most of the company's domestic traffic flows.

No doubt to Hayden's surprise, despite Nacchio's penchant for risk-taking, he declined to have anything to do with the agency illegally installing its monitoring equipment on the company's switching facilities. Although some international traffic passed through those switches—the traffic Hayden was interested in—they primarily transmitted only localized calls, such as neighborhood to neighborhood. While he never flatly said no, Nacchio wanted no part of the operation. Having spent his entire career in the long distance telephone business, he felt such an agreement would be illegal—a view shared by his in-house attorneys in Denver. They believed any such cooperation—even if limited to e-mail—would violate the Electronic Communications Privacy Act.

Enacted in 1986, the law extended the telephone wiretap provisions to include electronic information transmitted by and stored in computers. If the NSA wanted to obtain his data, Nacchio decided, all it had to do was enter the company through the front door with a warrant from the Foreign Intelligence Surveillance Court, not through the back door with a whisper and a wink. "Nacchio said it was a legal issue, and they should not do something their general counsel told them not to do," said Payne. "Nacchio projected that he might do it if they could find a way to do it legally."

According to Payne, the NSA did not take the rejection well. "Subsequent to the meeting," he said, "the customer came back and expressed disappointment at Qwest's decision." The agency, he said, would never let it drop. "It went on for years," said Payne. "In meetings after meetings, they would bring it up." At one point Payne suggested to Nacchio "that they just tell them no." But, Payne noted, he "realized at this time that 'no' was not going to be enough for them." While Qwest eventually was added as one of about thirty-five subcontractors for Groundbreaker, the company never received the other, larger slice of the action it was seeking. Later, when charged with insider trading, Nacchio would claim the rejection was retaliation for his refusing to go along with what his lawyers told him was an illegal request by the NSA.

Despite being turned down flat by Nacchio in 2001, Hayden was hoping that by waving the flag after the 9/11 attacks he could convince the wary executives to overlook a possible jail term and endless lawsuits by angry customers should the secret come out. Without their cooperation, there was no way to gain access to the critical fiber-optic transmission lines.

Cables

Once a lonely place with a few dozen copper cables carrying expensive conversations between continents, the seabed now resembles a ball of string and has truly become the world's information superhighway. There's the TAT-14 from Tuckerton, New Jersey, to Widemouth, England; the northern branch of Gemini from Charlestown, Rhode Island, to Porthcurno, England; and the southern branch from Manasquan, New Jersey, to Porthcurno. If you want to go to the Middle East and Asia you can hitch a ride on FLAG. And ARCOS-1 will take you from Miami to fourteen countries in Central America, South America, and the Caribbean.

As satellite dishes began sprouting like toadstools in the 1960s, undersea cables became almost an anachronism, like the telegraph. But thanks to the Internet and low-cost, high-density glass fiber, the volume of international communications transmitted over subsea cables zoomed from 2 percent in 1988 to 80 percent by 2000. At the same time, new technologies such as wave division multiplexing (WDM) and synchronous digital hierarchy (SDH) enabled companies to squeeze ever more information into the same cables without the need to expand their size.

The revolution was not limited to the deep seas. For decades, many of the world's domestic and regional communications were carried over microwaves. Pencil-thin signals that carried thousands of phone conversations, they were beamed between conical and horn-shaped antennas over giant networks of towers like needles on a porcupine. For the NSA, all that was required to tap into those communications was to hide their own antenna somewhere within the twenty-mile beam of the microwave signal as it zapped from one tower to the next.

Another advantage for the NSA was that microwaves traveled in a straight line. Thus, because of the curvature of the earth, they would eventually pass into deep space. By putting a geostationary satellite in their path, the agency would be able to relay all those conversations in real time down to a listening post and then to headquarters. This technique was a boon to the NSA during the Cold War. Because much of Russia's Siberia is permanently sealed under a deep layer of permafrost, burying landlines was impossible. Therefore, a series of microwave towers stretched from Moscow to its commands in the far eastern parts of the country, such as Vladivostok. As the microwave signals passed from tower to tower and on into space, the NSA was there, 22,300 miles above, listening in with a satellite named Rhyolite.

But as the fiber-optic revolution took hold, microwave towers around the world slowly began disappearing like steel dinosaurs, and satellite dishes gave way to underground trenches and cable-laying ships. Not only were the new cables more reliable than the satellites, which had to contend with atmospheric interruptions, they were also much faster—of critical importance for both standard voice communications and the rapidly growing Voice over Internet Protocol (VoIP). Satellite signals must travel at least forty-five thousand miles as they zap from caller to deep space and then back down to the receiver, producing an annoying time delay of between one-quarter and one-half a second. But the time delay across the ocean by cable is only about one-thirtieth of a second and unnoticeable.

Finally, there was the relatively low cost of undersea communications—partly as a result of massive overbuilding in anticipation of greater and greater Internet demand, such as that done by Nacchio's Qwest. Between 1999 and 2002, the capacity of the global undersea grid grew more than fifteen times, a development not lost on Michael Hayden.

In order to tap into the U.S. telecommunications system, the NSA studied a variety of "switches," central nodes and key crossroads where millions of communications come together before being distributed to other parts of the country. Among them were the half dozen or so cable landing stations on each coast. Like border crossings, they are the points of entry for all international cable communications. Small, nondescript buildings in little towns near the shore, they usually give no hint that tens of millions of communications are constantly passing through them—more than 80 percent of all international communications.

Typical is AT&T's landing station at Tuckerton, New Jersey, one of the busiest communications hubs in the world. It is the gateway for a number of international cables to Europe, the Caribbean, and South America, including TAT-14 (for Trans-Atlantic Telephone). Containing nearly ten million circuits and operating at 640 gigabits per second, TAT-14 connects the U.S. with Britain and much of Europe. Built as a nine-thousand-mile loop, it goes from Tuckerton to England, France, the Netherlands, Germany, Denmark, and back to New Jersey. Communications to and from the Middle East and elsewhere are funneled into and out of the European landing stations by microwave, landline, or satellite. TAT-14 then transports the traffic between those points and Tuckerton at the speed of light.

Tuckerton has a long history of international communications; in 1912 the nation's tallest radio tower was built just to the south. At the time, it was the only transmitter capable of broadcasting to Europe without a relay. Today the town still keeps the U.S. connected to Europe and beyond, but now instead of a giant transmitter, it does so from a nondescript, sandy-colored two-story building on a small rural road about a mile from the Jersey shore. Surrounded by pines, at first glance the AT&T landing station appears to be a modern apartment complex for beachgoers. But on closer examination, the windows are all blacked out and the heavy-duty, electrically operated gate looks more like it should be at an American embassy than a remote summer vacation spot. In reality, much of the facility is deep underground.

After transiting the Atlantic, the cable, buried in a trench in the sand, continues underground, where it is accessible through manhole covers, and then finally enters through the subterranean wall of the station. There the signals are converted and transmitted to other AT&T locations for further distribution around the country. Some customers connect directly to the station and then "backhaul" their data to a distant location, such as New York City. It is at switches such as these that the NSA began placing its equipment, capturing mirror images of what was coming in.

Then, over encrypted fiber-optic cables, it would backhaul the millions of phone calls and messages in real time to its headquarters in Fort Meade or to one of its key analytical facilities elsewhere in the country.

But while the consolidation of so much of America's worldwide communications into a few thin cables on each coast might make life easy for the NSA in its fight against terrorists, it also presents an extremely tempting target for terrorists. By 2002, the total capacity of the ten international cables entering the east coast was nearly 8.5 billion circuits, with the ability to transfer over 206 gigabytes of data per second. Six of the ten cables come ashore in a small cluster of just four cities on the east coast: Tuckerton, Manasquan, and Manahawkin along the Jersey coast, and Charlestown in Rhode Island. Like the Internet, AT&T's voice calls have also ballooned in recent years, from 37.5 million on an average business day in 1984 to 300 million in 1999.

"Theoretically, an attack on two or three of these sites—at the point where the cables come together in the undersea trench before coming ashore—could cause enormous damage to the entire system," said a 2002 RAND study. "For instance, a successful attack on trenches in Tuckerton and Manasquan and Charlestown would eliminate all but 11 gigabytes per second of carrying capacity in that region—a 95 percent cut." As an example of the chaos that might result from such a loss, a few years ago one cut cable on the SWM 3 network leading from Australia to Singapore caused Australia's largest Internet provider—Telstra—to lose up to 70 percent of its Internet capacity.

As the NSA began secretly approaching the telecommunications executives, once again Joe Nacchio and Qwest became a stumbling block. In early 2001 he had refused to allow the agency permission to install monitoring equipment on its Class 5 switching facilities, over which traveled primarily domestic communications. Now, approached again by the NSA following the 9/11 attacks, he again refused. "Mr. Nacchio made inquiry as to whether a warrant or other legal process had been secured in support of that request," said his lawyer, Herbert J. Stern. "When he learned that no such authority had been granted, and that there was disinclination on the part of the authorities to use any legal process," Nacchio concluded that the requests violated federal privacy requirements "and issued instructions to refuse to comply." But Qwest was a small player compared to some of the others and Hayden set his sights on them, especially AT&T and Verizon.

By then AT&T had discovered the answer to one of the key technical problems facing the NSA as its giant eavesdropping dishes became relics of a bygone time: how to tap into the delicate fiber-optic cables now linking continent to continent, country to country, and caller to caller.

Little ever happens in the sleepy town of Bridgeton, just outside of St. Louis, on the muddy banks of the Mississippi. "The original 15 blocks were platted in 1794, shortly after our nation was founded," its Web page proudly boasts. "We also hold the oldest continuous state charter, which was granted in 1843." But since then it had been quiet times, until 2002. That year a long-held secret was revealed, and another event became shrouded in utmost secrecy.

It had been a dry, hot summer, and as the chocolate river slowly retreated, the outline of a giant rib cage began to emerge. It was the skeletal hull of a nineteenth-century steamboat coming into view for the first time in 120 years. At 280 feet, the *Montana* had been one of the longest paddlewheelers ever to ply the Mississippi. It was a time of grandeur, when more than seven hundred steamboats regularly cruised the river, pulling into the Port of St. Louis to take on passengers and off-load cargo. Along the city's lively riverfront, colorful boats decked out with flags and bunting in red, white, and blue lined up for miles. But in June 1884, as the *Montana* neared Bridgeton, it collided with a railroad crossing, began taking on water, and sank into the gooey bottom. Soon the era of the steamboat came to an end, just as that of the telephone began to take hold.

That same summer, as Missourians from miles around crowded into Bridgeton to watch the river giving up its long-held secret, another group in Bridgeton was going to elaborate lengths to keep a secret. In a boxy, one-story redbrick building that once housed offices for the Western Union telegraph company, employees of AT&T were plastering over the windows, installing steel doors, and constructing a "mantrap." A bionic security portal containing retinal and fingerprint scanners, it was designed to keep curious workers out and allow the few with Top Secret NSA clearances in.

The secret hidden in the room had its beginnings five years earlier and 934 miles to the northeast, in a laboratory in New Jersey. In the mid-

1990s, the Internet revolution met the fiber-optic revolution, raising questions for scientists at AT&T regarding how fiber-optic systems operate under a variety of conditions. They needed ways to measure and analyze the photons as they flashed over the hair-thin strands of fiber bundled together inside the thick, heavily insulated cable. And the only way to conduct truly valid tests and measurements was to carry out the experiments on actual live and stored customer traffic, including that from other telecoms that passed data through AT&T equipment. This meant developing a way "to tap the network passively," according to confidential AT&T documents.

In 1996, the year AT&T inaugurated its WorldNet Internet service, the task of inventing the tap was given to a small team of scientists at AT&T's Research Labs in Florham Park, New Jersey. The leafy campus was once the estate of Vanderbilt descendants. What the team came up with was a device they called the PacketScope.

Among the locations chosen for the taps was AT&T's Bridgeton, Missouri, Network Operations Center. A one-story building with a two-story annex at 12976 Hollenberg Drive, it served as the telecom's technical command center, a major hub through which AT&T's domestic and international data circuits were managed. "They are in command of the network," said Mark Klein, a longtime AT&T employee. It was thus an ideal place to tap into and analyze a large portion of the system. Another location was its WorldNet Router Center at the AT&T Building at 32 Sixth Avenue in New York City, where most of the domestic and international cables converged. "The New York monitor taps into T3 [a high-speed cable] links connecting WN [WorldNet] to the rest of the Internet," according to the documents. And a third was set up at AT&T Labs in Florham Park, New Jersey.

At the Internet hubs in Bridgeton, New York City, and Florham Park, data flows through DSX-3 panels that are basically automatic switchboards redirecting the traffic to other locations. Each link in the panel has a jack through which the traffic could be monitored. To tap into the data, lines from the jacks were plugged into the PacketScope, which consisted of a Compaq 500-MHz UNIX workstation, 10-Gbyte striped disk arrays, and 140-Gbyte tape robots. As the systems became more complex, however, it would be necessary to actually tap into the cables themselves. "An approach others have used is to have an optical splitter, much like the tap for a T1 or T3 link," said the documents. This optical splitter would create a mirror image of the contents of the entire cable.

Once intercepted by the PacketScopes, the information was transmitted in real time to Florham Park, where AT&T constructed its WorldNet Data Warehouse to analyze and store information. According to one of the AT&T engineers working on the project, "The amount of data to be stored is truly enormous." To hold and manage it all, the warehouse was home to Daytona, AT&T's monster data storage computer. Engineers at the Data Warehouse could also remotely control the PacketScopes to target what to intercept. "That on-site presence of personnel to manage the monitoring equipment is not essential," said the AT&T documents.

For the AT&T engineers, ensuring the confidentiality of customers' e-mail and other data was critical. Thus only packet headers—the address information—were intercepted, not the full contents of the e-mail. The headers were then encrypted to further hide the true identity of the senders and receivers.

By the summer of 1997, the PacketScopes were fully in operation. But what the AT&T engineers never counted on was a massive terrorist attack and a president's decision to ignore existing privacy law. By the late fall of 2001, Hayden succeeded in gaining the secret cooperation of nearly all of the nation's telecommunications giants for his warrantless eavesdropping program. Within a year, engineers were busy installing highly secret, heavily locked rooms in key AT&T switches, among them Bridgeton, New York City, and the company's major West Coast central office in San Francisco. From then on the data—including both address information and content—would flow through the PacketScopes directly to the NSA. And Bridgeton would become the technical command center for the operation. "It was very hush-hush," said one of the AT&T workers there at the time. "We were told there was going to be some government personnel working in that room. We were told, 'Do not try to speak to them. Do not hamper their work. Do not impede anything that they're doing.' "

"Bridgeton, Missouri, was chosen" for the PacketScope, said Dr. Brian Reid, a former AT&T scientist at Bell Labs, "because it's roughly close to the center of North America geographically, and therefore if you're going to run a lot of wires to it, they don't have to be as long. Whereas if you put this in New Jersey, then the wires from Phoenix and Los Angeles would be too long. And so if you're going to build a hub for analysis, you put it somewhere in Missouri or Kansas, and they put it in Missouri . . . In the world of AT&T, all you had to do was go to Bridgeton and say, 'Hi guys, I'd like to listen,' and you would hear everything you needed to hear." The problem for the NSA today, says Reid, is the large number of other telecom companies, all of which would require separate secret agreements. "Now you'd have to go to the Qwest hub in Denver, and you'd have to go to the Sprint hub in St. Louis, and you'd have to go to the Vonage hub in Norway—it's increasingly global, it's increasingly decentralized, and there's no longer a small number of places to go to take advantage of other people's having drawn stuff together. There could be a hundred places."

Modeled after Bell Labs, birthplace of the transistor and winner of eleven Nobel Prizes for brilliant innovations in communications, AT&T Labs now spent much of its time helping the government conduct mass surveillance of its customers and seeking patents for ever more sophisticated bugs. One AT&T Labs patent application was called "Secure detection of an intercepted targeted IP phone from multiple monitoring locations," and another was titled "Monitoring selected IP voice calls through activity of a watchdog program at an IP-addressing mapping check point."

For decades, AT&T and much of the rest of the telecommunications industry have had a very secret, very cozy relationship with the NSA through the National Security Agency Advisory Board (NSAAB), made up of top company executives. With the advent of the warrantless eavesdropping program, the knowledge, expertise, and help of those executives became even more critical. Because of this, the agency has tried hard to keep the names of those industry leaders and details of their regular meeting at the NSA secret. Among the previous members was Dr. William O. Baker, who designed much of America's telecommunications infrastructure. During the two decades he served on the board he also served, at various points, as research chief, president, and chairman of the board of Bell Labs, long the epicenter of telecommunications research. Because the first operational fiber-optic system was developed under Baker at Bell Labs, the NSA had a large head start in finding ways to penetrate it.

The backgrounds of other recent members of the NSAAB also show the secret linkage between the NSA and the commercial telecom world. They include:

- Dr. Alf L. Andreassen, an information systems expert. In 1983 he founded and became director of Bell Labs Command, Control, Communication and Intelligence Center and later did similar intelligence work for AT&T.

- Dr. George H. Heilmeier, chairman emeritus of Telcordia Technologies, Inc., formerly known as Bell Communications Research, Inc. (or Bellcore). At the time of the breakup of AT&T, the highly regarded Bell Labs stayed with the parent company, and as a result the regional Bell operating companies, the Baby Bells, formed their own research and development company, which was Bellcore, later Telcordia. According to the company's literature, "We're one of the world's foremost providers of software and services for IP, wireline, wireless, and cable networks."

- David W. Aucsmith, security architect and chief technology officer for Microsoft Corp.'s Security Business & Technology Unit. From 1994 to 2002 he was the chief security architect for Intel Corporation, the company whose integrated circuit chips are in millions of personal computers around the world. Speaking of computer security, he once said, "The actual user of the PC—someone who can do anything they want—is the enemy."

- John P. Stenbit, on the board of directors of Loral Space & Communications Inc., a satellite communications company that owns and operates telecommunications satellites used to distribute broadband data and provide access to Internet.

As on the East Coast, during the late 1990s the amount of telephone and Internet traffic flowing across the Pacific to the United States boomed. Among the new pipes through which much of this communication passed was the eighteen-thousand-mile Southern Cross fiber-optic cable network, which offered a quantum leap in carrying capacity across the Southern

Pacific—up to 160 gigabytes per second. But the cable in which the NSA likely had the most interest was China-U.S., owned by a consortium of companies including AT&T and SBC Communications. Completed in 2000, the southern end of the fourteen-thousand-mile ring begins its long journey at a landing station in Shantou, a bustling port in the southern Chinese province of Guangdong known for its tea consumption.

While there was an obvious foreign intelligence value to monitoring that cable, there was also a terrorism connection. Many of the communications from Southeast Asia, including Indonesia and Malaysia, where al-Qaeda has been very active, were transmitted over the SEA-ME-WE 3 (Southwest Asia–Middle East–Western Europe) cable. That cable then linked to China-U.S. in Shantou.

Thus if an American businesswoman in Surabaya, Indonesia, sent an e-mail to her husband in Cincinnati, the signal would likely be routed first to the Ancol landing station on a beach area about five miles from the Indonesian capital of Jakarta. At Ancol, like a passenger boarding a very fast ship, it would travel over the SEA-ME-WE 3 cable to the Shantou landing station, arriving a millisecond or so later. At Shantou, the e-mail would transfer to the China-U.S. cable, which, in a few blinks of an eye, would transport it across the floor of the Pacific Ocean.

In the U.S., the message would arrive unceremoniously a few feet beneath a sandy beach at California's Montana De Oro State Park, near Morro Bay. Then, after another 2,200 feet inside a five-inch drill pipe under the drifting dunes, it would emerge in a manhole at the park's Sand Spit parking lot. Passing beneath the feet of surfers and beachcombers heading for the shore, the e-mail would zip another mile inland, arriving at 9401 Los Oso Valley Road in San Luis Obispo, a small, tan-colored windowless building surrounded by a high steel fence topped with barbed wire that is AT&T's landing station.

Despite its quiet surroundings, it is a very busy place. Five of the six transpacific cables pass under the beach and into that small building. Together, the cables contain 80 percent of all communications to and from virtually every nation in the Pacific and the Far East—dozens of countries, hundreds of languages, thousands of cities, tens of millions of simultaneous conversations and messages. Sealed in layers of polyethylene, Mylar tape, stranded steel wires, aluminum sheathing, copper tubing, and petroleum jelly are the heavily protected hair-thin glass fibers. Converted into photons and passing through them at the speed of light are cries and laughter, hopes and dreams, romance and commerce, voices and pictures, e-mail and faxes, bank statements and hotel reservations, love poems and death notices. The only thing they all have in common is a reasonable expectation of privacy.

From the landing station, the e-mail from Surabaya, together with millions of additional communications from all five cables, zaps 241 miles north to 611 Folsom Street in downtown San Francisco. Tall, forbidding, and nearly windowless, the titanium-colored nine-story building is, in essence, one big telecommunications switch—the nerve center where all of AT&T's regional trunk lines converge. Beneath the road, the message enters through the reinforced concrete walls of an underground vault. There it begins a climb toward the upper floors inside metal ductwork.

Along the way the messages pass floor after floor of wires—hanging like spaghetti from ceilings, tied in bundles along the floor, stretched like insulation along every wall. Old copper wire pairs, they connect neighborhood to neighborhood and local homes to the corner store. Another entire floor contains the actual "switch," a Northern Telecom DMS-100. Made up of rows of chocolate-brown cabinets that contain whirring drives and humming air conditioning, the superprocessor has the ability to juggle 100,000 calls while at the same time broadcasting annoying messages about misdialed calls and numbers no longer in service.

On the eighth floor, the cables finally emerge into the WorldNet Internet spaces where their signals are demultiplexed—sorted out between voice and data, various frequencies, and other details. Then they drop down to the seventh floor, an expansive space packed with gray electronic bays and steel racks. Stacked from floor to ceiling are Cisco routers and modems with flashing red, green, and yellow lights. It is the key choke point through which millions of e-mail and other data are constantly passing, from across the country and around the world. In addition to traffic from the international cables, the room is also a hub for a large percentage of America's domestic communications. The biggest "pipes" deliver 2.5 gigabits of data—the equivalent of one-quarter of the *Encyclopaedia Britannica*'s text—per second.

"There's lots of Internet traffic, as you can imagine, that goes in and out of this office," said Mark Klein, the AT&T technician in charge of the room. For over twenty-two years, Klein had worked for the company as a communications technician and computer network specialist, first in New York and then in California. "Probably hundreds of fiber-optic lines go out, carrying billions—that's billions with a B—of bits of data going in and out every second every day. So all the Web surfing you're doing, whatever you're doing on the Internet—the pictures, the video, the Voice over Internet—all that stuff's going in and out of there. And then of course there's also the traditional phone switch, which is doing what it's been doing since before the Internet—handling millions and millions of phone calls."

Following its merger with SBC, AT&T had become the biggest telecommunications company in the United States and one of the largest in the world, providing long-distance service to approximately 34.4 million customers. Its international voice service carried more than 18 billion minutes per year, reaching 240 countries, linking 400 carriers, and offering remote access via 19,500 points of presence in 149 countries around the globe. And much of those communications passed through its Folsom Street facility.

In a sense, the WorldNet Internet room was also a meeting place for dozens of the nation's major Internet service providers (ISPs). This was because only a fraction of all the Internet communications flowing into the room were from actual AT&T WorldNet customers. The rest were from customers of other Internet companies, such as Sprint, Level 3, and UUNET. In order to cheaply and efficiently exchange these packets, the companies enter into "peering" arrangements with one another and with AT&T, and then bring their pipes together in the WorldNet room at Folsom Street. Thus, when the e-mail from Surabaya arrives, it can quickly be shifted over to the businesswoman's own company, Sprint, for final delivery to Cincinnati.

At the same time, many other pipes are also entering Folsom Street from smaller ISPs. But rather than each running cables from their companies all the way to downtown San Francisco, they get together at central locations away from the city, known as Internet exchange points, or IXPs. There the companies exchange Internet traffic that is addressed to one another. By coming together, they need only lay a few feet of cable—to one another's routers—rather than many miles to a variety of locations. From the IXP, a single cable then goes to Folsom Street, which is another savings.

As the Internet has grown, so have the IXPs. Some have taken over entire buildings and become "carrier hotels." But historically, the two most important IXPs have been MAE (for Metropolitan Area Ethernet) East in Virginia and MAE West in California. MAE East began in the parking garage of a high-rise office building at 8100 Boone Boulevard in Vienna, Virginia, just outside Washington, D.C. "A group of network providers in the Virginia area got together over beer one night and decided to connect their networks," said the Internet architect Steve Feldman. It soon exploded as UUNET, MCI, Sprint, America Online, and others joined, turning it into the busiest Internet hub in the world, a sort of massive outlet mall for ISPs. It later moved up to a nicer set of offices on one of the upper floors, Suite 400. Then as it filled up, another major IXP, the Equinix colocation facility, opened at 21830 UUNET Way in Ashburn, Virginia. It is now overshadowing MAE East.

In California, MAE West developed in the heart of Silicon Valley and quickly became the second-busiest IXP in the world. As the World Wide Web grew, so too did the nation's "Internet backbone," which largely stretched between the two MAEs. Today MAE West sits on the eleventh floor of 55 Market Street, a gold-mirrored building in downtown San Jose. Every day, behind its steel door secured with a cyberlock, as much as 40 percent of the nation's Internet traffic speeds by. Inside are rows and rows of black cabinets, each containing a stack of quietly humming routers belonging to scores of different ISPs. Connected together with bright orange cables, they are constantly exchanging Internet packets. The routers, in turn, are all wired to the MAE, three bread-box-sized switches capable of handling a total of 30 billion bits a second. But like MAE East, MAE West is also becoming upstaged by another IXP: One Wilshire, in Los Angeles, where over 260 ISPs connect their networks to one another. It has become the main connecting point for the Pacific Rim countries.

From MAE West, a fiber-optic cable runs to AT&T's WorldNet Internet room on Folsom Street, where it joins more than a dozen other cables—"peering links"—from northern California IXPs. But rather than being connected directly to the routers, which would speed the Internet packets on to their ultimate destination—the e-mail from Surabaya to Cincinnati, for example—the cables instead pass into an odd, rectangular white box. Labeled "Splitter Cabinet," it is in reality a supersophisticated opto-electronic "bug" designed to tap into fiber-optic cables.

Splitter

In the old days of copper telephone wires, a basic tap consisted simply of attaching a pair of alligator clips to a telephone wire. Through induction, the clips pick up the conversations as they leak—or radiate—from the copper wire. But with glass fibers there is no leakage and thus tapping through induction is out. Instead, tapping into a fiber-optic cable literally requires major surgery.

After the NSA proposed its warrantless eavesdropping scheme to AT&T, the company's AT&T Labs in New Jersey drew up a step-by-step guide for the technicians who would carry out the task on the high-capacity cables. Titled "Splitter Cut-In and Test Procedure" and dated January 13, 2003, it said, "This procedure covers the steps required to insert optical splitters into select live Common Backbone (CBB) [AT&T's nationwide system] OC3, OC12 and OC48 optical circuits."

In preparing for the cut into the cable, the company took a number of precautions in the event the "surgery" went badly. Instructions were given to the technicians to begin the operation in the wee hours of the morning, around two o'clock, when there is the least amount of traffic moving through the cables.

Also, in the same way surgeons worry about patients losing too much blood during an operation, the AT&T cable tappers were concerned that the fibers would bleed too much light and thus they would lose their precious signal—and with it millions of e-mails and other data. There was no way to prevent some loss, but they needed to keep it below seven decibels—their unit of measurement—and preferably no more than six. As a precaution, one technician would keep constant track of the decibel level as the operation was taking place. Any significant decrease in the level was to be reported immediately to nervous engineers at AT&T's Network Operations Center in Bridgeton, Missouri, which coordinated the technical aspects of the program.

On the night of the operation, all went well inside the "splitter box." From the cut, mirrorlike images of the photons passing through the glass fibers were redirected within the box onto a second cable. Once this was completed, the signals then continued on to the WorldNet modems and routers. From there, the e-mail and other messages reached their final destination—and the businesswoman's husband in Cincinnati read the e-mail she had sent from Surabaya just moments before.

But the clone cable, with a duplicate copy of the woman's e-mail, took a different route. It descended one floor below to Room 641A, a small corner space on the sixth floor controlled not by AT&T, but by the NSA. Hidden behind the heavily secured orange door was the agency's warrantless listening post. Labeled SG3 (short for the cover name, Study Group 3), the 24-by-48-foot room was small and compact, like an electronic nest. Entering through the white panels of the false ceiling were clones of the cables containing the vast majority of all international and domestic communications entering Folsom Street.

Lining three walls of the bugging room were racks of high-tech electronic equipment. On one shelf sat several Juniper routers, including a powerful M40e, used by Internet service providers to launch and manage edge networks, and a Brocade Silk Worm 2800 switch for high-speed, block-level access to e-mail servers and databases. There was a meta-data cabinet; another for network management; and seven Sun computers, servers, and data storage devices. But the piece of equipment that most concerned the AT&T technician Mark Klein was the Narus STA 6400.

In the summer of 2002, Klein had been assigned to the company's Geary Street facility in San Francisco. "I was sitting at my workstation one day, and some e-mail came in," he said. "I opened it up, and it was just a notice saying that somebody from the National Security Agency, NSA, was going to come visit for some business. They didn't say what, of course . . . That struck me as a little odd to begin with, because I remember from back in the seventies, the NSA is not supposed to be doing domestic spying, so what were they doing in an AT&T company office?" A few days later, the NSA employee turned up and Klein introduced him to one of his colleagues, who was being processed for a Top Secret NSA clearance.

Then in January 2003, he and several other employees toured the company's giant switch on Folsom Street. "There I saw a new room being built adjacent to the 4ESS switch room where the public's phone calls are routed," he said. "I learned that the person whom the NSA interviewed for the secret job was the person working to install equipment in this room." Ten months later, Klein was transferred to the Folsom Street switch, where he was put in charge of the WorldNet Internet room, one floor above the secret NSA room. There, Klein took over responsibility for installing new fiber-optic circuits and troubleshooting those already in place.

"As soon as I saw the splitter," Klein said, "I knew this was completely unconstitutional and illegal because they were copying everything. I'm a technician, I know what this equipment does, and I traced the cable. This cable goes to that room, which we can't go into; that's a government room. And I knew what was on that cable. The documents gave me the list of sixteen entities whose data was being copied, and they were major carriers, and not just AT&T, including major exchange points, like MAE West. It was everything that went across the Internet then, which was Web browsing and e-mail and VoIP calls. The circuits listed were the peering links, which connect WorldNet with other networks and hence the whole country, as well as the rest of the world."

Klein also said that because they installed the taps in the AT&T facility in downtown San Francisco rather than at the cable landing station, a key target is domestic—not just international—traffic. "It struck me at the time that from what I knew of the network, if you just wanted to get international traffic, you would go to the cable stations and also the satellite stations, and you get all the international traffic you want, without having to mess it up with a whole bunch of domestic traffic that you would then have to waste your time sifting out. And it struck me at the time that they were putting this in places where they were bound to catch a lot of domestic traffic . . . The implication is that they want domestic traffic."

To Klein, there could be only one answer. "Based on my understanding of the connections and equipment at issue," he said, "it appears the NSA is capable of conducting what amounts to vacuum-cleaner surveillance of all the data crossing the Internet—whether that be people's e-mail, Web surfing, or any other data . . . What I saw is that everything's flowing across the Internet to this government-controlled room. The physical apparatus gives them everything. A lot of this was domestic."

When Klein retired, he took with him a stack of internal AT&T papers. "One of the documents listed the equipment installed in the secret room," he said, "and this list included a Narus STA 6400, which is a 'Semantic Traffic Analyzer.' The Narus STA technology is known to be used particularly by government intelligence agencies because of its ability to sift through large amounts of data looking for preprogrammed targets." Also in the room was a Narus Logic Server.

Like much of the equipment used for bugging, the Narus hardware and software was originally designed for a different purpose. With the growth of the Internet and digital communications, data began flowing over fiber-optic lines in "packets." The only way a company can determine exactly whom to bill for how much time is being used or how many megabytes are being sent is to analyze those millions of packets as they flow from the incoming cables to the routers at the speed of light. Thus, as the e-mail from Surabaya zaps through the room and onto a Sprint router, the Narus equipment can record its details—known as "metadata." With this information, AT&T can charge Sprint and Sprint is then reimbursed by the subscriber in Cincinnati.

Following the attacks on 9/11, Narus began modifying its system and selling it to intelligence agencies around the world, who used it not for billing purposes but for mass surveillance. Their top-of-the-line product became the secretive NarusInsight Intercept Suite, which the company claims is "the leader in carrier-class security and traffic intelligence for the world's largest IP networks."

The Intercept Suite, according to Narus, is "the industry's only network traffic intelligence system that supports real-time precision targeting, capturing and reconstruction of webmail traffic. Narus technology has long been recognized for its ability to identify and track almost all network and application protocols across very large networks. Targeting and capturing webmail traffic is a difficult challenge due to the proprietary and frequent changing nature of webmail services being monitored. The NarusInsight Intercept Suite (NIS) has solved this problem and is now capable of precision targeting, capturing and reconstructing numerous aspects of webmail traffic including email, chat, calendaring, draft folders, address books and much more. Traffic from all nodes and numerous protocols can be reassembled and viewed from a single management station or distributed across multiple stations. In addition, NIS supports a large percentage of all webmail services, including Google Gmail, MSN Hotmail, Yahoo! Mail, and Gawab Mail (English and Arabic versions)."

At the heart of the Intercept Suite is the NarusInsight computer, an enormously powerful machine capable of scanning the fastest transmission lines on the Internet, including OC-192 cables that carry 10 gigabits per second—10 billion bits of information per second. It can also carry almost 130,000 simultaneous telephone calls. According to the company, the Intercept Suite "uniquely provides insight into the *entire* network, ensuring that all targeted data is captured regardless of the size, speed, or asymmetric topology of the network. Any number of links, at any speed, with any routing architecture, can be simultaneously monitored." (Emphasis in original.)

"Anything that comes through [an Internet protocol network], we can record," boasts the company's vice president of marketing, Steve Bannerman. "We can reconstruct all of their e-mails along with attachments, see what Web pages they clicked on, we can reconstruct their [Voice over Internet Protocol] calls." Adds company CEO Greg Oslan, "The latest iteration of NIS follows a long line of powerful and unique products developed by Narus and once again raises the bar, providing unparalleled monitoring and intercept capabilities to service providers and government organizations around the world."

In its promotional literature to intelligence agencies, Narus claims it has the ability to analyze an astronomical number of records. "Narus is the recognized performance leader," it says, "with production environments exceeding 10 billion records per day, for global applications in wireless, WiFi, prepaid, broadband, voice and data."

To help ensure future contracts with the NSA, in September 2004 Narus appointed William P. Crowell, a former deputy director of the agency, to its board. Before becoming the agency's top civilian, Crowell had served as head of its signals intelligence operations. The Narus website also sheds light on additional qualities unique to its product:

One distinctive capability that Narus is known for is its ability to capture and collect data from the largest networks around the world. To complement this capability, Narus provides analytics and reporting products that have been deployed by its customers worldwide. They involve powerful parsing algorithms, data aggregation and filtering for delivery to various upstream and downstream operating and support systems. They also involve correlation and association of events collected from numerous sources, received in multiple formats, over many protocols, and through different periods of time.

By placing the Narus equipment in the secret room at AT&T, the NSA was spreading an electronic drift net across cyberspace. As data from the cables raced by at mega-Gbps speed, packets containing target names, addresses, key words, and phrases would be kicked out and forwarded to the NSA for further analysis. Among those who understand Narus's capabilities, as well as its dangers, is Dr. Brian Reid, the former scientist at Bell Labs, who also taught electrical engineering at Stanford and was a member of the team that built the first Cisco router.

"The Narus box allows you to find what you're looking for," said Reid. "It is a sifter—and its purpose is to winnow the information down to a low enough rate that it could be pumped to the other end of the wire, which we assume is the NSA. If they had enough capacity to deliver the information from the place where it was wiretapped to the place they were going to use it, they wouldn't need the Narus. Its only purpose is real-time sifting. And if you don't filter, then you have an information overload and you don't know what to send. They needed the Narus to know what to send. The Narus is an empty vessel waiting to be given instructions, and the hardware is simply a large number of parallel filters all of which can be programmed at once. It watches the data go by and compares what it sees to whatever it's been told to look for, and when it sees a match it notifies its parent computer by saying 'got one here,' and the parent computer responds by grabbing the thing it just got and sending it over the wire. All that could be done remotely—there's no need for any human in that room."

Reid added, "It looks at everything . . . Whatever question the NSA is trying to answer, that determines what they put in there. And whether they put in key words or address partial matches—there's no limit. You can look for whatever you want. And the thing that's great about the Narus box is that it gives you the freedom to pattern match on anything. So if you don't want to do key words, if you want to do a mixture of IP addresses and who's your ISP and whether it contained the word 'mother' in all caps, it can do that too."

Another expert familiar with Narus is J. Scott Marcus. One of the country's foremost experts on the Internet, from July 2001 to July 2005 he served as the senior advisor for Internet technology at the Federal Communications Commission. He analyzed Klein's documents and statement as an expert witness for the Electronic Frontier Foundation in a suit against AT&T over illegal surveillance. In his sworn declaration, he said that "the Narus system is well suited to process huge volumes of data, including user content, in real time. It is thus well suited to the capture and analysis of large volumes of data for purposes of surveillance."

Much of that "huge volume of data," according to Klein, came from the interception of traffic from AT&T's peering partners, such as Sprint and UUNET. And despite being turned down by Joe Nacchio, the NSA nevertheless got access to Qwest's communications because of its peering relationship with AT&T. Qwest's was among the cables placed through the "splitter box." Just as the AT&T documents outlined in detail how to tap into the cables, they also described which peering links to target. They included ConXion, Verio, XO, Genuity, Qwest, PAIX, Allegiance, Abovenet, Global Crossing, C&W, UUNET, Level 3, Sprint, Telia, PSINet, and MAE West. "It's not just WorldNet customers who are being spied on— it's the entire Internet."

Marcus, who holds a Top Secret clearance and has been a member of the FCC's Homeland Security Policy Council, agreed that the peering companies were indeed a key NSA target. "All of the networks with which AT&T peered in San Francisco had their traffic intercepted," he said, adding, "any AT&T peering partners whose traffic was not intercepted most likely were small networks that exchanged very little traffic with AT&T. The traffic intercepted at the facility probably represented a substantial fraction of AT&T's total national peering traffic."

Looking at the entire NSA setup, Marcus came away greatly concerned. He was especially surprised because it appeared that the system was not limited to international traffic but included all domestic U.S. communications as well—it all went into the secret room. The deployment, he said, "apparently involves considerably more locations than would be required to catch the majority of international traffic . . . This configuration appears to have the capability to enable surveillance and analysis of Internet content on a massive scale, including both overseas and purely domestic traffic . . . I conclude that AT&T has constructed an extensive— and expensive—collection of infrastructure that collectively has all the capability necessary to conduct large scale covert gathering of IP-based communications information, *not only for communications to overseas locations, but for purely domestic communications as well.*" (Emphasis in original.)

Secret cooperation with the telecom industry is only one method the NSA uses to penetrate the Internet and fiber-optic communications. Long before the warrantless eavesdropping program was inaugurated following the 9/11 attacks, the agency was covertly tapping into both. This was revealed in a highly classified closed-door discussion at the NSA on September 30, 1999, between the NSA deputy director for services Terry Thompson and members of the agency's technical workforce. "The projections that we made five, six, eight years ago," said Thompson in a videotape of the meeting obtained by the author, "about the increasing volumes of collection and what that's going to mean for our analysts have all come true, thanks in large part to the work that you all and others have done. We're much further ahead now in terms of being able to access and collect [Internet] network data, fiber optics, cellular data, all the different modalities of communications that we are targeting."

One of the ways to covertly penetrate both the Internet and fiber-optic communications is to target their weakest point, the point where the systems interconnect—the routers. Literally the heart of the Internet, they are the specialized microcomputers that link two or more incompatible computer networks together. They also act as a sort of postal service, deciding where to route the various messages carried over the network. "Virtually all Internet traffic travels across the system of one company: Cisco Systems," says a Cisco television ad. By discovering the weak spots and vulnerabilities in this "postal service," the NSA has the ability to target and intercept much of the electronic mail.

Thus, as Thompson further explained at the 1999 meeting, one of the NSA's goals should be to hire away, on a short-term basis, people from key companies such as Cisco. Having hired them, the agency could use their knowledge and expertise to "reverse engineer" the systems and find ways to install back doors. "I only need this person to do reverse engineering on Cisco routers," he said, "for about three or five years, because I see Cisco going away as a key manufacturer for routers and so I don't need that expertise. But I really need somebody today and for the next couple of years who knows Cisco routers inside and out and can help me understand how they're being used in target networks."

While there had always been movement back and forth between the NSA and the corporate world, for the most part agency officials considered the work too sensitive to hand out to contractors. But that changed in 2001 when Congress, worried that the NSA was falling far behind, insisted that the agency expand its domain to the private sector. In its budget authorization that year, the House Intelligence Committee listed fiber-optic communications and the Internet as among the key problem areas facing the NSA and recommended more outsourcing to the corporate world. "During the 1980s budget increases," said the committee, "NSA decided to build up its in-house government scientists and engineers and the agency now seems to believe that in-house talent can address the rapidly evolving signals environment better than outsiders can . . . The culture demanded compartmentation, valued hands-on technical work, and encouraged in-house prototyping. It placed little value on program management, contracting development work to industry, and the associated systems engineering skills."

The committee decided it was time for a change. "Today, an entirely new orientation is required," said the 2001 budget report. "The agency must rapidly enhance its program management and systems engineering skills and heed the dictates of these disciplines, including looking at options to contract out for these skills." According to Mike Hayden, "The explosive growth of the global network and new technologies make our partnership with industry more vital to NSA's success than ever before." As a result, in a troubling change, much of the NSA's highly sensitive eavesdropping has been outsourced to private firms in the same way it outsources copy machine repair.

Industry

The NSA's new willingness to outsource eavesdropping, plus the warrantless eavesdropping and other new programs, thus became a giant boon to a growing fraternity of contractors who make their living off the NSA. Headquarters for what might be termed the surveillance-industrial complex is the National Business Park, "NBP" in NSA lingo. Located just across the Baltimore-Washington Parkway from the agency's secret city, it is nearly as secret and nearly as protected as the agency itself. The centerpiece is NBP-1, a tall glass office building belonging to the NSA's Technology and Systems Organization.

Stretching out below NBP-1, hidden from the highway and surrounded by tall trees, National Business Park is a large compound of buildings owned by the NSA's numerous high-tech contractors. The NSA's problem is trying to keep up with the enormous volume of incoming information, including the warrantless monitoring, which, like any system when restraints are removed, tends to expand exponentially. NBP fills the need as a sort of private-sector NSA.

Among the companies with large, heavily protected buildings at NBP is Booz Allen with a 250,000-square-foot mausoleum. The company has long had very close ties to the NSA, especially since former director Mike McConnell left the agency in February 1996 to become a vice president and earn a $2-million-a-year salary. "At the National Business Park Campus, we apply Tomorrow's Technology Today," says the company's website, to deliver "Signals Intelligence Solutions to the government and private sector." Then, using head-hunting firms, it advertises for such positions as Internet eavesdroppers. One ad listed the job title as "Network Intelligence Analyst" and gave a description of the job:

• Provide network intelligence analysis support within multiple SIGINT development offices to high-profile government clients for a rapidly growing team.

• Provide wide range of network analysis, including basic research, protocol analysis, and network topology mapping of traffic through different layers of the OSI model and report the results of the analysis.

• Perform basic network and user discovery using various techniques, including domain name IP mapping, NS lookup, trace route analysis, and the analysis of network information, including operating systems and hosts from IP, TCP, and UDP headers.

Basic Qualifications:

• 3+ years of experience with intelligence analysis
• Knowledge of the TCP/IP protocols
• Ability to perform basic protocol and network analyses
• TS/SCI clearance

Additional Qualifications:

• BA or BS degree in a related field
• Experience with advanced telecommunications, LAN, WAN, routers, data communications, and connectivity
• Experience with SIGINT and intelligence analysis
• Knowledge of data and telephony networking
• Knowledge of basic data flow, including the OSI model and router, hub, and switched communications
• Experience with UNIX, including writing and modifying scripts for text data manipulation
• Possession of excellent technical writing skills

Clearance:

Applicants selected will be subject to a security investigation and may need to meet eligibility requirements for access to classified information; TS/SCI clearance is required.

Another Booz Allen listing was for a "SIGINT Network Analyst" and described the duties as possibly including monitoring phone calls. The person selected, said the ad, would "evaluate and analyze complex data and telecommunications networks within SIGINT offices for high-profile government clients." It's a competitive field. SAIC also advertises for network intelligence analysts, and another firm, SPARTA, was looking for a "Digital Network Intelligence Analyst . . . to pursue access and exploitation of targets of interest."

Making up the surveillance-industrial empire are both high-profile Wall Street giants and little-known industrial park dwarfs. What they have in common is great profits from the NSA's very deep pockets—more than ever since the start of the post-9/11 eavesdropping boom. By 2007, excluding the military, the intelligence community's budget was $43.5 billion, about a third larger than during the pre-9/11 years. Adding in the military and tactical intelligence budget brought the total to about $60 billion.

With the billions pouring in, Hayden launched the largest recruiting drive in the agency's history. In 2003, the agency's recruiters logged more than 290,000 miles on 268 recruiting trips to 102 schools in forty-four states and one territory. The efforts produced 820 new employees in 2002, another 1,125 in 2003, and 1,500 in 2004. By 2008, 40 percent of the NSA's workforce had been hired since 2001.

At the same time Hayden was building his empire within Fort Meade, he was also creating a shadow NSA: of the $60 billion going to the intelligence community, most of it—about $42 billion, an enormous 70 percent—was going to outside contractors. To some inside the agency, it seemed that any idea, no matter how pie-in-the-sky, regardless of its impracticality in the real world, got funded. The numbers told the story. In October 2001, the NSA had 55 contracts let out to 144 contractors. But by October 2005, the agency had 7,197 contracts and 4,388 active contractors.

Quick to get their share were the usual wingtip Goliaths, Booz Allen, L-3 Communications, Lockheed Martin, SAIC, and Northrop Grumman. Once focused primarily on management strategy for corporate board-rooms in Manhattan skyscrapers, Booz Allen realized that as the government slimmed down, they had a great opportunity to fatten up. Thus, in 1992 they moved their headquarters to Tysons Corner, Virginia. Now more than half of the company's $4 billion a year comes from the U.S. Treasury. And since 2000, Booz Allen's revenue has doubled. It is also the size of a city; in 2007 the company planned to increase its workforce of eighteen thousand by another four thousand. Among the surveillance projects in which the company has been heavily involved was John Poindexter's Total Information Awareness program.

Like the military-industrial complex warned of by President Dwight D. Eisenhower, the surveillance-industrial complex that has grown up since 2001 is a cozy club made up of business executives with close, expensive contractual ties to the NSA. A quick-turning revolving door allows frequent movement between the agency and industry as senior officials trade their blue NSA badges for green badges worn by contractors. As with Booz Allen, many firms have discovered that the fastest way into the NSA's cipher-locked door is by hiring a former director or other top executive.

Thus SPARTA hired Maureen Baginski, the NSA's powerful signals intelligence director, in October 2006 as president of its National Security Systems Sector. Applied Signal Technology put John P. Devine, the agency's former deputy director for technology and systems, on its board of directors. Likewise, TRW hired the former NSA director William Studeman, a retired navy admiral, to be vice president and deputy general manager for intelligence programs. Cylink, a major company involved in encryption products, hired McConnell's former deputy director, William P. Crowell, as vice president. Crowell had been through the revolving door before, going from a senior executive position at the NSA to a vice presidency at Atlantic Aerospace Electronics Corporation, an agency contractor, and back to the NSA as chief of staff. Another deputy director of the agency, Charles R. Lord, left the NSA and immediately became a vice president at E Systems, one of the NSA's biggest contractors.

With about forty-four thousand employees each, SAIC and NSA are both heavyweights, and they have a decidedly incestuous relationship.

After first installing the former NSA director Bobby Inman on its board, SAIC then hired top agency official William B. Black Jr. as a vice president following his retirement in 1997. Then Mike Hayden hired him back to be the agency's deputy director in 2000. Two years later SAIC won the $280 million Trailblazer contract to help develop the agency's next-generation eavesdropping architecture, which Black managed. Another official spinning back and forth between the company and the agency was Samuel S. Visner. From 1997 to 2001 he was SAIC's vice president for corporate development. He then moved to Fort Meade as the NSA's chief of signals intelligence programs and two years later returned as a senior vice president and director of SAIC's strategic planning and business development within the company's intelligence group.

For many years, the surveillance-industrial complex was managed from a white two-story office building at 141 National Business Park, just down the street from the NSA's NBP 1. Behind the double doors to Suite 112 was a little-known organization called the Security Affairs Support Association (SASA), which, since its founding in 1980, had served as the bridge between the intelligence and industrial communities. From 1999 to 2002, SASA's president was Lieutenant General Kenneth A. Minihan, who retired as director of the NSA in 1999. Its executive vice president for many years was retired air force major general John E. Morrison Jr., a former head of operations at the NSA and long one of the most respected people in the intelligence community.

In 2003, with an influx of money as a result of the post-9/11 intelligence boom, the organization changed its name to the Intelligence and National Security Alliance (INSA). It also moved closer to the centers of power, establishing itself in a nondescript building in Ballston, a nexus between the intelligence agencies, the Pentagon, and the contractors. Once a year, first as SASA and now as INSA, the organization holds the spy world's equivalent of the Oscars when it hosts the William Oscar Baker Award Dinner. The gala black-tie event attracts the Who's Who of both the intelligence community and the contractors seeking their money. "The effectiveness of the U.S. intelligence and national security communities depends on strong relationships within the industry," said the former NSA director McConnell, a member of SASA and then chairman of INSA before being named director of national intelligence.

For decades, the local business community viewed the NSA mostly with suspicion. It was a secretive Goliath that ate up a great deal of electricity but mostly kept to itself. But following the 9/11 attacks and Hayden's wild spending spree, the county quickly saw dollar signs and wanted to get in on the action. With Hayden's blessing and encouragement, county officials and local business leaders got together to create an industrial "incubator" for the agency called the Chesapeake Innovation Center. The idea was to establish a county-funded magnet that would attract scores of high-tech start-up firms seeking to invent a better signal trap and then sell it to the NSA. A brochure created by the CIC to attract the companies pointed out that wiretapping was the wave of the future. "Wiretapping activity—the capturing of communications made by suspected terrorists or criminals," said the glossy twenty-three-page booklet, "will grow 20–25% per year as new high-speed data and packet-based networks generate incremental demand for wiretapping software. This market is at historically high levels."

Excited local business leaders soon began hoping the center might be a way to turn the Baltimore–Washington corridor into the Silicon Valley of eavesdroppers. "Tech leaders want NSA to become Greater Baltimore's National Institutes of Health," gushed one article, "a government research facility that fuels the formation of a critical mass of high-tech companies, much the way NIH played a big role in spawning Montgomery County's bioscience cluster . . . NSA riches are flowing to local firms. Columbia's Raba Technologies landed a contract in August potentially worth $100 million for signals intelligence work." One local businessman boasted, "We're just scratching the surface with NSA."

The Fort Meade area had become a Klondike for data miners. But like many promising mines during the Gold Rush, the CIC incubator, housed in a pricey, brick-and-glass building at 175 Admiral Cochrane Drive in Annapolis, came up largely empty. The facility quickly began filling its twenty-seven thousand square feet of floor space but few tenants had anything useful to sell. The first year the incubator lost $60,000, the second $457,000, and the third between $150,000 and $200,000. By 2007, the CIC was forced to collapse its organization to one-fifth its original size, reducing its floor space to just 5,400 square feet.

The problems that led to 9/11, however, were never a lack of money or technology. During the late 1990s, on Hayden's watch, there were few targets as important as the Yemen ops center. It was known to be connected to both the African embassy bombings and the USS *Cole* attacks as well as serving as bin Laden's communications hub—with hundreds of calls to him and from him. Yet for nearly a year the agency intercepted phone calls between the house in Yemen and the suspected terrorists in San Diego without ever discovering their city code or even country code. With an annual pre-9/11 budget of more than $4 billion a year, and a constellation of satellites and listening posts around the world, obtaining that metadata should have been well within the agency's capabilities. If it wasn't, there was something seriously wrong with the agency.

By late 2003, many in the Republican Congress began seeing Hayden's bills and were stunned at the number of zeros before the decimal points. Few had ever witnessed such reckless spending with so little to show for it. Thus, in a highly unusual move, they snatched away his checkbook and credit cards, stripping him of his acquisition authority. From then on, if the agency needed new pencils, he would have to requisition them from Pentagon auditors with green eyeshades and the key to the cashbox. "We want to make sure that taxpayers get the intelligence systems that are needed at the best possible cost," said a spokesman for Senator John W. Warner, the Virginia Republican who headed the Senate Armed Services Committee, which led the push for the legislation. "Speed is important, but getting the right systems at the right cost is just as important, and they are not mutually exclusive." It was a rebuke to Hayden, but his career still seemed headed straight up.

As the founder of SASA, sixty-five-year-old Leonard Moodispaw might be considered the father of the surveillance-industrial complex. Tall and balding with rimless glasses and a white mustache, the thirteen-year NSA veteran was the CEO of Essex Corporation, one of the many secretive NSA contractors at NBP whose profits had exploded since the start of the warrantless eavesdropping program. A key reason was Essex's specialty: fiber optics. Moodispaw has a hearty laugh and a penchant for loud floral prints. He does not fit the bland stereotype of an electronic eavesdropper; a self-proclaimed Jimmy Buffett "Parrothead," he has stuffed parrots hanging from the ceiling in his lobby and calls himself a "flaming liberal." "I refuse to use Reagan's name unless I'm throwing up," he says. And he's not too fond of George W. Bush either. "The Bush administration is a very vindictive organization," he scowls.

First established in 1969, Essex spent its first several decades engaged in human factors research—exploring the pros and cons of such things as a third rear stoplight on automobiles. But sales were slow and the outlook grim—until the company hired Moodispaw, who brought in others from the agency and placed the company inside the NSA's rarefied orbit. In 2000 Moodispaw was named CEO and the next year the company's profits were soaring past 400 percent. One of thousands of companies on the NSA's contractor base, Essex was among the elite 30 percent who were regularly awarded competition-free no-bid contracts. Also like many of the others, Essex was the NSA in microcosm. Its name was virtually unknown beyond the secret city and its NBP suburb; most employees had superhigh NSA clearances and lived in Laurel or one of the surrounding towns; and its office was a high-security SCIF.

In contrast to Booz Allen and the other giants in the NBP, Essex was representative of the many smaller companies that also populated the office park. Rather than the thousands of contracts with the agency that a company like SAIC might have, the small firms would have maybe a dozen, and they would usually be narrowly focused. Also, many of the smaller NSA contractors tended to be made up largely of former NSA employees. At Essex, for example, James J. Devine, the executive vice president, was formerly the NSA's deputy director for support services, and his predecessor, Stephen E. Tate, was chief of the NSA's Strategic Directions Team. Terry Turpin, the company's chief technology officer, had headed the agency's advanced processing technologies division, and the former NSA director Ken Minihan serves as advisor to the company.

While the company had a seven-thousand-square-foot office at NBP, its main laboratory was a few miles away in the company's large SCIF. There, a key focus was developing ways to pack ever more data into cables—phone calls, Internet packets, and imagery—without expanding their physical size. At the same time, because of the sensitivity of the information, a way had to be found to scramble the photons with an all-optical encryption device. Such technologies are essential for the NSA to securely transfer massive volumes of data from the point of collection to the point of analysis. One system Essex was working on was hyperfine WDM technology. According to Chris Donaghey, an analyst with SunTrust Robinson Humphrey, "At its most promising, Essex's optical networking capability can improve the current amount of data on a fiber-optic cable by a factor of one thousand." The company's first patent for the technology, awarded on August 19, 2003, was intriguingly titled "Optical Tapped Delay Line."

Once the mega-volumes of data are transmitted through the cable, the NSA has to find ways to process it. For that, Essex was exploring a variety of optical signal-processing techniques—a method that actually dates back to Bletchley Park in England during World War II. British code breakers used optical signal processing to solve the enormously complex German cipher machine called Enigma. Today, it allows the NSA to process mountains of information at mind-numbing speeds.

Like most anything else in the arcane world of the supercomputer, optical signal processing has its own unique unit of measurement when it comes to speed. It is known as a "flop," for floating point operations per second. Thus, where it may take the average person several minutes to calculate with a pencil the correct answer to a single multiplication problem, such as 0.0572 X 8762639.8765, supercomputers are measured by how many times per second they can solve such problems. If it takes a second to come up with the answer, including where to place the "floating" decimal point, then the computer would be said to be operating at one flop per second. A teraflop is a trillion operations a second.

On a bench in Essex's lab was a 10-teraflop processor about the size of a standard desktop. It ran, however, about ten thousand times faster, at ten trillion operations a second. "We've developed a very sophisticated test called the 'holy shit test,' " said Moodispaw. "One day we had three different sets of government customers come in to see what we could do. They all said, 'Holy shit, you can do that?' We're getting results nobody else can on the technology side."

Eavesdropping has become one of the hottest sectors in the marketplace. By 2005, Essex's revenue shot up to $159.8 million, more than double that of the previous year and nearly ten times that of 2003. Profit grew even faster, rising to $8.6 million from $2.3 million in 2004. As the company skyrocketed, picking up another $47 million top-secret contract from the NSA, Moodispaw took the company public and moved it into a new thirty-nine-thousand-square-foot headquarters in Columbia and a year later added another twenty-five thousand square feet. Like Pac-Man, he also began gobbling up other smaller NSA contractors, such as Sensys Development Laboratories Inc. and Windermere, whose CEO was another former NSA deputy director, Raymond Tate. Then there were more acquisitions, including Adaptive Optics in Cambridge, Massachusetts, for $40.3 million.

By 2006, Moodispaw's once tiny company had gone from fewer than fifty people in 1969 to nearly a thousand employees, with revenue projections of $250 million to $260 million. It had become the fifth-fastest-growing company in the Baltimore region, and the surveillance-industrial complex continued to sizzle with no end in sight. Finally ripe for the plucking, Essex itself was purchased at the premium price of $580 million by Northrop Grumman, one of the giants in the surveillance world. "For our shareholders," said Moodispaw at the end of his short but very profitable ride, "we have increased the enterprise value of the company from less than $20 million in 2000 to approximately $580 million under the proposed acquisition." It was a price Northrop Grumman could easily afford; a month before its announcement, in October 2006, the NSA awarded the company a $220 million contract for a massive, new advanced information management and data storage system. At the NBP, as champagne corks flew in both neighboring companies, the business of tapping had become one of America's leading growth industries.

There was no celebration on the other side of the continent, however. As Mark Klein studied his schematics of the peering connections, and the splitter cabinet, and the cloned cable, and the secret room, he had one more shock coming. "I was talking to a technician on the phone back east," he said, "and I was trying to troubleshoot a problem because I couldn't get the splitter to work right. This technician tells me, 'Oh, yeah, we're having the same problem with the splitters going into other offices.' My hair just stood on end when the person said that. And I said, 'Other offices?' And she said, 'Yeah, in Seattle and San Diego and Los Angeles and San Jose,' all having the same problem . . . From all the connections I saw, they were basically sweeping up, vacuum-cleaning the Internet through all the data, sweeping it all into this secret room . . . It's the sort of thing that very intrusive, repressive governments would do, finding out about everybody's personal data without a warrant. I knew right away that this was illegal and unconstitutional, and yet they were doing it."

Transit

In addition to communications to and from the U.S., broad streams of telecommunications that transit the country are another key target of the NSA—calls and e-mails from one part of the world to another that simply pass through a U.S. switch. It is a greatly increasing phenomenon, making up about one-third of all communications entering and leaving the country, and one NSA has quietly been attempting to encourage. One of the agency's "greatest advantages," said Lieutenant General Keith B. Alexander, Hayden's successor as director of the NSA, was "the ability to access a vast portion of the world's communications infrastructure located in our own nation."

The problem for Hayden was that although the people he was targeting were foreigners in a foreign country communicating with foreigners in another foreign country, because the signal was on a cable—a wire—the FISA court consistently ruled that he must first obtain a warrant. "The issue was international communications are on a wire," said Director of National Intelligence Mike McConnell, "so all of a sudden we were in a position, because of the wording in the law, that we had to have a warrant to do that . . . Now if it were wireless, we would not be required to get a warrant . . . We haven't done that in wireless [satellite communications] for years." He added, "If Osama bin Laden in Pakistan call[ed] somebody in Singapore, and it passed through the United States, they had to have a warrant." Indeed, today most domestic and international communications at one point pass through a wire, such as a buried or undersea fiber-optic cable.

McConnell gave a preview of the cumbersome process now required when foreign-to-foreign communication is intercepted over a cable. "It takes about two hundred man-hours to do one telephone number," he said. "Think about it from the judges' standpoint. 'Well, is this foreign intelligence? Well, how do you know it's foreign intelligence? Well, what does Abdul calling Mohammed mean, and how do I interpret that?' So, it's a very complex process. And now you've got to write it all up and it goes through the signature process, take it through the Justice Department, and take it down to the FISA court. So all that process is about two hundred man-hours for one number."

One example might be a person in Tokyo sending an e-mail at three in the afternoon to someone in Beijing—a very busy, and expensive, time for the message to pass through an Asian switch. As a result, the ISP in Tokyo might instead automatically route all messages to Beijing at that hour via AT&T's WorldNet switch in San Francisco, or one of its peering partners there. At ten in the evening West Coast time, the communications traffic in San Francisco would be greatly reduced, and thus lessen the chance for a delay. Also, the off-peak time would provide a significant price break. Because the communications travel at the speed of light, and since both Japan–U.S. and China–U.S. fiber-optic cables pass through the San Luis Obispo landing station, there would be no time delay caused by the extra ten thousand or so miles.

The same principle would be true for European and Middle Eastern communications connecting through U.S. East Coast switches. A call from Yemen to Pakistan might pass through MAE East in Virginia or the 60 Broad Street "carrier hotel" in New York City. A call from Madrid to Beijing might also transit both MAE East and MAE West as it crosses North America. Cost has always been a factor helping the NSA in this regard. Pricing models, established by the International Telecommunications Union, have largely remained unchanged since they were established over a century ago. Based on those tariffs, smaller, less developed countries charge more to accept calls than U.S.-based carriers, providing a cost incentive to route phone calls through the U.S. rather than directly to a nearby country.

Another incentive for the NSA is America's advanced telecommunications infrastructure. According to Ethan Zuckerman, a computer expert at Harvard's Berkman Center who has spent a great deal of time working on technology issues in Africa, a large share of even local intra-African communications passes through U.S. switches due to the lack of local ISPs. "Because the Internet access terminates on a different continent," he said, "it's likely that two people in the same African city communicating via e-mail are routing their packets through the U.S., traveling tens of thousands of kilometers out of the way to have a chat across town." McConnell, pleased to see America become the world's switchboard, agreed. "Today a single communication can transit the world even if the two people communicating are only a few miles apart," he said. That may be true even if the two people are in the same city in the U.S., according to the former NSA deputy director Bill Crowell. "I have seen a communication that went from Memphis to Pakistan to Japan to whatever in order to get to another phone in Memphis," he said.

Like those from Africa, nearly all Latin American communications, internal and external, pass through a U.S. hub. It's a phenomenon with which Alan Mauldin, a researcher for the firm TeleGeography, which tracks global Internet traffic, is very familiar. "The U.S. does continue to play a major role in connecting the regions of the world together," he said. "For example, Internet traffic going between Latin America and Asia or Latin America and Europe is entirely routed through the U.S." Mauldin said that in 2005, an estimated 94 percent of that "interregional" traffic passed through U.S. switches. "Basically they backhaul to the United States, do the switch, and haul it back down since it's cheaper than crossing their international borders," said Bill Manning, a member of the research staff at USC's Information Sciences Institute and managing partner of ep.net.

That Latin American traffic—millions of calls and e-mails an hour—is funneled through a single building at 50 N.E. Ninth Street in Miami. Occupying an entire square block on the edge of the downtown area, the pastel-colored six-story structure bears no signs, no name, and no windows—just painted facsimiles. On its roof are three massive satellite dishes hidden in golf-ball-like white radomes. A 750,000-square-foot telecom fortress, it has seven-inch-thick, steel-reinforced concrete walls, numerous hidden cameras, and biometric-controlled security portals. The building was even designed to withstand a Category 5 hurricane, with nineteen million pounds of concrete roof ballast. From the outside, it could easily be mistaken for an NSA building at Fort Meade.

Known as the "NAP [National Access Point] of the Americas," like MAE East and MAE West it is one of the country's major Internet Exchange Points. According to Norm Laudermilch, one of the executives of Terremark, which owns the facility, "about 90 percent of the traffic between North and South America goes through our facility in Miami." The building also serves as a crossroads for communications heading for Europe and beyond. "Switching the majority of South America, Central America and the Caribbean's layer-1, layer-2 and layer-3 traffic bound to more than 148 countries in the world," says its sales literature, "makes the NAP of the Americas the unrivaled gateway to the Americas."

From cities and towns throughout Latin America, the calls and Internet traffic are funneled to landing stations linked to South America Crossing (SAC), a large cable that circles the continent and is owned by Global Crossing. At Hamm's Bay, St. Croix, in the U.S. Virgin Islands, SAC feeds all this data into another of the company's cables, Mid-Atlantic Crossing (MAC), which serves Central America and the Caribbean. After coming ashore at a landing station in Hollywood, Florida, one branch continues on to New York and then Europe. The other travels underground from the beach in Hollywood to the NAP of the Americas building in Miami, where Global Crossing is colocated. Thus, with a setup similar to San Francisco's in place at NAP of the Americas, the NSA would have access to virtually all communications in South America, Central America, and the Caribbean, internal and external—one-stop shopping.

The actual setup of the interception would be easy since under an agreement with the government, Global Crossing was forced to engineer its facility to be surveillance friendly—readily accessible to federal eavesdropping operations. Known as a "Network Security Agreement," required in order for the company to obtain its landing license, Global Crossing promised to provide a capability at its location "from which Electronic Surveillance can be conducted pursuant to Lawful U.S. Process." The company also agreed to "provide technical or other assistance to facilitate such Electronic Surveillance" to, among other organizations, the Defense Department, the NSA's parent.

The agreement took advantage of a federal statute passed in 1994 known as CALEA—the Communications Assistance for Law Enforcement Act. The law requires communications companies to engineer their facilities so that their network can easily be monitored. It even requires the company to install the eavesdropping devices themselves if necessary, and then never reveal their existence. According to the statute, the government is required to first provide a warrant from a federal judge—one from the FISA court, for example. But under the Bush administration's warrantless surveillance program, they presumably could simply order the company to comply.

With its virtual alligator clips secure on the great American trunk line, by 2002 the NSA was ingesting about 650 million intercepts a day—voice and data—the same as the number of pieces of mail delivered every day across the country by the U.S. Postal Service.

Partners

As the agency wired the country, it was no less concerned with the rest of the world. For forty years, the Echelon infrastructure had been in place and worked well. Countries would communicate, their signals would be transmitted to a satellite, and the NSA or one of its counterparts in Canada, Britain, Australia, or New Zealand would catch them. Other signals would be captured by the NSA's geostationary satellites, positioned like sentries at four points over the earth. Once the phone and Internet data was captured, it would be run through "Dictionaries," powerful computers loaded with watch-listed phone numbers, names, addresses, words, and phrases. Based on that greatly reduced end product, reports would be written and sent to the NSA and other members of the Five Eyes group.

But now that at least 80 to 90 percent of communications were transiting the seabed instead of outer space, Echelon needed to be completely revamped. Each member had to work out a secret arrangement with its respective cable companies, secret rooms had to be built, cables needed to be spliced into, data had to be backhauled to analysis centers, and faster processing facilities had to be constructed. In addition, because some of the critical connections were beyond reach of the members—no longer could they just plant a dish on a remote island—new secret partnerships had to be worked out with countries along cable routes.

In countries where no cooperation could be obtained, the NSA or one of its partners would have to surreptitiously recruit someone at a telecom switch to install a bug, or, as a last resort, attempt to physically tap the fiber-optic cable itself. "The best way to do it is to get in the switching station on the land. Find out where they are, bribe whoever you have to bribe, get access," said one knowledgeable intelligence official. One key problem when tapping any cable, he said, is not knowing what's going over it until going to all the trouble of gaining access to it. "Sometimes we don't know what's on them, we don't know what the traffic is, so our intelligence, in terms of telling you what's on the line, sometimes is good, sometimes is terrible. So you may be facing a situation, you spend several hundred million dollars in a year preparing to go do something and you find out that the take sucks."

Although tapping into underground fiber-optic lines is much more difficult than tapping into a copper cable, the technique has been perfected by the NSA. For cables buried in foreign countries, the task of gaining access to them was given to a unique covert organization named the Special Collection Service (SCS), which combined the clandestine skills of the CIA with the technical capabilities of the NSA. Its purpose is to put sophisticated eavesdropping equipment—from bugs to parabolic antennas—in difficult-to-reach places. It also attempts to target for recruitment key foreign communications personnel, such as database managers, systems administrators, and IT specialists.

The SCS is a key link in the NSA's transition from a traditional focus on information "in motion" to information "at rest." Since the first transatlantic intercept station was erected on Gillin farm in Houlton, Maine, just before the close of World War I, Sigint has concentrated on intercepting signals as they travel through the air or space. But as technology makes that increasingly difficult and cost prohibitive, the tendency, say senior intelligence officials, will be to turn instead to information "at rest"—the vast quantity of information stored on computer databases, discs, and hard drives. This may be done either remotely through cyberspace or physically by the SCS.

As encryption, fiber optics, the Internet, and other new technologies make life increasingly difficult for the NSA's intercept operators and code breakers, the SCS has greatly expanded and taken on an increasingly important role. "Yesterday's code clerk is today's systems administrator," said one very senior CIA official. The easiest way to a large amount of secret information is to get into foreign databases, and the best way to do that is to recruit—through bribes or other offers—the people who manage the systems. Also, by bribing someone to plant bugs in the keyboards or other vulnerable parts of a computer network, the NSA can intercept messages before the cryptographic software has a chance to jumble the text.

The position of SCS chief alternates between NSA and CIA officials. The service is headquartered in a heavily protected, three-hundred-acre compound consisting of three boxy low-rise buildings with an odd, circular park walled in between them. Located at 11600 Springfield Road in Laurel, Maryland, nine miles south of the NSA, the facility is disguised as a tree-lined corporate campus. In front is a sign with the letters "CSSG" that seems not to have any meaning. Inside, in what is known as "the live room," the electronic environment of target cities is re-created in order to test which antennas and receivers would be best for covert interception. Elsewhere, bugs, receivers, and antennas are incorporated into everyday objects so they can be smuggled into foreign countries. "Sometimes that's a very small antenna and you try to sneak it in," said former CIA director Stansfield Turner. "Sometimes the signal you're intercepting is very small, narrow, limited range, and getting your antenna there is going to be very difficult."

While in some places the NSA or SCS has compromised a nation's entire communications system by bribing an engineer or telecommunications official, in others much of the necessary eavesdropping can be done from special rooms in U.S. embassies. But in difficult countries clandestine SCS agents must sometimes fly in disguised as businesspeople and covertly implant the necessary eavesdropping equipment. The person might bring into the target country a parabolic antenna disguised as an umbrella. A receiver and satellite transmitter may be made to appear as a simple radio and laptop computer. The SCS official would then camouflage and plant the equipment in a remote site somewhere along the microwave's narrow beam—maybe in a tree in a wooded area or in the attic of a rented farm house. The signals captured by the equipment would be remotely retransmitted to a geostationary Sigint satellite, which would then relay them to the NSA.

In order to obtain access to fiber-optic cables in noncooperative or hostile foreign countries, the SCS would trace the cable to a remote area and then dig a trench to get access to it. Then the person would place an advanced "clip-on coupler" onto the cable. These commercially available devices, used to test fiber-optic systems, produce a microbend in the cable that allows a small amount of light to leak through the polymer cladding shell. The light can then be captured by a photon detector, a transducer that converts the photons into an electrical signal. This then connects to an optical/electrical converter that is plugged into a port on a laptop fitted with software allowing for remote control. Packed with super-long-life batteries, the entire system can be reburied with a camouflaged line running up a tree to an antenna disguised as branches. Signals from the bug can then be transmitted to an NSA satellite while remote-control instructions are broadcast back down to the computer. All of the equipment needed is commercially available.

To tap undersea fiber-optic cables in the Middle East and elsewhere, the navy secretly renovated the Seawolf-class submarine USS *Jimmy Carter* for such operations. In December 1999 Electric Boat was awarded a $887 million contract to extensively modify the sub with a special forty-five-meter-long section for "surveillance, mine warfare, special warfare, payload recovery and advanced communications." The sub would likely set down on the bottom over the cable while a special NSA team pulled it aboard in the newly installed section, tapped into it, and returned it to the bottom attached to a breakaway pod. A cable could then be covertly laid from the pod to a hidden shore location for clandestine transmission back to Fort Meade. The only problem is it hasn't yet worked. "Can't do it—doesn't have the ability to tap in. Won't be able to for a long time, if ever," said one knowledgeable intelligence official. "Tapping the cables underwater is extremely hard. I mean, it's hard enough doing it on land, but it's extremely hard to do it underwater. It's not like copper cable where you just go out and put something on it."

Fortunately for the NSA, industrial-strength cable tapping has always been a big business for countries around the world—and the agency has often been a beneficiary. In Britain, siphoning telegrams and later e-mail from incoming and outgoing cables has a long tradition, and GCHQ and the NSA have always been the closest of trading partners. In the 1960s, all cable traffic entering and leaving the United Kingdom was scrutinized by a special department of the post office, which controlled the cable system. "On the morning after they have been sent or received," said one report, "they are collected and sifted by a Post Office department concerned with security. Then any cables believed to be of special interest are passed to the Security Services. They are studied there, copied if necessary, and returned to the Post Office, which owns the former Cable and Wireless Company. Cables passed through private companies—mainly branches of foreign concerns operating in Britain—are collected in vans or cars each morning and taken to the Post Office security department. The probe is conducted under a special warrant, signed by a Secretary of State under Section 4 of the Official Secrets Act and regularly renewed to keep it valid." While communications technology has certainly changed since the 1960s, there is no indication that either the British policy or Section 4 of the Official Secrets Act has changed.

Just as the NSA and GCHQ are now attempting to find ways into the new world of fiber-optic cables, they faced similar challenges at the dawn of the satellite age forty years earlier. It was a time of enormous change; the U.S. and the UK would be directly connected for the first time, by both satellite and undersea cable. In 1962 the British Post Office Satellite Communications Station at Goonhilly Downs in Cornwall came online and its ninety-foot satellite dish began tracking Telstar, the world's first communications satellite. But because of Telstar's low orbit, communications could only be transmitted and received as the satellite passed overhead every 158 minutes.

The following year, the first submarine cable directly linking the two countries was completed. Known as TAT-3, the cable ran from Tuckerton, New Jersey, to Widemouth Bay near Bude in Cornwall. Then in April 1965, the first geostationary communications satellite, INTELSAT 1, nicknamed "Early Bird," was launched. At 22,300 miles in space over the equator, it was able to maintain a fixed position between the two continents. This allowed, for the first time, direct and continuous communications between Goonhilly Downs and the U.S. satellite ground station in Etam, West Virginia. Rapidly, other nations around the world began building ground stations and communicating with one another via Early Bird.

GCHQ needed no help from the NSA obtaining the communications coming over TAT-3. Since the UK end of the cable was under the control of the post office, it simply obtained the traffic directly from them—possibly at a GCHQ facility near the Bude landing station. The cable was one of the few communications links between countries in Europe and North

America and therefore proved a rich source of intelligence. But now much of Europe and beyond was bypassing England and communicating directly through Early Bird to other parts of the world. Without satellite dishes to intercept those signals, that widening stream of intelligence was out of GCHQ's reach—until the NSA came to the rescue.

At the time, the NSA was building its own satellite interception base at Sugar Grove, West Virginia, about fifty miles from Early Bird's downlink at Etam. Seeing the value in a worldwide network of such dishes—the eventual Echelon operation—the NSA agreed to help finance and build the station for GCHQ. The place chosen was Bude, possibly to place it near an existing interception facility for the TAT-3 cable. Today Widemouth Bay is the landing point for TAT-14 and a number of other major fiber-optic cables.

Once the two ninety-foot dishes at Bude were completed in the late 1960s, the director of GCHQ at the time, Sir Leonard Hooper, sent his personal thanks to NSA director Marshall "Pat" Carter. In his note he suggested that the original two dishes should be named after Carter and his deputy, Louis Tordella. "I know that I have leaned shamefully on you, and sometimes taken your name in vain, when I needed approval for something at this end," Sir Leonard wrote. "The aerials at Bude ought to be christened 'Pat' and 'Louis'!" Hooper added, "Between us, we have ensured that the blankets and sheets are more tightly tucked around the bed in which our two sets of people lie and, like you, I like it that way."

Sitting high above the Celtic Sea on the edge of Sharpnose Point, Bude today has nearly a dozen dishes pointed at various satellites, spanning the Indian Ocean to the South Atlantic. Since the opening of the space age, Goonhilly Downs had been a key link for Britain in satellite communications. But in 2008 the station was closed down. That left Madley, a village in Herefordshire about fifty miles from GCHQ headquarters, as the country's major satellite gateway.

After initial sorting at Bude, the intercepts are transmitted over an encrypted fiber-optic cable 171 miles northeast to a boxy, thirty-year-old building at GCHQ's Oakley complex in Cheltenham, Gloucestershire. There in X Division they are run through supercomputers, including a Cray 3, before being transferred by cable another four miles across town to the organization's new high-tech facility at Benhall. In 2004, most of Oakley and the agency's original headquarters at Benhall were destroyed by the wrecking ball as the new Benhall center opened for business. By then the supercomputers were also supposed to have been moved to the new facility. The massive undertaking, at a cost of $120 million, would have been the most expensive and delicate move in British history.

But as the transfer was about to take place, there was great concern that the critical flow of intelligence would be interrupted. In particular, it would have been impossible to monitor mobile phone chatter between suspected terrorists. Instead, it was decided to leave the machines in place at Oakley, along with several hundred staff, and spend $616 million on a fiber-optic cable linking the two centers. Over the following seven years, as the banks of supercomputers become obsolete, new machines will be installed directly at Benhall and thus guarantee continuity.

At the new center, the reams of intercepts would undergo final analysis by the agency's cryptolinguists, code breakers, and data miners and other members of the staff. Based on what information was contained in the messages and phone calls, the analysts would write up reports and forward them to the NSA and the other members of the Five Eyes pact.

Completed in 2003, GCHQ's $660 million new headquarters totaled 1.1 million square feet and covered 176 acres. It replaced more than fifty buildings on several sites. Many of the structures were huts similar to those that covered Bletchley Park, the secret World War II code-breaking center where the German Enigma code was solved. Far from Bletchley's solemn, monastery-like environment, the new GCHQ is a marvel of space-age construction. Made with steel, aluminum, glass, granite, Cotswold limestone, wood, and concrete, it is built in the shape of a modernistic silver-colored doughnut. The "hole" at the center is an open-air garden the size of London's Albert Hall. Inside the building are enough copper computer cables to stretch all the way to Rio de Janeiro, and surrounding the doughnut are parking lots with about twenty-nine hundred spaces.

The radical design by the British architect Chris Johnson was also intended to help foster interaction in a population known for security paranoia and eyes-lowered introversion. "It's a huge change for an organization whose traditional mentality was 'Shut the door behind you, and make sure no one follows you,' " he said. "They worked in an environment with their blinds down and doors locked. Not many people knew who their coworkers were, and there was no real sense of community or belonging." So today, although the building contains one million square feet of space stretched over four floors, the doughnut shape means that each employee is never any more than a five-minute walk from any colleague. Also included inside the doughnut is a six-hundred-seat restaurant, a health club, and a museum.

Security was also a key feature in the design, with eight inches of blast cladding fitted to all outer walls. As a further precaution, the deeper one goes into the doughnut, the higher the clearance required. And while the agency remains the blackest of Britain's spy agencies, it is also striving to be the greenest. The shell of each office chair is made from thirty-six large recycled plastic soft drink bottles; desks and table surfaces are made from 90 percent recycled wood; and all steel products are made from 30 percent recycled metal.

Though it was originally built to hold about four thousand people, the number of personnel crowding into the doughnut is now about fifty two hundred as a result of the buildup following the attacks on 9/11 and the London bombings in 2005. In an effort to attract new Web-savvy recruits, GCHQ has turned to ad campaigns within online computer games such as Tom Clancy's Splinter Cell Double Agent and Rainbow Six Vegas. And to find talented cipher-brains, the agency joined with the British Computer Society to sponsor a code-breaking competition called the National Cipher Challenge. Conducted on the Internet and lasting three months, the game involved cracking coded messages passed between Lord Nelson and naval intelligence as they tried to block a plot by Napoleon to obtain a mysterious Chinese weapon. To add to the complexity of the plot, the secret to the mystery lay in the encrypted two-hundred-year-old writings by the Elizabethan spy Christopher Marlowe.

GCHQ's biggest need, like that of the NSA, was for linguists, and in one recruitment pitch, the agency said it was seeking candidates fluent in Albanian, Amharic, any other African languages, Arabic, Azeri, Baluchi, Basque, Bengali, Brahui, Bulgarian, Chechen, Chinese, Dari, Georgian, Greek, Gujerati, Hindi, Indonesian, Japanese, Kashmiri, Kazakh, Korean, Kurdish-Sorani, Macedonian, Malay, Mirpuri, Nepali, Papiamento, Pashto, Patois/Creoles, Persian, Polish, Potohari, Punjabi, Romanian, Serbo-Croat, Shona, Somali, Swahili, Tamil, Turkish, Ukrainian, Urdu, Uzbek, and Vietnamese.

By 2007, Britain's security and intelligence budget had more than doubled to $4.2 billion from less than $2 billion before September 2001.

At $1.6 billion, GCHQ was the most expensive part of that budget, yet it was still overstretched. According to a report by the Parliamentary Intelligence and Security Committee, a key factor was the agency's continuous need to support MI5's domestic terrorism investigations. One of those was Operation Overt, a huge surveillance and intelligence effort targeting two cells of suspected Islamic militants who were believed to be plotting an attack on transatlantic airliners.

In light of these domestic terrorism threats, there has been a strong effort by the British attorney general to allow intercepts from GCHQ to be introduced in court as evidence during trial of terrorism suspects. But the move is greatly opposed by GCHQ officials, who claim the measure would jeopardize its intelligence collection techniques and divert substantial resources to prepare transcripts of thousands of hours of phone conversations for court cases. "GCHQ is, not unnaturally, nervous that its techniques might get into the public domain," said Shadow Home Secretary David Davis. Agreeing with Davis was Sir Swinton Thomas, whose odd title was Interception of Communications Commissioner. "The number of cases where intercept material would make a substantial difference are very few indeed or possibly even nonexistent," he said. And GCHQ officials told members of Parliament, "So far we do not believe that anything proposed passes the test of doing more good than harm."

Another problem is the long delay in developing a secure communications system to connect GCHQ with the other intelligence agencies and their overseas offices. Known as Scope, the system was supposed to be in place by 2004 but has now been delayed for another five years.

Leading the charge against using intercepted data in court was Sir David Pepper, who was named director of GCHQ in February 2003. Quiet and balding, Pepper spends his spare time taking long walks through the Cheltenham countryside, experimenting in the kitchen, and listening to music. With a doctorate in theoretical physics from St. John's College, Oxford, more than thirty years at "the Q," and a specialty in information technology, Pepper was the perfect technospy. Even though his agency was already outgrowing its new doughnut-shaped home, he knew it was destined to get fatter yet as MI5, the Security Service, continued to expand its domestic counterterrorism activities. By 2007, over two hundred domestic extremist groups, and some two thousand individuals, were being investigated by MI5. But as the GCHQ packed more and more eavesdroppers and analysts into the doughnut, the quality of the intelligence went down.

"How much we need to grow will depend more or less on how much ministers decide to grow the Security Service," said Pepper, who planned to retire in July 2008, after five years as head of GCHQ. "So our CT [counterterrorism] capability will need to keep pace so we can support the number of operations there that they are running . . . By the end of the year we had found that we were managing to support most of Security Service's highest-priority operations, but we were not achieving the quality of support that we and they had agreed we should aim for . . . essentially because we were spreading ourselves too thin . . . We do not have enough CT resources."

The biggest problem, according to Pepper, was the ever-expanding Internet and especially the increasing use of the Internet for phone calls. These VoIP calls frustrate the eavesdroppers at GCHQ because they bypass the traditional telecom hubs and gateways, such as Bude, that are piped to the agency. "The Internet uses a very different approach to communications," said Pepper, "in that, rather than having any sense of fixed lines like that, there is a big network with a number of nodes, but for any individual communicating, their communications are broken up into shorter packets. So whether you are sending an e-mail or any other form of Internet communication, anything you send is broken up into packets. These packets are then routed around the network and may go in any one of a number of different routes because the network is designed to be resilient . . . This [represents] the biggest change in telecoms technology since the invention of the telephone. It is a complete revolution."

In order to bring some relief to GCHQ, the Intelligence and Security Committee, which oversees the spy agencies, developed a Sigint modernization program. This included a twentyfold increase in the agency's ability to access, process, and store Internet and telephone data. It also led to "the automation of certain aspects of the analysis of communications, allowing improved identification of networks—a task that previously had to be performed manually. As a result, analysts now have more time to interpret the data and establish its significance."

The number of people in Britain whose communications were targeted had exploded in recent years. According to the 2007 report by the Interception of Communications Commissioner, the watchdog office that oversees eavesdropping by the intelligence community, over 439,000 requests were made to monitor people's telephone calls, e-mails, and letters by secret agencies and police departments in just over a year. The report also revealed that nearly four thousand errors were reported in a fifteen-month period. The author of the report, Sir Swinton Thomas, described the figures as "unacceptably high." Human rights groups labeled the revelations as signs of a "creeping contempt for our personal privacy."

Stretched along the curving Middle East seabed, the FLAG Falcon cable comes ashore in a number of countries with high intelligence value. Connecting Egypt to Mumbai, India, it traverses Oman, Bahrain, Kuwait, Qatar, and others. Of most interest to the NSA, however, are Iran, Iraq, Sudan, and Yemen, all of which have either joined or are eager to soon do so. The agency had long targeted Iran's nine Intelsat and four Inmarsat earth stations, and its microwave links to Turkey, Pakistan, and Afghanistan, but the thought of much of that traffic being transferred to a subsea cable has many at Fort Meade nervous.

Containing 120,000 voice and data circuits, the $1.2 billion cable is owned by FLAG (Fiber-optic Link Around the Globe), the world's largest private undersea cable system, with a vast network spanning forty thousand miles. Upon the completion of its newest cable, FLAG NGN, the company will soon have the capacity to carry a massive 2.5 billion simultaneous voice calls and 300 million simultaneous webchats in sixty countries on four continents. It is the Gulf region's most powerful cable, operating at a terabit per second, and its ring shape also provides redundancy, known as a self-healing capability.

For the NSA, as the Middle East seabed becomes layered with cables, it must begin establishing secret relationships with countries outside its exclusive Five Eyes club, something that is already happening, according to Keith Coulter, who, from 2001 until 2005, was director of the Canadian member of the group. According to Coulter, the Five Eyes "form the tightest and most historical partnership that we have had. It is strong." But, he noted, times are changing and his agency and the other members must also begin forming other cooperative arrangements. "The group," he said, "has been longstanding and successful but the world is evolving and so other partnerships are necessary, on our part and our allies' part. I belong to a European group that includes a number of countries, among which there is some sharing because there is much interest in terrorism."

Probably the best place within the entire region to install a listening post is the Indian city of Mumbai. It represents the kind of location where the NSA would seek to establish a secret presence; it is also an example of how many people may now be tapping into private phone calls and e-mail worldwide. From a listening post in Mumbai, eavesdroppers could listen to conversations between Europe and Asia, for example.

Mumbai contains the central switch for virtually all the cables in the Middle East and much of Asia, including FLAG, FLAG Falcon, SEA-ME-WE 3, and SEA ME-WE 4. SEA-ME-WE 3 alone is the longest system in the world at over twenty-four thousand miles—the distance around the earth. It has thirty-nine landing points in thirty-three countries on four continents, from Western Europe (including Germany, England, and France) to the Far East (including China, Japan, and Singapore) and Australia. Some of the cables connecting in Mumbai also have links to Iran, Pakistan, and other countries of great interest to the NSA.

The Mumbai switch is owned by VSNL, part of the Indian government. A few years ago the Indian NSA, Research and Analysis Wing (RAW), proposed tapping into it, according to Major General V. K. Singh, a former top official for RAW. "Sometime in 2000–2001," Singh said, "someone in RAW proposed that monitoring equipment should be installed at the VSNL gateway in Mumbai. When I joined RAW in November 2000, the project was still being discussed." VSNL, he added, "agreed to provide the facilities for installation of the interception equipment, but expressed misgivings about the presence of RAW personnel and equipment in its premises, which were frequently visited by foreign members of the consortium [that owned the cables]."

To alleviate the company's concern, RAW suggested that the company buy and install the equipment themselves and then apply for reimbursement from the intelligence agency. But while the company found the arrangement agreeable, Singh himself was troubled. "I had felt uneasy about the project right from the beginning," he said. "It would have been okay if we were going to intercept traffic going from or coming to India. One could always justify this on the ground that we wanted to monitor traffic related to terrorism . . . But the SMW 3 [Southeast Asia–Middle

East–Western Europe cable] was also carrying traffic that had nothing to do with India. What right did we have to monitor a call between a person in Germany who was talking to someone in Japan? . . . I expressed my misgivings several times . . . What we were planning to do was clearly another form of illegal interception. In fact, it was worse because we would not only be violating our own but also international laws. I was surprised when I found that other people in RAW not only disagreed but scoffed at my ideas."

General Singh was relieved when VSNL became privatized and was sold to the very large Indian company the Tata Group, thinking that the new company would not want to get involved in illegally spying on its customers. "But apparently this did not happen," he said. Agreements between the company and the government were signed. Singh left RAW in 2004, and he does not know if it is continuing. "But the fact that it was planned and approved raises many questions," he said. "Intelligence agencies need to be reminded, occasionally, that they are working not for themselves but the country and its citizens, who must never be humiliated by their actions."

More recently, the Indian government has become alarmed at the re- alization that BlackBerry users are able to evade its digital dragnet when sending e-mail. As a result, the government gave the four domestic mo- bile operators offering the service a deadline to detail precisely how they route their users' messages or have the system terminated. It is a preview of what may eventually happen in other democracies, including the U.S., as eavesdropping becomes all encompassing.

A key problem for New Delhi officials is the fact that BlackBerry's encrypted e-mail passes through servers all based outside the country. The system is licensed to India's mobile operators by Research in Motion (RIM), a Canadian company so confident in the security of its encryp- tion that it considers it virtually unbreakable. "Rumours speculating that [e-mail] can be intercepted and read by the National Security Agency in the U.S.," RIM has claimed, "or other 'spy' organisations are based on false and misleading information." In an extraordinary move, in an effort to resolve the impasse and prevent the mobile e-mail service from being shut down, Canada's electronic spies have agreed to help India's RAW intercept the BlackBerry messages.

Whether the NSA currently has its own equipment at the Mumbai landing station is unknown, but among the tools the Bush administration uses to get governments to cooperate in its eavesdropping operations are cash, equipment, and political pressure. The administration has recently used all three with Mexico, a country with an atrocious record of police corruption, torture, and human rights abuses. The State Department's Human Rights Report for 2006 said Mexico's "deeply entrenched culture of impunity and corruption persisted, particularly at the state and local level. The following human rights problems were reported: unlawful killings by security forces; kidnappings, including by police; torture; poor and over-crowded prison conditions; arbitrary arrests and detention; corruption, inefficiency, and lack of transparency in the judicial system; statements coerced through torture permitted as evidence in trials; criminal intimidation of journalists, leading to self-censorship; corruption at all levels of government; domestic violence against women often perpetrated with impunity; criminal violence, including killings against women; trafficking in persons, sometimes allegedly with official involvement; social and economic discrimination against indigenous people; and child labor."

There is also a long tradition of illegal eavesdropping in Mexico, especially on opposition political leaders. One case was accidentally discovered in 1998 in Campeche, a city on the Yucatán Peninsula surrounded by ancient Spanish walls and fortifications used centuries ago to protect the population from pirates and buccaneers. One night after sunset, Layda Sansores Sanroman rapped on the door of an old concrete house at the center of the city. When a janitor opened it, she walked into a government espionage center. Lining the back room walls were racks of electronic eavesdropping equipment. Another room was crammed with seven years' worth of transcripts from telephone taps—thousands of pages of private conversations from politicians, journalists, and everyday citizens.

"I was furious to discover my life on papers, documents, recordings and computer files," said Sansores, a fifty-two-year-old senator from an opposition political party who had been tipped off by an anonymous note. "Seven years of my life were there, tracked in detail." She and her aides later discovered that the equipment had been purchased by the government for $1.2 million from Israel.

More than a dozen other examples of systematic government eavesdropping around the country were also discovered about the same time—from hidden cameras and microphones uncovered in the offices of the

Mexico City government to interceptions of telephone calls by a state governor. "The discoveries—and the willingness of the targets to go public with evidence—confirmed many Mexicans' long-held suspicion that their government has acted as an omnipresent Big Brother spying on its citizenry, its perceived enemies and, frequently, on some of its own agencies and officials," said one news report at the time.

"Everything I say and do, I assume that I am being spied on," said Guanajuato state governor Vicente Fox, who would later be elected president, and whose phones were also tapped. Mariclaire Acosta, the president of the Mexican Commission for the Defense and Promotion of Human Rights, expressed a view felt by many. "It is a horrible, filthy method of political control," she said. "It's a fundamental violation of the right to privacy." She added that she was also a regular target of wiretaps. "The life of everybody in town is there."

Aware of Mexico's abysmal record in both human rights and in electronic surveillance, in 2006 the Bush administration entered into a quiet agreement with the Mexican government to fund and build an enormous $3 million telephone and Internet eavesdropping center that would reach into every town and village in the country. According to a State Department document used to solicit vendors for the system, the United States would provide Mexico "with the capability to intercept, analyze, and use intercepted information from all types of communications systems operating in Mexico." The document continued:

The U.S. Government intends to procure a communications intercept system that enables the timely receipt, processing, analysis, and storage of intercepted communications from the national telephonic and other communications service providers in Mexico. The proposed system must comply with the following AFI [Agencia Federal de Investigaciones, Mexico's Federal Investigative Agency] stated requirements for interception of target calls and sessions from (1) TELMEX PSTN network, through analog lines, (2) TELCEL TDMA and GSM network, (3) NEXTEL iDEIM/GSM network, (4) TELEFONICA network, (5) UNEFON network, (6) IUSACELL CDMA network and TDMA network, (7) Existing CISCO VoIP network at customer's premises, (8) packet data from the Mexico PRODIGY ISP network. Additionally the client desires the establishment of a central monitoring center with the capabilities of (1) real-time and off-line playback, (2) fax decoding, (3) packet data decoding, (4) storage of all calls for at least 25,000 hours, (5) storage of all session related information, (6) 30 monitoring stations and 30 printers, (7) cellular location and tracking. Capabilities must include TDMA, GSM, CDMA, iDEN, AMPS, PCS, landline, FAX, Email, chat, Internet, SMS and VoIP. The communications intercept system must include all necessary hardware, software and equipment required to provide a complete solution. Proposals must include pricing for the complete system, installation of the system, training in Spanish on use of the system and technical support.

The system the Bush administration wanted for Mexico was similar to its warrantless eavesdropping operation in the U.S. "The target phone database should be able to accommodate a maximum of 8,000,000 sessions," it added, "programmable by telephone service provider and monitoring center operators." The surveillance center would also have "the ability to generate a data bank for voices for the analysis of comparison, recognition and identification." This would give the center the capability to scan millions of telephone calls using voice prints of their targets. Another innovation was the ability to bring under surveillance ever widening circles of people—not just the target, but whoever called the target and then whoever called that person, and so on. "The ability," said the proposal, "to analyze calls (call crossovers) and the automatic generation of links between them." The system was also required to reach every phone in the country. "The Contractor shall be responsible," said the document, "for integrating into the telephone intercept system the required plans and maps of the entire Mexican Republic."

The deal underscores the close relationship between the country's conservative president, Felipe Calderon, and George W. Bush. In addition to the installation of the Bush administration's countrywide bugging system, Calderon was also attempting to amend the Mexican Constitution to allow the government to eavesdrop without a judge's approval under various conditions. While he argued that he needed the system and the freedom from court scrutiny in order to fight drugs and organized crime, many in Mexico were not buying it. Among them was Renato Sales, a former deputy prosecutor for Mexico City, who compared Calderon's plan to the Bush administration's warrantless eavesdropping program. "Suddenly anyone suspected of organized crime is presumed guilty and treated as someone without any constitutional rights," he said. Now a law professor at the Autonomous Technological Institute of Mexico, Sales added, "And who will determine who is an organized crime suspect? The state will."

Both sides have tried to avoid drawing attention to the agreement, however, because of the potential hostile reaction by the Mexican public to the possibility that all their phone calls and e-mail might be analyzed and stored not only by their own government but also by intelligence agents in Washington.

For the Bush administration and the NSA, there may be some significant strings attached to the offer to wire Mexico border to border and coast to coast with a free $3 million eavesdropping system. Most important, the U.S. will get full access to the data, possibly in a way similar to the setup with AT&T in San Francisco. It is the type of deal NSA may be working out with countries around the world as part of an Echelon II–style operation. A key problem with such a worldwide system is that it would supply countries with potentially even worse human rights and privacy records than Mexico with a critical means of internal repression.

The strings attached are contained in the part of the proposal labeled "Requirements." One of these items is a requirement "to disseminate timely and accurate, actionable information to each country's respective federal, state, local, private, and international partners." Since the U.S. certainly qualifies as an "international partner," it means Mexico is obligated to disseminate its data to a U.S. agency. But what is perhaps even more troublesome is the requirement to share its data with "private" partners—in other words private surveillance companies within the U.S.

This type of arrangement with Mexico and other countries may in fact be among the most secret parts of the Bush administration's entire warrantless eavesdropping program. That is because it completely bypasses the requirement for probable cause that one of the parties is connected to al-Qaeda. The intercepted data is gathered by Mexicans in Mexico—much of it involving calls to and from Americans across the border—and passed in bulk to the U.S., possibly to the NSA or FBI or Drug Enforcement Administration. Rather than al-Qaeda, it might involve drugs. According to a number of legal scholars, it may even be possible to introduce this type of information in U.S. courts. The protections offered by the Fourth Amendment, they say, do not apply outside the United States, especially when the surveillance is conducted by another country.

An indication of this can be seen in the evasive answers to questions put to the NSA general counsel Robert Deitz in 2006 by Congressman Robert C. Scott, a Virginia Democrat, during a congressional hearing. Scott attempted to pin Deitz down on whether there was a second, more secret element to the warrantless eavesdropping operation. "Is there another program?" he asked. "I mean you are using twenty questions. We are trying to get around to, if I can ask the right question, to target the right answer. Are you wiretapping people without an individual assessment of probable cause that they are a member of al-Qaeda or without a warrant?" Deitz responded, "I can't answer that." Nor did he volunteer to provide an answer in closed session.

But coming to his rescue was Steven G. Bradbury, the Justice Department point man on the warrantless surveillance program, who chose his words very carefully. "Well, if I might just jump in, Congressman. I think the president has made it clear that there is no other program that involves *domestic electronic surveillance of domestic communications,* and so the program that the President has described is the only program along those lines" [emphasis added]. By deliberately adding that caveat, "domestic" electronic surveillance, Bradbury appeared to be leaving open the possibility of foreign electronic surveillance of U.S. domestic communications.

Using non–U.S. citizens in a foreign country to evade the law and eavesdrop on Americans is not a new idea. In the 1970s, the Bureau of Narcotics and Dangerous Drugs (BNDD)—the predecessor of the Drug Enforcement Administration—was unable to obtain a judicial warrant to eavesdrop on a group of Americans within the U.S. As a result, they secretly turned to the NSA and asked them to conduct the illegal eavesdropping on their behalf. The NSA agreed, but the agency was nervous about giving the watch list containing the U.S. names to its intercept operators at the U.S. listening post (probably Sugar Grove, West Virginia). Because they were mostly military, they were worried about frequent turnover of personnel and the risk of the operation leaking out. Thus they asked the CIA to give help in conducting the eavesdropping with the watch list, which they agreed to do.

However, when the cooperation was discovered by the CIA's general counsel, Larry Houston, it was abruptly called to a halt. In Houston's opinion the activity possibly violated Section 605 of the Communications Act of 1934, prohibiting the unauthorized disclosure of private communications. He concluded, too, that since the intercepted messages were eventually given by the NSA to BNDD, the activity was for law enforcement purposes, which was outside the CIA's charter. As a result of Houston's memorandum, the CIA suspended any further collection.

But according to the NSA's deputy director at the time, Louis Tordella, the major reason for the CIA pullout was that the phone calls were being intercepted from American soil. "I was told that if they could move a group of Cubans up to Canada," Tordella said, "it would be quite all right, but they would not do it in the United States." Rebuffed by the CIA, the NSA continued the operation itself. A few years later it was among the many illegal programs uncovered by the Church Committee that led to FISA. Now the idea may have returned. If so, countries like Mexico and Britain could target American communications with their own nationals, on their own territory, and pass the information to the NSA.

Canada, however, despite Tordella's suggestion, seems an unlikely candidate to assist the NSA in spying on Americans, despite sharing our northern border. Since the very beginning, Canada's highly secret Communications Security Establishment (CSE) has been a key member of the Five Eyes partnership. During the Cold War, the organization played a large role in monitoring Soviet submarine and shipping activities in the Arctic. Then in August 2001 Keith Coulter became director and moved into his office in the Edward Drake Building, a modern six-story reinforced concrete and steel structure in the shape of a Y. Set in a modern, parklike landscape at the crest of a hill on Ottawa's Bronson Avenue, it was once the home of the Canadian Broadcasting Corporation. Today it pulls signals in rather than sending them out.

A onetime fighter pilot with the Snowbirds, the Canadian Forces Air Demonstration Team, and later a planner with the Treasury Board, Coulter was in office for just five weeks before the attacks of 9/11. Almost overnight, he was forced to put his agency into overdrive, to quickly move it into the twenty-first century. "Throughout the 1990s as CSE moved further away from its Cold War focus, the pace of change in the telecommunications world moved from evolutionary to truly revolutionary," he said. "The routing of messages became unpredictable. Anything could be anywhere in this new communications landscape." Coulter added, "Further, in the new environment, communications were moving in complex bundles that had to be mapped and analyzed before acquisition was even possible."

Another problem was legal—the CSE was prohibited from eavesdropping on not only domestic communications but also international, where one end of a conversation touched Canada. The law, Coulter said, "affected CSE in two ways. First, it prevented CSE from intercepting communications that an intelligence target abroad sent to or received from Canada. For example, CSE could not provide intelligence on a known terrorist group abroad if it was communicating with a member or accomplice in Canada. Second, this provision prevented CSE from intercepting any communications that might contain private communications. The difficulty here was that, in this new technological environment where anything could be anywhere in virtually endless communications haystacks and electronic highways, it was impossible for CSE to prove, before it acquired a communication, that both ends of the communication would be foreign. The result was that as technologies continued to evolve, CSE was increasingly unable to access valuable intelligence sources. By the time of the events of 9/11, all of CSE's international partners—the U.S., Britain, Australia, and New Zealand—had already found ways to deal with this issue. CSE was being left behind."

To catch up, Coulter was able to obtain changes in Canada's Anti-Terrorism Act that allowed CSE to begin targeting foreigners and foreign organizations abroad. "The act," he said, "allowed CSE to get back into the game . . . The authority that was given to us by Parliament allows us to get at that very rare but important call between, say, a terrorist group and a Canadian. It may be of international as well as national importance because of relationships."

But unlike the NSA's policy of warrantless targeting of Americans, CSE's ear is still welded to its base pointed outward. According to Coulter, his organization is forbidden from targeting Canadians either at home or abroad. "CSE is prohibited from directing its activities against Canadians or anyone else located within the twelve-mile limit that defines Canadian territory," he said. "CSE is also prohibited from directing its activities at Canadians abroad, defined in the act as Canadians or permanent residents." In addition, a National Defense Headquarters instruction also forbids domestic eavesdropping.

Coulter indicates that CSE, once seen as little more than the NSA's Canadian stepchild, has become more independent. He says the CSE even refuses to share with the NSA any communications touching Canadian territory, such as the international fiber-optic cables entering and leaving Pennant Point, near Halifax, Nova Scotia, or the satellite gateways at Pennant Point, Laurentides in Quebec, and Lake Cowichan in British Columbia. "We do not share with the United States anything that would involve one-end Canadian. I want to make it very clear, that is not something we do," he said. "The kind of thing we collect, that very small volume of information that we have that has an end in Canada, is shared within Canada and not within our partnership community." In fact, in 2003, during the United Nations Security Council debate over whether to invade Iraq, the NSA asked all Five Eyes countries to target the communications between diplomats on the Council. Canada, which had opposed the invasion, was the only member to refuse.

Today, CSE's budget has skyrocketed from the years before the 9/11 attacks, going from $140 million in 2000 to more than $200 million by 2007. It also increased its personnel by 80 percent to about 1,700.

To house them, the agency is constructing a new $62 million (Canadian dollars), 65,000-square-foot headquarters building in Ottawa. During the Cold War, one of the CSE's most important listening posts was in the far north at Alert, on the northeastern tip of Ellesmere Island in the Nunavut territory. The northernmost permanently inhabited settlement in the world—only about 450 miles from the North Pole—Alert was the perfect place to eavesdrop on the northernmost reaches of the Soviet Union because it was closer to Moscow than to Ottawa. There were about 215 intercept operators and support personnel posted there during the station's heyday. But the demise of the Soviet Union meant the end of Alert.

To eavesdrop on the Pacific, a station was established at Masset, at the top end of Graham Island off British Columbia. And the Atlantic region was monitored by a station at Gander in eastern Newfoundland. But in the late 1990s, both stations were, like Alert, largely shut down. They focused on high-frequency communications and the world had shifted to satellites and fiber-optic cables. Thus, what is left of the three stations is now remotely controlled by the CSE's principal listening post at CFS

Leitrim, located at 3545 Leitrim Road in Gloucester, just south of Ottawa. Originally opened in 1941, the station now has 450 military personnel and twenty-eight civilian employees and targets satellite communications with four radome-covered dishes behind the main building.

The current chief of CSE is sixty-six-year-old John L. Adams, who replaced Keith Coulter in July 2005. He dislikes the Orwellian image some people have of his agency. "I get very concerned about this 'Big Brother is watching me.' Nothing could be further from the truth," he says. The major problem, according to Adams, is volume. Even "with all of your fancy electronic filters," he says, "Big Brother would just be overwhelmed." Adams then gives the numbers. "There are one billion Internet users online right now," he says. "Over fifty billion e-mails are sent every day. The sheer volume, the variety, the velocity, the complexity of communications today would make this absurdly impossible. Especially for an organization of our small size."

Like Coulter, Adams also says that there are no agreements between the NSA and CSE to spy on each other's citizens. "There are all sorts of myths about CSE," he says. "One is that we ask our partner organizations in the Five Eyes community to target Canadian communications for us, or that we target their citizens for them. I can tell you that we do not."

An odd choice for chief, Adams had spent his career in the Canadian army largely as a bureaucrat and generalist. The five years prior to taking over the electronic spy agency he spent as a senior official in the fisheries and ocean department of the Coast Guard. In fact, prior to his appointment he didn't even know what the organization did. "It's very much a need-to-know business, and I didn't need to know, so I didn't know."

For those countries beyond the Five Eyes, without an NSA or a CSE or a GCHQ, there are a few companies that will build them the next best thing.

Wiretappers

Just across busy Interstate 395 from the Pentagon, Crystal City is a beehive of overweight contractors, military personnel in ill-fitting civilian clothes, and spooks behind Ray-Ban aviation-style sunglasses. In restaurants, walking down sidewalks, or filling up at gas stations, nearly everyone has a stack of playing-card-size badges hanging on black straps around their necks. Prestige is measured not in the make of their jeans, or the cut of their suits, but by the color and number of their badges, worn like battle ribbons from some secret war.

Once a desolate land of junkyards, drive-in movie theaters, used-car lots, and towing companies, crisscrossed by rusted railroad tracks, this area was transformed by the developer Robert H. Smith in the 1960s. Hoping to give his new community a fresh image, he hung an elaborate crystal chandelier in the lobby of the first building and named it Crystal House. Thereafter, every other building took on the Crystal theme—Crystal Gateway, Crystal Towers—until the entire area became Crystal City. Like the nature of the work that goes on there, much of the city is hidden from view.

On one level, Crystal City is a modern vertical village of sixty thousand daytime workers cocooned in odd-shaped dominos of glass, brick, and cement. Bland office towers connect to bland hotels that connect to bland no-name government high-rises. But below the buildings, streets, and sidewalks is a hidden, underground city of chophouses and flower-decorated boutiques, sushi dens and shoe repair shops. It is a place where people just back from the Green Zone bump into one another and others on their way to Afghanistan pick up electric transformers and have their body armor tailored.

Crystal City was thus an ideal venue for the Wiretappers' Ball. Known formally as the Intelligence Support System World Conference, it is a once-a-year secretive conclave of engineers and scientists in search of the ultimate bug. It is the place to come to discuss the latest developments in mass surveillance, how to listen in on entire continents at the least cost, and the best ways to tap into—or shut down—the newest Internet phone system. Picking up shiny brochures at booths and listening to the lectures are an assortment of doctoral-level computer scientists; electrical engineers with decades in the telecom business; government agents from superpowers and mini-states, democracies and dictatorships; and wealthy venture capitalists and start-up owners trying to impress them. The one group conspicuously absent is anyone even remotely connected to the media—a policy enforced by linebackers with earplugs and bulges under their blue blazers.

In 2006, the three-day Wiretappers' Ball was held in Crystal City's Hilton in late May. A sense of the atmosphere can be gleaned from the highly confidential program of lectures. On Monday, May 22, at 4:00, one could attend a talk on "Combining Data and Voice over Broadband into a Unified Interception Solution" given by an employee of Verint Systems. On Tuesday at 1:30, another Verint employee addressed "Broadening the Scope of Interception: Data Retention." A half hour later an employee of Agilent Technologies spoke about "Comprehensive Data Extraction for Flexible and Accurate Intelligence." Then at 2:45, still another Verint worker discussed "Comprehensive Solutions for Packet Data Collection: DEEPVIEW." "Verint's DEEPVIEW," said the description of the talk, "is a packet data collection system with the comprehensive functionality to penetrate deep into communications and turn raw, intercepted data into actionable intelligence and compelling evidence."

And on Wednesday, at 10:15, an employee of NICE Systems addressed the topic of "Unifying Telephony, VoIP and IP Interception for a Complete Overview of Your Target's Interactions." For those still awake, another Verint worker then took on the topic of "Challenges of Implementing Passive Interception for IMS [Instant Message Systems]." Next, the company NSC discussed locating keywords in masses of information in a lecture titled "NSC Spotter." "NSC's Key-Word Spotting (KWS) engine," said a company employee, "is designed for locating predefined words in audio conversations in real-time and off-line calls. The engine is used for speech analytics and call surveillance."

This hidden-from-view bugging industry got its start as a result of the passage of CALEA in 1994. The law mandated the telecom companies to configure their networks to supply the government with intercepts authorized by a court-issued warrant. But following the attacks on 9/11 and President Bush's secret order to begin massive warrantless eavesdropping, the industry began a period of explosive growth. Not only were sales booming, so was the competition to build bigger and better "mass surveillance systems" that incorporated both nationwide interception capabilities and advanced data-mining techniques. Once built, the systems were sold to whoever would buy them, including some of the most repressive and authoritarian governments on the planet.

Closer to home, America's two major telecom companies, AT&T and Verizon, have outsourced the bugging of their entire networks—carrying billions of American communications every day—to two mysterious companies with very troubling foreign connections. In AT&T's secret room in San Francisco, a mirror image of all data entering the building is filtered through surveillance equipment supplied and maintained by Narus. Verizon, which controls most of the rest of the country's domestic and international communications networks, chose a different company. According to knowledgeable sources, that company is Verint.

According to these sources, in 2006 Verizon constructed its "secret room" on the second floor of a nondescript two-story building at 14503 Luthe Road in Houston, Texas. Once Verizon receives watch-listed names from the NSA, it then reroutes their Internet communications into that room, which is packed with secret Verint machines and software. After passing through the Verint hardware, the messages are then transmitted in real time to a central government surveillance hub in Sterling, Virginia.

Run by the FBI, the hub is a newly built annex for the bureau's Engineering Research Facility (ERF), located on the grounds of the FBI Academy in Quantico, Virginia. Among the technologies developed by ERF is Carnivore, later given the more benign-sounding name DCS-1000, which is a sophisticated Internet "packet sniffer." While Verint and Narus sift through traffic at key Internet gateways around the country, Carnivore, or one of its successors, is used when the target has been narrowed down to a smaller, individual ISP. Thus, if Verint detects that a target is a subscriber to a small California-based Internet provider, the FBI can install its DCS-1000 at the company's office to record his activity. The device can also transmit the data back to the FBI in real time. An encrypted T1 cable connects the ERF Annex in Sterling directly to the NSA at Fort Meade.

Follow-on projects to the DCS-1000 include the DCS-5000, which is designed for FISA surveillance; the DCS-3000 for pen register (a device used to record all numbers dialed from a tapped phone) and trap-and-trace taps; and the DCS-6000, nicknamed Digital Storm, which intercepts the contents of phone calls and text messages. Once the information is sent back to the ERF, it is indexed and prioritized by the bureau's Electronic Surveillance (ELSUR) Data Management System. Other eavesdropping tools in the FBI's toolbox include a collection of intrusive spyware such as CIPAV, which stands for Computer and Internet Protocol Address Verifier. The program can be remotely implanted into a target computer to secretly send back to intelligence agents key details about the machine, including its IP address, operating system type, Internet browser, and a list of active programs. The CIPAV then transforms itself into a cyber pen register, logging the address information of every computer with which it comes into contact and then transmitting the details back to the ERF Annex in Sterling.

Another remotely installed and operated program, Magic Lantern, has the capability of recording and transmitting back in real time the target's every keystroke. Both spyware programs have likely been used on foreign targets, but only CIPAV appears to have been used domestically thus far. It was implanted in a target's MySpace account, and when he opened it, it launched in his system.

While Verizon's data network is centrally tapped at Luthe Road in Houston, it appears that the voice network is monitored from the company's sprawling facility on Hidden Ridge Avenue in Irving, Texas, near Dallas. It is there that the company's Global Security Operations Center keeps tabs on the entire Verizon system, looking for fraud. According to a sworn affidavit by Babak Pasdar, a computer security expert who has worked as a contractor for a number of major telecoms, he discovered a mysterious DS-3 line at the heart of one company's system—a link labeled "Quantico Circuit." His description of the company and the link seems to match that of Verizon as outlined in a lawsuit against the company. "The circuit was tied to the organization's core network," Pasdar said. "It had access to the billing system, text messaging, fraud detection, website, and pretty much all the systems in the data center without apparent restrictions." He added, "Everyone was uncomfortable talking about it."

While such tools as DCS-1000 and CIPAV are used on a small number of select targets, Verint and Narus are superintrusive—conducting mass surveillance on both international and domestic communications 24/7. What is especially troubling, but little known, is that both companies have extensive ties to a foreign country, Israel, as well as links to that country's intelligence service—a service with a long history of aggressive spying against the U.S. Equally troubling, the founder and former chairman of one of the companies is now a fugitive, wanted by the FBI on nearly three dozen charges of fraud, theft, lying, bribery, money laundering, and other crimes. Although there has long been Congressional oversight of the telecom industry, there is virtually no oversight of the companies hired to do the bugging.

Verint was founded by a former Israeli intelligence officer, Jacob Alexander, who often goes by the nickname "Kobi." His father, Zvi Alexander, was a wealthy Israeli oil baron and an international wheeler-dealer who ended up running the country's state-owned oil company. To win drilling franchises, he would make political payments to African cabinet ministers, often in partnership with the U.S. tax cheat Marc Rich, who became a fugitive and was given sanctuary in Israel. In his autobiography, the senior Alexander ridiculed America for criminalizing the bribery of foreign officials. The U.S., he wrote, is "very sanctimonious" and "refuses to accept the facts of life in the developing world."

Like his father, Kobi was also interested in making millions. After earning a degree in economics from the Hebrew University of Jerusalem in 1977 and spending several years in Israeli intelligence, he moved to New York, where he worked as an investment banker at Shearson Loeb Rhoades (now Smith Barney) while attending New York University at night for his MBA in finance.

Soon after completing his degree in 1980, Alexander returned to Israel and formed a voice- and fax-messaging company with two other Israelis,

Boaz Misholi and his brother-in-law, Yechiam Yimini. Called Efrat, the start-up was financed in part with subsidies from the Israeli government. Four years later, the three returned to New York and opened a company called Comverse, which was also incorporated in Israel. Its name a blend of "communications" and "versatility," Comverse became heavily involved in wireless technology, voice-mail software, and other areas of the telecom sector.

While deal making was taking place in the U.S., the secretive research and development was done in Comverse Technology's Israeli headquarters. Surrounded by sushi bars, gourmet coffee places, and a kosher McDonald's, the research center and other facilities are located in a cluster of seven buildings on Habarzel Street in Tel Aviv's high-tech Ramat Hahayal industrial park. In Israel, Alexander had become widely celebrated for his telecom fortune. "Kobi was an Israeli hero, one of our real high-tech pioneers," said Ron Tira, a Tel Aviv–based mutual fund manager with investments in Comverse.

One of the new products being developed in Tel Aviv was a digital surveillance device called AudioDisk that could monitor and record hundreds of telephone and fax machine lines simultaneously. The machine made the old reel-to-reel tape recorders obsolete: the data could be stored in "jukeboxes" and be available to the user instantly. The use of digital technology also meant that a key word or phrase could be located immediately, rather than by rewinding the tape to the right spot. The system was a major hit with intelligence agencies and police units in the U.S. and around the world, and ended up bringing in half of the company's revenues in 1993. Eventually, the business was spun off into a separate subsidiary called Comverse Infosys.

The security surge that followed the attacks on 9/11 sent the value of the company skyrocketing. Five months after the attacks, Alexander renamed the subsidiary Verint Systems, Inc. (short for Verified Intelligence), took over as chairman, and made plans to take it public. Named president and CEO was Dan Bodner, a former Israeli army engineer with degrees from the Technion and Tel Aviv University, and nearly fifteen years of experience at Comverse.

Soon, Verint was selling its "actionable intelligence solutions" to "more than 5,000 organizations in over 100 countries" around the world, according to the company, including the most repressive. For Kobi Alexander the war on terror was a boom time. He purchased a number of expensive condominiums in a luxury high-rise on New York's West 57th Street, bought a 25 percent stake in Tel Aviv's basketball team, entertained clients at Knicks games at Madison Square Garden, and bragged he could borrow oodles of money with a few business ideas scribbled on a napkin. No matter how much he had, Alexander's deep pockets could always hold more—and he decided the U.S. was the place to get it.

As his Israeli engineers in Tel Aviv built bigger and better bugs, Alexander wanted to attract the rapidly expanding U.S. intelligence community. He thus placed the former NSA director Lieutenant General Ken Minihan on the company's "security committee" and soon the NSA and other parts of the spy world were signing on. Then came the contract to install its machines at the heart of the Verizon network, the nation's second-largest telecom company. The Verint system chosen was STAR-GATE.

"With STAR-GATE," says the company's sales literature, "service providers can access communications on virtually any type of network, retain communication data for as long as required, and query and deliver content and data . . . Designed to manage vast numbers of targets, concurrent sessions, call data records, and communications, STAR-GATE transparently accesses targeted communications without alerting subscribers or disrupting service. Verint partners with leading switch and network equipment vendors across the globe to deliver passive, active, and hybrid solutions for a wide range of communication services and communication technologies . . . STAR-GATE can easily be customized to operate with any switch or storage platform type, model, or software version and can be easily integrated into any environment. Its modular architecture facilitates simple upgrade or adaptation to meet the demands of new communication protocols and technologies."

During a conference call with investors, company president and CEO Dan Bodner gave some examples of how customers used the company's mass interception equipment. One sounded like the NSA: "A multimillion-dollar expansion order for our Communications Interception Solution for an international government agency customer. This government customer is deploying our solution to enhance national security by improving its ability to intercept information, collect it from wireless, wireline, and cable networks." Another sounded like Verizon. "Examples of recent or-

ders for Verint's STAR-GATE solution for service providers include . . . a
multimillion-dollar expansion order for a U.S. wireless service provider."
Another could be Mexico or another of Verint's one hundred country customers. "An order for our Communications Interception Solution for a
new government agency customer in a new country for Verint. This new
customer is deploying our solution country-wide to enhance the national
security by intercepting and analyzing mass amounts of voice and data
collected from wireless networks."

Thus, by 2004, a large percentage of America's—and the world's—
voice and data communications were passing through wiretaps built,
installed, and maintained by a small, secretive Israeli company run by
former Israeli military and intelligence officers. Even more unnerving is
the fact that Verint can automatically access the mega-terabytes of stored
and real-time data secretly and remotely from anywhere, including Israel.
This was revealed in a closed-door hearing in Australia, another one of
Verint's customers. The hearing was held because Verint's system had
been called "a lemon" by the Australian government and they were about
to get rid of it. In a last-minute attempt to salvage the contract, company
executives flew to Australia to plead their case.

One of the problems that most concerned a government watchdog
group, the Corruption and Crime Commission (CCC) Subcommittee,
was the fact that while they themselves had difficulty getting access to
the intercepted data, Verint was accessing the data remotely from thousands of miles away. "The CCC," said subcommittee member Graham
Giffard, "has some issues," including "the fact that your company is
foreign owned . . . and that you can access data from overseas but the
CCC seems restricted in its ability to access data within that system." Zvi
Fischler, the company's Tel Aviv–based vice president for marketing and
sales, admitted the company conducts such activities. "We sometimes
operate by remote access," he said. "We connect to the system from remote in order to download some software." The explanation didn't seem
to satisfy the Australian officials, however, and Fischler agreed to stop.
"If the CCC finds it inappropriate to allow such access, we will of course
not do it this way," he said.

At the time, Verint in Australia was tapping only phone calls, but
Fischler offered to expand the monitoring system to include the Internet.
"Specifically addressing additional capacity," he said, "one issue could be

increasing the capacity in terms of number of interceptions. That is easily done. It could be done in a matter of a few weeks. Another upgrade that has already been offered is to increase the capacity to intercept different types of traffic that [are] not intercepted now. I mentioned broadband Internet access from the Internet service providers. We have indeed offered this kind of capacity increase."

While Verint can provide mass interception of data and phone calls, one of its Israeli spinoffs, PerSay, can go one step further and offer "advanced voice mining." The company, based in Tel Aviv, employs a system "that efficiently searches for a target's voice within a large volume of intercepted calls, regardless of the conversation content or method of communication." Thus, with remote access to the internal and international voice and data communications of over one hundred countries around the world, including the United States, Verint's headquarters in Tel Aviv has a capability rivaled only by NSA's, if not greater, especially when coupled with PerSay's voice-mining capability.

PerSay is an example of how close and interconnected these companies are with Israel's intelligence community—a factor of great concern considering how much of their bugging equipment is now secretly hardwired into the American telecommunications system. Among those on PerSay's board of directors is Arik Nir, a former senior official in Shin Bet, Israel's internal security service. Nir is also the managing director of PerSay's financial backer, Athlone Global Security, which counts former Mossad chief Ephraim Halevy on its advisory board. Athlone was one of the companies in the NSA's "incubator," the Chesapeake Innovation Center in Annapolis, Maryland.

Although there is no evidence of cooperation, the greatest potential beneficiaries of this marriage between the Israeli eavesdroppers and America's increasingly centralized telecom grid are Israel's intelligence agencies. "There is a huge, aggressive, ongoing set of Israeli [intelligence] activities directed against the United States," a former intelligence official told *Los Angeles Times* reporters Bob Drogin and Greg Miller in 2004. "Anybody who worked in counterintelligence in a professional capacity will tell you the Israelis are among the most aggressive and active countries targeting the United States." The former official discounted repeated Israeli denials that the country exceeded acceptable limits to obtain information. "They undertake a wide range of technical operations and human operations," he said. "The denials are laughable." In 2005, Lawrence A. Franklin, a senior Pentagon official, pled guilty to spying for Israel, and in 2008 two top officials of Israel's U.S. lobby, AIPAC, are scheduled for trial on similar charges.

The agency responsible for worldwide eavesdropping in Israel is the hypersecret Unit 8200, that country's NSA. "Unit 8200 is the technology intel unit of the Israeli Defense Forces Intelligence Corps," said Unit veteran Gil Kerbs. "In Israel," he said, "one's academic past is somehow less important than the military past. One of the questions asked in every job interview is: Where did you serve in the army? . . . When it comes to high-tech jobs, nothing can help you more than the sentence, 'I'm an 8200 alumnus.' "

According to a former chief of Unit 8200, both the veterans of the group and much of the high-tech intelligence equipment they developed are now employed in high-tech firms around the world. "Cautious estimates indicate that in the past few years," he told a reporter for the Israeli newspaper *Ha'aretz* in 2000, "Unit 8200 veterans have set up some 30 to 40 high-tech companies, including 5 to 10 that were floated on Wall Street." Referred to only as "Brigadier General B," he added, "This correlation between serving in the intelligence unit 8200 and starting successful high-tech companies is not coincidental. Many of the technologies in use around the world and developed in Israel were originally military technologies and were developed and improved by Unit veterans." Having both trained alumni of the organization and sophisticated eavesdropping equipment developed by Unit 8200 in foreign countries would be an enormous intelligence windfall, should Israel be able to harness it.

Retired Brigadier General Hanan Gefen, a former commander of Unit 8200, noted his former organization's influence on Comverse, which owns Verint, as well as other Israeli companies that dominate the U.S. eavesdropping and surveillance market. "Take NICE, Comverse and Check Point for example, three of the largest high-tech companies, which were all directly influenced by 8200 technology," said Gefen. "Check Point was founded by Unit alumni. Comverse's main product, the Logger, is based on the Unit's technology."

Check Point, a large Israeli-based company that sells firewalls and other Internet security software from an office in Redwood City, California, was founded by Unit 8200 veteran Gil Shwed. Today the four years he spent in the Unit go virtually unmentioned in his official biography. In 2006, the company attempted to acquire the firm Sourcefire, whose intrusion-prevention technology is used to protect the computer assets of both the Pentagon and NSA. Because of the potential for espionage, the deal set off alarm bells at the NSA and FBI and it was eventually killed by the Committee on Foreign Investments in the U.S., an oversight board. Alan T. Sherman, a specialist in information assurance at the University of Maryland, Baltimore County, noted the potential for "information warfare" was likely. "It's easy to hide malicious [software] code. Sometimes it just takes a few lines of malicious code to subvert a system." Nevertheless, despite the fact that many of the NSA's and the Pentagon's sensitive communications—like those of the rest of the country—travel across the tapping equipment of Verint and Narus, their links to Israel seem to have slipped below the radar.

The large Israeli firm NICE, like Verint and Narus, is also a major eavesdropper in the U.S., and like the other two, it keeps its government and commercial client list very secret. A key member of the Wiretappers' Ball, it was formed in 1986 by seven veterans of Unit 8200, according to the company's founder, Benny Levin. "We were seven people from the Unit," he said, "we all worked on a project for more than four years, we knew each other very well. We had very good complementary skills." Like a page out of Orwell, all their high-tech bugging systems are called "Nice." Nice Perform, for example, "provides voice content analysis with features such as: word spotting, emotion detection, talk pattern analysis, and state-of-the-art visualization techniques." Nice Universe "captures voice, email, chat, screen activity, and essential call details." Nice Log offers "audio compression technology that performs continuous recordings of up to thousands of analog and digital telephone lines and radio channels." And Nice VoIP "can use both packet sniffing and active recording methods for recording VoIP sessions (both by telephone and Internet)."

In 2006, Yiar Cohen, a brigadier general who served as head of Unit 8200 from 2000 to 2005, became chairman of the board of the Israeli company ECtel. Two years earlier, Verint had purchased that company's "government surveillance business" for $35 million. According to SEC documents filed by ECtel, "Our surveillance solutions enabled governmental agencies to perform real-time, comprehensive surveillance on telecommunications networks. We sold this business to Verint Systems in

March 2004." Verint said of the purchase, "The acquisition will provide Verint with additional communications interception capabilities for the mass collection and analysis of voice and data communications . . . These technologies will be integrated into Verint's portfolio of communications interception solutions and offered to Verint's global customer base."

That base, said Verint, included "new customers in new countries for Verint in the Asia Pacific and Latin America regions." Dan Bodner, president and CEO of Verint, noted the long and close relationship with ECtel. "We have been working with ECtel as a partner for a number of years and our knowledge of their products and familiarity with their employees will better enable us to integrate ECtel's communications interception business with Verint's operations."

ECtel's Cohen, who was head of Unit 8200 at the time of the 9/11 attacks, is also vice president of another Israeli telecom company, Elron. He noted the importance of placing veteran electronic spies from Unit 8200 in Israeli high-tech firms. "I think there's an axiomatic assumption that Unit alumni are people who bring with them very high personal and intellectual ability," he said. "They have a common background, and they know that 8200 has the privilege of sorting, choosing, and selecting the best group so that you don't have to invest so much in the selection yourself. I myself, after I came to Elron, brought five additional alumni with me." The ultimate winner in such an arrangement, according to Cohen, was Israel's economy. "Although 8200 doesn't directly enjoy the fruits, the state of Israel does, and in my opinion that's a complementary part of the Unit's task."

Unit 8200's revolving door with industry appears similar to that of the NSA. As both electronic intelligence organizations grow ever more dependent on the corporate world to conduct their eavesdropping, the line between government and industrial espionage blurs. This presents great opportunity for co-mingling personnel.

Similar to Verint, Narus was formed in November 1997 by five Israelis, with much of its money coming from Walden Israel, an Israeli venture capital company. At the time, most of the founders were working for the Israeli company VDOnet, which specialized in live video broadcasts on the Internet. Based in the Israeli city of Herzliya, the company also had offices in the Silicon Valley town of Palo Alto, California, not far from where Narus planted its flag in Mountain View. Among the five was Stanislav Khirman, a husky, bearded Russian who earned degrees in math at Ukrainian universities from 1980 to 1988. The next four years of his résumé are blank, but in 1992 he began working for Elta Systems, Inc. A division of Israel Aerospace Industries, Ltd., Elta specializes in developing advanced eavesdropping systems for Israeli defense and intelligence organizations. At Narus, Khirman became the chief technology officer.

Among the group of Israelis, Ori Cohen, a balding, dark-haired engineer with a PhD in physics from Imperial College in London, became president and chairman. He had spent a few years as CEO of IntelliCom Ltd., a company of which there is no record, and then became vice president of business and technology development at VDOnet with Khirman. That is all the information he has ever released about himself and, like Khirman, he makes no mention of his Israeli military service, if any. It seems the man whose system invades the privacy of hundreds of millions of Americans tries very hard to keep his own. Chief executive officer of Narus is Greg Oslan, who previously worked for a company owned by Haim Harel, an Israeli who spent much of his career specializing in electronic intelligence systems at the large Israeli defense firm Tadiran.

Thus, virtually the entire American telecommunications system is bugged by two Israeli-formed companies with possible ties to Israel's eavesdropping agency—with no oversight by Congress.

Also troubling are Verint's extremely close ties to the FBI's central wiretapping office, known as the CALEA Implementation Section (CIS). The CIS had long fought for greater access to the telecommunications switches—the same switches that Verint was tapping. The action by CIS was strongly resisted by the telecom industry and privacy groups who argued that the bureau was attempting to greatly exceed its legal mandate. "The FBI is committing the kind of dirty tricks more characteristic of scofflaws than cops," said a commentary in the industry publication *Wireless Week*. Taking aim at an FBI-crafted amendment to the wiretapping law, the article warned, "The proposed amendment would have created frightening police powers to track wireless users and prevented judicial or regulatory review of FBI compliance methods for telecommunications carriers." Al Gidari, a lawyer representing the wireless industry, said the FBI's list of requirements amounted to "the Cadillac of wiretaps." He added, "Everything they could ever think of to gold plate and put on the Cadillac was in that document."

The head of the FBI's liaison office with the telecom industry during much of the period leading up to implementation was David Worthley. What concerns many in the industry is that shortly after Worthley was removed from his liaison job in June 1997, he turned up as president of the Verint unit that sold its eavesdropping equipment and services to the FBI, NSA, and other agencies. The company set up its offices in Chantilly, Virginia—directly next door to the CIS and Worthley's old office. Thus, the company that secretly taps much of the country's telecommunications is now very closely tied to the agency constantly seeking greater access to the switches. This concern over the cozy relationship between the bureau and Verint greatly increased following disclosure of the Bush administration's warrantless eavesdropping operations. At the same time that the tappers and the agents have grown uncomfortably close, the previous checks and balances, such as the need for a FISA warrant, have been eliminated.

But as earphone-clad FBI agents were listening for terrorists and criminals through Verint's taps, top executives from the company and its parent, Comverse, were themselves engaging in an orgy of theft, bribery, money laundering, and other crimes.

For Kobi Alexander, chairman of Verint and CEO of Comverse, summers meant vacation and vacation often meant visiting relatives in Israel. Thus on June 28, 2006, as fierce rainstorms swept up and down the mid-Atlantic region, he, his wife, and their young daughter headed for Kennedy International Airport and a flight on El Al Airlines to sunny Tel Aviv. But unlike other trips back to his homeland, this time he sent ahead some extra cash: $57 million. Also unlike other vacations, this time it was going to be a one-way trip.

For Alexander, the storm clouds had been hovering overhead for months. On the other side of Manhattan, the Justice Department was in the final stages of preparing a thirty-two-count indictment charging him with masterminding a scheme to backdate millions of Comverse stock options. It was a crime, prosecutors say, that allowed Alexander to realize $138 million in profits—profits stolen from the pockets of the company's shareholders. The indictment also named as co-conspirators Comverse chief financial officer David Kreinberg, forty-one, and general counsel William Sorin, fifty-six. In addition, the trio of executives was accused of creating a secret slush fund to distribute options to favored employees,

options that could be exercised overnight for millions in profits. For Alexander, the charges had the potential of putting him away in prison for
as long as twenty-five years, and leveling fines and penalties of more than
$150 million.

To many who knew him, Alexander was the poster child for arrogance
and greed. "The one thing about Kobi is that he did have a sense of entitlement," said Stephen R. Kowarsky, a former colleague. "Most people
are a little bit shy or self-effacing about asking for something, but not
Kobi. It was easy for him to say, 'I want that. I deserve that.' "

In 2001, Alexander was the fourth most overpaid CEO in the U.S. telecom industry, making six times his deserved salary, in the view of the
Bloomberg News columnist Graef Crystal. That year his compensation
totaled $102.5 million, including $93.1 million in exercised stock options. The year before, he cashed in an additional $80 million worth of
options. Plus, until such actions were outlawed by the Sarbanes-Oxley
Act of 2002, he had packed the board with his father, Zvi Alexander,
and his sister, Shaula Alexander Yemini—who conveniently sat on the
board's remuneration and stock option committee. Yet despite their enormous wealth, around their luxury West 57th Street high-rise, where they
owned several condominiums and counted Goldie Hawn, Paul Allen, and
Al Pacino as neighbors, Kobi and his wife, Hana, were known as notori-
ously bad tippers. "They'd give us like $10 or $20 or $30 as a tip for the
holidays," scowled one worker at the building.

Alexander's sense of entitlement extended to escaping punishment.
Knowing he was likely to be indicted, he resigned his positions at Verint
and Comverse on May 1, 2006. Then, according to the Justice Department, Alexander offered a Comverse colleague $2 million to take the
blame and serve the prison time on his behalf. When that wasn't enough,
he upped the offer to $5 million, and then simply "told the individual he
can name his own price." But no offer was high enough, so Alexander
went to Plan B, fleeing to Israel with his family and transferring $57 mil-
lion from his bank in New York to an account in Israel.

Alexander believed Israel had become a safe haven for wealthy crooks
with ethnic or religious ties to the country, including Marc Rich, the business associate of his father. Also taking refuge from the law in Israel
was Leonid Nevzlin, the former deputy CEO of OAO Yukos Oil Company, who was facing tax evasion and murder conspiracy charges in Rus-

sia. Another was Pincus Green, like Rich a commodities trader charged with tax evasion in the U.S. Still another was Eddie Antar, the founder of the "Crazy Eddie" chain of electronics stores, who was charged with fraud and racketeering by the SEC. He was located in Israel following an intensive two-year international manhunt, but he asserted his Israeli citizenship and was allowed to stay. "He was Jewish, and the Israelis didn't want to extradite someone who was Jewish," said Jayne Blumberg, a former federal prosecutor in Newark who investigated and prosecuted the case. Antar, however, eventually decided against fighting extradition procedures and was returned to the U.S.

While Israel would be safe for a time, there were no guarantees it would remain that way; the country did have an extradition treaty with the U.S., and in both countries Alexander was a very high-profile figure. Thus, soon after his arrival he began intensively researching nations without an extradition agreement with the American government and, after a process of elimination, settled on the southwest African country of Namibia. Remote, sparsely populated, made up mostly of the bleak Kalahari Desert, it was also seemingly immune from the long arm of the FBI. On July 18, ten days before he was scheduled to return to New York from his vacation, he flew to the Namibian capital of Windhoek. A century earlier, the city was the seat of power in the German colony of South West Africa, and the country's influence was still very apparent in the architecture as well as the food. In addition to local dishes, most menus listed venison and sauerkraut as well as locally brewed beer.

It was the middle of the African winter and the days were mild when Alexander stepped off the plane at Windhoek Hosea Kutako International Airport. After making some initial contacts, he flew back to Israel and continued pushing his attorneys to negotiate a deal with federal prosecutors to avoid criminal charges. But in a July 21 conversation, the prosecutors would only agree to meet Alexander at JFK Airport and not arrest him at that time. Alexander agreed and provided evidence that he was ticketed on an El Al flight arriving in New York on July 28. But on July 27, he and his family instead flew from Tel Aviv to Frankfurt, Germany, where they transferred to Lufthansa for a nonstop flight to Windhoek.

After showing their Israeli passports, the Alexanders took a taxi to the posh Hotel Thule in Eros, a nearby suburb. Located high on a hill above Windhoek, the hotel offered vistas of the city below and the low-slung mountains in the distance. Flanked by stately palm trees, with guinea fowl and rock rabbits crawling about, it must have seemed a world away from their 57th Street apartment. The hotel literature boasted that Thule was "a mythical place . . . at the frontier of reality—the edge of the world." Alexander no doubt hoped so, but he must also have liked the part of the brochure that said the hotel was "an exclusive getaway."

Under the sheltering canopy of blue sky in Namibia, the staff of the Hotel Thule had no idea there was an international manhunt for their new guest. Nor did they think it suspicious that he shunned credit cards and paid cash in advance for two adjoining ground-floor rooms at $143 each a night. "We knew them as the Family Jacobs, that's how the booking agency gave it to us," said manager Wolfgang Balzer. "Alexander always looked very busy, and he insisted that the news channel on the satellite decoder always work. He was very anxious about that . . . I thought being from Israel, he was worried about Lebanon and all that."

Alexander bought a $107,000 Land Cruiser and began looking for a place to live. At the end of August he settled on Windhoek Country Club Estate, a gated community of fifty-seven block-style town houses that back up to the Windhoek Golf Course on the outskirts of the city. The family moved into number 19, a modern, five-thousand-square-foot, two-story house he purchased for $543,000. In the shadow of the Auas Mountains, the tan-colored house had a satellite dish perched on the roof and a basketball hoop hanging from the garage. Next door to the complex was the Desert Jewel Casino, which featured American roulette, stud poker, blackjack, and 290 slot machines. But perhaps the most important feature of the house was its proximity to Eros Airport, a private airstrip only about two hundred meters away, in the event he needed another quick escape.

Alexander knew it was only a matter of time before he was discovered and the United States began putting pressure on the Namibian government to toss him out. He therefore began investing large sums of money with powerful officials connected to the government, and making high-profile contributions to local civic projects. For Kobi Alexander, everyone had a price, a lesson he learned from his father's years of backroom payoffs to petty African officials for oil rights. After transferring about $16 million to a bank account in Namibia, he launched into a frenzy of investments and goodwill gestures, from developing $1.5 million in low-cost housing to $20,000 in yearly high school scholarships.

Alexander's principal business partners included Brigadier Mathias Sciweda of the Namibia Defence Force, who headed up the army's commercial arm and was known to be close to Namibia's powerful former president, Sam Nujoma. The two bought a number of properties, including one encompassing thirteen acres at Walvis Bay. In 2005, Sciweda's name had come up in a Namibian financial scandal involving an investment by Namibia's Social Security Commission of $4.3 million in a failed asset-management firm. Sciweda was named by the head of the firm to be among the shareholders. But he later testified that he never received any money from the firm.

On the other side of the world, when Alexander failed to show up at JFK Airport on July 28, the Justice Department immediately filed a criminal complaint charging him, Kreinberg, and Sorin with dozens of counts of fraud and other crimes. But instead of making the document public, they placed it under seal; thinking no charges had yet been filed, he might return voluntarily. Alexander, however, had no intention of ever returning to America and on July 31 attempted to transfer another $12 million out of his U.S. bank. By then, however, his remaining $50 million had been frozen by the prosecutors.

By August 9, the Justice Department concluded that Alexander was on the run and unsealed the indictment. At a press conference in Washington that day, Deputy Attorney General Paul J. McNulty made the dramatic announcement. "Three former executives of Comverse Technology," he said, "were charged today for their roles in orchestrating a long-running scheme to manipulate the grant of millions of Comverse stock options to themselves and to employees. Former chief executive officer Jacob 'Kobi' Alexander, former chief financial officer David Kreinberg, and former general counsel William F. Sorin allegedly orchestrated the scheme by fraudulently backdating the options and operating a secret stock options slush fund. An arrest warrant has been issued for Alexander." Acting assistant FBI director James "Chip" Burrus then added, "The alleged scheme of these defendants in backdating options victimized both Comverse shareholders and the American people."

The FBI slapped Alexander's face on its Most Wanted list and Interpol sent out a global "Red Notice" asking all cooperating countries to arrest him if he showed up at their border. Both Kreinberg and Sorin were arraigned in Brooklyn federal court within hours of the press conference and later pled guilty and faced prison sentences and millions of dollars in fines and penalties. Comverse and Verint were dumped from the Nasdaq Stock Market.

For a while, Alexander seemed safe. But as the millions began flowing into his Windhoek bank account, the transfers raised the suspicions of the country's bank regulatory agency and they notified Interpol. A few days later, on August 18, Interpol asked Namibian authorities to investigate whether Alexander was in the country. Within hours they reported back that he was and, at the request of the American government, Namibia's extradition laws were ordered changed to include the United States. The addition was approved by Namibia's president, Hifikepunye Pohamba, on August 31, but because it would take about a month for the modification to go into effect, it was decided not to alert Alexander. Two days earlier he had been granted a two-year work permit.

On September 27, the new extradition law went into effect and the news was reported in the local paper. Before Alexander could escape again, police arrested him at his home as he was having lunch with his wife and daughter. "He got very nervous when we handcuffed him," Namibia's chief inspector, William Lloyd, recalled. "He could see there was something serious coming at him." Placed in a patrol car, he was taken to Windhoek Central Prison, a desolate, overcrowded fortress encircled by razor wire and high-voltage electrified fences. There he was tossed into H-Section, where the average cell was packed with as many as thirty inmates. It was a long, hard fall for the man who had bugged America—and the world.

It was also a troubling insight into just how vulnerable America's voice and data communications systems have become. Unknown to the public, an entire national telecom network was channeled through a powerful foreign-made bug controlled by a corrupt foreign-based company with close links to a foreign electronic spy agency. As of 2008, the bug was still there and the only thing that had changed was a reshuffling of the company's top management.

Kobi Alexander's stay in prison was short; after six days he was released on $1.4 million in bail—the largest in the history of the country—and he has remained free ever since. As he keeps pumping tens of millions of dollars into Namibia's weak economy his extradition keeps getting pushed back further and further. "It looks like he's trying to influence the politics of Namibia to keep him there," said Patrick Dahlstrom, an attorney representing the financially harmed shareholders. Nonsense, replied Alexander's attorney, Richard Metcalfe, who saw no correlation between his client's newfound sense of generosity and his desire to stay in Namibia and out of an American prison. "I think it's typical of Kobi Alexander," he said. "I think it's part of that great Jewish ethos of generosity, of displaying generosity toward other people when you're doing well and when things go well with you. And I think that's part of the man and part of his psyche to be generous to people."

Technotyranny

Not only have Narus and Verint tapped virtually the entire American telecom system, between the two firms they have also wired much of the planet for sound—democracies as well as dictatorships, it doesn't seem to make any difference. Never before in history have so few people wiretapped so many. From China to America and from Europe to Southeast Asia and Australia, countries use Verint and Narus equipment to eavesdrop on—and in many cases repress—their citizens. Verint, for example, was the company that won the contract to build a secret nationwide eavesdropping system for the government of Mexico.

Verint's long list of customers also includes Vietnam, a place where the government makes no bones about eavesdropping on domestic communications, and putting in jail anyone caught opposing its policies. All Internet service providers (ISPs) there are state owned and they are required to provide technical assistance and workspace to public security agents to allow them to monitor Internet activities. The government also requires Internet agents, such as cybercafés, to register the personal information of their customers, store records of Internet sites visited by customers for thirty days, and cooperate with public security officials.

In July 2006, about the time Verint was taking Vietnam on as a client, the Ministry of Post and Telematics instructed all ISPs to install in their Internet kiosks new control software designed to record information on users and their Internet behavior and send the information to the ISPs' servers to be stored for a year. The software also contained an identification system that allows ISPs to identify the user and what the user does during an Internet session. To use Internet kiosks, customers must provide personal details to acquire a user name and password—both issued and controlled by the ISP. Customers then can use the issued user name and password to browse the Internet. In addition, at least some home Internet subscribers had all Internet usage monitored by the newly installed software and hardware system.

The new system worked well. On March 11, 2007, police raided a cybercafé and arrested an Internet user in Hanoi while he was taking part in a discussion forum on democracy. By the end of the year, his status was still unknown. Then, using the new equipment, the government installed firewalls to block websites that it deemed politically or culturally inappropriate, including sites operated by exile groups abroad. The government occasionally restricted access to the Radio Free Asia and Voice of America websites, as well as sites operated by overseas dissident groups. Among those affected were local newspapers that occasionally wrote stories based on RFA broadcasts. Finally, the government required owners of domestic websites, including those operated by foreign entities, to register their sites with the government and submit their website content to the government for approval.

Among those who must now watch his words is Le Quoc Quan, a political dissident who spends much of his time looking for safe places to talk about his opposition to the regime in power. He is far from paranoid; in 2007, Quan, a lawyer, was carted away to prison for one hundred days on suspicion of passing information to the CIA.

So pervasive is the new commercially available Internet censorship technology that dissidents are now arrested in Internet cafés, and state security agents show up at homes to seize computers. Around the same time Quan was arrested, the country's supreme court sentenced two other cyber-dissidents to jail for terms of three and four years for transmitting over the Internet "anti-government propaganda." To avoid the cyber-goons, Quan and a number of other protesters turned to VoIP. By communicating by phone over the Internet, their data packets become much harder to capture and their conversations are therefore more secure.

Among the most popular VoIP systems is Skype, which is a revolution in telecommunications. Not only are Skype calls cheap and easy to make, they are also virtually unbuggable—and the best way to defeat

Narus, Verint, and even the NSA. The company, acquired by eBay, Inc., provides free voice calls and instant messaging between users. There is a fee to talk to nonmembers. But the most unique feature is its security, which is achieved by end-to-end encryption for all calls to other members. Such technology makes it possible to fight back against the proliferating eavesdropping factories.

Skype and other VoIP calls have become life preservers for dissidents such as Quan in repressive countries around the world. The technology gives them the freedom necessary to plan demonstrations, enlist supporters, and organize meetings. "It's great. Amazing," says Quan. "Talking by phone is absolutely not safe in Vietnam. This way we can communicate more securely." Another option to further evade the authorities is to say parts of the message over the VoIP connection and then simultaneously write other parts on the Internet. Another advantage lies simply in the numbers—in 2007, there were about 17.9 million Internet users in Vietnam, nearly 21 percent of the country. "We can connect to a whole new generation," says Nguyen Thanh Giang, a seventy-one-year-old scholar and dissident who avoids the police patrols constantly watching his house by communicating over Skype. "More and more people are joining up."

The need for such protection is clear. In 2006, five dissident writers were jailed for planning to publish the newsletter *Tu Do Dan Chu* ("Freedom and Democracy"). About the same time another cyber-dissident, Truong Quoc Huy, twenty-five, who had spent nearly nine months in jail with his brother for chatting on a pro-democracy Internet forum, was re-arrested. The list of similar arrests is long, and Quan and Giang's days of dissent may, like that of Huy and his brother, be over. Verint's deal placed in the hands of the Vietnamese government the technology to block all VoIP calls from the Internet. This would force the dissidents to either use the monitored phone lines or the tapped Internet, both subject to Verint's intrusive technology.

The initial agreement between Verint and Vietnam's security chief in the Ministry of the Interior took place in 2002 and included two P-GSM stations, portable mobile phone listening devices, at $250,000 each. Since then, the company's involvement with the Communist government has grown substantially. Another company involved in the sale was Silver Bullet, a European company, and two Israeli companies acted as intermediaries. A few years later, the press freedom organization Reporters

Without Borders discovered the deal. For years the group had focused closely on Vietnam's harsh treatment of journalists and dissidents and they quickly issued a strong protest. "We are appalled to learn that our phone calls with Vietnamese cyber-dissidents have been monitored with equipment provided by European and U.S. companies," the organization said. "Coming a year after it emerged that Yahoo! cooperates with the Chinese police, this new case reinforces our conviction that telecommunications companies must be forced to respect certain rules of ethical conduct. In particular, they should be banned from selling surveillance equipment to repressive governments."

Although Verint refused to confirm the deal with the Vietnamese government, in 2002 it had issued a press release saying the company had been "selected to provide law enforcement communications interception solutions to a new customer in Asia Pacific," for "more than $1.5 million" but chose not to mention the name of the country. The system sounded very similar to the widespread surveillance network it installed in Mexico "Verint Systems," said the July 8, 2002, release, "a leading provider of analytic solutions for communications interception, digital video security and surveillance, and enterprise business intelligence . . . will provide a communications interception solution, including the 'front-end' interception system installed within the communications network of the service provider and the 'back-end' monitoring center used by multiple law enforcement agencies to collect and analyze intercepted communications from the specific network . . . Verint's software, which is used by over 800 organizations in over 50 countries worldwide, generates actionable intelligence through the collection, retention and analysis of voice, fax, video, email, Internet and data transmissions from multiple communications networks."

In 2007, First Consulting Group (FCG) Vietnam listed Verint as one of their key clients in Vietnam. "Verint is a leading global provider of Actionable Intelligence Software and Services," it said, adding that the company had been "engaged with FCG Vietnam for almost 4 years." As a sign of how much the company had grown in the country, FCG Vietnam noted that Verint had "started with 5 resources [personnel]; current team is over 120 resources."

Like Verint, Narus is branching out, looking to install its powerful tapping equipment deep within the world's telecommunications infrastructure. And also like its competitor, Narus has focused much of its attention on repressive countries, including China, with its forty million Internet users. "Narus' carrier-class IP platform is the first and only foreign IP management and security system ever certified by us," said Wang Haisheng, director of China's Internet police, the Information Technology Security Certification Center. "Narus' approach to IP data capture, analysis and management provides telecom carriers with a total network view to protect their network infrastructure. After months of rigorous testing and evaluation, Narus' solution proved to meet our stringent IT security criteria." The Chinese government has certified Narus for implantation in all its telecommunication organizations including China Telecom, China Netcom, China Mobile, and China Unicom. The services included "traffic analysis" and "interception."

The Narus spy equipment has had a devastating effect. According to a report by the State Department, "The authorities reportedly began to employ more sophisticated technology enabling the selective blocking of specific content rather than entire Web sites. Such technology was also used to block e-mails containing sensitive content . . . New restrictions aimed at increasing government control over the Internet included stricter Web site registration requirements, enhanced official control of online content, and an expanded definition of illegal online content. The country's Internet control system reportedly employed tens of thousands of persons. The government consistently blocked access to sites it deemed controversial, such as sites discussing Taiwan and Tibetan independence, underground religious and spiritual organizations, democracy activists, and the 1989 Tiananmen massacre. The government also at times blocked access to selected sites operated by major foreign news outlets, health organizations, and educational institutions."

In Shanghai, like in Vietnam, dissidents once used VoIP to avoid government-owned Shanghai Telecom's 6.2 million landlines—until the company installed the Narus software to prevent such calls and track them down. Now the dissidents face the same fate as their Vietnamese counterparts. Elsewhere in China in 2006, the dozens of Internet arrests included the former *Fuzhou Daily* journalist and Internet essayist Li Changqing, who was sentenced to three years in prison for "spreading alarmist information." His Internet articles supported jailed corruption whistleblower Huang Jingao. A few months later, the Internet essayist Yang Tongyan was sentenced to twelve years in prison for posting on overseas websites articles calling for the release of Chinese dissidents. About the same time, the Internet author Guo Qizhen was sentenced to four years' imprisonment on the charge of "inciting subversion of state power." By 2008, fifty-one cyber-dissidents and thirty-five journalists were sitting in Chinese prisons, according to Reporters Without Borders.

Narus has also quietly sold similar equipment to many of the most repressive governments of the Middle East, from Pakistan to Egypt to Saudi Arabia to Libya, some known to torture opponents. In 2005, Narus announced "a multimillion-dollar agreement with Giza Systems of Egypt, licensing Narus' comprehensive portfolio of IP management and security products in the Middle East region. Giza Systems, a world-class systems provider of telecommunications solutions in the Middle East, delivers IP management and security solutions in Egypt, Saudi Arabia, Palestine, and Libya using the Narus system. Narus and Giza Systems formalized this exclusive relationship after working together for more than two years providing Voice over IP (VoIP) detection, mediation, and protection to the largest IP carriers in the Middle East, Telecom Egypt and Saudi Telecom are already benefiting from Narus' carrier-class applications for analysis, security, monitoring and mediation of IP traffic in combination with Giza Systems' technical and commercial capabilities."

According to James Mullins, Narus's vice president of sales for Europe, the Middle East, and Africa, "Collaborating with a recognized leader in deploying IP services gives Narus a clear advantage in meeting the needs of Middle Eastern carriers . . . Teaming up with Giza Systems to target the Middle East region enables Narus to extend its worldwide leadership position in unified IP Management and Security. It ensures that customers get both the solutions and support for their IP networks that they require."

Shortly after installing the Narus system, the Egyptian Ministry of Communications and Information issued a decree asserting the government's right to block, suspend, or shut down any website deemed to threaten national security. Then on October 30, 2006, Reporters Without Borders published a list of thirteen countries it labeled as "enemies of the Internet," a list that included Vietnam and also Egypt due to the recent imprisonment of pro-democracy bloggers. On January 27, 2006, the Egyptian government reportedly had blocked the website Save Egypt Front (saveegyptfront.org). And on May 7, security forces had arrested prominent blogger Alaa Seif Al-Islam (www.manalaa.net) and detained him at Tora Prison until June 22 without charges. Many other bloggers were also arrested and at least one was tortured, according to a U.S. State Department report.

Not only is Narus selling interception and VoIP-blocking software to these countries, it is also selling an extremely intrusive package known as Forensics. Designed for one of the largest telecommunications networks, Tier-One, the system enables the owner to do "Web page reconstruction, playback of VoIP traffic and e-mail reconstruction." An associated program called Narus Directed Analysis "provides a flexible, targeting component designed to surgically capture traffic around a specific event [such as a demonstration], anomalous behavior or specific computer. Among the possible targeting criteria are client identity, server identity, protocol, network link." These two pieces of software, Narus says, "are currently deployed in Tier-1 Carrier-Class networks around the world including Asia and EMEA [Europe, the Middle East and Africa]."

Not to be outdone, Verint offers its "VANTAGE Mass Interception Solutions" for any country interested in total control of its citizens. "Verint Communications Interception Solutions extract intelligence from virtually any type of network," its sales literature says. "VANTAGE is a mass interception system that intercepts, filters and analyzes voice and data for intelligence purposes, with sophisticated probing technology for collecting maximum communications, Verint's real-time filtering mechanisms to extract the most important information, and stored data analysis for generating intelligence from data collected over time. Access sources range from passive trunk monitoring at the operator's facility to microwave and satellite interception."

The Verint sales brochure goes on to say:

VANTAGE features include:

- Mass interception of communications related to specific areas of interest
- Passive monitoring of virtually any type of network
- Sophisticated filtering for high-throughput networks and to track known targets and network events in real time
- Processing engines to organize mass amounts of collected unstructured data into a format that enables rule-based retrieval and interactive analysis

- Interactive analysis tools, including free text search, visual link analysis, location tracking, and reporting
- Built-in support for various intelligence methodologies

Once the phone calls and Internet activity are captured, Verint gives its customers the tools to deeply mine the information for whomever or whatever it is targeting. "DEEPVIEW," says Verint, is a "packet data collection system with the comprehensive functionality to penetrate deep into communications." It also contains a "powerful decoding engine that addresses such services as VoIP, email, webmail, chat, web surfing, instant messaging, and more."

For the companies, marketing their mass interception systems to dictatorships and authoritarian governments to enhance their police states and to jail opponents is just business. "Once, our customers buy our product, it's relatively opaque to us," said Steve Bannerman, vice president of marketing at Narus.

But while the physicists and engineers at Narus had discovered the key to secretly intercepting massive amounts of communications, what they were lacking was an efficient method of picking out the targeted names, e-mail addresses, and phone numbers and packaging the data for their customers in the U.S. and overseas. To help them solve that problem, the company turned to a part-time vintner attempting to grow grapes on a scruffy patch of tired Nebraska soil. For a company founded by Israelis and used to the fast-paced life of Silicon Valley, Bennet, Nebraska, population 685, was a long way away—both in miles and culture.

Miners

In the summer of 2006, Mike Murman's big concern was getting a permit from the Otoe County commissioners for a building to house a grape-crushing machine for the winery he had been trying to start for six years. "I call it Glacial Till Vineyards," he said. Murman also wanted permission for an open-lagoon wastewater treatment system on the premises. A native Nebraskan from Hastings, Murman, forty-nine, graduated from the University of Nebraska-Lincoln in 1979 with a degree in business and marketing and began working for Selection Research, Inc., a Nebraska-based market research and personnel testing firm, and a few years later he decided to start up his own company, Measurement Systems Corp. But because its work was similar to that of Selection Research, the company sued Murman for his alleged use of trade secrets.

As the lawsuit dragged on for five years, Murman created a new company called Pen-Link that developed software to analyze phone call patterns from wiretaps. The company developed computer programs to find links between the numbers—who's being called by whom, and who they are calling. "We would give them an automated way to load telephone records and provide an analysis tool for that information," he said.

When not acting as an amateur vintner, Murman runs his bugging and link-analysis firm from its small headquarters at 5936 VanDervoort Drive in Lincoln, Nebraska, about fifteen miles from Bennet. A regular at the Wiretappers' Ball, he says Pen-Link has about a hundred large wiretap installations and thousands of customers, including seven thousand who are still using the company's first product. The latest products are the Lincoln System, used in phone taps, and the Predator, for Internet eavesdropping. Among his customers are the CIA and a number of other lettered government agencies, as well as eight foreign countries, mostly in Latin America, and he is actively marketing to the Middle East. "Every government in the world does interception of communications, some lawfully, some not," Murman candidly admits. "We realized that our growth shouldn't just be in the United States, but everywhere."

As for most participants in the Wiretappers' Ball, the Bush administration's warrantless eavesdropping program has meant boom times for Pen-Link. In 2003, the company's sales were $6.9 million; by 2006 they had grown 121 percent to $15.2 million. Nevertheless, Murman prefers to keep a low profile. "Nobody knows much about who we are," he says. "We like being private and under the radar in Lincoln, Nebraska."

By the summer of 2006, however, Narus was looking for new ways to mine the data it was collecting and came knocking at Murman's door with a collaboration deal. Murman accepted and on June 13, Narus announced "a strategic agreement with Pen-Link, Ltd. to market NarusInsight Intercept Suite software in conjunction with Pen-Link's LINCOLN® 2 intercept collection and reporting solution." The announcement said marrying Narus's powerful intercept capability with Pen-Link's sophisticated analysis software "combined best-of-breed technologies." Narus also boasted of its capability to do "deep packet inspection"—the analysis not just of the address information but of the entire content of traffic. "NarusInsight is unique in its ability to simultaneously provide deep packet inspection from layer 3 to layer 7 and complete correlation across every link and element on the network."

As the NSA obtained access to virtually all domestic and international communications through the Narus and Verint bugs, analysts next turned their focus to mining that information for intelligence.

What both the NSA and the FBI were most interested in was "link analysis"—building ever-expanding lists of names emanating outward from their original target, like circles in a pond from a dropped stone. If John was the target, who were the people John called the most, what time were the calls, what was their frequency and their duration? Then each of these people—John's "community of interest" in NSA lingo—would be targeted, and on and on like an endless chain letter.

The FBI began flooding the telecoms with emergency "exigent circumstances" letters asking for calling records on long lists of targets. "Due to exigent circumstances it is requested that call detail records for the attached list of telephone numbers be provided," said the letters. "Additionally, please provide a community of interest for the telephone numbers in the attached list." The operation was conducted from Room 4315, the Communications Analysis Unit, at FBI headquarters in Washington.

Verizon alone received over 239,000 "requests and demands for customer information" from federal and state officials between January 2005 and September 2007. But because its database was designed simply for billing purposes, the company was not able to provide the "community of interest" data requested. According to Randal S. Milch, Verizon's general counsel, the company also received requests "containing 'boilerplate' language directing us, for instance, 'to identify a "calling circle" for the foregoing telephone numbers based on a two generation community of interest; provide related subscriber information.' " In a letter to members of Congress looking into the requests, Milch said, "Because Verizon does not maintain such 'calling circle' records, we have not provided this information in response to these requests; we have not analyzed the legal justification for any such requests, been offered indemnification for any such requests, or sought our customers' consent to respond to . . . any such requests."

One solution to the problem was for the NSA to secretly obtain massive amounts of current and past billing information from the telecoms and then use their own personnel and supercomputers to identify the calling circles around their targets. Because of an FCC rule requiring the telecoms to keep these records for seven years, there was a vast supply. And because the NSA was principally interested only in international links, the companies they approached were AT&T, MCI WorldCom (which later became part of Verizon), and possibly Sprint. AT&T and MCI apparently agreed.

"The president's program uses information collected from phone companies," said Senator Kit Bond, the ranking member of the Senate Intelligence Committee. "The phone companies keep their records. They have a record. And it shows what telephone number called what other telephone number." Director of National Intelligence Mike McConnell also indicated that the warrantless eavesdropping program was only one program of many highly secret NSA programs approved by Bush following the attacks on 9/11. "This is the only aspect of the NSA activities that can be discussed publicly, because it is the only aspect of those various activities whose existence has been officially acknowledged," he said.

For the NSA, the most valuable source of this information was AT&T. "The AT&T network, on a busy workday, gets around 300 million calls," said Rick Greer of AT&T Labs in 2001. Two years later that figure had grown to 400 million calls and billions of e-mail messages a day. To store over a trillion records a year, Greer spent much of the last two decades building Daytona, AT&T's monster in-house database management system. Housed at the AT&T Labs Florham Park complex, the same place that controlled the company's PacketScope cable-tapping operation, the data warehouse contains an astronomical number of phone records, including over 312 terabytes of information and 2.8 trillion records. By comparison, the 28 million books in the U.S. Library of Congress contain a total of approximately 20 terabytes of text. Among the databases managed by Daytona was the company's Security Call Analysis and Monitoring Platform (SCAMP), WorldNet IP data warehouse, and Hawkeye, a gargantuan database containing all of AT&T's phone call records.

While AT&T uses Hawkeye to store years of compressed, inactive records, the company keeps the most recent two years' worth of phone data on SCAMP, which was designed to be accessed frequently. Once a call has been completed, its details—the phone number called, time of call, and duration of call—are instantly entered into the SCAMP database. Another system, possibly Hawkeye, contains the name and address data. The NSA obtained direct access to both systems and may have downloaded massive amounts of the data in order to conduct their own "calling circle" analysis. "An analyst can query the system for all calls made to a country from a specific area code during a specific month and get an answer within a minute," said an AT&T specialist. Thus, the NSA could check all calls made to Afghanistan from New York City during September 2001, and have an answer almost instantly. Once the "calling circles" were created, the NSA began its eavesdropping on the American names and phone numbers inside—one, two, or three steps removed from the original target.

Because of the enormous volume of call records to analyze, NSA is now outsourcing much of the work to private contractors, a fact that raises serious additional questions about oversight and concerns over who is given access to the most private information about Americans. For example,

SAIC recently placed an advertisement for a "geo metadata/global network analyst." The requirements include: "Must be able to manipulate GEO data, follow and reacquire targets, operationalize analysis, manipulate call records and conduct call chaining with the purpose of identifying targets." "Call chaining" is the term used for creating the "calling circles" and the SAIC office placing the ad was in Columbia, Maryland, near the NSA.

By 2003, both the NSA and SCAMP were drowning in records. That year, according to AT&T, SCAMP became "the world's largest publicly known database by far as verified by being awarded two Grand Prizes in the 2003 Winter [Corp.] Top 10 Very Large Database contest. Data management for SCAMP is provided by Daytona." Although AT&T may have won the top prize for the largest "publicly known database," the NSA would have likely won the award for the largest database known or unknown—likely in the mega-petabytes (a petabyte is 1,000 terabytes). "It's the largest database ever assembled in the world," said one person about the NSA's phone-record program, adding that it was the agency's goal "to create a database of every call ever made" within the U.S. "Having lots of data gives you lots of power," warned one AT&T official. Even those involved in the NSA program are becoming "uncomfortable with the mountain of data they have now begun to accumulate," according to a lawyer for one.

This calling-circle program was one of the key reasons that the agency began bypassing the FISA court and launched its warrantless eavesdropping program. Unable to show probable cause, or even reasonable suspicion—simply a link to a name or a phone number—the NSA was on an expansive fishing expedition, an activity strictly prohibited by both FISA and the Fourth Amendment. People became NSA targets simply because they happened to call a target, subjecting all of their international communications to warrantless tapping, whether they were simply a neighbor or a friend. The agency termed the activity "hot pursuit" and argued that it provided "early warning." "The president determined that it was necessary following September 11 to create an early-warning detection system," said Assistant Attorney General William E. Moschella. "FISA could not have provided the speed and agility required for the early-warning detection system."

While the NSA focused on the international communications of those within the calling circles, it also passed on the U.S. phone numbers to the FBI as unsolicited leads so they could begin a domestic investigation, including tapping their domestic phone calls. But soon after the program started, bureau agents began getting swamped with thousands of these blind names and numbers a month, virtually all of which, according to some of those involved in the program, led nowhere—to a babysitter or the local pizza joint. The result was frequent complaints to the bureau's NSA liaison that the unfiltered and unanalyzed data was flooding them and keeping them from pursuing more productive work. "We'd chase a number, find it's a schoolteacher with no indication they've ever been involved in international terrorism—case closed," said one former FBI official knowledgeable about the program. "After you get a thousand numbers and not one is turning up anything, you get some frustration."

Thus, of the approximately five thousand NSA warrantless taps conducted between September 2001 and December 2005, fewer than ten Americans a year drew enough suspicion to move to the next level. That involved obtaining a FISA order to begin targeting their domestic communications. While it could be argued that obtaining those ten was worth the effort, others would argue that at least that number may have been lost by flooding the FBI with so much useless information, thus preventing them from pursuing more promising leads.

Another problem was the secretive way in which the agency passed the data to the FBI. At first, because the agents were not cleared for the program, they were only given the names and phone numbers without any details as to where they came from or why they might be useful. The NSA simply told them that it was "information whose source we can't share, but it indicates that this person has been communicating with a suspected al-Qaeda operative."

The program raised serious concerns about issues of privacy. At one point FBI Director Robert S. Mueller III questioned senior administration officials about "whether the program had a proper legal foundation." But the Justice Department, which at about the same time was finding little problem with torture, told Mueller the department's legal memorandums supported it. Nevertheless, Mueller's concerns were well founded. Among the places that received data from the NSA's program was the Defense Intelligence Agency, which, on occasion, used the material to conduct physical surveillance of people and vehicles within the U.S.

By 2008, the idea of communications privacy in the United States had literally become a joke. A group calling itself the Billboard Liberation Front began putting up large billboards bearing the AT&T logo with ad copy such as: "AT&T works in more places, like NSA HEADQUAR- TERS." The group said it was offering its help to the phone company for free to "promote and celebrate the innovative collaboration of these two global communications giants." According to the group's minister of pro- paganda, Blank DeCoverly, "These two titans of telecom have a long and intimate relationship dating back to the age of the telegraph. In these dark days of terrorism, that should be a comfort to every law-abiding citizen with nothing to hide."

Rather than hide its partnership with the NSA, the group suggested that AT&T should place it at the center of a new ad campaign and even offered a suggested tagline: "Modern life is so hectic—who has time to cc the feds on every message? It's a great example of how we anticipate our customers' needs and act on them."

But for many, allowing the NSA to plunder everyone's private commu- nications is not a laughing matter, especially if the agency begins tapping into such companies as Google. In addition to having millions of e-mail customers through their Gmail service, the company maintains records of trillions of Internet searches by hundreds of millions of Americans. For many, every time they have a question they turn to Google, giving the com- pany—and thus the NSA—an enormous insight into everyone's thinking.

According to a former Google executive who left in 2004, the thought that the NSA's data miners could begin ordering them to install a secret pipeline to the agency has many in the company worried. "During my time at Google," he said, "we actually had committee meetings to plan strategy for what to do if the NSA came to us with a demand—and I left kind of in the middle of this. We started making process changes to the way we handled information to make sure that information that the NSA wanted wouldn't be there. The right thing to do would be to erase everything, but the founders of Google are such information freaks they couldn't do that. So they wanted to find ways to make it so that the NSA couldn't benefit from [the stored data] but Google could. And by the time I left, they hadn't located that boundary . . . They were really worried about what would happen if the NSA learned what could be done with in- formation that Google had. And they figured that they only had a couple of years before somebody in the government figured it out."

BOOK FOUR

DISCOVERY

Fractures

For Joe Tomba, it was a homecoming of sorts. Twenty-eight years earlier he had turned in his security badge and driven away from NSA headquarters for the last time, never thinking he would ever return. But now in 2004, both he and the NSA had come full circle. In 1976 the agency was facing the potential of a major scandal involving warrantless eavesdropping on millions of Americans. At the same time, Donald Rumsfeld at the Pentagon and Dick Cheney at the White House were urging the president to stonewall any congressional inquiry. At the center of the controversy, facing a congressional subpoena to testify about the secret program, was Joe Tomba. But under orders from President Gerald R. Ford, he refused, and was subsequently cited for contempt of Congress by a congressional subcommittee.

By 2004, three years after Mike Hayden launched the NSA's warrantless eavesdropping program, the chest-thumping, freewheeling days of anything-in-the-name-of-security were coming to a close. Fractures were now beginning to appear in the thick wall of secrecy surrounding the program and Hayden began to think the unthinkable, that details of the program would leak and suddenly the agency would be back reliving the nightmare years of the mid-1970s. Back to the time when the director was forced to answer hostile questions in front of an angry, open hearing in Congress and stone-faced FBI agents read the Miranda rights to senior agency officials facing possible arrest and imprisonment. With those thoughts in mind, the agency began putting together a video to help guide a new generation of NSA employees through the minefields of congressional inquiries and subpoenas. Thus, the agency invited Joe Tomba to lend his thoughts to the film: thoughts on what to expect when the wall of secrecy comes tumbling down around a warrantless eavesdropping program.

Now Tomba was back at Fort Meade, Cheney was back at the White House, Rumsfeld was back at the Pentagon, and the NSA was back on the verge of another eavesdropping scandal. As he looked around at the agency, which had grown into a sprawling city, Tomba's thoughts likely drifted back three decades, back to that cold day in February when he was ordered to defy Congress and protect the program and the senior officials behind it.

The troubles, as they often do, began with a leak. On July 22, 1975, the *New York Daily News* charged that for at least five years the NSA routinely eavesdropped on commercial cable traffic to and from the United States. The news shocked many around the country and prompted the House Government Operations Subcommittee on Government Information and Individual Rights to launch an investigation. At the time, few people in Washington generated as much fear in government circles as Bella S. Abzug, the subcommittee's hat-wearing chairwoman. To those occupying the seats of power she was like an ammunition-laden cargo plane out of control.

Realizing the difficulty in directly calling NSA officials to testify, Abzug decided to try a different tack. She would instead drag before the committee, in open session, the executives from the international communications companies who either knew about the massive eavesdropping operation code-named Operation Shamrock, or had participated in it. Whereas the NSA might be able to hide behind the shields of classifications and executive privilege, the same protection was not available to private corporations.

But when Don Rumsfeld, the White House chief of staff, first became aware of the Abzug investigation in late October, he urged President Ford to launch a major counterattack. As a result, RCA Global and ITT World Communications, two of the companies that had cooperated with the agency and had been called to testify, suddenly informed the subcommittee that they would refuse to send officials unless so ordered by a subpoena. Then on the day before the start of the scheduled hearings, a platoon of officials from the White House, NSA, Pentagon, and Justice Department converged on the chairwoman in an effort to change her mind about holding public sessions. In the delegation were NSA director Lew Allen, Pentagon intelligence chief Albert Hall, Deputy Attorney General Harold Tyler, Special Counsel to the President John Marsh, and White House congressional liaison Charles Leppert. Their argument was that such hearings would jeopardize either a current Justice Department criminal investigation or the national security.

Unimpressed, Abzug refused to cancel or postpone the hearings. So, in a last-ditch effort, only moments before the congresswoman gaveled the hearing to order, Attorney General Edward H. Levi personally came to the hearing room and tried his own appeal. He fared no better than the others, and at eleven o'clock on October 23, 1975, the hearings began as scheduled—but without the main witnesses. The only testimony came from two representatives of AT&T and one of its subsidiaries, Chesapeake & Potomac Telephone Company.

Conceding the first round to the administration, the combative New York Democrat offered both Allen and Levi a chance to come before the committee and state their case for the record. Both refused. Thus, on February 4, 1976, subpoenas were issued to Joe Tomba and executives of ITT World Communications, RCA Global, and Western Union International. By then, Rumsfeld had become secretary of defense, putting him in charge of the NSA, and Dick Cheney had become the White House chief of staff, replacing Rumsfeld. Both believed in maximum executive power and thus encouraged Ford to flex his presidential muscle and fight back as hard as possible. Thus, on February 17, in an extraordinary and unprecedented expansion of the doctrine of executive privilege, Ford instructed Rumsfeld and Attorney General Levi to inform Tomba and the company executives "that they should decline to comply."

The following day Rumsfeld instructed Tomba that, inasmuch as President Ford has asserted executive privilege in the matter, the subpoenas were not to be complied with. Then, for the first time in history, the concept of executive privilege was extended to a private corporation: Attorney General Levi, in a letter to the attorney for Western Union, wrote, "On behalf of the President, I hereby request that Western Union International honor this invocation of executive privilege."

With the stage set for a major battle between the Congress and the executive branch, on February 25 the Manhattan congresswoman once again called the hearings to order and the subcommittee turned its attention to Joseph J. Tomba, a dark-haired, middle-level NSA employee in his mid-thirties. An engineer with sixteen years of service at the NSA, he had been recruited during his senior year at West Virginia University in 1960. Assigned in the mid-1960s to the C1 Group in PROD, the NSA's operations division, he eventually was promoted to a supervisory position. In 1970 he apparently took over management of Operation Shamrock from a Mr. Feeney, who had held the position for eighteen years, from the time the NSA was created in 1952. So compartmented was the program that besides the middle-level manager, the only other persons exercising responsibility over the operation were the director and deputy director.

Under orders from Rumsfeld and the president, Tomba sought refuge behind executive privilege, but not before he drew the ire of the subcommittee with a brief opening statement. "General Allen has asked me to convey to you," he told a surprised Abzug, "his willingness to attempt to meet the requirements of your subcommittee along with the necessary safeguards applicable to any classified information. To this end, his staff is available to work with your people to define more precisely your exact information requirements." "I certainly appreciate your bringing that message to us personally," the chairwoman responded after stating that the subcommittee already had invited the general on several occasions, "particularly since it is quite obvious that apparently no telephone communication can be made without interception." A few minutes later, by a vote of 6 to 1, the subcommittee voted to recommend to the full committee that Tomba and the other witnesses be cited for contempt of Congress.

Stonewalled by the government, the subcommittee next turned to the telegraph companies. On March 3, Thomas S. Greenish, executive vice president of Western Union International, testified before the panel and turned over an eight-year-old list of NSA targets, an action that Ford, Cheney, and Rumsfeld had vigorously attempted to block by asking the corporation to honor Ford's all-embracing claim of executive privilege.

Following Greenish to the witness table was Howard R. Hawkins, chairman of the board and chief executive officer of RCA Global Communications, along with several of his subordinates. Their testimony represented still another defeat for the administration. Attorney General Levi had earlier asked, "on behalf of the President," that representatives of the corporation neither testify before the subcommittee nor produce documents, "until procedures can be agreed upon to assure that the president's invocation of executive privilege is not effectively undone." Apparently fearing the stormy congresswoman more than the president and attorney general, Hawkins and his associates went ahead with their testimony and also produced an assortment of records. About a week later, George Knapp, president of ITT World Communications, and several other employees also testified about Shamrock. By then the administration seemed to have thrown in the towel; it made no attempt to prevent their appearance.

After the hearings, the subcommittee staff began work on a draft report, to be issued by the Government Operations Committee, that examined the NSA's eavesdropping activities on communications entering and leaving the country. But a controversy soon arose over whether the report should be released, and, following its completion in the fall of 1977, the decision was made to quietly kill it. Titled "Interception of International Telecommunications by the National Security Agency," the draft of the report pointed to the NSA's "extraordinary capability to intercept" and concluded that "no other agency of the federal government undertakes such activity on such an immense scale." Calling the enormous secrecy surrounding the agency "obsessive and unfounded," the report went on to charge that the NSA's appeal to the Congress and the public that they simply "trust us" was totally unjustified when viewed in light of the agency's long record of privacy violations.

The report was particularly critical of the agency's constant attempts to hide behind semantics. Pointing to a statement by Vice Admiral Bobby Inman, General Allen's successor as NSA director, in which he stated: "Let there be no doubt . . . there are no U.S. citizens now targeted by the NSA in the United States or abroad, none," the report called the declaration "misleading." It added that "while an American citizen or company might not be targeted by name, by virtue of his international activities, his communications might be selected by the NSA on the basis of its 'foreign intelligence' criteria. The NSA has not denied that it, in fact, 'selects' U.S. messages of this nature."

Although spared the final indignity of a public report on Shamrock by the Abzug subcommittee, the NSA was not yet out of the fire. The Rockefeller Commission, ironically set up by the White House under Vice President Nelson A. Rockefeller to counter the congressional investigations, came up with its own allegations of questionable activities on the part of the NSA.

As a result, Attorney General Levi established a top-secret task force made up of Justice Department prosecutors and FBI agents to investigate the commission's findings. It was the first time that any law enforcement agency had ever been charged with investigating the legality of the NSA's operations, and the reaction within the agency was predictably hostile. Noting that "attitudes ranged from circumspection to wariness," Dougald D. McMillan, author of the task force's final report, wrote that "one typically had to ask the right question to elicit the right answer or document." He pointed out that "it is likely, therefore, that we had insufficient information on occasion to frame the 'magic' question. One also had to ascertain the specific person or division to whom the right question should be addressed, since compartmentalization of intelligence-gathering often results in one hand not knowing what the other is doing."

Nevertheless, over the course of twelve months, the handpicked, specially cleared team of lawyers and agents gradually pulled back layer after layer of secrecy cloaking some of the NSA's most advanced eavesdropping technology and supersecret processing techniques. The final report of the task force, classified Top Secret Umbra/Handle via Comint Channels Only, and excluded from declassification, was considered so sensitive that only two copies were ever printed. In the end, despite the fact that the task force had managed to uncover numerous examples of potentially illegal eavesdropping activities, the report concluded with the recommendation that the inquiry be terminated. "There is likely to be much 'buck-passing' from subordinate to superior, agency to agency, agency to board or committee, board or committee to the President, and from the living to the dead."

In addition, calling the subject matter of the report "an international cause célèbre involving fundamental constitutional rights of United States citizens," the task force pointed to the likelihood of "graymail" and the possibility that defense attorneys would probably subpoena "every tenuously involved government official and former official" to establish that authority for the various operations emanated from on high. "While the high office of prospective defense witnesses should not enter into the prosecutive decision," the report noted, "the confusion, obfuscation, and surprise testimony which might result cannot be ignored." Rather than point a finger at any one official or any one agency, the task force instead indicted the national security system as a whole, a system that granted the agencies "too much discretionary authority with too little accountability . . . a 35-year failing of Presidents and the Congress rather than the agencies."

While on the one hand charging that those NSA and cable company employees who participated in Shamrock apparently violated several sections of the Communications Act of 1934, the "Prosecutive Summary" pointed to the NSA's highly secret executive branch "charter," National Security Council Intelligence Directive (NSCID) No. 9 (later NSCID No. 6), which gave the agency virtual carte blanche to disregard legal restraints placed on the rest of the government. "Orders, directives, policies, or recommendations of any authority of the Executive branch relating to the collection   of intelligence," the top-secret document reads, ". . . shall not be applicable to [the NSA's] Communications Intelligence activities, unless specifically so stated." The summary concluded: "Its birth certificate [which was, by the way, top secret] said it did not have to follow the limitations in the NSES [National Security Electronic Surveillance] area that limited other agencies unless it was expressly directed to do so."

Another reason for recommending against prosecution with regard to Shamrock was far less complex: "It is not illegal to 'ask' a company to give out copies of cables. If the company complies, it may be violating the statute but the recipient would not."

Mike Hayden knew the history of Shamrock as if it were tattooed on his eyelids. And he knew that once a scandal flared, it could quickly turn into a firestorm and level everything in its path. It was largely because of Shamrock that FISA and the FISA court were created in the first place. And it was one of the reasons that Congress put sharp teeth in the law, making violation a felony punishable by five years in prison for every count—every warrantless intercept.

In March 2004, a nervous Mike Hayden began seeing the first sign of fractures in the wall of secrecy protecting his own Shamrock, his warrantless eavesdropping program.

Emergency

Stretched along Washington's Pennsylvania Avenue, the Justice Department has the appearance of a place that can hold a secret. Its doors are two stories tall and made of high-strength aluminum, and its walls are Indiana limestone over a steel frame. By 2004, the building was holding a great many secrets, the most sensitive of which was the presidential authorization directing the NSA to bypass the FISA court and launch a wide-ranging list of warrantless eavesdropping and data mining programs. So great was the secret that even James Comey, the deputy attorney general and the number two law enforcement official in the country, was not cleared for the program until late in his tenure.

Tall and lanky with a touch of Jimmy Stewart, Comey, the forty-five-year-old grandson of an Irish cop, had come a long way. But in the Bush administration, access to the innermost secrets was a decision based less on loyalty to the law than loyalty to the lawyer, specifically David Addington, the counsel to Dick Cheney (later his chief of staff). Then forty-seven, Addington had worked for Cheney much of his adult life, and both shared a common belief that over the past few decades the power of the president had been reduced to that of a petty bureaucrat. Their goal was to restore both power and grandeur to the office, and scuttling the FISA court, with its nitpicky judges, was one step down that road. "We're going to push and push and push until some larger force makes us stop," he once said. Comey, a straight-arrow government worker without a political agenda, did not fit into Addington's world. As long as Attorney

General John Ashcroft could rubber-stamp the program's renewal every forty-five days, there would be no need to brief him. Nor had his predecessor, Larry Thompson, ever been cleared for the program. It was only at the insistence of Jack Goldsmith, the assistant attorney general in charge of the Office of Legal Counsel, that Comey was read in on it. "There was a little bit of a struggle getting Mr. Comey read into the program," said Goldsmith.

Forty-one-year-old Jack Goldsmith, stocky and rumpled like a doddering uncle, had solid conservative credentials. But his loyalty, like that of his boss Comey, was to the statue of Lady Justice in the building's Great Hall, not to Addington and Cheney. Nor did he share their fever for turning the presidency into a monarchy. Instead, he helped lead a small coterie of lawyers who were repelled by the Bush administration's use of bureaucratic strong-arm tactics to bend, twist, and break the laws they had little use for, such as FISA. And Goldsmith also did not buy into the legal somersaults required to justify the warrantless surveillance program the Bush administration later tagged the Terrorist Surveillance Program (TSP).

Calling Addington "the chief legal architect of the Terrorist Surveillance Program," Goldsmith added, "he and the vice president had abhorred FISA's intrusion on presidential power ever since its enactment in 1978." Addington and Cheney had originally wanted John Yoo, the architect of the legal justification for the NSA's warrantless program, to be promoted to head the office, but Ashcroft thought Cheney was already interfering too much in his department and that was never going to happen.

Since he first arrived in October 2003, Goldsmith had been reviewing the administration's warrantless eavesdropping program, and he didn't like what he saw. "It was the biggest legal mess I've ever encountered," he said, and submitted his view to Ashcroft in a top-secret draft memorandum titled "Review of Legality of the [NSA] Program." By early March 2004, both he and Comey concluded the Justice Department could no longer certify the program as legal. "There were certain aspects of programs related to the TSP that I could not find a legal support for," said Goldsmith.

As a result, a decision had to be made—and made quickly—as to whether to recommend that Ashcroft refuse to recertify it. "The program had to be renewed by March the 11th—which was a Thursday—of 2004," said Comey. "And we were engaged in a very intensive reevaluation of the matter." About a week before, on Thursday, March 4, Comey met with Ashcroft for an hour to pass on his and Goldsmith's analysis of the NSA's warrantless programs. "We had concerns as to our ability to certify [their] legality," said Comey. Ashcroft agreed and decided he was not going to sign the recertification form the next day. It was a program he had never liked from the beginning but felt he was ordered to go along with. The White House had "just shoved it in front of me and told me to sign it," he told several associates.

A few hours later Ashcroft was in his office preparing to announce the convictions of three defendants linked to an alleged "Virginia jihad network." Suddenly he began experiencing increasing pain in his stomach. A call was made to White House physician Daniel Parks, who examined Ashcroft and advised him to go to the hospital. At George Washington University Hospital, he was admitted to a special four-room "pod" in the intensive care section that was cordoned off and designed to protect VIP patients. Following an examination, doctors determined that the attorney general had a severe case of gallstone pancreatitis, an inflammation of a digestive organ that can be very painful. Back at the Justice Department, Comey became the acting attorney general.

By Monday doctors had decided that, as a precautionary measure, they needed to remove Ashcroft's gallbladder to prevent a recurrence of the painful gallstones, and on Tuesday, March 9, Dr. Bruce Abell began the operation, inserting a narrow instrument into the attorney general's abdomen through the navel and extracting the gallbladder. It was a major procedure lasting about an hour and a half that left Ashcroft weak and in guarded condition.

At noon, shortly after Ashcroft was wheeled into his intensive care suite, Comey was at the White House taking his seat in the West Wing office of Andy Card, the president's chief of staff. At fifty-six, Card knew George W. Bush almost as well as a brother. He was seated with Bush's father, the former president, when he vomited on the Japanese prime minister; he was standing next to father and son as they shed tears in the Oval Office on Inauguration Day 2001; and he was the one who whispered in George W.'s ear on 9/11 that the country was under attack. Now his job was to keep the president's warrantless eavesdropping program going despite the warning signals from Comey.

So secret was the program that a good percentage of those officials cleared for it were also present in the room, including Cheney, Addington, Hayden, FBI Director Robert Mueller, CIA Deputy Director John McLaughlin, and White House Counsel Alberto Gonzales. The news was not good. Comey told the group that the department had determined the NSA program had no legal basis and he would not renew it. "As acting attorney general," he said, "I would not certify the program as to its legality."

Without Comey's signature, the NSA would have to immediately pull the plug on the operation or possibly face criminal charges. Worse, Cheney and Card suddenly realized that their tightly controlled White House now had a loose cannon atop the Justice Department. Four hours later, Comey was back in Card's office with Cheney, Hayden, Addington, and the others, but this time he brought with him his top legal experts from Goldsmith's office to explain in detail why the NSA program was not legal.

On Wednesday morning the *Washington Post* ran an article about the attorney general indicating that he was having a rough time. "Ashcroft in Guarded Condition After Surgery," said the headline on page two. And at the Justice Department there appeared to be an odd calm, with no communication from the White House concerning the program's renewal, which was scheduled for the following day.

Far from calm, there was near panic at the White House as Card and Gonzales feared that a shutdown of the NSA program was only hours away. Pulling out all the stops, late in the afternoon they called an emergency meeting in the Situation Room with the "Gang of Eight." That included the top Democrat and Republican in both the Senate and House, and in the Senate and House intelligence committees. "We informed the leadership that Mr. Comey felt the president did not have the authority to authorize these activities," said Gonzales, "and we were there asking for help, to ask for emergency legislation." According to Gonzales, "the consensus in the room from the congressional leadership is that we should continue the activities, at least for now, despite the objections of Mr. Comey. There was also consensus that it would be very, very difficult to obtain legislation without compromising this program, but that we should look for a way ahead."

But West Virginia senator Jay Rockefeller, the ranking Democrat on

the Senate Intelligence Committee, later all but accused Gonzales of lying. Rockefeller, who was at the meeting, insisted he had "never heard of"
Comey at the time and that they were never told of any infighting at the
Justice Department over intelligence programs. He also denied that they
were asked to enact legislation to overcome Comey's resistance. "They
were not telling us what was really going on," Rockefeller said. Another
person at the meeting who disagreed with Gonzales's assessment was the
California Democrat Nancy Pelosi, then the House minority leader and
later speaker. "I made clear my disagreement with what the White House
was asking," she said.

Gonzales and Card had one last desperate option. Race to the hospital,
tell Ashcroft about the congressional support, and get him to reclaim his
authority as attorney general and then recertify the program. But first they
would have to call him up to ask him to see them. And that call would
have to come from Bush himself.

By 7:00 p.m. it was dark, and Comey decided to head for home. He
climbed into his black Justice Department SUV, which was driven by an
FBI agent and trailed by a follow-up car. Soon after the car turned onto
Constitution Avenue, however, his cell phone rang. On the other end was
David Ayers, Ashcroft's chief of staff. "He had gotten a call from Mrs.
[Janet] Ashcroft from the hospital," recalled Comey. "She had banned all
visitors and all phone calls. So I hadn't seen him or talked to him because
he was very ill. And Mrs. Ashcroft reported that a call had come through,
and that as a result of that call Mr. Card and Mr. Gonzales were on their
way to the hospital to see Mr. Ashcroft." Comey added, "I have some
recollection that the call was from the president himself."

Now Comey understood the calm. Rather than wait until Thursday
and have the NSA program declared legally unsupportable and scrapped,
the president and his men had decided to make an end run around him
the night before. "I was concerned that, given how ill I knew the attorney general was, that there might be an effort to ask him to overrule me
when he was in no condition to do that," said Comey. "So I hung up the
phone, immediately called my chief of staff, told him to get as many of
my people as possible to the hospital immediately. I hung up, called [FBI]
Director Mueller." At 7:20, Mueller received the call while having dinner
in a restaurant with his wife and daughter. "I'll meet you at the hospital
right now," Mueller responded. Comey then turned to his security detail.

"I need to get to George Washington Hospital immediately," he told them as they turned on the car's emergency equipment.

With the siren wailing and red and blue lights flashing from the roof and grille of the car, Comey was at the hospital within just a few minutes. "I got out of the car and ran up—literally ran up the stairs with my security detail," he said. "And so I raced to the hospital room, entered. And Mrs. Ashcroft was standing by the hospital bed, Mr. Ashcroft was lying down in the bed, the room was darkened. And I immediately began speaking to him, trying to orient him as to time and place, and trying to see if he could focus on what was happening, and it wasn't clear to me that he could. He seemed pretty bad off."

The White House was just blocks away and Comey knew that the president's men could arrive any minute. He needed some muscle to keep from being removed from the room when they arrived. "Director Mueller instructed the FBI agents present not to allow me to be removed from the room under any circumstances," said Comey, who took a seat in an armchair by the head of the bed with his two aides standing behind him. It was a short wait. A few minutes later, Gonzales and Card stormed in.

"How are you, General?" Gonzales asked, the envelope containing the unsigned NSA recertification in his hand. "Not well," Ashcroft replied, flatly refusing to sign the document. "But that doesn't matter, because I'm not the attorney general. There is the attorney general," he said, pointing at Comey. Their ambush foiled, Comey could feel the room turn to ice. "The two men did not acknowledge me," he said. "Be well," Card said to Ashcroft as the two turned and walked from the room.

A few minutes later, at 7:40, FBI director Mueller arrived at the intensive care suite and Comey filled him in on what had taken place. Mueller then went into Ashcroft's room and saw him sitting in a chair. "Feeble, barely articulate, clearly stressed," he noted. To Mueller's surprise, Ashcroft complained that even he, the attorney general, was never able to get the full details of the NSA program from the White House. Mueller would later note, "The AG also told them [Card and Gonzales] that he was barred from obtaining the advice he needed on the program by the strict compartmentalization rules of the WH [White House]." As Mueller was in with Ashcroft, an FBI agent notified Comey that he had an urgent call in the command center that had been set up next to Ashcroft's room.

"I took the call," said Comey. "And Mr. Card was very upset and demanded that I come to the White House immediately." But in an unprecedented act of distrust at the highest levels of government, the nation's top law enforcement official refused to meet alone with the president's chief of staff in the White House. "I responded that, after the conduct I had just witnessed, I would not meet with him without a witness present . . . I was concerned that this was an effort to do an end run around the acting attorney general and to get a very sick man to approve something that the Department of Justice had already concluded—the department as a whole—was unable to be certified as to its legality."

Comey was boiling. "After what I just witnessed," he told Card, "I will not meet with you without a witness. And I intend that witness to be the solicitor general of the United States." At the time, the solicitor general was Ted Olson, whose wife, Barbara Olson, died on 9/11 when her American Airlines jet smashed into the Pentagon. "Until I can connect with Mr. Olson, I'm not going to meet with you." Card asked Comey if he was refusing to come to the White House, a fireable offense. "No, sir, I'm not. I'll be there. I need to go back to the Department of Justice first," said Comey.

At about 11:00, the FBI security detail drove Comey and Olson to the White House. "We went into the West Wing," said Comey. "Mr. Card was concerned . . . he had heard reports that there were to be a large number of resignations at the Department of Justice." Comey reiterated his belief that the NSA program was outside the law and said he would not sign the certification. With the issue still unresolved, the group departed the White House as the clock neared midnight and the deadline for approval arrived.

On Thursday, Bush decided to reauthorize the NSA program in spite of the view by his own Justice Department that it was not legal. It had not been legal from the start, but Bush and Hayden had at least taken comfort from the fact that the attorney general would put his stamp of approval on it every forty-five days. Now they didn't even have that. Worse, they were on notice that they were breaking the law.

At the Justice Department, it was the final straw for Comey. "The program was reauthorized without us and without a signature from the Department of Justice attesting as to its legality," he said. "And I prepared a letter of resignation, intending to resign the next day, Friday, March the 12th . . . I didn't believe that as the chief law enforcement officer in the country I could stay when they had gone ahead and done something that I had said I could find no legal basis for . . . It was going forward even though I had communicated, 'I cannot approve this as to its legality.' "

Not only was Comey planning to resign, so were Mueller, Goldsmith, and a slew of other Justice Department officials, including the attorney general himself. "Mr. Ashcroft's chief of staff asked me something that meant a great deal to him," said Comey. "And that is that I not resign until Mr. Ashcroft was well enough to resign with me. He was very concerned that Mr. Ashcroft was not well enough to understand fully what was going on. And he begged me to wait until—this was Thursday that I was making this decision—to wait until Monday to give him the weekend to get oriented enough so that I wouldn't leave him behind, was his concern." Both Comey and Ashcroft's chief of staff were convinced the attorney general would join in the mutiny. "Friday would be my last day and Monday morning I would resign," said Comey.

Never in history had so many senior government officials threatened to resign to protest an administration's disregard for the law. That the top leadership of the Justice Department and the FBI had agreed to a mass resignation, led by the attorney general, indicates the seriousness with which they viewed the misconduct of both the Bush White House and Hayden's NSA.

Bush knew what happened following the "Saturday Night Massacre" at Justice during Nixon's Watergate years, when top officials quit rather than fire the special prosecutor, and he had no stomach to fight an almost certain call for his impeachment. In addition, it was an election year and in a few months he would be fighting John Kerry to remain in the White House, and a messy scandal at the Justice Department would be just what the Democrats would like.

On Friday morning, Comey, together with Mueller, went to the Oval Office to brief Bush and Cheney on counterterrorism issues. But after the short session, this time there was something different. "As I was leaving, the president asked to speak to me, took me in his study, and we had a one-on-one meeting," said Comey. During their meeting, Comey told Bush what changes the NSA would have to make in order to bring the program back within the law—changes Cheney still opposed. At the end of the session, Bush was still noncommittal but agreed to talk to Mueller, who was waiting for Comey in the White House lobby. "I'll talk to Director

Mueller," said Bush. At 9:45, Mueller gave the president a similar appraisal of the NSA program's lack of legal standing and Bush, overruling
Cheney, finally agreed to implement the changes.

The changes involved scrapping several of the NSA's most illegal data
mining operations, reworking others, and more fully justifying the program not just under the president's Article 2 inherent authority argument,
but also under an even less valid argument. This was the congressional
authorization to use force against al-Qaeda—which few even in Congress
believe granted authority for eavesdropping on Americans. But according
to Comey, it would be three weeks or so before the Justice Department
was able to recertify the program—three weeks in which the NSA and
the White House were operating a surveillance system without legal authorization.

Despite the changes, the NSA's warrantless program continued to be
operated outside the law. While a few of the most egregious aspects had
been eliminated or modified, it was still in violation of FISA, which required all national security eavesdropping to be approved by the FISA
court—under penalty of imprisonment and with no exceptions. But because of the Bush administration's trademark go-it-alone policy, the program would continue in violation of FISA. And Hayden's wall of secrecy
surrounding it would remain intact. But not for long.

Exposure

In the late summer of 2004, Hayden received a call from James Risen, forty-eight, a reporter at the *New York Times*, about an NSA program to eavesdrop on Americans without a warrant. Hayden was stunned. Without confirming anything, he said that whatever the NSA might be doing was "intensely operational" and, he added quickly, "legal, appropriate, and effective." He then quickly ended the conversation.

As Hayden hung up the phone he could see his foot-thick wall of secrecy finally crumbling around him. It was time to start preparing his employees for possible hearings and investigations. Time to explain the dos, don'ts, and dodges to those potentially facing subpoenas; time to recall Joe Tomba to NSA to help explain what to expect and what not to expect when staring up at a half circle of angry members of Congress. Some NSA officials even began seeking out defense lawyers.

The phone call touched off a quiet, escalating, and long-running game of cat and mouse in which the NSA and later the White House alternated between threats and pleas to convince the *Times* to scrap the story. In the beginning, the officials would only discuss the eavesdropping in hypotheticals, telling the *Times* that "if" such a program existed, "disclosure would do serious and perhaps irreparable harm to national security." Eventually the hypotheticals were dropped and replaced by actual details.

After sitting on the story for more than a year, the *Times* again got in touch with the NSA in the fall of 2005, and Hayden and the Bush administration once again went to battle stations, inviting *Times* editors and reporters to a power session at the White House. There to greet them was Hayden; newly appointed Secretary of State Condi Rice; National Security Advisor Stephen Hadley; John Negroponte, the director of national intelligence; and Harriet Miers, the White House counsel. Cheney, along with Hayden the architect of the plan, had considered attending but wisely, given his reputation within the press, decided to sit out the session.

At the meeting, the *Times*'s executive editor, Bill Keller, was warned that publication of the story would alert the terrorists and "shut down the game." "It's all the marbles," said one official cryptically, adding, "The enemy is inside the gates." For Hayden, among his most serious concerns was not releasing the fact that most international communications pass through U.S. switches, making them vulnerable to NSA's eavesdropping. In sum, the consensus was that if there was another 9/11, the *Times* would share in the blame. But by the time the meeting ended, the White House realized that they had reached a dead end.

Within hours, however, officials were requesting one final summit—a showdown of sorts between President George W. Bush and *Times* publisher Arthur Sulzberger Jr. A few days later in the Oval Office, on Monday, December 5, Hayden, carrying a heavy black briefing book, took a seat near the fireplace a few feet from the president. Looking at Sulzberger, Bush said that if the paper went ahead with publication and another attack took place, they would be sitting alongside each other in a congressional hearing room explaining why it happened and how they missed it. Bush then added, "There'll be blood on your hands."

But in the end, Keller and Sulzberger agreed that they had heard nothing new to make them change their minds. The White House asked for more meetings but the decision was to publish immediately. Thus, on Friday, December 16, the *Times* rolled out its story.

The next day Bush discussed the NSA program in his Saturday radio address. "In the weeks following the terrorist attacks on our nation," he said, "I authorized the National Security Agency, consistent with U.S. law and the Constitution, to intercept the international communications of people with known links to al-Qaeda and related terrorist organizations. Before we intercept these communications, the government must have information that establishes a clear link to these terrorist networks."

He also said, "The activities I authorized are reviewed approximately every forty-five days. Each review is based on a fresh intelligence assessment of terrorist threats to the continuity of our government and the threat of catastrophic damage to our homeland. During each assessment, previous activities under the authorization are reviewed. The review includes approval by our nation's top legal officials, including the attorney general and the counsel to the president. I have reauthorized this program more than thirty times since the September the 11th attacks, and I intend to do so for as long as our nation faces a continuing threat from al-Qaeda and related groups."

The following month, concerned about Congress, the press, and the public using the terms "warrantless wiretapping" and "warrantless surveillance" to refer to the program, Bush attempted to rebrand it. His new name was the "Terrorist Surveillance Program (TSP)," something it had never been called before. Later, Attorney General Alberto Gonzales would obliquely make a distinction. He would indicate that the TSP—mostly voice and data eavesdropping activities—was the program that began around April 2004, following reforms after the infamous Ashcroft hospital visit. The NSA program that was in existence from October 2001 until then—largely highly questionable data mining activities—he would simply call "other intelligence activities."

At the NSA there was shock and outrage by many employees who believed that the NSA had long ago learned from its past mistakes and put an end to warrantless eavesdropping on Americans and looking for ways to evade the law. Many believed Hayden had squandered thirty years of hard work to restore the NSA to a place where it could be trusted again by the American public. Some even protested to the agency's inspector general, asking for an internal investigation, a serious indication of how far the agency's star had fallen even within its own secret city.

"Until the story broke in the *New York Times*," Hayden said, "no one who was asked to be part of this program inside the National Security Agency expressed any reservations about being part of this program. After the story broke, people who were not part of the program were quite understandably concerned about what might be going on; they then went to the NSA IG to ask questions about it." At a time when the NSA needed a Jim Comey or a Bob Mueller, it had only a three-star sycophant unwilling to protect the agency from the destructive forces of Cheney and Addington.

Within days of the report, the once solid and airtight FISA court began developing cracks. U.S. District Judge James Robertson, one of the eleven Top Secret–cleared members of the panel, sent a letter to Chief Justice John G. Roberts Jr. notifying him that he was quitting the court. Though he gave no explanation, two of his colleagues who were familiar with his decision said that Robertson was deeply troubled by the warrantless surveillance, which he found legally questionable. He was also concerned that the program may have compromised the work of the court by using information from illegally obtained taps in applications for FISA orders. "They just don't know if the product of wiretaps were used for FISA warrants—to kind of cleanse the information," said one person familiar with the court. "What I've heard some of the judges say is they feel they've participated in a Potemkin court."

In August 2006, the NSA and the Bush administration began looking ahead with considerable concern. That month a judge ruled in the first lawsuit brought against the NSA over the warrantless surveillance program, launched by the American Civil Liberties Union shortly after the *New York Times* article. The organization asked the federal courts to rule that the program was illegal and to bring it to an end. Among the plaintiffs were individuals and groups across the political spectrum, including scholars, lawyers, and journalists (including the author).

On August 17, 2006, U.S. District Court Judge Anna Diggs Taylor, seventy-three, rejected almost every argument from the Bush administration, including the "inherent powers" of the president, and the "authorization to use military force against al-Qaeda" arguments, and found in favor of the ACLU. Ruling that the NSA program was illegal, violating both FISA and the Fourth Amendment of the Constitution, she ordered it shut down. "It was never the intent of the framers to give the president such unfettered control, particularly when his actions blatantly disregard the parameters clearly enumerated in the Bill of Rights," she wrote. "The three separate branches of government were developed as a check and balance for one another." Rejecting the idea that the president can eavesdrop on Americans simply as a result of his "inherent powers," Judge Taylor ruled, "There are no hereditary Kings in America and no powers not created by the Constitution. So all 'inherent powers' must derive from that Constitution." Upon hearing the decision, Attorney General Alberto Gonzales called an impromptu news conference. "As you know, today, a district court judge in Michigan ruled that the program was unlawful," he said. "We disagree with the decision."

Shaken by the court's decision, the NSA immediately asked Judge Taylor to stay the ruling so the program could continue until a decision by an appeals court, which was granted. But the agency faced another major blow in November when the congressional elections gave both houses to the Democrats—representatives and senators who were champing at the bit to begin holding hearings in January on such Bush administration programs as the NSA's warrantless eavesdropping operation. Also in January was the federal appeals court hearing in which the Bush administration was going to try to convince a panel of three judges to overturn Judge Taylor's ruling. An unfavorable ruling by the appeals court, and the only salvation would be a positive ruling by the U.S. Supreme Court.

Given the many storm clouds on the horizon, and growing pressure from the telecoms who were being sued by angry customers and public interest groups, the NSA and the Justice Department began looking for a way out. Eventually, on January 10, 2007, they got one of the eleven judges on the FISA court, who rotate in and out of Washington, to interpret as permissible a key aspect of the warrantless program. This involved working with a friendly judge to come up with an "innovative" way to interpret the FISA statute so that the agency could target foreign-to-foreign communications that simply transit a U.S. switch—and the interception is done on U.S. soil—without going to the court for every name.

Under the traditional interpretation of FISA, the NSA would need to get a warrant from the FISA court before targeting the transit communication of either foreign individual as long as it enters the U.S. on a wire, such as an undersea fiber-optic cable, and also as long as it is intercepted inside the U.S.—for example, at the switch or at a listening post such as NSA Georgia. The new "innovative" approach may involve a reinterpretation of the law to include a "programmatic" or blanket approach. Thus the NSA would program into its intercept equipment the names and phone numbers of foreigners whom they have probable cause to believe are members of al-Qaeda or an associate terrorist organization. Under the new interpretation, the NSA may not need to submit an application for these foreign-to-foreign communications, except when one end reaches a U.S. phone. In that case the agency can begin eavesdropping immediately as long as an emergency application is made within three days.

Once the procedures were worked out, the agency only needed to wait until the friendly judge began his or her rotation onto the court—which took place on January 17. Then the judge simply issued the prearranged order and the NSA was in business. "We got a favorable ruling from the court, and in essence, we could conduct our mission," said Mike McConnell.

There was thus no longer any need to operate outside the FISA court. Finally, on January 17, Attorney General Gonzales announced that the warrantless eavesdropping program was coming to an end and the NSA's eavesdropping activities from then on would once again come under the FISA court. "All surveillance previously occurring under the Terrorist Surveillance Program (TSP) would now be conducted subject to the approval of the FISC," Gonzales said. "Under these circumstances, the President had determined not to reauthorize the TSP when the then current authorization expired."

The only problem with the NSA's approach was that the program had to be renewed every few months and that other, less friendly judges might not come to the same interpretation—which is what happened just a few months later. "The second judge looked at the same data and said, 'Well, wait a minute. I interpret the law, which is the FISA law, differently,'" recalled McConnell. "And it came down to, if it's on a wire and it's foreign in a foreign country, you have to have a warrant." Suddenly the NSA was back to the pre-9/11 days—at the same time it was racing to find American soldiers kidnapped in Iraq. And their kidnappers' Iraq-to-Iraq communications were transiting the U.S.—on a wire.

Extremis

Nineteen-year-old Steven D. Green sat in a Midland, Texas, recruiter's office with a photo of George W. Bush smiling down from the wall. Like the president, Green was a native son of the West Texas oil town, where his schoolmates nicknamed him "the drifter." By January 2005, the once-proud U.S. Army had been reduced to emptying jail cells and drunk tanks to fill its quota of Iraq-bound soldiers. Criminals, dropouts, and the unemployable were now sought after, given bonuses, outfitted with deadly weapons, and then set loose in a crowded land with few rules, less oversight, and a license to kill.

A few days before, Green, a bony-faced, unemployed tenth-grade dropout, had been behind bars in a grimy lockup on alcohol-possession charges, his third time under arrest. He was troubled from an early age, one neighbor said. "I don't know if he killed small cats or anything, but that's the kind of kid he was." Nevertheless, like 11,017 others in 2005, many with felony convictions, Green was granted a "moral waiver" by the army and was soon wearing the American flag on his shoulder as he kicked in doors in Baghdad and aimed his M-249 belt-fed machine gun at petrified women and children.

"I came over here because I wanted to kill people," he casually told a reporter over a mess-tent dinner of turkey cutlets in February 2006. "The truth is," he said, shrugging, "it wasn't all I thought it was cracked up to be. I mean, I thought killing somebody would be this life-changing experience. And then I did it, and I was like, 'All right, whatever.' I shot a guy who wouldn't stop when we were out at a traffic checkpoint and it was like nothing. Over here, killing people is like squashing an ant. I mean, you kill somebody and it's like 'All right, let's go get some pizza.' " Green concluded, "See, this war is different from all the ones that our fathers and grandfathers fought. Those wars were for something. This war is for nothing."

Despite the fact that Green made no effort to hide his blood lust, the reporter, Andrew Tilghman from the army's *Stars and Stripes* newspaper, found the violently psychotic conversation little more than routine. "I just saw and heard a blunt-talking kid," he said, and thought little more of it.

A few months later, the "blunt-talking kid" saw an attractive fourteen-year-old Iraqi girl and ran his index finger down her cheek as she stood frozen in fear. Thin and tall, Abeer Qasim Hamza al-Janabi lived with her family in a farmhouse about a thousand feet from the checkpoint where Green worked, just outside the sunbaked Sunni village of Mahmudiyah, twenty miles from Baghdad. The soldiers would enter the farmhouse frequently under the pretext of searching for "terrorists" but were in reality attempting to get close to Abeer, which means "fragrance of flowers." They would smile, give her the thumbs-up sign, and say, "Very good, very good."

Then, on the night of March 12, 2006, Green and four of his army buddies, including Specialist James Barker, twenty-three, and Sergeant Paul Cortez, drank cheap local Iraqi whiskey mixed with an energy drink and played cards. Between hands, they planned an attack on the girl and her family. After hitting golf balls, they changed into dark clothing and abandoned the checkpoint to go "kill and hurt a lot of Iraqis," according to one of the men involved. Green grabbed a loaded Russian-made AK-47 rifle, snatched from a dead Iraqi, to use for the killing, figuring the murders would be blamed on fellow Iraqis. Another conspirator stayed behind to monitor the radio and warn them if there was trouble.

Inside Abeer's house, Green forced the girl's parents and five-year-old sister into a bedroom, where he shot the father several times in the head, the mother several times in the abdomen, and the sister in the head and shoulder. "I just killed them, all are dead," Green boasted to his friends. As Green killed her family, Abeer was in another room being brutally gang-raped by Cortez and Barker. "Cortez pushed her to the ground. I went towards the top of her and kind of held her hands down while Cortez proceeded to lift her dress up," Barker later admitted. Cortez added, "I lifted up her skirt and took off her stockings while Barker held her hands with his knees. After I was done, myself and Barker switched spots." As Abeer screamed and cried, Barker shouted at her to "shut up" in Arabic. Then as Cortez stood lookout, Green raped Abeer and then shot her in the head. Cortez poured kerosene onto her body and attempted to light her and the house on fire to cover up the massacre. On the way back to the checkpoint, where Barker grilled chicken wings, Green tossed the AK-47 into the canal.

Despite a clumsy attempt by army superiors to cover up the crime, details of the grisly murders and the premeditated involvement of U.S. soldiers eventually came to light. Brutalized by the long occupation and outraged by the rape and murders, local farmers became part of the Islamic State of Iraq (ISI), a large umbrella group of Sunni insurgents created as a reaction to the U.S. invasion and occupation. Meeting in the fields near the Euphrates River, their operational plan tacked to a tree, the men set their sights on avenging the death of Abeer and her family. They chose the early morning hours of May 12, 2007, near Mahmudiyah, not far from where the slaughter took place.

On the night of May 11, 2007, two U.S. Humvees took up positions on a lonely stretch of asphalt road in the lush agricultural area on the outskirts of Mahmudiyah. Located in the flat and arid Euphrates River Valley, this area is where the Iraqi desert gives way to soggy irrigation canals and palm trees towering above tall grass. At twilight and in the early morning, it bore an odd resemblance to the rice fields of Vietnam. Parked about 165 feet apart, with their vehicles and gun turrets facing opposite directions, the men, four in each vehicle, were there to keep a lookout for anyone planting explosive devices in the road. It was the third night in a row soldiers had parked in the same spot.

Just after 4:00 a.m. on Saturday, a sleepy time in the morning when no one in either vehicle was up in the gun mounts keeping a lookout, about fifteen Iraqis met at a farmhouse, picked up their weapons, and then quietly made their way to the road. Once there, they cut through razor-wire coils, snuck into the unguarded space between the two vehicles, and hurled grenades into the open turrets. The muffled blasts shattered the tranquil night and plumes of fire shot out of the open turrets like the flick of a lighter in a darkened room. From inside each burning hulk came the sound of machine-gun fire as the heat cooked off rounds of ammunition. While most of the men were killed instantly, or died in the subsequent firefight, a few managed to escape and were quickly captured at gunpoint—one of the key aims of the ambush. The Iraqis then planted explosive booby traps around the burning vehicles, hoping to slow down any responding U.S. troops. "The attack was extremely bold," said Major Robert Griggs, the group's operations officer. "It really is amazing how good the enemy was."

Among the first to arrive after the attack was First Lieutenant Morgan Spring-Glace, who expected to find eight bodies. "No one thought there would be an abduction," he said. Among the missing was nineteen-year-old Byron W. Fouty, a private from Waterford, Michigan, who dropped out of high school, had trouble finding work, and joined the army as a last resort. "Maybe he thought by joining the army it was regular pay," said Cathy Conger, the mother of one of Fouty's close friends. Once in Iraq, however, Fouty quickly realized he had made a big mistake, especially after learning that his tour there had been extended from twelve months to fifteen months. "George W. Bush has decided that another 3 months in this [expletive] is worthwhile," he wrote on his MySpace blog a month before the attack. "This pisses me off to a level I haven't been in a long time." He added, "Last June I decided to join the Army. Ha, another wrong turn."

Another missing soldier was Private First Class Joseph J. Anzack Jr. of Torrance, California. A high school football player with little interest in academics, he was gung ho to join the army soon after graduation. But like Fouty, he also quickly began developing second thoughts, which he expressed when he came home for Thanksgiving about six months before the attack. "He kept saying, 'God, I don't want to go back,' " said his aunt, Debbie Anzack. "It was going to another country, everything that was expected of him, the fact that people were trying to blow him up." Finally there was Specialist Alex R. Jimenez, twenty-five, of Lawrence, Massachusetts, who as a boy played regularly with little green plastic soldiers and dreamed of joining the military. It was a dream he accomplished when he signed up with the army following high school in June 2002.

In the days and weeks following the ambush and kidnapping, four thousand U.S. troops and two thousand Iraqi soldiers were mobilized for a massive door-busting dragnet throughout the region, with some houses being raided multiple times. Women and children were interrogated, thumbprinted, and forced to submit to retinal scanning, while more than a thousand Iraqi men were detained for questioning. At the time, the government of Iraq was already holding at least twenty-four thousand prisoners, nearly all of whom had not been convicted of any crime or even had a trial. The United States was holding approximately twenty-six thousand prisoners under the same conditions.

Instead of finding cooperative residents, the battalion only found the body of one of the missing soldiers floating half naked in the Euphrates River, a few kilometers south of where the battle took place. The lifeless remains were those of Private First Class Joseph J. Anzack Jr., the high school football player from Torrance, California. In a posting on their website, the captors gave the reason for the attack. "You should remember what you have done to our sister Abeer in the same area," it said. They also released a videotape that showed the military identification badges of the two missing soldiers, above which was Arabic script. "Bush is the reason for the loss of your prisoners," it said. The voice then said, "After the three soldiers were alive as prisoners they became dead bodies." The speaker also referred to the inability to obtain the bodies of their own dead from the U.S. military. "Because you disdain to give us the corpses of our dead," he said, "so we will not give you the corpses of your dead, and their residence will be under the soil, God willing."

As the six thousand U.S. and Iraqi troops pounded on doors and placed handcuff straps on hundreds of suspects, the NSA was also searching for anyone involved in the kidnappings. Immediately after receiving word of the capture on Saturday, May 12, the agency began focusing both regional and national intercept capabilities on the area. At NSA Georgia, all ears were on Mahmudiyah. By Sunday, intercept operators were beginning to develop a number of leads connected to the Islamic State of Iraq, and on Monday agency officials went to the FISA court and asked to amend an existing order—apparently adding ISI to a list of terror groups. Approval was granted within hours.

A short time later, analysts came up with a list of names associated with ISI, including the name of one of the suspected kidnappers, a man who went by the moniker Abu Rus. Intelligence officials believed he had masterminded an earlier assault in the area and he was also a suspect in the downing of a U.S. helicopter in April 2006. Army general David H.

Petraeus, the top U.S. commander in Iraq, would later confirm that the military had identified the person chiefly responsible for the abduction. "We know who that guy is," he said. "He's sort of an affiliate of al-Qaeda. He's the big player down in that area. We've tangled with him before."

But targeting the suspects proved a problem. That spring, several FISA court judges reviewed the opinion of the friendly judge who ruled in the administration's favor in January and came up with a very different inter-pretation. "We have to get an update every ninety days," said McConnell. "Subsequent judges started to define it a little more narrowly." In fact they rejected the earlier interpretation and insisted that a strict reading of FISA required an order, including a showing of probable cause, before the NSA could begin intercepting the ISI e-mail traffic. "Originally the court seemed to be complicit in what Bush and those guys were doing but then they got a ruling saying, knock it off," said one senior intelligence official.

It all had to do with location. At least some of the e-mail likely passed through U.S.-based ISPs, such as Yahoo or Gmail, triggering the statute. "So what we found is we were actually going backwards in our ability to conduct our surveillance," McConnell complained, "which was requiring a warrant for a foreign target in a foreign country. And the issue was the wording of the law from '78. If it touched a wire in the United States, we had to have a warrant. That was the basic issue."

A second problem stemmed from the fact that the actual intercept was conducted on U.S. soil, either at NSA Georgia or in one of the NSA's secret telecom rooms. "Where we intercept the communications has be-come a very important part of the determination," said McConnell. It was a section of FISA that was little noticed during the Cold War because nearly all of the NSA's listening posts were located overseas, and thus unaffected by the restriction. But beginning in the mid-1990s under Mc-Connell, most of the NSA's foreign bases were closed and consolidated stateside in Georgia, Texas, Colorado, and Hawaii. Later, secret intercept rooms were established in domestic telecom facilities, such as the AT&T hub in San Francisco.

Despite the unfavorable ruling, the FISA court gave the NSA a grace period of a few weeks. "We had a stay until the end of May," said McCon-nell. After that, the agency was back to operating as it did pre-9/11. Thus, with every minute counting, attorneys in the NSA's Office of General

Counsel quickly began to put together an emergency FISA application. All that was required was the signature of the attorney general before the targeting could begin. The agency would then have three full days before it would be required to obtain a regular FISA order. At 10:00 a.m. on Tuesday, representatives from the NSA met with other intelligence officials to discuss how best to target the ISI suspects. Fifty-two minutes later, the agency formally notified Justice of its desire to begin the intercept operation. To the agency's surprise, some of the names were already being surveilled under a preexisting FISA order. Finally, at 12:53 p.m., the NSA's general counsel signed off on the emergency FISA request to begin targeting of the remaining names, certifying that all of the probable cause requirements had been met.

But rather than quickly get the document signed and start the surveillance, Bush administration lawyers and intelligence officials spent the next four and a half hours debating and discussing how to go about it. Thus it was not until 5:15 p.m. that they began looking for a signature and by then key officials were out of reach. Attorney General Gonzales was in Texas addressing a United States attorneys' conference and the solicitor general, who was then the acting attorney general, had already left for the day. Rather than call him back in, the decision was made to attempt to reach Gonzales in Texas. That mistake cost another two hours as the Justice Department's command center called back and forth to the staff but were unable to actually speak to the attorney general. Finally, at 7:18 p.m., Gonzales authorized the emergency request and the FBI was immediately contacted. Ten minutes later, bureau officials notified the NSA and at 7:38 p.m. the names were placed on the watch list and the targeting finally began.

The system had descended into chaos, and this time lives depended on it. Because of the spring FISA court ruling "we lost about two-thirds of our capability," complained McConnell. "We were in a situation where we couldn't do our basic function of providing warning or alert to stop an attack." This was because so much of the world's communications—especially Internet traffic—passes through U.S. switches and routers. "If you were to look at a map of the world by bandwidth, it would show that the United States is the center of the world," said McConnell.

Then, once the new court ruling took effect on June 1, the agency had to begin performing a sort of triage on the intercepts. Massive amounts were flowing in, but analysts were able to target only a small number because of the need to obtain a FISA order on those selected. "We were in extremis," McConnell complained. "American soldiers were captured in Iraq by insurgents and we found ourselves in a position where we had to get a warrant to target the communications of the insurgents . . . What we did do was, as the numbers got smaller, we prioritized in a way that we kept the most important, the most threatening, on coverage. And we worked very quickly to try to catch up, and what we found is [that] there's so much volume that we were falling further and further behind."

Realizing the mess that was developing, a few months earlier the Bush administration had finally decided to go to Congress and seek to modify FISA—something they could have done at the very beginning. Six years earlier, following the 9/11 attacks, the administration could have simply and quickly updated the law with virtually no opposition. Instead, led by Cheney and Hayden, the White House came up with its supersecret make-up-the-rules-as-you-go warrantless eavesdropping program. Now, more than half a decade later, the program was no longer secret because of the *New York Times* leaks—leaks driven by its illegal nature. At the same time, the war was in an upward death spiral, the president's national ratings were below sea level, and Congress was in the hands of angry Democrats. It was a bad time to at last seek legislation, especially where much of it involved "trust us."

"In his normal dick-measuring contest with Congress, Cheney's big mantra was trying to reclaim executive power that he thinks the executive branch lost after Watergate," said one senior intelligence official. "And so their whole thing was we don't need your permission or your cooperation. He completely overplayed his hand, they painted themselves into this corner, and I would argue that they would ultimately get less out of this than they would have gotten if they brought Congress in early on. I would argue that they would have gotten more than they're going to end up getting."

Immunity

Chosen as the administration's chief lobbyist for the NSA eavesdropping program was the former NSA director and retired vice admiral Mike McConnell, now the newly appointed director of national intelligence (DNI). Born on July 26, 1943, in the foothills of the Blue Ridge Mountains in Greenville, South Carolina, McConnell was the son of a progressive textile worker who, in the 1930s, promoted union organization and civil rights. In the early 1960s he attended the local college, Furman University, where he slept in a closet in the school's gym while managing the basketball team. After graduating with a degree in economics in 1966, during the war in Vietnam he joined the navy. "My father was in World War II, my uncles were in Korea," McConnell said, "and so it was a war and it never entered my mind that I wouldn't do anything other than what my family had done, [which] is to volunteer."

Shortly afterward, McConnell shipped off to Vietnam as a damage control officer on the USS *Colleton,* a ship attached to the Mobile Riverine Force in the Mekong Delta. A decade later, while assigned as the operations officer for the Fleet Ocean Surveillance Information Facility in Rota, Spain, in 1976, McConnell received his first initiation into the world of signals intelligence. "Four navy chiefs and one NSA civilian took me under their wing to teach me Sigint," he recalled. "I learned as a young navy lieutenant that Sigint is hard; it is complex, esoteric, and difficult to understand over its depth and breadth . . . It changed my understanding, respect for, and use of Sigint for the rest of my professional life."

In 1992 McConnell was named director of the NSA, where he oversaw the downsizing of the agency at the start of the post–Cold War years. He also found that it was far easier to eavesdrop than to convert the intercepts into finished, usable intelligence. As always, code breaking—referred to as processing—was the hardest part. "I have three major problems," McConnell was often heard declaring, "processing, processing, and processing." He also got his first taste of the new world of communications. "When I went there, it was all wireless. We listened to people around the world. I left four years later, it was all wire."

After retiring from the NSA, McConnell became a senior vice president at Booz Allen Hamilton, where, during the war in Iraq, he pocketed $2 million a year selling intelligence and defense services to the Pentagon and the spy community. Among the company's major contracts was a $63 million data mining operation for John Poindexter's discredited Total Information Awareness program.

Personable, soft-spoken, and courtly, with a mouth that seems constantly in a frown, McConnell has light-brown hair and a slight stoop when he walks. He took over as spy czar in February 2007. With the bulk of the intelligence work now being outsourced to private industry, it came as little surprise that Bush would choose an industry kingpin to run the intelligence community. But the driving force behind McConnell's selection was actually Cheney, who needed a good salesman to push Congress into passing a weakened and watered-down FISA bill to the administration's liking. The two had become close when Cheney was secretary of defense under the first President Bush and was responsible for McConnell's appointment as NSA director. In his new job, McConnell had to change his sleep patterns. "I get up at 4:00 every morning," he said. "I try to get to bed by 10:00 or 11:00 at the latest. And you do the math; that kind of makes it a full day. Why do I get up at 4:00? I have to brief the president at 7:30 to 8:00, six days a week."

McConnell argued against having a public debate on the issue of warrantless eavesdropping. Nevertheless, like Cheney and Bush, McConnell decided to use fearmongering as his principal marketing tool. During an address at his alma mater, Furman University in Greenville, South Carolina, for example, the DNI warned the students that a horde of Iraqi and Pakistani terrorists might be conspiring to wipe out their university and kill them all. "Today, terrorists in Pakistan . . . would like nothing more

than to obliterate this campus," he said. "If they're planning with the terrorists in Iraq, more often than not, the communications will flow through
the United States. So we've got foreign terrorists in Pakistan talking to a
foreign terrorist in Iraq who wants to attack the members of this audience
and a law said, 'Mike McConnell, you can't listen to that.' "

Then following the kidnapping of the soldiers in Iraq, McConnell
made the incident a part of the administration's sales pitch to Congress.
In closed session, he warned legislators that the NSA had lost precious
time in the first critical hours—time that could have been spent looking
for the suspects. "It took time," he said, because of the FISA requirement,
to demonstrate to the attorney general that the target was likely an agent
of a foreign power. By the time the NSA obtained the legal permission
for the tap, he said, it was no longer useful. "Some Americans are going
to die," he said, unless the administration got its way.

The theme was then picked up and spread by the Republicans, who
eventually convinced many in the public that FISA was responsible for the
soldiers' fate. "The intelligence community was forced to abandon our soldiers because of the law," a senior congressional staffer told the *New York
Post.* "How many lawyers does it take to rescue our soldiers?" he asked sar-
castically. "It should be zero." The family members of the kidnapped soldiers, understandably upset, also joined in. "This is terrible. If they would
have acted sooner, maybe they would have found something out and been
able to find my son," said Alex Jimenez's mother, Maria Duran. "Oh my
God. I just keep asking myself, where is my son? What could have happened to him? . . . They should change the law, because God only knows
what type of information they could have found during that time period."

But the reality was far different from the sales pitch. It wasn't until
10:00 a.m. Tuesday morning, three days after the attack, that the NSA
first began working on the paperwork for the emergency application and
by 12:53 p.m. they were finished. All that was needed was the signature of the attorney general or the acting attorney general. According to
Royce Lamberth, the former presiding judge of the FISA court, "The
attorney general can immediately implement a surveillance by notifying
the court." But rather than get that done and begin the surveillance, the
Justice Department wasted the afternoon talking about the issue, then
couldn't locate the acting attorney general, and spent another two hours
trying to find Gonzales. Rather than blame the delay on the slow-moving

Justice Department, however, McConnell argued to Congress that it was the new FISA requirement that was gumming up the works and risking the lives of American soldiers.

The tactics worked. As members of Congress were racing for the door to start their August recess, the Bush administration was able to ramrod through both chambers a temporary FISA reform containing the changes they wanted. These included giving the NSA, for the first time, the authority to eavesdrop without a warrant not just on overseas targets calling or e-mailing into the country, but also on Americans communicating overseas, as long as the target is "a person reasonably believed to be located outside of the United States." Thus, if a person in Chicago calls or e-mails someone in London, the NSA could now eavesdrop on that conversation or read that message without a warrant, as long as the agency's target is the person in London.

This was a substantial expansion of the law and basically stripped authority away from the FISA court by giving the attorney general and McConnell the power to approve international surveillance, rather than the eleven judges. The only role for the court would be to review and approve the procedures used by the NSA after the eavesdropping had been conducted. It would have no authority to examine the justification for the individual cases. The law also gave the Bush administration additional power to force the telecom industry to cooperate with such spying operations. The companies could now be compelled to cooperate by orders from the attorney general and McConnell.

The Protect America Act was passed during a Saturday session on August 4 but not signed into law by President Bush until the next morning. At that point, the NSA raced to get back up to speed. "It actually took us about five days to get it all done," said McConnell, "because there were new procedures, and we had to be very careful, so we had the highest priority on coverage, and then it took us about five days or so get back to where we were in January."

Ironically, it turned out that the changes in FISA apparently had nothing to do with the search for the missing soldiers. The kidnapping took place on May 12 and the new interpretation of the law didn't go into effect until June 1. Also, according to Colonel Michael Kershaw, one of the regional commanders in Iraq who helped lead the search, the key suspect involved and the initial target of the NSA's search, Abu Rus, was quickly captured, and it turned out that he had nothing to do with the kidnapping. "The terrorist that really had led the attack against our predecessor unit," said Kershaw, "we detained him about three weeks after the attack on our soldiers. We went after his group immediately and were able to capture him. But the information that we found that was associated with him led us to believe that he was not involved directly in the attack on our soldiers."

Nevertheless, the scare tactics worked and the bill was passed—but only as a placeholder until permanent legislation could be debated and enacted. Thus it was set to self-destruct in just six months, at midnight on Saturday, February 16. As the date approached, the Senate complied fully and passed the administration's bill, complete with immunity from prosecution for the telecoms that assisted with the warrantless eavesdropping program. "Under the president's program, the terrorist surveillance program," McConnell acknowledged, "the private sector had assisted us. Because if you're going to get access you've got to have a partner." The House, however, showed signs of balking. Many members had been severely criticized for running out of town in August instead of fighting against the Protect America Act and now they were going to take their time. The House asked for a three-week extension of the act so it could study the Senate bill, but the White House said it would veto any such extension, despite the claim that the country would be in mortal danger if the legislation expired.

The key issue was immunity for the telecoms, which the House had refused to put in its version of the bill—the Restore Act—and they weren't budging, despite the fact that it was approved by the Senate. Many believed that the issue needed to be settled in the courts, not on Capitol Hill, and it was also an issue important for a number of Democratic support groups. "The House should stand up to the bullying from the president and reject the administration's lies and fearmongering," said Caroline Fredrickson, director of the American Civil Liberties Union's legislative office in Washington. "Let the American system of justice decide this case. Do not give the phone companies a 'get out of jail free' card. If the companies really 'did the right thing' as the president said, then they have nothing to fear from going to court." She added, "Terrorism is a threat. But ignoring the Constitution is also a threat."

At the White House, the anger and frustration was growing. On Thursday, two days before the deadline, President Bush said he would delay his planned five-nation tour of Africa to continue pressuring the House over the immunity issue. "If these companies are subjected to lawsuits that could cost them billions of dollars, they won't participate, they won't help us, they won't help protect America," Bush said. He then continued his fearsome warnings. "At this moment, somewhere in the world, terrorists are planning new attacks on our country. Their goal is to bring destruction to our shores that will make September the 11th pale by comparison." He added, "There is really no excuse for letting this critical legislation expire." Nevertheless, as in a high-stakes game of poker, he again refused to agree to a three-week extension, insisting on an up-or-down vote before the expiration of the deadline.

As the administration's fearmongering escalated, a number of national security experts, including some who had served in the Bush administration, publicly challenged the allegations. Among them was Richard Clarke, the former head of counterterrorism at the National Security Council under Bush; Rand Beers, the former senior director for combating terrorism at the National Security Council during the Bush administration; Lieutenant General Don Kerrick, former deputy national security advisor; and Suzanne Spaulding, the former assistant general counsel at the CIA. All had worked with McConnell in the past. Nevertheless, they wrote that McConnell and the Bush administration were distorting the truth about NSA surveillance capabilities after the Protect America Act expired. "The sunset of the Protect America Act (PAA) does not put America at greater risk," they wrote. "The intelligence community currently has the tools it needs to acquire surveillance of new targets and methods of communication."

They also rejected the administration's claim that it was crucial to national security that the telecoms receive retroactive immunity. "Telecommunications companies will continue to cooperate with lawful government requests, particularly since FISA orders legally compel cooperation with the government. Again, it is unclear to us that the immunity debate will affect our surveillance capabilities . . . The Administration has made it clear it believes this entire debate hinges on liability protection. As previously stated, it is unclear that liability protection would significantly improve our surveillance capabilities. It is wrong to make this one issue an immovable impediment to Congress passing strong legislation to protect the American people."

Finally, at midnight on Saturday, February 16, 2008, the law expired. Thus, six and a half years after Cheney and Hayden secretly took NSA off course, sending its reputation—and Americans' trust in the agency—plunging, and possibly violating the law and the Constitution, they were back to square one. "We have to work the dark side, if you will," Cheney had said back then. "Spend time in the shadows . . ."

But with the elections coming up and Democrats worried about being labeled weak on national security, the Bush administration largely got its way on July 9 when the Senate went along with the House and passed the FISA Amendments Act. The new law provides what amounts to legal immunity to the telecoms, weakens the authority of the FISA court, and gives freer range to NSA in targeting suspected terrorists abroad.

To end the more than forty lawsuits brought against them by public interest groups, the telecoms need only to show a federal judge that they received written assurance from the Bush administration that the eavesdropping was legal, which is basically a formality. Although the NSA will still have to obtain a FISA order to target Americans, they can now target foreigners outside the country simply by submitting to the court a list of suspected terrorist groups rather than individual names. It will be up to NSA shift supervisors to determine who is a member of the group. But in a significant concession, Americans abroad now come under the protection of the FISA court for the first time. Previously, all that was needed to eavesdrop on Americans outside the country was the permission of the attorney general; now to listen in on Americans overseas the NSA will have to obtain a FISA order.

The vote was seen as both a win for the Bush administration and a litmus test for Senator Barack Obama, the Democratic candidate for president. Although Senator John McCain had long supported the bill, but never bothered to vote on it, Obama had long opposed it and at one point even threatened a filibuster. But as the date for the vote approached, Obama said he would support the legislation, causing uproar among his most ardent followers—more than seven thousand of whom expressed their frustration on his own Web site and called for him to reverse his decision. "I have watched your campaign with genuine enthusiasm," wrote Robert Arellano, "and I have given you money. For the first time in my life, I have sensed the presence of a presidential candidate who might actually bring some meaningful change to the corrupt cesspool of national politics. But your about-face on the FISA bill genuinely angers and alarms me."

Despite the protest, Obama voted in favor of the bill. His only concession was a vow, if elected, to have his attorney general do a fresh review of the NSA's eavesdropping activities. "Given the choice between voting for an improved yet imperfect bill, and losing important surveillance tools, I've chosen to support the current compromise," he said. "I do so with the firm intention—once I'm sworn in as president—to have my attorney general conduct a comprehensive review of all our surveillance programs, and to make further recommendations on any steps needed to preserve civil liberties and to prevent executive branch abuse in the future."

And so the post-9/11 battle for civil liberties is lost with a promise that the war will continue behind the scenes of another president's administration. It is ironic, for if there is a lesson of the FISA Amendments Act, it is that presidential power is abundant; it is political courage that is in short supply.

BOOK FIVE

———————— ■ ————————

FUTURE

Exabytes

With the Middle East destined to be the central focus of NSA operations for the foreseeable future, shortly after the 9/11 attacks Mike Hayden took a close look at his limited and dilapidated facilities at NSA Georgia and called in the architects. As more trailers were set up to accommodate the growing overflow of personnel, work began on the blueprints for a sprawling new operational center to eavesdrop on target countries stretching from Pakistan to Libya.

Code-named Sweet Tea, the new listening post will include a 501,699-square-foot operations building containing a workout room, a credit union, a mini-shopping area, nursing facilities, an eight-hundred-seat cafeteria, and a new 7,600-square-foot Visitor Control Center. Located at the corner of 16th Street and Lane Avenue, the new NSA/CSS Georgia was also designed with the NSA's all-hearing antennas in mind. The location, said agency documents, "provides the perfect look angles with no possibility for encroachment to their required line-of-sight in the future." While the cost of the project has been pegged at $340.8 million, that figure excludes the purchase and installation of all the new equipment. Once the costly computers and expensive analytical equipment have been acquired and wired in place, officials believe the final total could be closer to $1 billion. The latest projections in 2008 were that the center would be fully up and running by 2012 and employ more than four thousand workers, making it the agency's largest facility outside of Fort Meade.

Inside, the workstations of voice interceptors and data miners that once looked like battlefield command centers, with multiple computers and monitors crammed together, will now have a single monitor and hard drive. Until now, for security reasons, separate computer systems have been needed for different highly classified programs, thereby creating a physical firewall between them. One system might be used exclusively for an operation targeting a high-level encrypted Egyptian diplomatic network while another, less sensitive computer might be used on intercepts from an Iranian naval base. A third might be an unclassified system connected to the Internet. Switching between hard drives or computers was both time-consuming and cumbersome.

But the NSA is now developing a secure "virtualization" platform able to combine multiple special-access programs on a single workstation. Analysts will only be able to enter the various sections of the computer hard drive with unique IDs and passwords. They can also quickly form password-protected "communities of interest" in the system, such as one in which only personnel cleared for Operation Highlander intercepts have access. "What's nice about this platform is I can form these communities of interest on the fly, make sure that they are secure, and begin to share information very quickly with other members of that community," said Chris Daly of IBM's Software Group, which is developing the system with General Dynamics Corporation's C4 Systems. "Secure virtualization ensures that one virtual space on my machine doesn't get contaminated by another."

Another innovation for Arabic voice interceptors at NSA Georgia, who must sift through at least twenty different dialects, is a new reference manual called the Arabic Variant Identification Aid (AVIA), which describes six dialects, Baghdadi Arabic being the latest addition. The system, created by NSA's Center for Advanced Study of Language, also comes with voice samples to help identify the origin of the speaker. A center document says, "A speaker who claims to be Egyptian but who speaks with a Yemeni 'accent' is probably lying. Linguists can use the AVIA to determine that such a person's speech is really Yemeni rather than Egyptian."

The intercept operators will also soon be carrying around Top Secret BlackBerry-type smart phones. Also built by General Dynamics' C4 Systems, the secure mobile device, known as the Sectéra Edge, will be capable of handling a variety of classifications, including voice communications at the Top Secret level and e-mail and Web access at the Secret level and below. "For the first time, authorized military and government personnel can now wirelessly access both classified and unclassified voice and data communications on the same device," said John Cole, vice president of C4 Systems for information assurance. "The Sectéra Edge is an all-in-one communications solution, allowing users to easily switch between classified and unclassified information by pressing a single key." Like a BlackBerry, the smart phone can synchronize information with a computer and, soon, will be able to accommodate WiFi networks.

At the quiet groundbreaking ceremony on March 26, 2007, NSA director Keith Alexander showed up with Georgia Republican Senator Saxby Chambliss. Before scooping some dirt with a golden shovel, Chambliss told the group of electronic spies, "You're doing the Lord's work." Someone then asked Alexander about the warrantless eavesdropping program. "We don't want to spy on Americans, now do we," he said. "We want to spy on terrorists."

While NSA Georgia has its ears cocked toward the Middle East and North Africa, NSA Texas eavesdrops on Central and South America as well as the Caribbean from a series of buildings and satellite dishes on the Medina Annex of Lackland Air Force Base. Since the attacks on 9/11, however, and with Latin America low on the priority list, the facility has been playing an increasing role in helping NSA Georgia target the Middle East and also hot spots in Europe such as Bosnia. Like Georgia, the facility is a consolidation of army, navy, marine, and air force Sigint specialists, with the air force taking the lead role. And also like Georgia, San Antonio is about to get an influx of NSA money and personnel.

The third major listening post in the U.S., focusing on Asia and the Pacific, is NSA Hawaii. For decades, the facility has been buried underground in a bunker in Kunia, in the center of the island of Oahu, about fifteen miles west of Honolulu. Originally constructed as an underground tunnel shortly after the Japanese attack on Pearl Harbor in December 1941, the $23 million cavern was built to house a bomb-proof aircraft assembly plant. But rather than drill into the ground, the engineers decided instead to erect a three-story hangarlike structure with a large open bay area and reinforced concrete walls and then cover it with earth.

Nicknamed "The Hole," the 250,000-square-foot facility was instead used as a map-making plant, producing 2,700,000 maps during one very busy month. Then following the war, the navy used the subterranean compound to store torpedoes and ammo, and later, after extensive renovations, it became a command center for U.S. Pacific forces. Then in January 1980, the NSA took it over, packed it with receivers and computers, put the army (and later the navy) in charge, and began eavesdropping on much of Asia.

But with the sudden windfall of post-9/11 cash, NSA architects drew up plans for a massive new facility, similar to NSA Georgia. On August 30, 2007, Director Keith Alexander, wearing a lei around his neck and holding a long 'O'o stick, an early Hawaiian digging tool, broke ground on the new facility. "Because of the mind-boggling changes in communication technology over the last two decades, coupled with the disturbing social and political dynamics, we need more, newer, and better ways to process intelligence," said Alexander. "This building and its design, infrastructure, capabilities, and location will support and protect an unparalleled intellectual combine."

Located off Whitmore Avenue in Wahiawa, the new 234,000-square-foot, two-story building is to be surrounded by an "Exclusive Standoff Zone," an empty area the width of a football field between the facility and the tall fence that encircles it. The seventy-acre site was formerly the home of a giant "elephant cage," an enormous circular antenna used for eavesdropping and direction finding over much of the Pacific. Once the $318 million facility is completed in September 2010, the twenty-seven hundred Kunia workers will leave their old bunker and enter the new one, which will be built partly underground.

Another highly secret NSA facility undergoing extensive expansion is its Denver Security Operations Center, located at 18201 East Devils Thumb Avenue on Buckley Air Force Base in Aurora, just outside Colorado's capital city. For decades, a series of four large satellite dishes in golf-ball-like radomes have served as the downlink for a number of the agency's most powerful eavesdropping spacecraft. These include a microwave-only eavesdropping system known as Vortex or Mercury, and a multifrequency giant known as Magnum or Orion. The two geosynchronous satellites were such behemoths they needed to be launched on the powerful Titan-IV rocket. The take from these satellites is analyzed in the attached Aerospace Data Facility, which in 2000 employed about twenty-nine hundred analysts from all branches of the service as well as NSA civilians. But like the other listening posts, the Denver center is undergoing a large expansion.

At the time of the attacks, the NSA had only about 7 percent of its facilities outside of the Baltimore-Washington area. The realization that a series of similar attacks could virtually wipe out the agency caused Mike Hayden to begin thinking seriously about moving critical parts of the agency to other areas of the country. Another reason to relocate large chunks of the agency was power. As the agency began digging through massive amounts of data, its energy-hungry thinking machines were put on overdrive. What is likely the world's largest collection of superpowerful computers is housed in the Tordella Supercomputer Building, a windowless, two-story, 183,000-square-foot facility on Ream Road at NSA Headquarters. Keeping the whirring machines from melting is an eight-thousand-ton chilled water plant. Even before the attacks, all that number crunching consumed enormous amounts of energy—about the same amount of electricity as half the city of Annapolis, Maryland's capital.

Following the attacks, as the NSA began plowing through mountains of data in its search for terrorists, the agency's already enormous power demands began running up against Baltimore Gas & Electric Company's finite amount of energy. The problem was so serious that agency technicians were unable to install two new multimillion-dollar supercomputers in the Tordella Building out of fear that the NSA's power grid would collapse, blowing the fuse on the entire agency.

By 2006, the estimates were that such a calamity could be anywhere from two months to less than two years away. "If there's a major power failure out there, any backup systems would be inadequate to power the whole facility," said Michael Jacobs, who was in charge of the code-making side of the NSA until 2002. Another longtime agency executive, William Nolte, pointed to the danger of erratic power surges. "You've got an awfully big computer plant and a lot of precision equipment, and I don't think they would handle power surges and the like really well," he said. "Even recalibrating equipment would be really time-consuming—with lost opportunities and lost up-time."

As a short-term fix, the agency began considering buying additional generators and pulling the plug on a number of older computers designed for code-breaking attacks on Cold War targets. They even began raising the temperature two degrees during the summer to help alleviate the strain on the electrical system. Some current and former government officials pointed the finger at General Hayden for not taking greater action when the energy problems first began to surface in the late 1990s. "It fits into a long, long pattern of crisis-of-the-day management as opposed to investing in the future," said one. Also alarmed was Senator John D. Rockefeller IV, the chairman of the Senate Intelligence Committee. The NSA officials "were so busy doing what various people wanted that they forgot to understand that they were running out of power, and that's sort of a national catastrophe," he said, warning, "We cannot have that place go dark."

One potential solution involved an enormous building boom, creating a poweropolis with a new 50-megavolt amp substation, a 50-megawatt generator plant, and another 36-megawatt generator plant, on top of the agency's existing city-size capacity. The other answer was to begin moving much of the data mining out of Fort Meade to more energy-friendly parts of the country.

After months of searching, it was decided to relocate the data center to a former Sony Electronics computer chip plant not far from NSA Texas. In what had become a common practice, once the NSA approved of the new building, it was purchased by Corporate Office Properties Trust (COPT), a Columbia, Maryland, real-estate investment company that specialized in leasing buildings to the NSA and its contractors. The firm also owned much of National Business Park, the office complex across from the NSA where many of the companies doing business with the agency leased buildings. The NSA would then lease the former Sony plant from COPT at a nice profit for the company. "We have become increasingly reliant on intelligence and defense tenants," said Randall Griffin, president and CEO of COPT, "particularly due to the increased activity in those sectors following the events of September 11, 2001."

COPT paid $30.5 million for the 470,000-square-foot facility, which Sony vacated in 2003. Located on fifty acres of land, it consists of two connected former research and development buildings at 1 Sony Drive, located at NW Loop 410 and Military Drive in northwestern Bexar County. The company also placed under contract another twenty-seven acres of adjoining land with the understanding the NSA would likely expand the facility and construct additional buildings. The NSA's plan was to spend about $100 million to renovate what it was calling the Texas

Cryptology Center, and then employ about fifteen hundred people to work there, many hired locally. An initial group of experienced agency workers would come down to train the new hires in another leased building, an old Albertsons grocery store near Interstate 10 and Wurzbach Road in San Antonio.

The timing of the move was interesting. Although the agency began looking at the property in 2005 and even signed a lease for the Sony building, it seemed to be holding back. When asked if the project was still on track, NSA spokesman Don Webber issued a noncommittal response regarding the move. "I will not speculate about any changes to NSA's plans for a new facility for NSA/CSS Texas," said Webber. "As with any government program, shifting priorities, funding availability, and mission essentials could always alter the scope or schedule of a planned project." City officials, worried about losing the facility, traveled to NSA headquarters in early January 2007. "We told them we were going to get Microsoft, and that really opened up their eyes," said Bexar County judge Nelson Wolff. Then on January 18, Microsoft formally announced its decision to move to San Antonio. Three months later, on April 19, the NSA issued a quiet press release saying it had finally agreed on the San Antonio location.

Both the NSA and Microsoft had been eyeing San Antonio for years. The city had the cheapest electricity in Texas and the state had its own power grid, which made it less vulnerable to rippling outages on the national power grid. Nevertheless, it seemed that the NSA wanted to be assured that Microsoft would also be there before making a final commitment.

For an agency heavily involved in data harvesting, there were many advantages to having their miners virtually next door to the mother lode of data centers. Microsoft's plan was to build a $550 million, two-building complex on a forty-four-acre site at 5150 Rogers Road. At 470,000 square feet, the facility was the exact same size as the NSA's data center, with each almost the size of the city's Alamodome. One big difference, however, was in the number of personnel to be employed. As with most data centers, virtually everything in the Microsoft complex was automated and thus the company intended to hire only about seventy-five people to keep the equipment humming. The NSA, however, was planning to employ about fifteen hundred—far more than was needed to babysit a warehouse of routers and servers but enough to analyze the data passing across them.

On July 30, 2007, under mostly sunny skies, a white stretch Hummer pulled up to a vacant field in the Westover Hills section of San Antonio. As the door opened, a woman dressed in a white shirt, khaki pants, and cowboy boots stepped out and surveyed the vast open area. Debra Chrapaty, Microsoft's corporate vice president for global foundation services, then opened the groundbreaking ceremony for the new complex that, she said, would contain the digital brain for the world's largest software company.

"We're building a cloud," Chrapaty said. "The cloud is not the cloud in the sky, it's what we're about to break ground on in San Antonio." Inside the virtual cloud, she said, were tens of thousands of computer servers through which will pass e-mail, instant messages, photos, videos, software programs, and details on the Internet searches of millions of users worldwide. Chrapaty noted that Microsoft has more than 280 million Hotmail customers, and its computer systems handle eight billion message transactions per day. She also said the current plant was only the beginning and that Microsoft hoped to build a second, identical facility, bringing the total investment close to $1 billion. The new data center will be a place "where the Internet lives," said another company executive.

Microsoft hoped the first phase of the complex would "go live" in July 2008. When completed, the building will be a mirror image of the company's new data center in Quincy, Washington, which went live on March 27, 2007. Like Quincy, the San Antonio complex will be low-key and secretive, without even a sign to identify it. On the outside, the windowless, beige-colored building will be wrapped in a tall security fence.

Inside, employees will have to pass through a telephone-booth-sized security portal containing a biometric scanner that will take a hand impression to match one in the computer. They will also wear badges with radio-frequency-identification smart chips. Past the lobby, a small group of workers will oversee the operations of the data center in a glass-enclosed control room with a wall of monitors. Elsewhere, the building will consist of long hallways between huge brain centers containing tens of thousands of computer servers. To keep them a cool sixty to sixty-eight degrees, each center will have a room with refrigerator-sized air-conditioning units. In the event of a power failure, another room will contain giant blocks of batteries that would automatically come to life for eighteen seconds before the SUV-sized backup generators kick in.

As Microsoft broke ground on Rogers Road, 7.3 miles away workers were tearing walls and replacing floors at the NSA's future data center. In addition to tapping into American communications without a warrant, General Hayden also wanted to know exactly what Americans were doing day by day, hour by hour, and second by second. He wanted to know where they shopped, what they bought, what movies they saw, what books they read, the toll booths they went through, the plane tickets they purchased, the hotels they stayed in, and the restaurants where they ate. In other words, Total Information Awareness, the same Orwellian concept that John Poindexter had tried to develop while working for the Pentagon's DARPA.

Following the scandal that erupted after public exposure of his TIA project, Poindexter resigned and Congress killed any further money for the project. But surveillance projects have an uncanny way of coming back, and rather than die, many of the ideas and concepts simply migrated to the NSA, an agency with a far better track record than DARPA for keeping secrets. Even though Congress cut off funding for the stillborn program in 2003, it nevertheless authorized some of the research to continue and allowed TIA technology to be used in the NSA's foreign surveillance operations. Thus, just as the NSA can rifle through millions of phone calls under the Bush administration's warrantless surveillance program, it can also sift through billions of records, such as those stored at Microsoft's data facility. Such "transactional" data includes websites visited, queries to search engines, phone records, credit card usage, airline passenger data, banking transfers, and e-mail header details.

Even without the warrantless powers granted by President Bush, obtaining personal information has become much easier with the passage of the Patriot Act and the frequent use of "national security letters," which do not require probable cause or court approval. In 2000, the number of NSLs issued was 8,500, a large number. But between 2003 and 2005 the requests had skyrocketed to 143,074, according to a 2007 Justice Department inspector general's report. The audit found that 60 percent of a sample of these subpoenas were not in compliance with the rules, and another 22 percent contained unreported possible violations of the law, including improper requests and unauthorized collections of information.

The revised CALEA not only makes it a crime for any company, such as Microsoft, to refuse to cooperate, it also makes it a crime for company officials to disclose such cooperation.

While the revelations of such widespread abuse may have come as a surprise to most Americans, they did not surprise the president of a small Internet access and consulting business who was one of the many recipients of a national security letter. "The letter ordered me to provide sensitive information about one of my clients," he said. "There was no indication that a judge had reviewed or approved the letter, and it turned out that none had. The letter came with a gag provision that prohibited me from telling anyone, including my client, that the FBI was seeking this information. Based on the context of the demand—a context that the FBI still won't let me discuss publicly—I suspected that the FBI was abusing its power and that the letter sought information to which the FBI was not entitled."

The executive went to court and fought the order and the FBI eventually dropped the matter. "But the FBI still hasn't abandoned the gag order that prevents me from disclosing my experience and concerns with the law or the national security letter that was served on my company," he said. "Living under the gag order has been stressful and surreal. Under the threat of criminal prosecution, I must hide all aspects of my involvement in the case—including the mere fact that I received an NSL—from my colleagues, my family, and my friends. When I meet with my attorneys I cannot tell my girlfriend where I am going or where I have been. I hide any papers related to the case in a place where she will not look. When clients and friends ask me whether I am the one challenging the constitutionality of the NSL statute, I have no choice but to look them in the eye and lie. I resent being conscripted as a secret informer for the government and being made to mislead those who are close to me, especially because I have doubts about the legitimacy of the underlying investigation." He added, "At some point—a point we passed long ago—the secrecy itself becomes a threat to our democracy."

Another 2007 study, this one by the Congressional Research Service examining the federal government's data mining practices, gave a hint at the NSA's data dragnet. It cited a statistic from the Web page (now removed) for the NSA's Advanced Research and Development Activity

(ARDA): "Some intelligence data sources grow at a rate of four petabytes per month now," the study said, "and the rate of growth is increasing." As noted in the opening of this book, in a year at that rate, the database would hold at least 48 petabytes, the equivalent of nearly one billion four-door filing cabinets full of documents. It would also be equal to about twenty-four trillion pages of text.

Eric Haseltine noted in 2004 that even the NSA's enormous computer power has trouble keeping up with the flow. "We can either be drowned by it or we can get on our surfboard and surf it and let it propel us. And, of course, that's what we're trying to do."

According to a University of California, Berkeley, study that measured data trends around the globe, the NSA does a lot of surfing. In 2002, there were 1.1 billion telephone lines in the world producing close to 3,785 billion minutes—equivalent to 15 exabytes of data. At the same time, there were also 1.14 billion mobile cellular phones producing over 600 billion wireless minutes, or another 2.3 exabytes. Then there's the Internet, which in 2002 contained about 32 petabytes of data and had about 667 million users who sent and received about 532,897 terabytes of information, including 440,606 terabytes of e-mail.

To analyze such amounts of information flowing into the agency's rapidly filling databases, the NSA and ARDA came up with a number of TIA like exploitation systems including one called Novel Intelligence from Massive Data (NIMD). The program focused on the development of data mining and analysis tools to be used in working with enormous quantities of information. "Novel Intelligence" refers to a potential key piece of a puzzle that had not previously been known. "Massive Data" is measured either by size—one petabyte and above—or by complexity, such as multimedia, audio, maps, graphics, video, spoken text, equations, and chemical formulas or a combination all jumbled together.

At the heart of NIMD is a piece of software called the Glass Box that sits on analysts' workstations and captures much of their online research process—the searches, results, downloads, documents viewed, and locations where data is sent. Based on the data captured in the Glass Box, models are created to automate and improve upon the analysts' techniques. Similar analytic functions can then be automated and implemented on vast bodies of data. The ultimate goal would be to have, in essence, robotic analysis "of streaming petabytes of data"—such as that flowing across the Microsoft servers or through AT&T's OC-192 pipes. This "data triage" would then make "decisions about which data to store, which to elevate for immediate analysis, and which to delete without further attention." If fully implemented on U.S. communications and data links, it would create a society where everyone's words and actions would be screened by secret surveillance machines programmed to watch-list anyone who matches a complex algorithm created by a secret agency.

In the same way that the NSA is drowning in useless data, it is also unable to keep its head above water in analyzing voice communications. Despite decades of research, the agency has still not perfected the capability to effectively spot key words or phrases in voice telephone conversations. There are just too many and they go by too fast. Even at the agency's Middle East listening post in Georgia, where the hunt for Osama bin Laden was priority one, the eavesdropping was still conducted the old-fashioned way—analysts such as Adrienne Kinne would manually listen to each call. There were far more calls, however, than there were analysts to listen.

Nevertheless, the science of telephonic word spotting is progressing both within the agency and in the outside world. Among the leading companies in the field is Natural Speech Communication (NSC), which, like Verint, Narus, and NICE, is a company based in Israel, the eavesdropping capital of the world. Founded by Ami Moyal, a participant in the Wiretappers' Ball, the company has sold its eavesdropping products to a number of unidentified Western intelligence services. "The NSC Spotter is currently deployed in several agencies around the world," says the company. According to Moyal, "We don't pretend that we can compete against the U.S. National Security Agency, but we have a supplementary product." Like the other Israeli bugging companies, NSC also has extremely close ties to Israeli intelligence. Among the five members of the company's board of directors is Shabtai Shavit, who served as head of Mossad from 1989 until 1996, and since then has been an advisor to the Israeli National Security Council and to the subcommittee on intelligence of the Knesset.

"NSC's technology is a fascinating technology that can upgrade intelligence and monitoring systems all over the world," said Shavit. "NSC has a unique solution for the analysis of huge amounts of audio data in real time for security operations that depends on immediate response. Also, word-spotting technology has big potential in additional markets dealing with large quantities of audio and video data. I believe that the right use of this technology will create a big change in the way audio is analyzed and mapped these days and will enable the full utilization of valuable information hidden in audio data."

According to the company, NSC's keyword-spotting technology has the capability to monitor in real time an enormous number of phone calls. "With increasing volumes of audio streams that require monitoring," says the company, "keyword spotting is the only way to address the need of handling hundreds of thousands of calls per day. KWS can assist human agents to focus on the most relevant calls thereby optimizing the monitoring process. This frees the agents from working on irrelevant material, leading to better utilization of human resources . . . These organizations are inundated with a huge amount of audio sources that require constant monitoring. Since there is such a large amount of data, using only human resources is not an option. KWS technology enables these organizations to scan and prioritize the audio material so that the most significant conversations are handled first."

For the NSA, a particularly appealing feature of the NSC keyword-spotting software is its availability in a variety of Arabic dialects. "This included recording a large, representative database of Arab speakers of the Levantine dialect," says the company, "spoken by Israeli Arabs, Jordanians, Lebanese, and Palestinians. A particular problem was collecting the colloquial spoken form of the language as used in everyday speech, and not the classical standard forms found in read speech."

Another company deeply involved in targeting phone calls, and closely linked to the NSA, is Nexidia Inc. But rather than conducting real-time word spotting on multiple voice communications channels, Nexidia specializes in analyzing, at enormous speed, the content of calls already recorded. According to the company, it can search through phone calls "169,000 to 548,000 times faster than real time." Thus, says Nexidia, "the technology can render over eight thousand hours of audio data searchable per day." Among the company's first customers was the NSA, and sitting on the board of directors is the NSA's former director Ken Minihan.

Also, among the grants and contracts awarded to the company's founder, Mark A. Clements, were several from the NSA, including one titled "Analysis of Whispered Speech," which he worked on from January 2000 until August 2003. From the title, the NSA might have had George Orwell's classic dystopian novel *1984* in mind. In his book, Orwell wrote, "Any sound that Winston made, above the level of a very low whisper, would be picked up by it . . . You had to live—did live, from habit that became instinct—in the assumption that every sound you made was overheard and, except in darkness, every movement scrutinized." Mindful of the limitations of Orwell's Big Brother, the NSA is apparently determined to prevent even low whispers from escaping their microphones.

Trailblazer

Well beyond word spotting, NSA is also developing another tool that Orwell's Thought Police might have found useful—an artificial intelligence system designed to know what people are thinking. With the entire Internet and thousands of databases for a brain, the device will be able to respond almost instantaneously to complex questions posed by intelligence analysts. As more and more data is collected—through phone calls, credit card receipts, social networks like Facebook and MySpace, GPS tracks, cell phone geolocation, Internet searches, Amazon book purchases, even E-Z Pass toll records—it may one day be possible to know not just where people are and what they are doing, but what and how they think. The system is so potentially intrusive that at least one researcher has quit, citing concerns over the dangers in placing such a powerful weapon in the hands of a top-secret agency with little accountability.

Known as Aquaint, which stands for "Advanced QUestion Answering for INTelligence," the project was run for many years by John Prange, an NSA scientist at the Advanced Research and Development Activity. Headquartered in Room 12A69 in the NSA's Research and Engineering Building at 1 National Business Park, ARDA was set up by the agency to serve as a sort of intelligence community DARPA, the place where John Poindexter's infamous Total Information Awareness project was born. Later named the Disruptive Technology Office, ARDA has now morphed into the Intelligence Advanced Research Projects Activity (IARPA).

A sort of national laboratory for eavesdropping and other spycraft,

IARPA will move into its new 120,000-square-foot home in 2009. The building will be part of the new M Square Research Park in College Park, Maryland. A mammoth two-million-square-foot, 128-acre complex, it is operated in collaboration with the University of Maryland. "Their budget is classified, but I understand it's very well funded," said Brian Darmody, the University of Maryland's assistant vice president of research and economic development, referring to IARPA. "They'll be in their own building here, and they're going to grow. Their mission is expanding."

If IARPA is the spy world's DARPA, Aquaint may be the reincarnation of TIA. After a briefing by Hayden, Cheney, and Tenet on some of the NSA's data mining programs in July 2003, Senator Jay Rockefeller IV, the vice chairman of the Senate Intelligence Committee, wrote a concerned letter to Cheney. "As I reflected on the meeting today," he said, "John Poindexter's TIA project sprung to mind, exacerbating my concern regarding the direction the administration is moving with regard to security, technology, and surveillance."

The original goal of Aquaint, which dates back to the 1990s, was simply to develop a sophisticated method of picking the right needles out of a vast haystack of information and coming up with the answer to a question. As with TIA, many universities were invited to contribute brainpower to the project. But in the aftermath of the attacks on 9/11, with the creation of the secret warrantless eavesdropping program and the buildup of massive databases, the project began taking on a more urgent tone.

In a 2004 pilot project, a mass of data was gathered from news stories taken from the *New York Times,* the AP news wire, and the English portion of the Chinese Xinhua news wire covering 1998 to 2000. Then, thirteen U.S. military intelligence analysts searched the data and came up with a number of scenarios based on the material. Finally, using those scenarios, an NSA analyst developed fifty topics, and in each of those topics created a series of questions for Aquaint's computerized brain to answer. "Will the Japanese use force to defend the Senkakus?" was one. "What types of disputes or conflicts between the PLA [People's Liberation Army] and Hong Kong residents have been reported?" was another. And "Who were the participants in this spy ring, and how are they related to each other?" was a third. Since then, the NSA has attempted to build both on the complexity of the system—more essay-like answers rather than yes or no—and on attacking greater volumes of data.

"The technology behaves like a robot, understanding and answering complex questions," said one former Aquaint researcher. "Think of *2001: A Space Odyssey* and the most memorable character, HAL 9000, having a conversation with David. We are essentially building this system. We are building HAL." A naturalized U.S. citizen who received her PhD from Columbia, the researcher worked on the program for several years but eventually left due to moral concerns. "The system can answer the question, 'What does X think about Y?' " she said. "Working for the government is great, but I don't like looking into other people's secrets. I am interested in helping people and helping physicians and patients for the quality of people's lives." The researcher now focuses on developing similar search techniques for the medical community.

A supersmart search engine, capable of answering complex questions such as "What were the major issues in the last ten presidential elections?" would be very useful for the public. But that same capability in the hands of an agency like the NSA—absolutely secret, often above the law, resistant to oversight, and with access to petabytes of private information about Americans—could be a privacy and civil liberties nightmare. "We must not forget that the ultimate goal is to transfer research results into operational use," said Aquaint project leader John Prange, in charge of information exploitation for IARPA.

Once up and running, the database of old newspapers could quickly be expanded to include an inland sea of personal information scooped up by the agency's warrantless data suction hoses. Unregulated, they could ask it to determine which Americans might likely pose a security risk—or have sympathies toward a particular cause, such as the antiwar movement, as was done during the 1960s and 1970s. The Aquaint robospy might then base its decision on the types of books a person purchased online, or chat room talk, or websites visited—or a similar combination of data. Such a system would have an enormous chilling effect on everyone's everyday activities—what will the Aquaint computer think if I buy this book, or go to that website, or make this comment? Will I be suspected of being a terrorist or a spy or a subversive?

Collecting information, however, has always been far less of a problem for the NSA than understanding it, and that means knowing the language. To expand its linguistic capabilities, the agency established another new organization, the Center for Advanced Study of Language (CASL), and housed it in a building near IARPA at the M Square Research Park. But far from simply learning the meaning of foreign words, CASL, like Aquaint, attempts to find ways to get into someone's mind and understand what they're thinking. One area of study is to attempt to determine if someone is lying simply by watching their behavior and listening to them speak. According to one CASL document, "Many deception cues are difficult to identify, particularly when they are subtle, such as changes in verb tense or extremely brief facial expressions. CASL researchers are studying these cues in detail with advanced measurement and statistical analysis techniques in order to recommend ways to identify deceptive cue combinations."

Another area of focus explores the "growing need to work with foreign text that is incomplete," such as partly deciphered messages or a corrupted hard drive or the intercept of only one side of a conversation. The center is thus attempting to find ways to prod the agency's cipher-brains to fill in the missing blanks. "In response," says the report, "CASL's cognitive neuroscience team has been studying the cognitive basis of working memory's capacity for filling in incomplete areas of text. They have made significant headway in this research by using a powerful high-density electroencephalogram (EEG) machine acquired in 2006." The effort is apparently directed at discovering what parts of the brain are used when very good cryptanalysts are able to guess correctly the missing words and phrases in a message.

Like something out of a B-grade sci-fi movie, CASL is even trying to turn dull minds into creative geniuses by training employees to control their own brain waves: "The cognitive neuroscience team has also been researching divergent thinking: creative, innovative and flexible thinking valuable for language work. They are exploring ways to improve divergent thinking using the EEG and neurobiological feedback. A change in brain-wave activity is believed to be critical for generating creative ideas, so the team trains its subjects to change their brain-wave activity."

Now that the NSA has begun undertaking remote assassinations, CASL is also attempting to find ways to better identify who exactly is speaking before the CIA blows him or her up with a Hellfire missile, as they did with al-Harethi and his companions in Yemen. "CASL researchers," says the report, "are applying sociolinguistic knowledge to speaker recognition and identification technology. The team developed a protocol for conducting a forensic exam to bring in insights from phonetics, socio-linguistics, speech analysis and culture. In addition, the team is working on a sociolinguistic ontology, or an organized system for representing the social variables—race, gender, age, etc.—that interact with linguistic variation."

Aquaint, Novel Intelligence from Massive Data, Glass Box, cognitive neuroscience research, brain-wave control, speaker recognition, and many more projects are all part of Trailblazer, the code name for the NSA's rapid push to modernize its eavesdropping operations in a digital, cellular, fiber-optic world. Hayden had originally picked Trailblazer over the rival system Thinthread, which would have given the agency a greater ability to trace the origins and destinations of phone calls and e-mail. Unfortunately, Trailblazer, launched in 2000, started out bad and only got worse.

The first contracts, worth $197 million, went to a little known soft ware company that only eighteen months earlier was operating out of the owner's basement. The company, Conquest, was founded in 1989 by Norman G. Snyder, a former agency employee, in the basement of his Severna Park, Maryland, house. It had the advantage of being close to the Denny's restaurant in Laurel, where the company's executives held their weekly meetings. "Five or ten years ago NSA would have never chosen a company like Conquest," said Snyder, who later moved the company to the agency's National Business Park.

Later, many of the NSA's giants—SAIC, Boeing, Computer Science Corporation, IBM, Litton—came on board. But Trailblazer was plagued from the start with huge cost overruns and long delays and things never got better. Hayden indicated that one of the key problems was that they were eavesdropping on far more information than they could ever process. "We've had pretty good success with the front end in terms of collection," he said. "The more success you have with regard to collection, the more you're swimming in an ocean of data. So what Trailblazer was essentially designed to do was to help us deal with masses of information and to turn it into usable things for American decision makers. There is no other element out there in American society that is dealing with volumes of data in this dimension."

Hayden and his corporate partners quickly realized they were no longer swimming but drowning in that data ocean as the cost overruns began mounting. When the agency's inspector general looked at the problem, he found "inadequate management and oversight" of private contractors and overpayment for the work that was done. "The costs were greater than anticipated, to the tune of, I would say, in the hundreds of millions," Hayden acknowledged. "The slippages were actually more dramatic than the costs. As we slipped, the costs were pushed to the right. But we underestimated the costs by, I would say, a couple to several hundred million in terms of the costs. Again, it was what we actually encountered doing this. It was just far more difficult than anyone anticipated." Hayden also said that the agency tried to do too much too fast. "We learned," he said, "that we don't profit by trying to do moon shots, by trying to take the great leap forward, that we can do a lot better with incremental improvement, spiral development."

Turbulence

Upon becoming director in August 2005, Lieutenant General Keith Alexander decided to learn from Hayden's mistakes and take a much more piecemeal approach to the problem of the three troublesome Vs of signals intelligence—volume, velocity, and variety. Rather than one unified theory of Sigint, as Trailblazer was intended to be, Alexander focused more on mastering the individual pieces of the system. "I think the way to do it efficiently is smaller steps, more rapidly done, rather than try to take one big jump and make it all the way across," he said, "[in terms of] how you handle data, how you visualize that data and how we jump from industrial-age analysis to the information-age analysis that our country needs."

"The new idea of Trailblazer, the follow-on to Trailblazer, the big pie-in-the-sky supersecret follow-on is now called Turbulence," said one senior official familiar with the program. Soon after it was established, Turbulence lived up to its name as Congress began raising questions. "NSA's transformation program, Trailblazer, has been terminated because of severe management problems, and its successor, Turbulence, is experiencing the same management deficiencies that have plagued the NSA since at least the end of the Cold War," said one document prepared by the Senate Armed Services Committee in March 2007.

A month later, Alexander received the results of an internal survey that appeared remarkably similar to a nearly identical study carried out when Hayden first arrived at the agency eight years earlier. "What we need is fundamental change in the way we manage NSA and what we expect of management and ourselves," said the task force, which was led by George "Dennis" Bartko, the agency's deputy chief of cryptanalysis. The agency lacked a "unity of purpose," was facing an "identity crisis," and failed to produce a "fundamental management culture change." The twenty-eight-page classified document referred repeatedly to a lack of direction and cohesion among both management and the workforce. "We do not trust our peers [coworkers] to deliver," it said. "Fragmentation has undermined corporate [NSA management] trust. Lack of trust is on display in NSA organizational structures [and] behaviors across the Enterprise."

Among their solutions, the twenty-four members of the panel recommended that the agency "decide upon a common purpose, develop plans and strategies aligned with that purpose, manage all of our resources, and tie rewards to successful execution of our plans." Bartko, in a separate column he wrote in an agency publication, pointed out the seeming lack of progress from the earlier, Hayden-era report. "If these recommendations were made before, what's different this time?" he asked rhetorically, adding, "Now is the time" for change. "It has to be. The Nation is depending on us not only today, but tomorrow as well."

But most troubling was the lack of oversight. "There is no clear measurement and no accountability for execution performance," said the task force. That may have been a factor in another report that measured morale within the intelligence community. The survey found that only 46 percent of senior managers within the intelligence community were satisfied with the "policies and practices of your senior leaders," and only 43 percent of NSA managers.

Ironically, despite the call for accountability, the room within the agency reserved for the Government Accountability Office, the Congressional watchdog agency, remains vacant. "We still actually do have space at the NSA," said Comptroller General David M. Walker, the director of the GAO. "We just don't use it and the reason we don't use it is we're not getting any requests [from Congress], you know. So I don't want to have people sitting out there twiddling their thumbs."

At the same time that the NSA is becoming less accountable, it is becoming more and more depended upon—due in large part to the lack of useful human intelligence coming from the CIA. Now just one agency among many in the intelligence community, the CIA's lackluster performance became starkly clear when it was forced to shutter nearly all of its multimillion-dollar front companies throughout Europe because they were not producing any useful intelligence. The fronts, posing as investment banks and other companies, were to serve as cover for clandestine service officers attempting to develop sources and information. But instead of intelligence the front companies only produced large bills, leading to the closure of ten out of a dozen offices. Critics saw the failure as just one more example of an agency out of touch with the times. "I don't believe the intelligence community has made the fundamental shift in how it operates to adapt to the different targets that are out there," said Republican congressman Peter Hoekstra of Michigan, the number two person on the House Intelligence Committee and normally a strong defender of the agency.

Considering the CIA's failures leading up to the attacks on 9/11, its bumbling on the weapons of mass destruction question leading to the war in Iraq, and now its lack of credible human intelligence on terrorism despite billions being added to its budget, the agency was quickly becoming more of a liability than an asset. As a result, Bush and Cheney began turning instead to the NSA and Turbulence to lead both the intelligence war and the cyberwar. "Bush told Alexander that he wanted 'a Manhattan Project' on this," said the senior official with knowledge of the program. Bush as well as Cheney, who had become very close to Alexander, pushed the NSA chief to go hard on the offensive.

Not only is Alexander the country's top eavesdropper as director of the NSA, he is also the nation's hacker in chief as commander of the little-known Joint Functional Component Command for Network Warfare (JFCC-NW). A highly secret element of the U.S. Strategic Command, it is America's cyberwar center, located at the NSA. While the air force also runs a cyber operations center at Lackland Air Force Base in Texas, the Air Force Information Warfare Center, its focus is largely defensive. At the NSA, the emphasis is penetration, exploitation, and attack. "They have had some pretty good success in terms of monitoring networks and going in and collecting and going in and leaving things behind," said the official.

In addition to viruses designed to covertly tap into networks, the things left behind could also potentially include such things as virulent strains of software viruses and logic bombs that remain dormant until a predetermined time. Once they come to life, they destroy a computer's data from the inside. Shortly after he retired as director of the NSA, Mike McConnell, now the director of national intelligence, said he knew of more than a dozen people who could "do major damage" to a nation by mounting a computer attack with just a few weeks' preparation.

Aware of the NSA's increasing involvement in cyber warfare, in March 2008 Russian president Vladimir Putin signed several executive orders designed to protect secrets on government computer networks from attack by restricting connections between international and domestic computer networks. Similar to a practice long employed by U.S. intelligence agencies, the measures restrict the ability of computers with access to "state or official secrets" to connect with networks that travel outside of the country. The decree stipulates that all "information systems, information and telecommunications networks, and computer equipment used to store, process or transmit information that contains state secrets or information from a state agency that contains official secrets," may not operate on networks connected to others that travel outside Russia's borders.

The NSA's heavy involvement in cyber warfare dates back to 1996, when then CIA director John Deutch announced plans to create a "cyberwar" center at the NSA. "The electron," Deutch warned, "is the ultimate precision-guided weapon." The Information Operations Technology Center was created at the NSA in 1999 and became the leading organization for network exploitation and attack. Then in July 2002, President Bush signed a top-secret order directing the national security community, including the NSA, to develop, for the first time, rules and policies governing how the United States would launch cyberattacks against foreign computer networks.

Known as National Security Presidential Directive 16, the order allows the president to launch a secret preemptive cyberwar against any number of foreign countries, from China to Pakistan. "I think the presidential directive on information warfare is prima facie evidence of how seriously the government does take cyber warfare," said John Arquilla, an associate professor of defense analysis at the Naval Postgraduate School and an expert on unconventional warfare. "It also marks a shift away from a far more prudential approach to information warfare. In the last administration, there was a great concern about using techniques of cyber warfare that would then be emulated by others, and, by suggesting to the world that the Americans think this is a legitimate form of warfare, others might want to begin doing this as well. There was a great deal of concern about that." As the most cyber-connected country in the world, the U.S. has more to lose by starting an endless cyberwar than any other nation.

The NSA sends its "global network exploitation analysts" to train at the agency's Network Exploitation and Target Development Bootcamp. Then, at the National Cryptologic School, they take such courses as "Ultimate Web Hacking" and "Ultimate Web Hacking Advanced." Many of the cyber warriors are outsourced from the agency's major contractors lining its National Business Park.

"Turbulence is working much better," said a knowledgeable official in 2008. "Trailblazer they tried to start off too comprehensively. What they're doing with Turbulence is they're starting out with little test programs and trying to take those and see where they go and expand on them. If they work, expand them, if they don't work, ohitoan them. Spend small amounts of money on certain ideas, see if they work, if they don't work, forget it; if they do work, move on to the next idea. And they try to expand those things out through the system. With Trailblazer, they tried to design a comprehensive system from day one. Alexander's thing is don't start with the big concept, start with little ideas, see how they work and see if you can sustain them." Most of the new Turbulence projects, he said, deal with network attacks. "They are mainly more ways of automating things to go into computers, burrow into computers, and then confuse the computer once you get it going. More sophisticated ways to do that kind of thing."

By moving into the world of cyberwar, the NSA has crossed another dangerous threshold. Corrupting or destroying another nation's data network is considered by most countries an act of war. And in a world where all networks are intertwined like a ball of string, once a well-disguised virus is set loose on one system, it may quickly spread to others, including those in the U.S. Like warrantless eavesdropping and mega–data mining, it is a legal and technical landscape virtually unexplored by Congress and society.

But if the NSA is light-years ahead of the laws of the United States, it still must obey the laws of physics—although it is coming close to getting around those laws also. According to an internal study, in order for the agency to be able to handle the enormous amounts of data projected in the near future, its computers will have to accelerate enormously—to petaflop speed, a quadrillion mathematical operations a second, long the Mount Everest of computing. With such a capability, the agency would likely be able to search through much of the world's telecommunications and computer networks looking for keywords on a real-time basis. But as silicon chips reach their finite limit in capacity, and as the supercomputer industry gives way to massively parallel computing, the agency is looking for ways to reinvent the computerized wheel.

In the spring of 1976 the first Cray-1 rolled out of the Cray Research production plant in Chippewa Falls, Wisconsin, and directly into the basement of the NSA. A second was quietly delivered to the NSA's secret think tank, the Communications Research Division of the Institute for Defense Analysis at Princeton University. With a random-access semiconductor memory capable of transferring up to 320 million words per second, or the equivalent of about twenty-five hundred three-hundred-page books, the computer could not have been a disappointment. And when it was hooked up to the computer's specialized input-output subsystem, the machine could accommodate up to forty-eight disc storage units, which could hold a total of almost thirty billion words, each no farther away than eighty millionths of a second.

By the mid to late 1980s, the pace of supercomputer development was barely giving the NSA enough time to boot up its newest Cray megamachine before a new one was wheeled into its basement "flophouse." But as the demand grew for faster—and cheaper—machines in the 1990s, universities and high-end companies turned to massively parallel computers containing a thousand or more processors, each as powerful as a traditional minicomputer. The shift meant trouble for Cray as the world turned to subcompacts, with fewer and fewer takers for its supercharged Rolls-Royces.

Following the worst financial year of its life, in which it was forced to cut nearly a quarter of its employees, and facing an uncertain future, Cray Research called it quits. It was acquired by Silicon Graphics Inc.—later known simply as SGI—a Mountain View, California, manufacturer of powerful, high-performance workstations, the sort of machines that became Cray's greatest competitor.

As the supercomputer business began crashing, worries increased at the NSA. Massively parallel processing might have been a good solution for some high-end commercial businesses, but it was insufficient for the NSA's specialized needs. "High end computing systems don't scale well when they're put in clusters, and they tend to be fragile, with a lot of reliability issues," said Steve Scott, chief technology officer at Cray. According to a Pentagon report on supercomputing and the NSA, "Large supercomputers have always been the only way to solve some really big 'capability' problems." These massive number crunchers, known as vector computers, were the engines that powered the agency's unique codebreaking machines—machines that stripped away the tightly welded steel that encased the secret intercepted messages flowing into the NSA. As a result, for decades the agency had quietly underwritten a large portion of the supercomputer industry.

The nervousness at the NSA increased substantially in 1999 as SGI appeared to be on the verge of going belly up while still under contract to build the agency's newest supercomputer, the Cray SV2. At the Pentagon, a special task force of the Defense Science Board was convened to look into pumping cash into the company to keep the SV2—and NSA codebreaking—alive.

"The Task Force concluded that there is a significant need for high performance computers that provide extremely fast access to extremely large global memories. Such computers support a crucial national cryptanalysis capability," said the study. "The vector supercomputing portion of the capability segment of the high performance technical computing market is at a critical juncture as far as U.S. national security interests are concerned. If the current Cray SV2 development slips its schedule or is unsuccessful, this vector market will be lost to the U.S. with the result that only foreign [Japanese] sources will be available for obtaining this critical computing capability . . . While the Task Force considers the development of the SV2 to be a very high-risk venture, we believe the DoD should continue to pursue its development because the potential payoff is so great—two orders of magnitude improvement—and the required investment is reasonable."

The decision to underwrite the SV2 was welcomed at the NSA with a collective sigh of relief. "The United States is committed to maintaining and building on its long-held position as the global leader in supercomputing," said the NSA's chief scientist, George Cotter. "These powerful computers are absolutely essential to U.S. national security interests. To that end, the U.S. government is committing significant support to SGI's Cray SV2 program." The new system was expected to dramatically extend the capability of the NSA's supercomputers with exceptional memory bandwidth, interconnections, and vector-processing capabilities. Its peak speed was estimated to be in the tens of teraflops (trillions of calculations per second), faster than any supercomputer in existence.

In 2000, SGI finally threw in the towel and sold Cray Research to the Seattle-based Tera Computer. In a sense, Cray had gone full circle, ending up in the hands of another maverick with a dream of building the fastest machine on earth. This time it was Tera's founder and chief scientist, Burton J. Smith, a large, rumpled man who had stunned many in the field by building a machine that in 1997 set a world speed record for sorting integer numbers. The rebirth of what was now called Cray Inc. was good news for the NSA. The agency was said to have played a quiet role in making the deal happen "because it wants at least one U.S. company to build state-of-the-art supercomputers with capabilities beyond the needs of most business customers." Work would thus continue on the NSA's SV2 with a delivery date scheduled for 2002.

Another major Cray customer, not surprisingly, was Australia's Defence Signals Directorate, their NSA. A Cray document bluntly stated the DSD's mission: the organization, it said, "filters all telephone conversations, fax calls and data transmissions, including e-mail."

Following the attacks on 9/11, with the NSA increasing its data intake exponentially, Hayden began looking beyond the SV2, rechristened the Cray X1. What he now needed was a new customized system capable of much greater bandwidth and able to process the Nile Rivers of data gushing in from the NSA's front-end collection facilities both in the U.S. and around the world. He also wanted a system that would be a hybrid, combining the best of both parallel and vector processing. The answer was a colossal Cray machine code-named the Black Widow. Made up of sixteen tall cabinets crammed with thousands of processors, the computer was painted jet black with a splash of red. In September 2003 Hayden gave his approval for the system, for which the NSA was paying $17.5 million—about the size of the agency's entire budget in its early years.

According to an Office of Science and Technology document, the Black Widow system "will provide outstanding global memory bandwidth across all processor configurations and will be scalable to hundreds of teraflops. Should be the most powerful commercially available system in the world at that time." Also called the Cray XT5h, the Black Widow was targeted to scale to 32,000 processors, versus 4,096 for the X1, and employ new multistreaming processors (MSPs) allowing it to achieve the enormous speeds. But while the sixteen closet-sized cabinets were to roll into the agency's Tordella supercomputer building in 2006, by early 2008 the agency was still waiting for the truck to arrive. Cray hoped to have the Black Widow in place sometime that year.

Then in 2010, the NSA expects delivery of the Cray X-3, known as Cascade. Funded with $250 million from DARPA, it will likely be the most expensive computer ever created, and the fastest—designed to break the petaflop barrier with a sustained speed of more than a quadrillion calculations a second. It had been a long struggle. In 1971, the agency's CDC 7600 broke the megaflop barrier and fifteen years later, in 1986, its Cray-2 cracked the gigaflop limit. Then in 1997 its Intel ASCI Red crossed the teraflop line.

Finally, in 2008, a military supercomputer called Roadrunner reached the petaflop milestone. The $133 million computer, built by scientists at IBM and Los Alamos National Laboratory, will be used to solve problems related to nuclear weapons. But if history is any judge, it is likely that the NSA will also get their own Roadrunner. If so, they will have to again increase their power supply; the machine uses up about three megawatts of power, about what a large shopping mall consumes. According to Thomas D'Agostino, the administrator of the National Nuclear Security Administration, the amount of calculation the Roadrunner can do in a day is the equivalent to everybody on the planet—six billion people—using hand calculators to perform calculations twenty-four hours a day, seven days a week, for forty-six years. But while Roadrunner hit 1.026 quadrillion calculations a second, what the NSA needs is a computer that will operate at that speed or above constantly, and that is what they hope Black Widow and Cascade will do.

But for the NSA, the petaflop barrier may be only a brief way station. The agency has quietly made it known within the Pentagon that by 2018 it will need a computer capable of exaflop speed—one quintillion (1,000, 000,000,000,000,000) operations a second. To build such a machine for both the NSA and the Department of Energy, a new computer research center was launched in 2008. Known as the Institute for Advanced Architectures, the facility is run jointly by Sandia and Oak Ridge national laboratories. "We are faced with some problems for which petaflop supercomputers will not be fast enough," said the Sandia National Laboratory computer architect Doug Doerfler. "That's why we need to start designing an architecture now for exaflop-caliber computing." Among those potential problems, according to Sandia's Sudip Dosanjh, is power consumption. "An exaflop supercomputer might need 100 megawatts of power, which is a significant portion of a power plant," he said. "We need to do some research to get that down. Otherwise no one will be able to power one." After exaflops come zettaflops (a billion trillion) and yottaflops (a trillion trillion) and beyond that, the numbers haven't yet been named.

With its secret intercept rooms, its sprawling data farms, and its race for exaflop speeds, the NSA is akin to Jorge Luis Borges's "Library of Babel," a place where the collection of information is both infinite and at the same time monstrous, where the entire world's knowledge is stored, but not a single word understood. In this "labyrinth of letters," Borges wrote, "there are leagues of senseless cacophonies, verbal jumbles and incoherences."

Abyss

Like a pint-size brain surrounded by a heavily protected, half-million-square-foot body, a diminutive Dell computer in the basement of the National Counterterrorism Center is at the core of the Bush administration's war on terror. Contained on its tape drive is "the watch list"—the group of people, both American and foreign, thought to pose a threat to the nation. At one time the list could be contained on a small 3x5 card with a great deal of space left over. Today it has grown to more than half a million names, and it is expanding by the thousands every month. Known as the Terrorist Identities Datamart Environment, or TIDE, it is the last stop for the thousands of names vacuumed up in the NSA's warrantless eavesdropping program as well as its other eavesdropping operations.

"This is the list that the Do Not Fly list comes from," said one senior intelligence official concerned about the integrity of the system. "When that data comes in, it goes out to about six different watch lists. They're all drawn from that central database. It is an Oracle database sitting in a Unix operating system. In a nutshell, NCTC is functionally a huge data warehouse. The only thing that makes NCTC worth anything is the database, the TIDE database. This is the most important data since 9/11. If you screw this up, we know they're out there, we know they're operating, we know they're trying to get back in. The data is buried in this database."

Nevertheless, he said, the system is a disaster. The database is incompatible with both the NSA and the CIA systems. Despite the ocean of data collected by the NSA, he pointed out, "there really are no interfaces now so even if they want to send every bit of signal intelligence they have, we don't have the database structure that can match up the records. There are point-to-point interfaces between NSA and CIA. It doesn't exist from NSA to NCTC. That's the problem with data in the intelligence field—there is no leadership right now."

The problem, he said, goes back years. "Prior to ODNI [Office of the Director of National Intelligence] there was no organization that would say, 'All of you guys have to play together electronically.' There were all these memorandums of agreement that were one-off. The CIA director would meet with NSA and they'd do a handshake, and NSA would meet with DIA [Defense Intelligence Agency] and they'd do a handshake. So if you have sixteen of these major collection systems out there, you can just see how many of these memorandums of agreement exist today. There should have been a data architect . . . It's the worst technical screwup I've ever seen . . . The brains of the U.S. intelligence community reside in that building out there. The lights are on but nobody's home."

When CIA employees around the world write intelligence reports, they send one copy to the CIA's main computer database, code-named Quantum Leap, which is located on a secure floor in an office building in Reston, Virginia. Another copy goes to the NCTC. But because of the incompatibility, at NCTC the reports must be printed off the computer, manually reviewed, and then physically typed into the TIDE database. "The investment in it's been a couple of hundred million dollars," said the senior intelligence official. "Not so much the software and even the machines, but it's all of the people. The CIA had a budget of about a hundred million a year just converting documents to get it in there—basically cables out of the field. The transmission of those documents to NCTC was by hand. They literally had no way to connect the two networks, so they'd print out a big stack of documents and they'd get reentered in the system. Then they had teams of dozens of analysts going through the cables . . . They sit there and read them and highlight things with yellow highlighters and then they go to a data entry team. And then it goes into an Oracle database, a relational database. And in that kind of database you can't do a lot of connect[ing] the dots."

The official also had great concerns about the civil liberties dangers of the massive database. "The core group is about 40,000, which is the hard-core, identified," he said. "When you go out at two degrees or three degrees, meaning friends, family, business associates, it grows to almost 120,000. When you go out four degrees, you're upwards of 400,000. Four degrees is—I know you, you live in the building, and it so happens that there is a business in that building that allows me to connect the owner of that business to another group of another cell. So it's really just using this technology to establish these connections."

Because of changes in the law, the rules changed at the NCTC and U.S. names no longer had to be removed. "Before the FISA thing came down you would get U.S. citizens and they would have to be flagged and then they're removed," he said. "When the Patriot Act started it didn't matter. Before that if someone was a U.S. citizen whether they were hanging out with Saddam Hussein in Sudan or not, you were required by law to delete their record in that database. You could not have U.S. citizens in a collection database. The Patriot Act said if someone's a person of interest and has a known affiliation to a suspected group, you can track them when the initial encounter occurred outside the U.S. If it occurred inside the U.S., you immediately had to turn it over to the FBI."

The official said the NSA ran a test with the NCTC in order to see whether it would be possible to match the NSA's enormous database of phone numbers—acquired from the phone companies—with the NCTC list of names. The test was apparently part of the warrantless eavesdropping program. "We ran a pilot where we ran the data and connected it with cell phone records. So we knew these people in the U.S. and they got a whole bunch of cell phone records—matched the names to numbers. Pretty much we know every cell phone number in the world. But the cell phone numbers allowed us to connect them to calls inside. So all of a sudden we had a rich pattern of connectivity. So we have some guy living in Frankfurt—he makes a lot of calls to six or seven people in Chicago all the time. Bingo, now you're able to notify the FBI that, hey, you know those two guys you were looking for? Here's their address.

"It's what NSA's been doing since 9/11," the official continued. "They're just sweeping the stuff up. Now you don't have to put in sweeper rooms to collect this stuff; in many cases you can just go to the phone company and say, 'Give me only those records associated with outbound calls to this number in Frankfurt.' You get the same data. Frankly, that's a much better way. All of the telephone company equipment has been standardized since about '86. The telecommunications act. Prior to '86 every switch had its own peculiar data format."

But the law and policy, he said, have not kept pace with the technological developments. "They could be snooping on just about anything right now and not be accountable and be able to hold up their hands and go, 'Our system doesn't track that,'" he said, "when in many cases the system does but the code is so convoluted you could never know it. What concerned me is that I started to realize the linkage between what they were trying to do with the technology and what was going on up on the policy and the legal level with law. You can't build these systems without safeguards and controls and they don't have any of that in place right now."

Rather than focusing on legal, policy, and civil liberties issues, the NCTC is focusing its attention on building a bigger database—this one code-named Railhead—which will absorb TIDE. "The metaphor was that the Railhead program would be this intersection, this railhead, where all these data interfaces would converge into the equivalent of a railhead in a train network," said the senior intelligence official. "It's the largest program at NCTC, and Railhead and TIDE are about to be fused. Railhead is about to eat the TIDE database and when it does that, the TIDE database will just cease to exist."

So loose are the criteria for being tossed into the vast sea of names that in 2007, over twenty-seven thousand were removed, for a variety of unnamed reasons, because they should not have been in there. How many other innocent people remain on the list is unknown, but with upwards of a thousand new names a day being added, the number is likely substantial. Unlike a bad credit report, there is no way for anyone to ever know they are in the system—and few ways out of it.

More than three decades ago, when the NSA posed a fraction of the privacy threat it poses today with the Internet, digital communications, and mass storage, Senator Frank Church, the first chairman of the Senate Intelligence Committee, investigated the NSA and issued a stark warning:

> That capability at any time could be turned around on the American people and no American would have any privacy left, such [is] the capability to monitor everything: telephone conversations, tele-

grams, it doesn't matter. There would be no place to hide. If this
government ever became a tyranny, if a dictator ever took charge in
this country, the technological capacity that the intelligence community has given the government could enable it to impose total
tyranny, and there would be no way to fight back, because the most
careful effort to combine together in resistance to the government,
no matter how privately it was done, is within the reach of the government to know. Such is the capability of this technology.

There is now the capacity to make tyranny total in America. Only law
ensures that we never fall into that abyss—the abyss from which there is
no return.

Notes

Unless otherwise noted, the day-to-day activities of the hijackers are derived primarily from *The Chronology of Events for Hijackers* (November 14, 2003), a formerly secret three-hundred-page chronology released by the FBI under the Freedom of Information Act.

Introduction

1 "A lot of time you could tell": Interview with Adrienne J. Kinne (March 13, 2008).

2 "Black Widow"; it will soon break the petaflop barrier: Interview with a senior intelligence official.

2 "Whereas some observers once predicted": Congressional Research Service, "Data Mining and Homeland Security: An Overview" (January 18, 2007).

2 the equivalent of nearly one billion four-door filing cabinets: From Whatsabyte website at: http://www.whatsabyte.com/.

2 "We in the NSA are encountering problems": C. E. Unterberg, Towbin/Chesapeake Innovation Center, "The Business of Connecting the Dots: The $1 Billion Intelligence and Security Informatics/Analytics Market" (November 17, 2005).

3 By way of perspective, 200 petabytes: University of California, Berkeley, "How Much Information, 2003" (October 30, 2003).

3 Details on NSA purchase of plant; almost the size of the Alamodome: L. A. Lorek, "S.A. Lands Microsoft's $550 Million Facility," *San Antonio Express-News* (January 18, 2007); "Sony Electronics Campus Sold for $30.5 Million," *San Antonio Business Journal* (March 31, 2005).

3 Details on Terrorist Identities Datamart Environment: Interview with a senior intelligence official.

Sanaa

8 Details on bin Laden's purchase of satellite phone: See Mark Morris, " 'Jihad Phone' Linked to Former Missouri Student," *Kansas City Star* (September 19, 2001).

8 bin Laden and his top aides made a total of 221 calls: Mark Hosenball and Daniel Klaidman, Periscope, *Newsweek* (October 29, 2007).

8 al-Mihdhar began life atop Yemen's: National Commission on Terrorist Attacks upon the United States. *Final Report* (Washington, D.C.: U.S. Government Printing Office, 2006). Outline of the 9/11 Plot, Staff Statement no. 16. Hereafter referred to as 9/11 Commission report.

9 "well-behaved, nice young men": "Not My Sons, Says Al-Hazmi, Doubting FBI's Suspect List," *Saudi Gazette* (September 23, 2001).

9 "I went to Peshawar": Saqr Al-Amri, "FBI Photos Are Not of His Sons, Says Suspects' Father," *Arab News* (September 20, 2001).

10 "My Muslim Brothers of the World": Osama bin Laden, "Declaration of War Against America" (August 23, 1996).

11 Bin Laden would call them "The Founders": "Bin Ladin's Former 'Bodyguard' Interviewed on Al-Qa'ida Strategies," *Al-Quds Al-'Arabi* (August 3, 2004).

Intercept

13 Inside, upwards of 30,000 employees: Extrapolation from a chart, "Relative Personnel and Funding Sizes of Major Intelligence Agencies," contained in the report *Preparing for the 21st Century: An Appraisal of U.S. Intelligence* (March 1, 1996), p. 132. The report was prepared by the Commission on the Roles and Capabilities of the U.S. Intelligence Community. Another 8,000 employees work at other U.S. and overseas locations.

13 more than four dozen buildings: NSA, Dana Roscoe, "NSA Hosts Special Partnership Breakfast," *National Security Agency Newsletter (NSAN)* (January 2000), p. 4.

13 more than 700 uniformed officers: NSA, Andrew Plitt, "Emergency! Emergency!," *NSAN* (September 1991), pp. 8–9.

13 Its fire department responded to 168 alarms: NSA, "Fire Prevention Week," *NSAN* (January 2000), p. 11.

14 But hidden beneath the dark reflective finish: NSA, "On a Clear Day You Can See the Washington Monument?," *NSAN* (April 1984), pp. 4–5; protective shielding: Barton Reppert, Associated Press, " 'Electromagnetic Envelope' for NSA," *Washington Post* (March 30, 1984).

14 Tempest: During much of the 1980s the NSA wasted millions of dollars on "Tempest protection." All computers, monitors, and other electronic equipment the agency bought would have to be refitted with copper shielding on the remote chance that an enemy might be able to capture some stray electrons. This tripled the cost of each piece of equipment. Eventually, after making many of the NSA's contractors rich, the Tempest paranoia subsided. "As far as I know, nobody ever found any Russians sitting out in a parking lot in a van, and you almost can't do it anyway," said one security expert.

14 "engages in the interception of literally millions of communications"; "It is intolerable to think of the United States Government, of big brother": *Congressional Record* (House) (May 13, 1999), pp. H3112–H3141.

15 "Is Uncle Sam illicitly reading your e-mail?": David Ruppe, "Big Brother Is Listening," ABCNews.com (July 27, 1999).

15 "They're Listening to Your Calls": Otis Port with Inka Resch, "They're Listening to Your Calls: Echelon Monitors Phones, E-Mail, and Radio Signals," *BusinessWeek* (May 31, 1999).

16 "Jam Echelon Day": James Glave, "Hackers Ascend Upper 'Echelon,' " *Wired News* (October 6, 1999).

16 In response, the EU announced it was also launching a full-scale investigation: See *An Appraisal of Technologies of Political Control*, European Parliament, Scientific and Technological Options Assessment (STOA), Luxembourg (January 6, 1998).

16 "All e-mail, telephone and fax communications are routinely intercepted": Ibid.

16 "Almost by accident we've stumbled on to what we believe is a substantial problem": Andrew Wood, BBC Dispatches (December 18, 1997).

16 identified the two people who would be traveling to Southeast Asia by their first names: 9/11 Commission report, p. 353.

17 analysts felt it was not their job to research the suspected terrorists' identities: Ibid.

17 "like an ATM for signals intelligence": U.S. Senate Select Committee on Intelligence and U.S. House Permanent Select Committee on Intelligence, *Report of the Joint Inquiry into the Terrorist Attacks of September 11, 2001*, Part 1, Findings and Conclusions, p. 64, at: http://www.gpoaccess.gov/serialset/creports/911.html.

17 "suspected al-Qa'ida logistics facility": *Joint Inquiry*, Part 2, Narrative: The Attacks of September 11, 2001, p. 151.

18 "We knew that some guys that looked as though they were al-Qaeda": Interview with a senior CIA official.

18 "Activities of Bin Ladin Associate Khalid Revealed": National Commission on Terrorist Attacks upon the United States. *Terror and Travel Monolog*, chap. 2, footnote 15.

18 "something nefarious might be afoot": 9/11 Commission report, p. 353.

18 Hazmi flight details: 9/11 Commission report, Staff Statement no. 2.

19 "pls hold off on CIR for now per Tom Wilshire": Department of Justice, Office of the Inspector General, "A Review of the FBI's Handling of Intelligence Information Related to the September 11 Attacks" (November 2004), p. 240.

19 "Doug came to me and said, 'What the fuck?' ": Interview with Mark Rossini (April 8, 2008).

20 "They refused to tell us because they didn't want the FBI . . . muddying up their operation": Interview with FBI agent.

20 "What we had was an al-Qaeda guy, all his passport information, and a visa to the U.S.": Interview with senior CIA official.

21 "Is this a no-go or should I remake it in some way?": Department of Justice, Office of the Inspector General, "A Review of the FBI's Handling of Intelligence Information Related to the September 11 Attacks" (November 2004), p. 241.

San Diego

22   "Some See U.S. As Terrorists' Next Big Target": John-Thor Dahlburg, "Some See U.S. As Terrorists' Next Big Target," *Los Angeles Times* (January 13, 2000).

23   Mihdhar Mohammad al-Mihdhar Zaid: "Mihdhar" is also transliterated into English as "Mihdar," and it was as Mihdar Mohammad al-Mihdar Zaid that he entered the U.S. Khalid al-Mihdhar has also used the spelling "Mihdar." For example, when he obtained a Visa credit card, number 4217-6612-7663-2585, he spelled his last name "Midhar." FBI, *Chronology of Events for Hijackers* (November 14, 2003), p. 53.

23   Mihdhar Zaid was born May 8, 1978, in a remote part of South Yemen; details on Mihdhar Zaid: See *U.S. v. Mohdar Mohamed Abdoulah,* United States District Court, Southern District of California, Case No. 01-CR-3240-W (May 13, 2002).

23   the same day, according to an FBI chronology: FBI, *Chronology of Events for Hijackers* (November 14, 2003).

23   to acclimate Mihdhar and Hazmi to San Diego: 9/11 Commission report, p. 516, note 20. The opposite seems more likely: that Mohamed asked Bayoumi to acclimate Khalid and Hazmi. This could be the reason that Bayoumi may have, in the Commission's words, "dissembled about some aspects of his story, perhaps to counter suspicion."

24   "They never gave me any indication of hate": Kelly Thornton, "Muslim Regrets Renting to Hijackers: Lemon Grove Man Feels Betrayed, Has Fears About Safety," *San Diego Union-Tribune* (October 31, 2001).

25   On March 20, for example, Mihdhar used the cell phone: FBI, *Chronology of Events for Hijackers* (November 14, 2003), p. 57.

25   "Anytime you saw them": Johanna McGeary and David Van Biema, "The New Breed of Terrorist," *Time* (September 24, 2001).

25   Shaikh, their landlord, also noticed something odd: Department of Justice, Office of the Inspector General, "A Review of the FBI's Handling of Intelligence Information Related to the September 11 Attacks" (November 2004), p. 261.

25   In March 2000, Mihdhar signed up for WebTV Networks: FBI, *Chronology of Events for Hijackers* (November 14, 2003), p. 56.

26   Bangkok station reported to Alec Station: Department of Justice, Office of the Inspector General, "A Review of the FBI's Handling of Intelligence Information Related to the September 11 Attacks" (November 2004), p. 248.

Deaf

28   "I'll state right up front": NSA, "DIRNSA's Desk," *NSAN* (May 1999), p. 3.

29   "He was so interested in history": Scott Shane, "C.I.A. Pick Dazzles Many, but Critics See Mixed Résumé," *New York Times* (May 18, 2006).

30   "I've crawled in the mud to take pictures": U.S. Senate Select Committee on Intelligence, Hearings on the Nomination of General Michael V. Hayden to Be the Director of the Central Intelligence Agency (May 18, 2006).

31   "Other than the affront to truthfulness": Interview with Lt. Gen. Michael V. Hayden (February 2, 2000).

31   But Hayden's decision to secretly turn a deaf ear to nearly all international communications entering and leaving the U.S.: See U.S. Congress, House Permanent Select Committee on Intelligence and Senate Select Committee on

Intelligence, Report of the Joint Inquiry into the Terrorist Attacks of September 11, 2001 (December 2002), p. 73: "Before September 11, it was NSA policy not to target terrorists in the United States, even though it could have obtained a Foreign Intelligence Surveillance Court order authorizing such collection. NSA Director Hayden testified that it was more appropriate for the FBI to conduct such surveillance because NSA does not want to be perceived as targeting individuals in this country and because the intelligence produced about communicants in the United States is likely to be about their domestic activities."

31 "No one from the commission—no one": Philip Shenon, *The Commission: The Uncensored History of the 9/11 Investigation* (New York: Twelve, 2008), p. 155.

32 But the problem was that Hayden did not coordinate coverage with the bureau either: See U.S. Congress, House Permanent Select Committee on Intelligence and Senate Select Committee on Intelligence, Report of the Joint Inquiry into the Terrorist Attacks of September 11, 2001 (December 2002), p. 249: "NSA Director Hayden testified before the Joint Inquiry that the collection of communications between the United States and foreign countries will most likely contain information about . . . domestic activities and thus . . . is the responsibility of the FBI, not NSA. General Hayden contrasted the foreign intelligence value of such intercepts and their domestic security value. If the former is at stake, he asserted, NSA should intercept the communications; if the latter, the FBI.

"General Hayden, senior NSA managers, NSA legal staff, and NSA analysts made clear in Joint Inquiry testimony and interviews that they do not want to be perceived as focusing NSA capabilities against 'U.S. persons' in the United States. The Director and his staff were unanimous that lessons NSA learned as a result of Congressional investigations during the 1970s should not be forgotten.

"Whatever the merits of this position, it was incumbent on NSA and the FBI to coordinate so that the full range of intelligence collection weapons in the arsenal of the Intelligence Community could have been deployed against the terrorist threat. NSA routinely gave the FBI intelligence reporting, and that reporting contained leads about foreign terrorist-related communications. In addition, NSA responded to requests from the FBI for such information . . . The FBI used NSA-supplied information to advance its investigative interests. However, there was no inter-agency procedure in effect to ensure that the FBI made an informed decision to cover communications that NSA was not covering."

33 "Give me a sense"; "The whole system is down": Vernon Loeb, "Test of Strength," *Washington Post Magazine* (July 29, 2001).

33 "How many computers are down?" . . . "All of them": "National Security Nightmare," *60 Minutes II,* CBS (February 13, 2001).

33 "It was the whole net by which we move . . . Everything on the Fort Meade campus went down"; details of the NSA crash: Interview with Lt. Gen. Michael V. Hayden (February 2, 2000).

33 "NSA headquarters was brain-dead": "National Security Nightmare," *60 Minutes II,* CBS (February 13, 2001).

33 "I called [NSA director of corporate communications]": Interview with Lt. Gen. Michael V. Hayden (February 2, 2000).

34 "I said the fact that we're down is an operational secret": Interview with Lt. Gen. Michael V. Hayden (February 2, 2000).

34 he received a call from his deputy director for technology: Vernon Loeb, "Test of Strength," *Washington Post Magazine* (July 29, 2001).

34 "We actually got in touch with them": Ben Macintyre, "UK Spied for US as Computer Bug Hit," *The Times* (London) (April 27, 2000).

35 enough data every three hours to fill the Library of Congress; memory buffers capable of storing five trillion pages of data: Vernon Loeb, "Test of Strength," *Washington Post Magazine* (July 29, 2001).

35 "We had the ability to store": NSA, "DIRNSA's Desk," *NSAN* (May 1999), p. 3.

35 "The network outage was a wake-up call": Lt. Gen. Michael V. Hayden, address to the Kennedy Political Union of American University (February 17, 2000).

35 "We went deaf for seventy-two hours": Vernon Loeb, "Test of Strength," *Washington Post Magazine* (July 29, 2001).

36 "There are concerns that the NSA operates": U.S. House of Representatives Permanent Select Committee on Intelligence, hearings on the NSA (April 12, 2000).

36 "What I'm here to tell you today": Ibid.

37 Just two days earlier in San Diego; And three days later: See FBI director Robert S. Mueller III, statement for the record, Joint Intelligence Committee Inquiry (September 26, 2002).

38 "Mike Hayden's challenge": U.S. House of Representatives Permanent Select Committee on Intelligence, hearings on the NSA (April 12, 2000).

Mesa

39 One stood . . . with a video camera: Lisa Myers, Jim Popkin, and the NBC Investigative Unit, "Did the 9/11 Hijackers Have a U.S. Accomplice?" *NBC Nightly News* (September 8, 2006).

41 "It was a massacre": Robert Fisk, "Massacre in a Sanctuary: Eyewitness," *The Independent* (April 19, 1996).

42 "How easily we killed them": James Walsh, "Anatomy of a Tragedy," *Time* (international edition) (May 20, 1996).

42 "Around the Middle East": James Walsh, "Anatomy of a Tragedy," *Time* (international edition) (May 20, 1996).

42 Grapes of Wrath; "enraged": Richard Miniter and Hartwig Nathe, "God's Warrior," *Sunday Times* (London) (January 13, 2002).

42 signed his last will and testament: Atta's last will and testament was dated April 11, 1996, the same day Israel launched Operation Grapes of Wrath.

43 "longtime friend from Saudi Arabia": 9/11 Commission report, p. 223.

Thinthread

44 Taylor background: NSA, "National Security Agency's Deputy Director for Operations Retires," *NSAN* (January 31, 2001).

44 "We need help": NSA, Secret Memorandum, Taylor to Hayden, "Thoughts on Strategic Issues for the Institution" (April 9, 1999).

47 "very emotional debate": Siobhan Gorman, "NSA Rejected System That Sifted Phone Data Legally," *Baltimore Sun* (May 18, 2006).

47 "We are digging out of a deep hole": U.S. Senate Select Committee on Intelligence and U.S. House Permanent Select Committee on Intelligence, Joint Inquiry, testimony, Lt. Gen. Michael V. Hayden (October 17, 2002).

Totowa

48 Boeing 737-200 Systems Ground Training; "Steep Turns"; "Hani absorbed a great deal of information": Jet Tech International file for Hani Hanjour included in *U.S. v. Moussaoui.*

49 "I asked him to come back to my car": Nolan Clay and Randy Ellis, "Terrorist Ticketed Last April on I-40," *Daily Oklahoman* (January 20, 2002).

49 Oklahoma Highway Patrol trooper, Charles Hanger: See testimony of Charles Hanger, *U.S. v. Terry Lynn Nichols,* Criminal Action No. 96-Cr-68, United States District Court for the District of Colorado (November 5, 1997).

50 Hillwood Motor Lodge: 6301 Arlington Boulevard, Falls Church, Virginia, 22044. The facility has since closed.

51 Details on Rababah: Brooke A. Masters, "High Price of Opening a Window on Terror," *Washington Post* (May 5, 2002).

51 "behaved very gentle-like": Andrew Brophy, "Hijackers: Fairfield Stay Still Jolts Some," *Connecticut Post* (Bridgeport, CT) (July 23, 2004).

52 Modesta Gomez would sell them packs of Salem or Parliament cigarettes and Budweiser beer: Fredrick Kunkle, "N.J. Neighborhood Was Suspects' Inconspicuous Hub," *Washington Post* (October 1, 2001).

54 "a very sharp person"; "You are here because there is some material": Peter Bergen, *The Osama Bin Laden I Know: An Oral History of al Qaeda's Leader* (New York: Simon & Schuster, 2006), p. 285.

54 "The coming weeks will hold important surprises"; "happy with the talk of his aides": Jason Keyser, "Defense Minister Warns of Threat from bin Laden," Associated Press Worldstream (June 25, 2001).

54 "dismantle their equipment and move to other hideouts": Anwar Iqbal, "Bin Laden Forms a New Jihadi Group," United Press International (June 26, 2001).

Chatter

55 "Unbelievable news coming in weeks," said one intercept: Condoleezza Rice, testimony before the 9/11 Commission (April 7, 2004).

55 "To all the mujahideen, your brothers"; "Video Shows bin Laden Urging Muslims to Prepare for Fighting," CNN (June 20, 2001).

56 "Threat UBL Attack Against US Interests Next 24–48 Hours": 9/11 Commission report, p. 534.

57 "had reached a crescendo": 9/11 Commission report, p. 257.

57 "we had more than thirty warnings that *something* was imminent": U.S. Senate Select Committee on Intelligence and U.S. House Permanent Select Committee on Intelligence, Joint Inquiry, testimony, Lt. Gen. Michael V. Hayden (October 17, 2002).

Warning

63 As an act of revenge, he ordered Khalid Shaikh to immediately launch the attack in the U.S.: 9/11 Commission report, p. 250.

64 "but will still happen": 9/11 Commission report, p. 260.

64 "Bin Ladin Determined to Strike in U.S.": 9/11 Commission report, p. 260.

68 "Except for information reflecting": Department of Justice, Office of the Inspector General, "A Review of the FBI's Handling of Intelligence Information Related to the September 11 Attacks" (November 2004), p. 38.

68 "I plan to write something up": Department of Justice, Office of the Inspector General, "A Review of the FBI's Handling of Intelligence Information Related to the September 11 Attacks" (November 2004), p. 299.

69 "We are going to be struck soon": U.S. Senate Select Committee on Intelligence and U.S. House Permanent Select Committee on Intelligence, Joint Inquiry, testimony, Cofer Black (September 26, 2002).

69 "it all click[ed] for me": Department of Justice, Office of the Inspector General, "A Review of the FBI's Handling of Intelligence Information Related to the September 11 Attacks" (November 2004), p. 301.

Discovery

75 "I am still looking at intel": Department of Justice, Office of the Inspector General, "A Review of the FBI's Handling of Intelligence Information Related to the September 11 Attacks" (November 2004), p. 304.

Laurel

77 "because [Hanjour] was a gentleman": Laura Mansnerus and David Kocieniewski, "A Hub for Hijackers Found in New Jersey," *New York Times* (September 27, 2001).

77 "They left as quietly as they came in": Fredrick Kunkle, "NJ Neighborhood Was Suspects' Inconspicuous Hub," *Washington Post* (October 1, 2001).

79 "How are you doing today?": Maryland State Police video (September 9, 2001).

80 "A stand-up meeting in here with just my personal staff": Interview with Lt. Gen. Michael V. Hayden (February 2, 2000).

80 "Tomorrow is zero hour"; "The match begins tomorrow": David Ensor, "More Clues Before September 11 Surface," *Newsnight with Aaron Brown,* CNN (June 19, 2002).

81 Among the items inside was a handwritten letter in Arabic from Mihdhar to his wife: The FBI mistakenly attributed this letter to Hazmi. FBI, *Chronology of Events for Hijackers* (November 14, 2003).

81 "It is finally going to happen": 9/11 Commission report, p. 250.

Surprise

82 "Defense secretary Donald Rumsfeld says he can trim a billion dollars": *Morning Edition,* NPR (September 11, 2001).

82 Hayden morning routine: Interview with Lt. Gen. Michael V. Hayden (February 2, 2000).

84 Hayden was surrounded by the accoutrements of power: Personal observation during several visits to Hayden's office.

86 "It's something I started here": Interview with Lt. Gen. Michael V. Hayden (February 2, 2000).

87 "The immediate image I had was a light plane": Interview with Lt. Gen. Michael V. Hayden (January 20, 2004).

87 "American 77 cleared direct um Falmouth": Transcript, American Airlines Flight 77.

88 "You guys never been able to raise him at all?": Transcript, American Airlines Flight 77.

Pentagon

89   "One plane's an accident, two planes is an attack": Interview with Lt. Gen.
     Michael V. Hayden (January 20, 2004).
89   "I saw the second plane hit in the office and it was like, oh my God, we're under
     attack": Interview with Mark Rossini.
90   "Barbara is on the phone": This and other details concerning Ted and Barbara
     Olson are derived from Ted Olson interview, *Larry King Live,* CNN (Septem-
     ber 14, 2001).
91   "I don't think any fighter pilot": Jack Sullivan, "Fargo Pilots Remember Sept.
     11 Duty," Associated Press (August 19, 2002).
91   "Fast-moving primary target"; "Oh my God!": "Get These Planes on the
     Ground," *20/20,* ABC News (October 24, 2001).
92   "One of the more emotional": Interview with Lt. Gen. Michael V. Hayden
     (January 20, 2004).
92   "He's twelve miles west": "Get These Planes on the Ground," *20/20,* ABC
     News (October 24, 2001).
93   "We thought it was coming for the CIA": Interview with Mark Rossini.
93   "so that when and if we died": Judith Miller, Jeff Gerth, and Don Van Natta
     Jr., "Planning for Terror but Failing to Act," *New York Times* (December 30,
     2001).
93   "We're moving now, sir; we're moving": Nancy Gibbs, "Special Report: Day
     of the Attack," *Time* (September 12, 2001).
93   "Women, drop your heels": Transcript, "The President's Story," *60 Minutes II,*
     CBS (September 10, 2002).
94   "Six miles"; "And we waited": "Get These Planes on the Ground," *20/20,* ABC
     News (October 24, 2001).
94   "It's an American Airlines plane": Transcript, Arlington, Virginia, police de-
     partment, September 11, 2001, Associated Press (September 18, 2001).
94   "Dulles, hold all of our inbound": "Get These Planes on the Ground," *20/20,*
     ABC News (October 24, 2001).
95   "I did and I didn't want to": Ted Olson interview, *Larry King Live,* CNN (Sep-
     tember 14, 2001).
95   "heard good news": CBS News (September 4, 2002).
95   "I got in touch with George Tenet"; "Number one, security": Interview with Lt.
     Gen. Michael V. Hayden (January 20, 2004).

Opportunity

99   "Mark is okay"; "I realized this was a well-coordinated attack"; "I stayed most
     of the day"; "A Manhattan Project for Counter-Terrorism": Shane Harris, "Sig-
     nals and Noise," *National Journal* (June 16, 2006).
102 "How are we going to find terrorists and preempt"; "the decision-making head":
     Robert O'Harrow Jr., "U.S. Hopes to Check Computers Globally: System
     Would Be Used to Hunt Terrorists," *Washington Post* (November 12, 2002).
102 "Our task is akin to finding dangerous": DARPA, Information Awareness Of-
     fice, address by Ted Senator, "Evidence Extraction and Link Discovery Pro-
     gram" (2002).
104 "the supersnoop's dream": William Safire, "You Are Suspect," *New York Times*
     (November 14, 2002).

Hunters

105 "We had all the senior leadership of the agency in this room"; "We could not squeeze any more juice out of retraining"; "We were a third smaller": Interview with Lt. Gen. Michael V. Hayden (January 20, 2004).

106 "We let the hiring program atrophy": Anne Baye Ericksen, "Spies Like You," *Graduating Engineer Online* (November 15, 2001).

107 "Anyone with a little computer understanding": Laura Sullivan, "National Security Agency Retreats into Secrecy Shell," *Baltimore Sun* (November 3, 2001).

107 "On the thirteenth of September"; "I had an agency": U.S. Senate Select Committee on Intelligence, Hearings on the Nomination of General Michael V. Hayden to Be the Director of the Central Intelligence Agency (May 16, 2006).

108 "We're going to live on the edge": Kenneth Roth, "The Mukasey Nomination Should Hinge on More Than Water-Boarding," *Huffington Post* (November 2, 2007).

108 "playing a little offense": Transcript, Hayden interview, *The Charlie Rose Show*, PBS (October 23, 2007).

108 "I called Mike to relay the vice president's inquiry"; "We went to see the vice president together": George Tenet with Bill Harlow, *In the Center of the Storm: My Years at the CIA* (New York: HarperCollins, 2007), p. 237.

108 "The volumes and routing of data": NSA, "Transition 2001" (December 2000), pp. 31, 32.

109 "Mikey": Bill Gertz, "Hayden Applauded for Military Service," *Washington Times* (June 21, 2008).

109 "Is there anything more we could be doing, given the current laws?": The White House, "President Discusses War on Terror and Operation Iraqi Freedom" (March 20, 2006).

109 "He showed me the plans for this country to pick up a conversation": The White House, "President Discusses Global War on Terror Following Briefing at CENTCOM" (February 17, 2006).

110 "When the law was passed": U.S. Senate Committee on the Judiciary, "FISA for the 21st Century," testimony, Gen. Michael V. Hayden (July 26, 2006).

110 "hot pursuit": The White House, "President Discusses War on Terror and Operation Iraqi Freedom" (March 20, 2006).

110 "From that decision to coverage is measured in minutes": U.S. Senate Select Committee on Intelligence, Hearings on the Nomination of General Michael V. Hayden to Be the Director of the Central Intelligence Agency (May 16, 2006).

110 "The problem with the seventy-two-hour rule": U.S. House of Representatives Committee on the Judiciary, statement for the record, Robert L. Deitz, General Counsel, National Security Agency (September 6, 2006).

111 "We've done it in a matter of a day": "Spying on the Homefront," *Frontline*, PBS (May 15, 2007).

111 "The Congress in 1978": "Spying on the Homefront," *Frontline*, PBS (May 15, 2007).

FISA

112 "Either we're serious about fighting": The White House, "Vice President's Remarks to the Traveling Press" (December 20, 2005).

112 who became the chief legal architect; "We're one bomb away from getting rid of that obnoxious [FISA] court"; "He and the vice president had abhorred FISA's intrusion": Jack Goldsmith, *The Terror Presidency: Law and Judgment Inside the Bush Administration* (New York: W. W. Norton, 2007), p. 181.

113 In its first twenty-two years; FISA application details: U.S. Department of Justice, Office of Legislative Affairs, annual FISA reports.

113 "When I first went into the FISA court": U.S. House of Representatives Committee on the Judiciary, hearings, "Constitution in Crisis: Domestic Surveillance and Executive Power" (January 20, 2006).

114 "My wife, Janis"; "Those who know me": Speech by Judge Royce C. Lamberth before the University of Texas Law Alumni Association (April 13, 2002).

114 In March, he sent a letter to Attorney General John Ashcroft: David Johnston and James Risen, "Officials Say 2 More Jets May Have Been in the Plot," *New York Times* (September 19, 2001).

115 "Sigint is even more important in this war": John Yoo, *War by Other Means: An Insider's Account of the War on Terror* (New York: Atlantic Monthly Press, 2006), p. 113.

115 "The government had to figure out": "Spying on the Homefront," *Frontline,* PBS (May 15, 2007).

115 "electronic surveillance techniques and equipment that are more powerful": John Yoo, *War by Other Means: An Insider's Account of the War on Terror* (New York: Atlantic Monthly Press, 2006), pp. 99–199.

116 "It appears clear that the Fourth Amendment's warrant requirement": U.S. Senate Select Committee on Intelligence, testimony, John Yoo (October 30, 2003).

116 "Our office recently concluded": The comment was included in a thirty-seven-page memo dated October 23, 2001, titled "Authority for Use of Military Force to Combat Terrorist Activities Within the United States." On April 2, 2007, Justice Department spokesman Brian Rochrkasse said that statement does not reflect the current view of the department's Office of Legal Counsel.

116 "Three guys": U.S. Senate Select Committee on Intelligence, Hearings on the Nomination of General Michael V. Hayden to Be the Director of the Central Intelligence Agency (May 18, 2006).

116 "Before I arrived": Jack Goldsmith, *The Terror Presidency: Law and Judgment Inside the Bush Administration* (New York: W. W. Norton, 2007), p. 182.

116 "They did not want the legal analysis scrutinized": U.S. Senate Committee on the Judiciary, hearing, "Preserving the Rule of Law in the Fight against Terrorism" (October 2, 2007).

116 "It was clear no one was asking him to approve it": Eric Lichtblau, *Bush's Law: The Remaking of American Justice* (New York: Pantheon Books, 2008), p. 162.

117 "We have to understand you can fight the war": Speech by Judge Royce C. Lamberth before the American Library Association (June 24, 2007).

117 between 10 and 20 percent of all the requests: Eric Lichtblau, *Bush's Law: The Remaking of American Justice* (New York: Pantheon Books, 2008), p. 162.

118 "you indicated that you had been operating": Eric Lichtblau and Scott Shane, "Files Say Agency Initiated Growth of Spying Effort," *New York Times* (January 4, 2006).

Mission

119 Hayden made participation in it voluntary: Interview with Senator Bill Frist, *Late Edition with Wolf Blitzer,* CNN (May 14, 2006).

119 "Let me tell you what I told them when we launched the program": U.S. Senate Select Committee on Intelligence, Hearings on the Nomination of General Michael V. Hayden to Be the Director of the Central Intelligence Agency (May 18, 2006).

120 "I don't make those decisions": U.S. Senate Select Committee on Intelligence, Hearings on the Nomination of Lieutenant General Michael V. Hayden, USAF, to Be Principal Deputy Director of National Intelligence (April 14, 2005).

120 "I'm trying to communicate to you": Hayden press conference quoted on *Democracy Now!* (January 24, 2006).

120 "this isn't simply Liberty Hall": U.S. House of Representatives Committee on the Judiciary, statement for the record, Robert L. Deitz, General Counsel, National Security Agency (September 6, 2006).

120 "The standard that is most applicable to the operations of NSA": U.S. Senate Select Committee on Intelligence, Hearings on the Nomination of Lt. Gen. Michael V. Hayden, USAF, to Be Principal Deputy Director of National Intelligence (April 14, 2005).

121 "When we didn't find the weapons after the invasion and the occupation": U.S. Senate Select Committee on Intelligence, Hearings on the Nomination of Lt. Gen. Michael V. Hayden, USAF, to Be Principal Deputy Director of National Intelligence (April 14, 2005).

122 "There were other circumstances in which clearly"; "I can demonstrate": U.S. Senate Select Committee on Intelligence, Hearings on the Nomination of Lt. Gen. Michael V. Hayden, USAF, to Be Principal Deputy Director of National Intelligence (April 14, 2005).

Highlander

124 "She told me to turn on the television": This and all subsequent quotes from John Berry came from interviews with John Berry (June 15, 2008, and June 20, 2008).

126 "It's like one day we're going to go off": This and all subsequent quotes from Adrienne Kinne came from an interview with Adrienne J. Kinne (March 13, 2008).

Assassination

135 "He knew this guy's phone number": Interview with a senior intelligence official.

136 On January 13, 2006, for example; "an alarming precedent [and] a clear case": Josh Meyer, "CIA Expands Use of Drones in Terror War," *Los Angeles Times* (January 29, 2006).

137 "A Sigint agency can't wait for the political decision": Bob Woodward, *Plan of Attack* (New York: Simon & Schuster, 2004), p. 214.

137 "Rock Drill": Bob Woodward, *Plan of Attack* (New York: Simon & Schuster, 2004), p. 216.

137 "Having had about four years' ": Vice Admiral William O. Studeman, address before the Association of Former Intelligence Officers, February 4, 1991; reprinted in *NCVA Cryptolog* (Fall Extra, 1991), pp. 2, 11.

138 "I agreed to stay army because": John F. Berry, "Army Asks Another Year from Reservist," *Press-Enterprise* (Southern California) (September 29, 2002).
139 "When I asked our best analysts to characterize our Sigint now": Interview with Lt. Gen. Michael V. Hayden (January 20, 2004).
140 "Statement of Director's Intent": Bob Woodward, *Plan of Attack* (New York: Simon & Schuster, 2004), p. 269.
140 "Beware, your office is bugged": Kim Sengupta and Kathy Marks, "Britain and US shared transcripts after Bugging Blix's Mobile Phone," *The Independent* (February 28, 2004).
141 "The UK in this time was also spying": Ed Johnson, "Britain Spied on UN's Annan," Associated Press (February 26, 2004).
141 "serious consequences": Raymond Whitaker and Andy McSmith, "The Whistleblower, the Loose Cannon, and the Case for War," *The Independent* (February 24, 2004).
142 "You should know that we don't like the idea": Martin Bright, Peter Beaumont, and Jo Tuckman, "British Spy Op Wrecked Peace Move," *The Observer* (February 15, 2004).
142 "As you've likely heard by now": Martin Bright, Ed Vulliamy, and Peter Beaumont, "Revealed: US Dirty Tricks to Win Vote on Iraq War," *The Observer* (March 2, 2003).

War

143 "every statement I make today": Transcript, Secretary of State Colin Powell address before the United Nations Security Council (February 5, 2003).
144 "We were asked, what do you have": Interview with Lt. Gen. Michael V. Hayden (January 20, 2004).
146 "We're going to bomb those barbarians": Interview with Adrienne J. Kinne (March 13, 2008).
149 "When suspected terrorists go to great lengths"; "After information is collected". i2 Inc. website at: http://www.i2inc.com/solutions/counterterrorism/.
149 Agility, AMHS, Anchory, ArcView, Fastscope, Hightide, Hombase, Intelink, Octave, Document Management Center, Dishfire, CREST, Pinwale, COASTLINE, SNACKS: L-3 Communications Services Group recruitment advertisement, "Senior Operations (SIGINT) Analyst: L-3 Communications Services Group," at: http://hotjobs.yahoo.com/job-JWLBJDI9483.
149 "And I just kind of saw in those two years": Adrienne J. Kinne, address at the Dartmouth Impeachment Forum, Hanover, New Hampshire (November 26, 2007).
150 "Where the information goes is a bank of computers": Interview with a senior intelligence official.
151 "Hayden wanted to really get": Interview with Eric Haseltine (April 8, 2008).
153 "What can be more important for Iraq today": Bob Fonow, "Hidden Surprises: Update on Iraq's Defense and Security Communications," Iraq Development Program (March 2, 2008).
154 "You didn't know it was going to happen?": Gen. Michael V. Hayden appearance on *Meet the Press,* NBC (March 30, 2008).
154 "The money is incredible": Interview with a former CIA official.
155 "The DO's chunk of the budget": Interview with a senior intelligence official.

155   "The first contract I was on I left": Interview with a former CIA operations of-
      ficer.
156   "We were talking to teams in the field": Interview with a former CIA opera-
      tions officer.
158   "How do you do your job that way?": Interview with a former CIA operations
      officer.

Shamrock

161   "The powers that be are trying to kill it": Interview with a senior NSA official
      (August 2001).
162   "There are still things that you can pick up": Interview with a senior intelli-
      gence official.
162   "Today you have no idea where that information is being routed": Interview
      with intelligence official.
162   "The need for a court order should not depend": U.S. House of Representatives
      Committee on the Judiciary, statement for the record, Robert L. Deitz, General
      Counsel, National Security Agency (September 6, 2006).
164   "had put all our cards on the table": U.S. Army Security Agency, *Historical
      Background,* vol. 3, p. 80.
165   Corderman; "the necessary contacts"; "very definitely and finally refused":
      U.S. Senate Select Committee on Intelligence, *Supplementary Detailed
      Staff Reports on Intelligence and the Rights of Americans,* Book 3, pp. 767–
      68.
166   "the intelligence constituted a matter of great importance"; "so long as the
      present attorney general"; "while it was always difficult": U.S. Department
      of Justice, prosecutive summary (March 4, 1977), pp. 33–34. This report, la-
      beled Top Secret/Handle via Comint Channels Only, was prepared for Robert
      L. Keuch, deputy assistant attorney general, Criminal Division, by George W.
      Calhoun, chief, special litigation. It analyzed the feasibility of bringing crimi-
      nal charges against members of the intelligence community during the mid-
      1970s for questionable and illegal intelligence activities.
168   "OK'd by the President and Tom Clark": U.S. Department of Justice, prosecu-
      tive summary (March 4, 1977), p. 33.

Qwest

169   1.5 million calls; it would have greater capacity than those of AT&T: Rachael
      King, "With Five New Networks Crisscrossing the Continent, America Is
      Awash in Fiber," *Fortune* (March 15, 1999).
169   thirteen-thousand-mile network: Brent Schlender, "Cool Companies," *Fortune*
      (July 7, 1997).
170   A general, said the caller, would like to meet with him: Shane Harris, "NSA
      Sought Data Before 9/11," *National Journal* (November 3, 2007).
170   "informed opportunism"; "I feel like an emerging oil baron": Greg Griffin,
      "Until the Denver Detour That Could Put Him in Prison, His Story Was as
      American as Apple Pie," *Denver Post* (December 25, 2005).
171   "Qwest is all about being aggressive": Miles Moffeit and Kris Hudson, "Wired
      for Trouble," *Denver Post* (December 15, 2002).
171   Qwest's extensive network was capable of carrying all the voice and data traf-

fic in the entire U.S.: Mark Gimein with research associate Doris Burke, "What Did Joe Know?" *Fortune* (May 12, 2003).

171 "most important thing we do is make our numbers": Greg Griffin, "Until the Denver Detour That Could Put Him in Prison, His Story Was as American as Apple Pie," *Denver Post* (December 25, 2005).

171 During a sales conference at the swank Bellagio Hotel: Mark Gimein with research associate Doris Burke, "What Did Joe Know?" *Fortune* (May 12, 2003).

172 "Our experience told us": Miles Moffeit and Kris Hudson, "Wired for Trouble," *Denver Post* (December 15, 2002).

172 Qwest executives and auditors began worrying about what the SEC would find: Mark Gimein with research associate Doris Burke, "What Did Joe Know?" *Fortune* (May 12, 2003).

172 Nacchio quietly began unloading more than $100 million: Greg Griffin, "Until the Denver Detour That Could Put Him in Prison, His Story Was as American as Apple Pie," *Denver Post* (December 25, 2005).

172 Known as Project Groundbreaker: Project Groundbreaker grew out of Project Breakthrough, which in 1998 outsourced twenty NSA legacy software systems.

172 "the problem for this agency is we downsized": George Cahlink, "Breaking the Code," *Government Executive* (September 1, 2001).

173 they primarily transmitted only localized calls, such as neighborhood to neighborhood: Eric Lichtblau, James Risen, and Scott Shane, "Wider Spying Fuels Aid Plan for Telecom Industry," *New York Times* (December 16, 2007).

173 "Nacchio said it was a legal issue": Shane Harris, "NSA Sought Data Before 9/11," *National Journal* (November 3, 2007).

173 "Subsequent to the meeting": Ryan Singel, "NSA Domestic Surveillance Began 7 Months Before 9/11, Convicted Qwest CEO Claims," Wired.com blog (October 11, 2007).

Cables

178 By 2002, the total capacity: F. W. Lacroix, *A Concept of Operations for a New Deep-Diving Submarine* (RAND Corporation, 2002), p. 142.

178 from 37.5 million on an average business day: AT&T website at: http://www.corp.att.com/history/nethistory/switching.html.

178 "Theoretically, an attack on two or three of these sites": F. W. Lacroix, *A Concept of Operations for a New Deep-Diving Submarine* (RAND Corporation, 2002), p. 142.

178 refused to allow the agency permission to install monitoring equipment on its Class 5 switching facilities: Eric Lichtblau, James Risen, and Scott Shane, "Wider Spying Fuels Aid Plan for Telecom Industry," *New York Times* (December 16, 2007).

178 "When he learned that no such authority had been granted": Quoted in *McMurray v. Verizon Communications Inc.,* United States District Court, Southern District of New York, Amended Complaint.

179 "The original 15 blocks": Bridgeton website at: http://www.bridgetonmo.com.

180 "to tap the network passively": Nikos Anerousis, Ramón Cáceres, et al., "Using the AT&T Labs PacketScope for Internet Measurement, Design, and Performance Analysis," Network and Distributed Systems Research Laboratory, AT&T Labs-Research, Florham Park, NJ (October 1997).

180 "They are in command of the network": Interview with Mark Klein (April 16, 2008).

180 "The New York monitor taps into T3": Nikos Anerousis, Ramón Cáceres, et al., "Using the AT&T Labs PacketScope for Internet Measurement, Design, and Performance Analysis," Network and Distributed Systems Research Laboratory, AT&T Labs-Research, Florham Park, NJ (October 1997).

181 "on-site presence of personnel to manage the monitoring equipment": Nikos Anerousis, Ramón Cáceres, et al., "Using the AT&T Labs PacketScope for Internet Measurement, Design, and Performance Analysis," Network and Distributed Systems Research Laboratory, AT&T Labs-Research, Florham Park, NJ (October 1997).

181 "It was very hush-hush": Kim Zetter, "Is the NSA Spying on U.S. Internet Traffic?" Salon.com (June 21, 2006).

181 "Bridgeton, Missouri, was chosen": Interview with Dr. Brian Reid (April 16, 2008).

182 "Secure detection of an intercepted targeted IP phone": AT&T Patent Application no. 376459, granted December 17, 2002.

182 "Monitoring selected IP voice calls": AT&T Patent Application no. 375754, granted April 30, 2002.

183 Dr. Alf L. Andreassen: Paladin Capital Group, Paladin Team, at: http://www.paladincapgroup.com/team.htm.

183 Dr. George H. Heilmeier: Mitre Board of Directors (July 8, 2005); Mitre website at: http://www.mitre.org/about/bot/heilmeier.html.

183 David W. Aucsmith: Georgia Tech, College of Computing, "The New Face of Computing," at: http://www.cc.gatech.edu/events/symposium/david-aucsmith-bio.

183 "The actual user of the PC": Mary Ellen Zurko, "Listwatch," IEEE (March 11, 1999), at: http://www.ieee-security.org/Cipher/Newsbriefs/1999/990314.LISTWATCH.html.

183 John P. Stenbit: Loral Space & Communications, Inc., press release (June 20, 2006).

185 611 Folsom Street: Until 2005 this was the SBC Communications Building, and AT&T occupied three floors. In 2005, SBC bought AT&T and changed its name, and that of the building, to AT&T.

185 "There's lots of Internet traffic": "Spying on the Home Front," Frontline, PBS (May 15, 2007).

Splitter

189 "I was sitting at my workstation one day": "Spying on the Home Front," Frontline, PBS (May 15, 2007).

190 "As soon as I saw the splitter": Interview with Mark Klein (April 17, 2008).

191 "What I saw is that everything's flowing across the Internet": James Risen and Eric Lichtblau, "Ex-Worker at AT&T Fights Immunity Bill," New York Times (November 7, 2007).

191 "the leader in carrier-class security and traffic intelligence": Narus brochure.

191 "the industry's only network traffic intelligence system": Ibid.

192 "uniquely provides insight into the entire network": Ibid.

192 "Anything that comes through": Robert Poe, "The Ultimate Net Monitoring Tool," Wired News (May 17, 2006).

192　"The latest iteration of NIS": "Narus Extends Traffic Intelligence Solution to Webmail Targeting," *Wireless News* (December 11, 2007).

192　Narus appointed William P. Crowell: "Narus Appoints Former Deputy Director of the National Security Agency to Its Board of Directors," Narus press release (September 29, 2004).

193　"The Narus box allows you": Interview with Dr. Brian Reid (April 16, 2008).

194　"the Narus system is well suited to process huge volumes of data"; Marcus comments: declaration of J. Scott Marcus, *Tash Hepting et al. v. AT&T Corp.,* United States District Court for the Northern District of California, Case No. C-06-0672-VRW.

195　"The projections that we made"; "I only need this person": NSA, videotape, "A Conversation Between the Deputy Director for Services and the NSA Technical Work Force" (September 30, 1999).

196　"During the 1980s budget increases"; "Today, an entirely new orientation is required": U.S. House of Representatives Permanent Select Committee on Intelligence, report, *Intelligence Authorization Act for Fiscal Year 2001,* 106th Cong., 2nd Sess. (May 16, 2000).

196　"The explosive growth of the global network": NSA, "DIRNSA's Desk," *NSAN* (July 2000), p. 3.

Industry

197　earn a $2-million-a-year salary: Bernard Wysocki Jr., "Is U.S. Government 'Outsourcing Its Brain'?" *Wall Street Journal* (March 30, 2007).

197　"we apply Tomorrow's Technology Today": Booz Allen Hamilton website.

198　"Network Intelligence Analyst": *Washington Post* "Jobs" section at: http://www.washingtonpost.com/wl/jobs/JS_JobSearchDetail?jobid=25263621&job SummaryIndex=0&agentII)=&xteed=1 (January 24, 2008).

199　intelligence community's budget was $43.5 billion: Office of the Director of National Intelligence, press release (October 30, 2007).

199　total to about $60 billion. "ODNI Document Suggests a Larger Intelligence Budget," *Secrecy News* (June 5, 2007).

199　the agency's recruiters logged more than 290,000 miles: U.S. House of Representatives Permanent Select Committee on Intelligence, hearings, "Building Capabilities: The Intelligence Community's National Security Requirement for Diversity of Languages, Skills, and Ethnic and Cultural Understanding," testimony, William B. Black, Deputy Director, National Security Agency (November 5, 2003).

199　But by October 2005, the agency had 7,197 contracts: NSA, Deborah Walker, Acquisition Resource Center, slide presentation (2006).

200　Now more than half of the company's $4 billion a year: Barnaby Wickham, "Bright Lights, Big Future," *Baltimore SmartCEO* (February 2005).

200　Details on SAIC: Donald L. Barlett and James B. Steele, "Washington's $8 Billion Shadow," *Vanity Fair* (March 2007); Matthew Swibel, "SAIC Hits the Street," Forbes.com (October 11, 2006).

201　"effectiveness of the U.S intelligence and national security communities": "Booz Allen Senior VP McConnell Elected Chair of Prominent Intelligence Community Advocacy Group," at: http://www.boozallen.com/capabilities/Industries/industries_article/1077809?lpid=659025.

202　"Wiretapping activity—the capturing of communications": C. E. Unterberg,

Towbin/Chesapeake Innovation Center, "The Business of Connecting the Dots: The $1 Billion Intelligence and Security Informatics/Analytics Market" (November 17, 2005).

202 "Tech leaders want NSA to become": Robert J. Terry, "National Security Agency Reaching Out to Maryland's Tech Companies," *Baltimore Business Journal* (November 7, 2003).

202 "The first year the incubator lost $60,000": Katie Arcieri, "In Budget Maneuver, County Consolidates Incubator," *Capital* (April 17, 2007).

203 "We want to make sure that taxpayers": Ariel Sabar, "Change at NSA Causes Concern," *Baltimore Sun* (November 25, 2003).

203 "flaming liberal"; "I refuse to use Reagan's name": Barnaby Wickham, "Bright Lights, Big Future," *Baltimore SmartCEO* (February 2005).

204 "At its most promising, Essex's optical networking": Ibid.

205 "Optical Tapped Delay Line": Securities and Exchange Commission 10K form for 2003.

205 "We've developed a very sophisticated test": Barnaby Wickham, "Bright Lights, Big Future," *Baltimore SmartCEO* (February 2005). [The word "shit" was not spelled out in the cited work.]

206 "For our shareholders": Allison Connolly, "Northrop to Buy Columbia Intelligence Firm Essex," *Baltimore Sun* (November 9, 2006).

206 NSA awarded the company a $220 million contract for a massive, new advanced information management and data storage system: "Information Management and Storage for Security Agency," *Signal Connections* (November 15, 2007).

206 "I was talking to a technician on the phone back east": "Spying on the Home Front," *Frontline,* PBS (May 15, 2007).

Transit

207 making up about one-third of all communications entering and leaving the country: TeleGeography Inc. survey cited in Barton Gellman, Dafna Linzer, and Carol D. Leonnig, "Surveillance Net Yields Few Suspects," *Washington Post* (February 5, 2006).

207 "greatest advantages": U.S. Senate Committee on the Judiciary, statement for the record, Lt. Gen. Keith B. Alexander, Director, National Security Agency (July 26, 2006).

207 "The issue was international communications": Chris Roberts, "Debate on the Foreign Intelligence Surveillance Act," *El Paso Times* (August 22, 2007).

207 "If Osama bin Laden in Pakistan": U.S. House of Representatives Committee on the Judiciary, hearing, "Warrantless Surveillance and the Foreign Intelligence Surveillance Act: The Role of Checks and Balances in Protecting Americans' Privacy Rights," Part 2 (September 18, 2007).

208 "It takes about two hundred man-hours to do one telephone number": Chris Roberts, "Debate on the Foreign Intelligence Surveillance Act," *El Paso Times* (August 22, 2007).

209 "Because the Internet access terminates on a different continent": Ethan Zuckerman, "A Peaceful EASSy Feeling," at http://ethanzuckerman.com/blog/?p=856.

209 "I have seen a communication": William P. Crowell, RSA Conference, San Francisco (April 9, 2008).

209 "The U.S. does continue to play a major role": Declan McCullagh, "NSA Eavesdropping: How It Might Work," *CNET News* (February 7, 2006).

209 "Basically they backhaul to the United States": Ryan Singel, "NSA's Lucky Break: How the U.S. Became Switchboard to the World," Wired.com (October 10, 2007).

210 "about 90 percent of the traffic between North and South America goes through our facility in Miami": Donnie Johnston, "Giant Data Firm Makes Its Mark ABOUT Terremark," *Free Lance-Star* (Fredericksburg, VA) (January 17, 2008).

210 "Switching the majority of South America": Terremark Web page at: http://www.terremark.com/technology-platform/nap-of-the-americas.aspx.

210 "Network Security Agreement": Securities and Exchange Commission, Global Crossing 10K form (December 8, 2003), p. 8.

211 650 million intercepts a day: Scott Shane, "C.I.A. Pick Dazzles Many, but Critics See Mixed Résumé," *New York Times* (May 18, 2006).

Partners

213 "The best way to do it": Interview with a senior intelligence official.

214 "Sometimes that's a very small antenna": "Spy Machines," *Nova*, PBS (1987).

215 "Can't do it—doesn't have the ability to tap in": Interview with a senior intelligence official.

215 "On the morning after they have been sent": Chapman Pincher, "Security Check on Private Messages Out of Britain," *Daily Express* (February 21, 1967).

217 "I know that I have leaned shamefully on you": Sir Leonard Hooper to Lt. Gen. Marshall Carter, letter (July 27, 1969), author's private collection.

218 GCHQ move to Benhall: Michael Evans, "GCHQ's £1bn Doughnut Is Filled with Everything but Computers," *The Times* (London) (June 14, 2003).

218 "It's a huge change for an organization": Dave Barista, "Spy Central," *Building Design and Construction* (August 1, 2004).

219 more than doubled to $4.2 billion: Nigel Morris, "Defence: Anti-terror Measures to Cost £2bn," *The Independent* (December 7, 2006).

220 "The number of cases where intercept material": "Watchdog Rejects Phone Tap Claims," BBC News (November 21, 2006).

220 "So far we do not believe": James Chapman, "Phone-Tap Evidence in Court Will Hit Terror War, Say Spies," *Daily Mail* (February 6, 2008).

220 over two hundred domestic extremist groups: Lewis Page, "VOIP and the Web Baffle Brit Spook Wiretappers," *The Register* (January 30, 2008).

221 "How much we need to grow will depend more or less"; Pepper comments: (UK) Intelligence and Security Committee, *Annual Report 2006–2007* (January 2008).

221 "the automation of certain aspects of the analysis of communications": Ibid.

222 439,000 requests were made; "unacceptably high": (UK) *Report of the Interception of Communications Commissioner for 2005–2006* (February 17, 2007).

222 "form the tightest and most historical partnership": (Canada) "Proceedings of the Special Senate Committee on the Anti-terrorism Act," testimony, Keith Coulter (April 11, 2005).

223 "Sometime in 2000–2001": Maj. Gen. V. K. Singh, *India's External Intelligence: Secrets of Research and Analysis Wing* (RAW) (New Delhi: Manas Publications, 2007), p. 139.

223 "I had felt uneasy about the project right from the beginning": Ibid., p. 140.

224 "But apparently this did not happen": Ibid., p. 141.

224 "Rumours speculating that [e-mail] can be intercepted": Rhys Blakely, "India Turns to Canada's Spies to Avert Threat of Espionage via BlackBerry," *The Times* (London) (March 10, 2008).

225 "deeply entrenched culture of impunity": U.S. Department of State, *2006 Country Reports on Human Rights Practices,* Mexico (March 6, 2007).

225 "I was furious to discover my life on papers": Molly Moore, "Spy Network Stuns Mexicans; Raid Opens Door to Exposure of Government Snooping," *Washington Post* (April 13, 1998).

226 "The discoveries—and the willingness of the targets"; "Everything I say and do": Ibid.

226 "with the capability to intercept": U.S. State Department, U.S. AID, Federal Business Opportunities website: FedBizOpp.gov.

228 "Suddenly anyone suspected of organized crime": Sam Enriquez, "Mexico to Boost Tapping of Phones and E-mail with U.S. Aid," *Los Angeles Times* (May 27, 2007).

228 "to disseminate timely and accurate": U.S. State Department, U.S. AID, Federal Business Opportunities website: FedBizOpp.gov.

229 "Is there another program?": U.S. House of Representatives Committee on the Judiciary, Subcommittee on Crime, Terrorism, and Homeland Security, Hearings on Legislative Proposals to Update the Foreign Intelligence Surveillance Act (FISA) (September 6, 2006).

229 "Well, if I might just jump in, Congressman": Ibid.

230 "if they could move a group of Cubans": U.S. Senate Select Committee on Intelligence, *Supplementary Detailed Staff Reports on Intelligence and the Rights of Americans,* Book 3 p. 755, note 76.

230 "Throughout the 1990s as CSE moved further away": (Canada) "Proceedings of the Special Senate Committee on the Anti-terrorism Act," testimony, Keith Coulter (April 11, 2005).

231 "Further, in the new environment": Keith Coulter, the John Tait Memorial Lecture, CASIS Conference, "CSE's Post-9/11 Transformation" (October 15, 2004).

231 "affected CSE in two ways": (Canada) "Proceedings of the Special Senate Committee on the Anti-terrorism Act," testimony, Keith Coulter (April 11, 2005).

231 "allowed CSE to get back into the game": Ibid.

231 "prohibited from directing its activities against Canadians": Ibid.

232 "We do not share with the United States": Ibid.

232 to more than $200 million by 2007: John L. Adams, CCSE speech to Université Laval students (February 6, 2007).

232 To house them: Stewart Bell, "Secretive Canadian Spy Agency to Get $62-Million HQ," *National Post* (Canada) (May 22, 2008).

233 " 'Big Brother is watching me' ": Michelle Shephard, "Web Snoop Vital, Spy Boss Says," *The Star* (October 22, 2005).

233 "one billion Internet users online right now": John L. Adams, CCSE speech to Université Laval students (February 6, 2007).

233 "all sorts of myths about CSE": Ibid.

Wiretappers

237 Computer and Internet Protocol Address Verifier: U.S. District Court, Western District of Washington, Affidavit for a Search Warrant, Case 3:07-mj-05114-JPD (June 12, 2007).

237 implanted in a target's MySpace account: Ibid.

238 "The circuit was tied to the organization's core network": Affidavit of Babak Pasdar for the Government Accountability Project, a Washington-based whistleblower organization (February 29, 2008). The legal case in which the description of the company is similar is *McMurray v. Verizon,* United States District Court, Southern District of New York, Case 1:06-cv-03650-WHP-RLE, Document 16, filed June 23, 2006.

238 "very sanctimonious"; "refuses to accept the facts of life in the developing world": Zvi Alexander, *Oil· Israel's Covert Efforts to Secure Oil Supplies* (Jerusalem: Gefen Publishing House, 2004).

239 Dan Bodner, a former Israeli army engineer: Securities and Exchange Commission 10K form (May 28, 2003).

239 "more than 5,000 organizations in over 100 countries": Verint website at: http://verint.com/corporate/index.cfm.

240 He thus placed the former NSA director Lieutenant General Ken Minihan on the company's "security committee": Securities and Exchange Commission 10K form (May 28, 2003).

240 "service providers can access communications": Verint website at: http://verint.com/communications_interception/.

240 "A multimillion-dollar expansion order": "Conference Call to Discuss Selected Unaudited 1st Quarter Results—Final," *FD Wire* (June 22, 2006).

241 "The CCC has some issues": (Australia) Subcommittee of the Joint Standing Committee on the Corruption and Crime Commission, closed session, transcript of evidence taken (October 18, 2004).

242 "advanced voice mining": PerSay website at: http://www.persay.com/spid.asp.

242 former Mossad chief Ephraim Halevy; Chesapeake Innovation Center: Athlone Global Security Inc., press release, "Major General Doron Almog, Founder of Athlone Global Security, Honoured by Israel for His Work Heading Investigation of Lebanon/Israel Conflict" (June 21, 2007).

242 "huge, aggressive, ongoing set of Israeli [intelligence] activities": Bob Drogin. and Greg Miller, "Israel Has Long Spied on U.S., Say Officials," *Los Angeles Times* (September 3, 2004).

243 "Unit 8200 is the technology intel Unit": Gil Kerbs, "The Unit," *Forbes Israel* (February 8, 2007).

243 "Cautious estimates indicate": Yuval Dror, "Intelligence Unit Fights for Tomorrow's Engineers," *Ha'aretz* (November 8, 2000).

243 "Take NICE, Comverse and Check Point": Gil Kerbs, "The Unit," *Forbes Israel* (February 8, 2007).

243 was founded by Unit 8200 veteran Gil Shwed; four years he spent in the Unit go virtually unmentioned: Lea Goldman, "A Fortune in Firewalls," Forbes.com (March 18, 2002).

244 "We were seven people from the Unit": Stacy Perman, *Spies, Inc.: Business Innovation from Israel's Masters of Espionage* (Saddle River, NJ: Pearson Prentice Hall, 2005), p. 182.

244 "provides voice content analysis with features": Securities and Exchange Commission form 20-F (June 29, 2005).

245 "I think there's an axiomatic assumption": Gil Kerbs, "The Unit," *Forbes Israel* (February 8, 2007).

245 Narus was formed in November 1997 by five Israelis: Raphael Fogel, "Ori Cohen, Private Eye," *Ha'aretz* (July 11, 2006).

245 much of its money coming from Walden Israel: Walden Israel website at: http://www.walden.co.il/pages/ShowPort.asp?Id=105.

245 Details on Stanislav Khirman: Khirman bio at: http://www.linkedin.com/in/khirman.

246 Elta specializes in developing advanced eavesdropping systems: Israel Aerospace Industries website at: http://www.iai.co.il/ELTA.aspx?FolderID=17887&lang=EN.

246 "The FBI is committing the kind of dirty tricks": Judith Lockwood, "Opinion: FBI Losing Credibility," *Wireless Week* (July 27, 1998).

246 "the Cadillac of wiretaps": Shane Harris, "Surveillance Standoff," *National Journal* (April 4, 2008).

247 Worthley was removed from his liaison job in June 1997: Edward Warner, "FBI Shakes Up Staff, Bureau Reassigns Its Liaison Chief," *Wireless Week* (June 16, 1997).

248 "The one thing about Kobi": Julie Creswell, "At Comverse: Many Smart Business Moves and Maybe a Bad One," *New York Times* (August 21, 2006).

248 In 2001, Alexander was the fourth most overpaid CEO: Zvika Paz, "Zaki Rakib, Kobi Alexander Lead Most Overpaid CEO List," *Globes* (Tel Aviv) (October 16, 2001).

248 That year his compensation totaled $102.5 million: Ken Schachter, "CEO's Dad, Sister Quit Comverse Technology Board," *Long Island Business News* (November 1, 2002).

248 The year before, he cashed in an additional $80 million: Julie Creswell, "At Comverse: Many Smart Business Moves and Maybe a Bad One," *New York Times* (August 21, 2006).

248 "They'd give us like $10": Janet Whitman and Tom Liddy, "Sly as a Fox—Kobi Giving Feds a Fit," *New York Post* (October 8, 2006).

248 Also taking refuge from the law in Israel was Leonid Nevzlin; "He was Jewish": Jim Cohen, "Kobi Alexander: Once Wooed by World Leaders, Now Chased by FBI," Bloomberg News (August 31, 2006).

250 "a mythical place": Hotel Thule website.

250 "We knew them as the Family Jacobs"; "I thought being from Israel, he was worried about Lebanon and all that": John Grobler, "U.S. Fugitive Made Powerful Alliances," *International Herald Tribune* (October 3, 2006).

250 "Alexander always looked very busy": "Comverse's Alexander Was in Namibia as Charges Neared," NYSSCPA.org news staff (September 29, 2006).

250 $20,000 in yearly high school scholarships: Surihe Gaomas, "Kobi Launches New Bursary Fund," *New Era* (Windhoek) (November 29, 2007).

251 Alexander's principal business partners included Brigadier Mathias Sciweda: Werner Menges, "A US Fugitive, a Namibian Brigadier, and Dollars Galore," *Namibian* (October 3, 2006).

251 Sciweda's name had come up in a Namibian financial scandal: Tangeni Amupadhi, "Scandal claims Namibian MP," *Mail & Guardian* (South Africa) (September 5, 2005).

251 By then, however, his remaining $50 million had been frozen by the prosecutors: "US Seizes $50m from Kobi Alexander's Bank Accounts," *Globes* (Tel Aviv) (September 11, 2007).

251 "Three former executives of Comverse Technology": U.S. Department of Justice, press release, "Former Executives of Comverse Technology Inc. Charged with Backdating Millions of Stock Options and Creating a Secret Stock Options Slush Fund" (August 9, 2006).

252 Comverse and Verint were dumped from the Nasdaq: Michael Cohn, "Comverse Taps New Leader," *Red Herring* (February 7, 2007).

252 "He got very nervous when we handcuffed him": John Grobler and Julie Creswell, "U.S. Fugitive in Options Case Displeased by His African Jail," *New York Times* (September 29, 2006).

252 overcrowded . . . average cell was packed with as many as thirty inmates: John Winterdyk, *Adult Corrections: International Systems and Perspectives* (Monsey, NY: Criminal Justice Press, 2004), p. 286.

252 "trying to influence the politics of Namibia": Scott Cohn, "Accused of Fraud, Kobi Alexander Escapes to Namibia," *NBC Nightly News* (June 8, 2007). See also Scott Cohn, "Reporter's Diary: 'Kobi' Alexander's Namibia," *CNBC* (June 7, 2007).

Technotyranny

255 Le Quoc Quan, a political dissident: Marcus Gee, "Using VoIP to Talk over the Internet, Vietnam's Small, Aging Dissident Community Recruits a New Generation," *Globe and Mail* (Canada) (June 12, 2007).

255 "anti-government propaganda": Ibid.

256 "It's great. Amazing": Ibid.

256 five dissident writers were jailed for planning to publish the newsletter *Tu Do Dan Chu*: "Media Rights Group Urges Vietnam to Stop Jailing Journalists," Agence France-Presse (August 25, 2006).

256 took place in 2002 and included two P-GSM stations, portable mobile phone listening devices, at $250,000 each: Robert Karniol, "Vietnamese Army Enhances Mobile Phone Monitoring," *Jane's Defence Weekly* (October 31, 2005).

257 "We are appalled to learn that our phone calls": "UK and US Sold Mobile Phone Tapping Equipment to Vietnam," Reporters Without Borders website at: http://www.rsf.org/article.php3?id_article=18648 (August 24, 2006).

257 "selected to provide law enforcement communications interception": "Verint Selected to Provide Law Enforcement Communications Interception Solution to a New Customer in Asia Pacific," *Business Wire* (July 8, 2002).

257 "Verint is a leading global provider of Actionable Intelligence": First Consulting Group Vietnam, "Outsourcing Alternatives Vietnam" (October 30, 2007) at: http://investmentmart.gov.vn/Speeches/30th%2016h30%20workshop6%20Ngo%20Hung%20Phuong.pdf.

258 "Narus' carrier-class IP platform": Narus, press release, "Narus Unifies IP Management" (July 13, 2005).

258 "The authorities reportedly began to employ more sophisticated technology":

U.S. Department of State, *Country Reports on Human Rights Practices* (March 6, 2007).

258 until the company installed the Narus software to prevent such calls: "Network Monitoring Technology Provider Narus Secures $30 Million in New Funding," Associated Press (October 29, 2006).

258 "spreading alarmist information"; details on dissidents: U.S. Department of State, *Country Reports on Human Rights Practices* (March 6, 2007) at: www.state.gov/g/drl/rls/hrrpt/2006/78771.htm.

259 By 2008, fifty-one cyber-dissidents and thirty-five journalists: "China Releases 'Spy' Reporter," Reuters (February 6, 2008).

259 "a multimillion-dollar agreement with Giza Systems of Egypt": "IP Management and Security Solutions to the Middle East," *VoIP Monitor* (September 13, 2005).

259 "Collaborating with a recognized leader": "IP Management and Security Solutions to the Middle East," *VoIP Monitor* (September 13, 2005).

260 selling an extremely intrusive package known as Forensics: "Narus Develops New Forensics Software for Tier-One Carrier-Class Networks," *Business Wire* (February 15, 2005).

260 "VANTAGE Mass Interception Solutions": Verint Systems, Inc., "VANTAGE Mass Interception Solutions" (2006).

260 "VANTAGE features include": Ibid.

261 "Once our customers buy our product": Matt Marshall, "The Secret Narus Spy Software," *Venture Beat* (April 12, 2006).

Miners

262 getting a permit from the Otoe County commissioners: Notice of Meeting, Otoe County Courthouse, Nebraska City, Nebraska (July 25, 2006).

262 "I call it Glacial Till Vineyards": Richard Piersol, "Pen-Link Chairman Shares the Wealth," *Lincoln Journal Star* (September 15, 2007).

262 "an automated way to load telephone records": Chet Mullin, "Tapping into New Possibilities: Pen-Link Employees Cash In on Growing Surveillance Business," *Omaha World-Herald* (September 26, 2007).

263 "Every government in the world does interception": Ibid.

263 "Nobody knows much about who we are": Richard Piersol, "Pen-Link Chairman Shares the Wealth," *Lincoln Journal Star* (September 15, 2007).

263 "a strategic agreement with Pen-Link, Ltd.": "Narus Teams with Pen-Link," *Business Wire* (June 13, 2006).

264 "Due to exigent circumstances it is requested": FBI, redacted letter from unit chief, Communications Analysis Unit (June 10, 2005); the letter was part of a response by the FBI to a Freedom of Information Act request by the Electronic Frontier Foundation.

264 "requests and demands for customer information": Randal S. Milch to Congressman John D. Dingell et al., letter (October 12, 2007).

264 "The president's program uses information": "NSA Wire Tapping Program Revealed," *NewsHour*, PBS (May 11, 2006).

265 "the only aspect of the NSA activities that can be discussed": J. M. McConnell, Director of National Intelligence, to Senator Arlen Specter, ranking member, Committee on the Judiciary, letter (July 31, 2007).

265 "The AT&T network, on a busy workday": Stacy Hunter, "The Mediated IP

Data Battle Strategy: Divide and Conquer, or Partition and Store?" *Billing World* (June 1, 2001).

265 Two years later that figure had grown: "Bigger, Better," *Information Week* (March 22, 2004).

265 including over 312 terabytes of information and 2.8 trillion records: AT&T, "AT&T Daytona System," at: http://www.research.att.com/~daytona.

265 While AT&T uses Hawkeye to store years of compressed, inactive records: AT&T Labs, "Major Technological Contributions from AT&T Labs Research," at: http://www.research.att.com/index.cfm?portal=27.

265 "An analyst can query the system for all calls": "Bigger, Better," *Information Week* (March 22, 2004).

266 "Must be able to manipulate GEO data": Jobster website at: http://www.jobster.com/job/permalink/47433797-geo-metadata-global-network-analyst--saic--columbia--md.

266 "the world's largest publicly known database by far": AT&T Labs, "Major Technological Contributions from AT&T Labs Research," at: http://www.research.att.com/index.cfm?portal=27.

266 "It's the largest database ever assembled in the world": Leslie Cauley, "NSA Has Massive Database of Americans' Phone Calls," *USA Today* (May 11, 2006).

266 "Having lots of data gives you lots of power": "Bigger, Better," *Information Week* (March 22, 2004).

266 "uncomfortable with the mountain of data": Barton Gellman, Dafna Linzer, and Carol D. Leonnig, "Surveillance Net Yields Few Suspects," *Washington Post* (February 5, 2006).

266 "The president determined that it was necessary following September 11": Assistant Attorney General William E. Moschella to the Honorable Pat Roberts, et al., letter (December 22, 2005).

267 "We'd chase a number, find it's a schoolteacher": Ibid.

267 fewer than ten Americans a year drew enough suspicion: Barton Gellman, Dafna Linzer, and Carol D. Leonnig, "Surveillance Net Yields Few Suspects," *Washington Post* (February 5, 2006).

267 "information whose source we can't share": Lowell Bergman, Eric Lichtblau, Scott Shane, and Don Van Natta Jr., "Spy Agency Data After Sept. 11 Led F.B.I. to Dead Ends," *New York Times* (January 17, 2006).

267 "whether the program had a proper legal foundation": Ibid.

268 "AT&T works in more places, like NSA HEADQUARTERS": Elizabeth Olson, "Advertising Advice? Thanks, but No Thanks," Portfolio.com (March 6, 2008).

268 "Modern life is so hectic": Elizabeth Olson, "Advertising Advice? Thanks, but No Thanks," Portfolio.com (March 6, 2008).

268 "During my time at Google": Interview with a former Google executive.

Fractures

273 "that they should decline to comply": U.S. House of Representatives Committee on Government Operations, Subcommittee on Information and Individual Rights, hearings, "Interception of Nonverbal Communications by Federal Intelligence Agencies" (1976), p. 99.

273 "On behalf of the President": Ibid.

274 "General Allen has asked me to convey to you": Ibid., pp. 80–81.

275 "Interception of International Telecommunications by the National Security

Agency": U.S. House of Representatives Committee on Government Operations, Subcommittee on Information and Individual Rights, "Interception of International Telecommunications by the National Security Agency," Draft Report (1976). This report was prepared in the fall of 1977 by professional staff member Robert S. Fink but was never published or released to the public.

275 The Rockefeller Commission: Commission on CIA Activities Within the United States, *Report to the President* (June 5, 1975).

276 "attitudes ranged from circumspection to wariness"; "There is likely to be much 'buck-passing'": Top Secret Umbra/Handle Via Comint Channels Only, U.S. Department of Justice, Report on Inquiry into CIA-Related Electronic Surveillance Activities (June 30, 1976).

277 "Orders, directives, policies, or recommendations"; "It is not illegal to 'ask' ": U.S. Department of Justice, prosecutive summary (March 4, 1977), pp. 12, 38.

Emergency

278 "We're going to push and push and push": Jack Goldsmith, *The Terror Presidency: Law and Judgment Inside the Bush Administration* (New York: W. W. Norton, 2007), p. 126.

279 "There was a little bit of a struggle"; "the chief legal architect"; Goldsmith comments: U.S. Senate Judiciary Committee, hearing, "Preserving the Rule of Law in the Fight Against Terrorism" (October 2, 2007).

279 "The program had to be renewed by March the 11th": Unless otherwise noted, all quotes from James Comey are derived from: U.S. Senate Judiciary Committee, hearing, "U.S. Attorney Firings" (May 15, 2007).

280 "just shoved it in front of me": Eric Lichtblau, *Bush's Law: The Remaking of American Justice* (New York: Pantheon Books, 2008), p. 162.

281 "Ashcroft in Guarded Condition After Surgery": Dan Eggen, "Ashcroft in Guarded Condition After Surgery," *Washington Post* (March 10, 2004).

281 "We informed the leadership that Mr. Comey felt": U.S. Senate Judiciary Committee, "Oversight of the U.S. Department of Justice," testimony, Attorney General Alberto Gonzales (July 24, 2007).

282 "never heard of": John Bresnahan, "Rockefeller Says March 2004 'Gang of Eight' Meeting Was Not as Gonzales Described," *Politico* (July 24, 2007).

282 By 7:00 p.m. it was dark, and Comey decided to head for home: Unless otherwise noted, all details of the events at the hospital are derived from: U.S. Senate Committee on the Judiciary, hearing, "U.S. Attorney Firings," testimony of James Comey (May 15, 2007).

282 At 7:20, Mueller received the call while having dinner: FBI, Richard C. Powers to Congressman John Conyers Jr., letter, with attachment, "RSM Program Log" (August 14, 2007).

283 "How are you, General"; "Be well": Comey response to "Written Questions to Former Deputy Attorney General James B. Comey Submitted by Senator Patrick Leahy" (May 22, 2007).

283 "Feeble, barely articulate, clearly stressed"; "The AG also told them [Card and Gonzales] that he was barred from obtaining the advice": FBI, Richard C. Powers to Congressman John Conyers Jr., letter, with attachment, "RSM Program Log" (August 14, 2007).

Exposure

287   "intensely operational"; "disclosure would do serious and perhaps irrepara-
      ble harm to national security": Eric Lichtblau, *Bush's Law: The Remaking of
      American Justice* (New York: Pantheon, 2008), pp. 193–94.

288   "shut down the game"; "There'll be blood on your hands": Ibid., pp. 207–8.

288   "I authorized the National Security Agency": The White House, President's
      radio address (December 17, 2005).

289   "Until the story broke in the *New York Times*": Hayden comments, *The Charlie
      Rose Show,* PBS (October 22, 2007).

290   "They just don't know if the product of wiretaps": Carol D. Leonnig and Dafna
      Linzer, "Spy Court Judge Quits in Protest," *Washington Post* (December 21,
      2005).

290   "It was never the intent of the framers to give the president such unfettered
      control": *American Civil Liberties Union v. National Security Agency,* United
      States District Court, Eastern District of Michigan, Southern Division, Case
      No. 06-CV-10204 (August 17, 2006).

290   "As you know, today": U.S. Department of Justice, "Remarks of Attorney Gen-
      eral Gonzales at Press Briefing on the Terrorist Surveillance Program Ruling"
      (August 17, 2006).

292   "We got a favorable ruling from the court": Mike McConnell, interview by J. J.
      Green on WTOP-Radio, Washington, D.C. (February 26, 2008).

292   "All surveillance previously occurring": U.S. Justice Department, Alberto
      Gonzales to Patrick Leahy and Arlen Specter, letter (January 17, 2007).

292   "The second judge looked at the same data": Chris Roberts, "Debate on the
      Foreign Intelligence Surveillance Act," *El Paso Times* (August 22, 2007).

Extremis

293   "the drifter": Steve Quinn, "Soldier Charged in Iraq Was a 'Drifter,' " Associ-
      ated Press (August 5, 2006).

293   "I don't know if he killed small cats"; Nevertheless, like 11,017 others: Jim
      Dwyer and Robert F. Worth, "Accused GI Was Troubled Long Before Iraq,"
      New York Times (July 14, 2006).

293   "I came over here because I wanted to kill people"; "I just saw and heard a
      blunt-talking kid": Andrew Tilghman, "I Came Over Here Because I Wanted
      to Kill People," *Washington Post* (July 30, 2006).

294   "Very good, very good": Julie Rawe with Bobby Ghosh, "A Soldier's Shame,"
      Time (July 9, 2006).

294   "kill and hurt a lot of Iraqis": *American Morning,* CNN (August 8, 2006).

294   "I just killed them, all are dead": Ibid. See also United States District Court,
      Western District of Kentucky, *U.S. v. Steven D. Green,* Criminal Complaint
      (June 30, 2006).

294   "Cortez pushed her to the ground": Charles Laurence, "The Rape That Shames
      America," *Daily Mail* (November 18, 2006).

295   Court case: Specialist James Barker pleaded guilty in the case in November
      2006 and was sentenced to ninety years' imprisonment. Sergeant Paul Cortez
      pleaded guilty February 20 to conspiring to rape, conspiracy to obstruct justice,
      violation of a general order, murder, rape, arson, unlawful entry, and obstruc-
      tion of justice. Cortez was sentenced to one hundred years in prison. Private

First Class Bryan Howard, twenty, of Fort Campbell pleaded guilty March 21 to being an accessory to the rape and murder of a fourteen-year-old Iraqi girl and the slaying of her family. Howard was sentenced to twenty-seven months in prison. Private First Class Jesse Spielman, twenty-two, of Chambersburg, Pennsylvania, was found guilty August 4 of conspiracy to commit rape, rape, housebreaking with intent to commit rape, and four counts of felony murder. He was found guilty and sentenced to 110 years. Former Private First Class Steven Green awaits trial in federal court, now set for April 13, 2009, in Paducah, Kentucky. Green, twenty-two, is accused of being a central figure in the case.

296   "The attack was extremely bold": Thomas Frank, "The Trail Is Cold but a Platoon Searches On for Two U.S. Soldiers," *USA Today* (August 8, 2007).

296   "Maybe he thought by joining the army it was regular pay"; he was gungho to join the army: Marnie Eisenstadt and John O'Brien, "Anguished Families Hope, Pray for Release of Four Fort Drum Soldiers," *Post-Standard* (Syracuse, NY) (May 17, 2007).

296   "George W. Bush has decided": Korie Wilkins, "Family Copes Best It Can 4 Months After Soldier Vanishes," *Detroit Free Press* (September 4, 2007).

296   "He kept saying, 'God, I don't want to go back' ": Ann Scott Tyson, "Those at Home Await Word on the Missing," *Washington Post* (May 16, 2007).

297   Women and children were interrogated: Joshua Partlow, "Insurgent Video Claims Captured U.S. Soldiers Are Dead," *Washington Post* (June 5, 2007).

297   more than a thousand Iraqi men were detained for questioning: Thomas Frank, "The Trail Is Cold but a Platoon Searches On for Two U.S. Soldiers," *USA Today* (August 8, 2007).

297   the government of Iraq was already holding at least twenty-four thousand prisoners: Solomon Moore, "11 in Mahdi Militia Die in Clash with US Force," *International Herald Tribune* (December 28, 2007).

297   "You should remember what you have done to our sister Abeer": Gina Cavallaro, "DoD Releases Names of Ambushed Soldiers," *Army Times* (May 17, 2007).

297   "Bush is the reason for the loss of your prisoners": Joshua Partlow, "Insurgent Video Claims Captured U.S. Soldiers Are Dead," *Washington Post* (June 5, 2007); see also, Damien Cave, David S. Cloud, Richard A. Oppel Jr., and Ahmad Fadam, "Iraq Insurgent Group Claims It Killed Missing U.S. Soldiers," *New York Times* (June 5, 2007).

298   "We know who that guy is": Garrett Therolf, "Army Hopeful for Captives," *Los Angeles Times* (May 20, 2007).

298   "We have to get an update every ninety days": U.S. House of Representatives Committee on the Judiciary, hearings, "Warrantless Surveillance and the Foreign Intelligence Surveillance Act," testimony, Mike McConnell (September 18, 2007).

298   "the court seemed to be complicit": Interview with a senior intelligence official.

298   "Where we intercept the communications": U.S. Senate Select Committee on Intelligence, hearings, "Proposed FISA Modernization Legislation," testimony, Mike McConnell (May 1, 2007).

298   It was a section of FISA that was little noticed during the Cold War: See for

example, U.S. Department of Justice, William E. Moschella, assistant attorney general, letter to the Honorable Arlen Specter, chairman, Committee on the Judiciary (March 24, 2006). In answer to a list of questions, the DOJ says, "The installation or use of a surveillance device inside the United States to acquire information could, under some circumstances, require a FISA order, regardless of the location of the target of the surveillance." This refers to 50 U.S.C. § 1801(f)(4), which defines "electronic surveillance" as "the installation or use of an electronic, mechanical, or other surveillance device in the United States for monitoring to acquire information, other than from a wire or radio communication, under circumstances in which a person has a reasonable expectation of privacy and a warrant would be required for law enforcement purposes."

298 "We had a stay until the end of May"; "We were in a situation": U.S. House of Representatives Committee on the Judiciary, hearings, "Warrantless Surveillance and the Foreign Intelligence Surveillance Act," testimony, Mike McConnell (September 18, 2007).

300 "We were in extremis": Chris Roberts, "Debate on the Foreign Intelligence Surveillance Act," *El Paso Times* (August 22, 2007).

300 "In his normal dick-measuring contest with Congress": Interview with a senior intelligence official.

Immunity

301 "My father was in World War II": McConnell remarks at Furman University (March 28, 2008).

301 "Four navy chiefs and one NSA civilian": NSA, "The Magic of CSGs," *Communicator* (March 4, 1996).

302 "When I went there, it was all wireless"; "I get up at 4:00 every morning": McConnell remarks at Furman University (March 28, 2008).

302 "Today, terrorists in Pakistan . . . would like nothing more than to obliterate this campus": Ibid.

303 "Some Americans are going to die": Dan Eggen, "Iraq Wiretap Delay Not Quite as Presented," *Washington Post* (September 29, 2007).

303 "The intelligence community was forced to abandon our soldiers", "This is terrible": Charles Hurt, " 'Wire' Law Failed Lost GI: 10-Hour Delay As Feds Sought Tap," *New York Post* (October 15, 2007).

303 "The attorney general can immediately implement a surveillance": Speech by Judge Royce C. Lamberth before the University of Texas Law Alumni Association (April 13, 2002).

305 "The terrorist that really had led the attack": Department of Defense, Special Defense Department Briefing (October 5, 2007).

305 "Under the president's program": Chris Roberts, "Debate on the Foreign Intelligence Surveillance Act," *El Paso Times* (August 22, 2007).

305 "The House should stand up to the bullying": "Bush Spy Bill Stance Called Fear-Mongering," CBS/AP (February 14, 2008).

306 "If these companies are subjected to lawsuits": Ibid.

306 "The sunset of the Protect America Act": Rand Beers, Richard A. Clarke, Don Kerrick, Suzanne Spaulding, letter to Mike McConnell (February 25, 2008).

307 "We have to work the dark side, if you will": *Meet the Press,* NBC (September 16, 2001).

307 "I have watched your campaign with genuine enthusiasm": James Risen, "Obama Voters Protest His Switch on Telecom Immunity," *New York Times* (July 2, 2008).

308 "Given the choice between voting for an improved yet imperfect bill": Posted on My.BarackObama.com.

Exabytes

311 "perfect look angles with no possibility for encroachment": Corey Pein, "Out of Thin Air," *Metro Spirit* (Augusta, GA) (December 14, 2006).

312 "What's nice about this platform": David Hubler, "Secret Sharers Gain Security, Time," *Washington Technology* (March 8, 2008).

312 "A speaker who claims to be Egyptian": University of Maryland, Center for Advanced Study of Language Web page at: http://www.casl.umd.edu/work/ ProjectDetail.cfm?project_ id=166.

313 "For the first time, authorized military and government personnel": Ty Young, "General Dynamics Unit Gets Clearance to Provide NSA Communications," *Phoenix Business Journal* (March 6, 2008).

313 "You're doing the Lord's work": Corey Pein, "Top Spies Come to Town to Cheer Big New Intel Facility," *Metro Spirit* (Augusta, GA) (March 28, 2007).

315 "If there's a major power failure out there": Siobhan Gorman, "NSA Risking Electrical Overload," *Baltimore Sun* (August 6, 2006).

316 "It fits into a long, long pattern": Ibid.

316 new 50-megavolt amp substation: Department of Defense, "Intent to Prepare an Environmental Impact Statement for Power Upgrades Project Within the Fort Meade Complex," *Federal Register* (January 2, 2008).

316 "We have become increasingly reliant": William Wan and Melissa Harris, "National Security Agency Leases Texas Plant for Expansion Project," *Baltimore Sun* (April 16, 2005).

317 "I will not speculate about any changes to NSA's plans": L. A. Lorek, "NSA Plan for S.A. Is on Hold," *San Antonio Express-News* (January 29, 2007).

317 Microsoft data center: "Microsoft Confirms Huge San Antonio Data Center," Datacenterknowledge.com (January 19, 2007).

318 "We're building a cloud": L. A. Lorek, "Microsoft Groundbreaking," *San Antonio Express-News* (July 31, 2007).

319 But between 2003 and 2005 the requests had skyrocketed: U.S. Department of Justice, Office of the Inspector General, "A Review of the Federal Bureau of Investigation's Use of National Security Letters" (March 2007).

320 "The letter ordered me to provide sensitive information": "My National Security Letter Gag Order," *Washington Post* (March 23, 2007).

321 the equivalent of nearly one billion four-door filing cabinets: From Whatsabyte website at: http://www.whatsabyte.com/.

321 "We can either be drowned by it": C. E. Unterberg, Towbin/Chesapeake Innovation Center, "The Business of Connecting the Dots" (November 17, 2005).

321 In 2002, there were 1.1 billion telephone lines: University of California, Berkeley, "How Much Information, 2003" (October 30, 2003).

322 "of streaming petabytes of data": Advanced Research and Development Activity, "Call for 2005 Challenge Workshop Proposals," ARDA website at: http:// www.ic-arda.org.

322 "NSC's technology is a fascinating technology": NSC, press release, "Mr.

Shabtai Shavit, Former Head of Israeli MOSSAD, Joined NSC's Board of Directors" (July 17, 2007).

323 "169,000 to 548,000 times faster than real time": Nexidia, press release, "Nexidia Increases Index Speed of Audio Files by 24%" (February 21, 2007).

323 Among the company's first customers was the NSA: Go2Gear, press release, "Media Entrepreneur Launches Go2Gear" (October 3, 2003).

323 "Analysis of Whispered Speech": Résumé of Mark A. Clements.

323 "Any sound that Winston made": George Orwell, *1984* (New York: Signet Classic, 1950), p. 3.

Trailblazer

326 "Their budget is classified": Joe Coombs, "Intel Agency Slips into M Square Research Park," *Washington Business Journal* (December 21, 2007).

326 "As I reflected on the meeting today": Rockefeller to Cheney, letter (July 2003).

326 "Will the Japanese use force to defend the Senkakus?'": U.S. National Institute of Standards and Technology, "2004 Pilot for Evaluation of Relationship Questions."

327 "The technology behaves like a robot"; "I don't like looking into other people's secrets": Eben Harrell, "2001: A Web Odyssey for NSA," *The Scotsman* (October 8, 2005).

327 "We must not forget that the ultimate goal": Office of the Director of National Intelligence, ARDA, PowerPoint presentation, "Advanced Question Answering: Plenty of Challenges to Go Around" (March 25, 2002).

328 "Many deception cues are difficult to identify": University of Maryland, Center for Advanced Study of Language, 2007 Annual Report (2008).

328 "growing need to work with foreign text": Ibid.

328 "CASL's cognitive neuroscience team": Ibid.

328 "CASL researchers": Ibid.

329 "Five or ten years ago NSA would have never chosen": Len Lazarick, "Conquest Is Trailblazing for NSA," *Business Monthly* (November 2001).

329 "We've had pretty good success with the front end in terms of collection": U.S. Senate Select Committee on Intelligence, Hearings on the Nomination of Lieutenant General Michael V. Hayden, USAF, to Be Principal Deputy Director of National Intelligence (April 14, 2005).

330 "inadequate management and oversight": Siobhan Gorman, "NSA's Terror Detector Is Fading Fast," *Baltimore Sun* (January 29, 2006).

330 "The costs were greater than anticipated": U.S. Senate Select Committee on Intelligence, Hearings on the Nomination of Lieutenant General Michael V. Hayden, USAF, to Be Principal Deputy Director of National Intelligence (April 14, 2005).

Turbulence

331 "I think the way to do it efficiently is smaller steps": Siobhan Gorman, "System Error," *Baltimore Sun* (January 29, 2006).

331 "The new idea of Trailblazer": Interview with a senior intelligence official.

331 "NSA's transformation program, Trailblazer": Document prepared for the Senate Armed Services Committee, Hearing on the Nomination of James R. Clapper Jr. to Be Undersecretary of Defense for Intelligence (March 27, 2007).

331 "What we need is fundamental change": Siobhan Gorman, "Management

Shortcomings Seen at NSA," *Baltimore Sun* (May 6, 2007).

332 "We still actually do have space at the NSA": U.S. Senate Subcommittee on Oversight of Government Management, the Federal Workforce, and the District of Columbia, Committee on Homeland Security and Governmental Affairs, testimony, Comptroller General David M. Walker (February 29, 2008).

333 "Bush told Alexander that he wanted": Interview with a senior intelligence official.

333 "They have had some pretty good success": Interview with a senior intelligence official.

334 "do major damage": Bradley Graham, "Authorities Struggle to Write the Rules of Cyberwar," *Washington Post* (July 8, 1998).

334 "state or official secrets": Matt Siegel, "Government Computers Face Anti-Espionage Restrictions," *Moscow Times* (March 31, 2008).

335 "Turbulence is working much better": Interview with a senior intelligence official.

337 "High end computing systems don't scale well": Terry Costlow, "Breaking the Next Flop Barrier," *Design News* (July 18, 2005).

337 "Large supercomputers have always been": U.S. Department of Defense, Office of the Under Secretary of Defense for Acquisition, "Report of the Defense Science Board Task Force on DoD Supercomputing Needs" (October 11, 2000).

337 "The Task Force concluded that there is a significant need": Ibid.

337 "These powerful computers": "U.S. Government to Support SGI Vector Supercomputer," *Mainframe Computing* (November 1, 1999).

338 Tera Computer acquired SGI: "Tera Computer Company to Acquire Supercomputer Pioneer Cray from SGI," *Business Wire* (March 2, 2000).

338 "because it wants at least one": Steve Alexander, "Struggling Firm Buys Struggling Cray Research," *Minneapolis Star Tribune* (March 3, 2000), p. 1D.

338 "filters all telephone conversations": Cray Annual Report, 2004.

339 Details on Roadrunner: John Markoff, "Supercomputer Sets Record," *International Herald Tribune* (June 9, 2008).

340 "An exaflop supercomputer might need 100 megawatts of power": Thomas Claburn, " 'Exaflop' Supercomputer Planning Begins," *InformationWeek* (February 22, 2008).

340 "labyrinth of letters": Jorge Luis Borges, "The Library of Babel," quoted in Emir Rodriguez Monegal, *Jorge Luis Borges: A Literary Biography* (New York: E. P. Dutton, 1978), p. 26.

Abyss

341 "This is the list that the Do Not Fly list comes from": Interview with a senior intelligence official.

344 "That capability at any time": NBC, *Meet the Press* (August 17, 1975).

Index

ALSO BY JAMES BAMFORD

BODY OF SECRETS
Anatomy of the Ultra-Secret National Security Agency

The National Security Agency is the world's most powerful, most far-reaching espionage organization. Now with a new afterword describing the security lapses that preceded the attacks of September 11, 2001, *Body of Secrets* takes us to the inner sanctum of America's spy world. Bamford reveals the NSA's hidden role in the most volatile world events of the past, and its desperate scramble to meet the frightening challenges of today and tomorrow. Here is a scrupulously documented account—much of which is based on unprecedented access to previously undisclosed documents—of the agency's tireless hunt for intelligence on enemies and allies alike. *Body of Secrets* is a riveting analysis of this most clandestine of agencies, a major work of history and investigative journalism.

Current Affairs/978-0-385-49908-8

A PRETEXT FOR WAR
*9/11, Iraq, and the Abuse of America's
Intelligence Agencies*

In *A Pretext for War*, James Bamford draws on his unparalleled access to top intelligence sources to produce a devastating exposé of the intelligence community and the Bush administration. *A Pretext for War* reveals the systematic weaknesses behind the failure to detect or prevent the 9/11 attacks, and details the Bush administration's subsequent misuse of intelligence to sell preemptive war to the American people. Filled with unprecedented new revelations, from the sites of "undisclosed locations" to the actual sources of America's Middle East policy, *A Pretext for War* is essential reading for anyone concerned about the security of the United States.

Current Affairs/978-1-4000-3034-7

ANCHOR BOOKS
Available at your local bookstore, or visit
www.randomhouse.com